OECD ECONOMIC OUTLOOK

108

DECEMBER 2020

This work is published under the responsibility of the Secretary-General of the OECD. The opinions expressed and arguments employed herein do not necessarily reflect the official views of OECD member countries.

This document, as well as any data and map included herein, are without prejudice to the status of or sovereignty over any territory, to the delimitation of international frontiers and boundaries and to the name of any territory, city or area.

The statistical data for Israel are supplied by and under the responsibility of the relevant Israeli authorities. The use of such data by the OECD is without prejudice to the status of the Golan Heights, East Jerusalem and Israeli settlements in the West Bank under the terms of international law.

Note by Turkey
The information in this document with reference to "Cyprus" relates to the southern part of the Island. There is no single authority representing both Turkish and Greek Cypriot people on the Island. Turkey recognises the Turkish Republic of Northern Cyprus (TRNC). Until a lasting and equitable solution is found within the context of the United Nations, Turkey shall preserve its position concerning the "Cyprus issue".

Note by all the European Union Member States of the OECD and the European Union
The Republic of Cyprus is recognised by all members of the United Nations with the exception of Turkey. The information in this document relates to the area under the effective control of the Government of the Republic of Cyprus.

Please cite this publication as:
OECD (2020), *OECD Economic Outlook, Volume 2020 Issue 2*, No. 108, OECD Publishing, Paris, *https://doi.org/10.1787/39a88ab1-en*.

ISBN 978-92-64-68013-5 (print)
ISBN 978-92-64-86175-6 (pdf)

OECD Economic Outlook
ISSN 0474-5574 (print)
ISSN 1609-7408 (online)

Table of contents

FIGURES

TABLES

Follow OECD Publications on:

http://twitter.com/OECD_Pubs

http://www.facebook.com/OECDPublications

http://www.linkedin.com/groups/OECD-Publications-4645871

http://www.youtube.com/oecdilibrary

http://www.oecd.org/oecddirect/

This book has...

StatLinks

A service that delivers Excel® files from the printed page!

Look for the *StatLinks* at the bottom of the tables or graphs in this book. To download the matching Excel® spreadsheet, just type the link into your Internet browser, starting with the *https://doi.org* prefix, or click on the link from the e-book edition.

Conventional signs

$	US dollar	.	Decimal point
¥	Japanese yen	I, II	Calendar half-years
£	Pound sterling	Q1, Q4	Calendar quarters
€	Euro	Billion	Thousand million
mb/d	Million barrels per day	Trillion	Thousand billion
. .	Data not available	s.a.a.r.	Seasonally adjusted at annual rates
0	Nil or negligible	n.s.a.	Not seasonally adjusted
–	Irrelevant		

Editorial

Turning hope into reality

For the first time since the pandemic began, there is now hope for a brighter future. Progress with vaccines and treatment have lifted expectations and uncertainty has receded. Thanks to unprecedented government and central bank action, global activity has rapidly recovered in many sectors, though some service activities remain impaired by physical distancing. The collapse in employment has partially reversed, but large numbers of people remain underemployed. Most firms have survived, albeit financially weakened in many cases. Without massive policy support, the economic and social situation would have been calamitous. The worst has been avoided, most of the economic fabric has been preserved and could revive quickly, but the situation remains precarious for many vulnerable people, firms and countries.

The road ahead is brighter but challenging. At the time of writing, the global death toll has risen to 1½ million, subsequent waves have hit many countries and the first one continues unabated in others. While waiting for effective vaccinations to be widely distributed or some breakthrough in treatment, hopefully in the course of 2021 for most, managing the pandemic will still impose strains on the economy. Economic activity will continue with fewer face-to-face interactions and partly-closed borders for a few more quarters. Some sectors will regain strength, others will be on standstill. Developing or emerging-market economies, where tourism is important, will continue to see their situation deteriorate and will require more international aid. Policies will have to continue to sustain economic activity forcefully, all the more so with the end of the health crisis in sight.

The global economy will gain momentum over the coming two years, with global GDP at pre-pandemic levels by the end of 2021. After a sharp decline this year, global GDP is projected to rise by around 4¼ per cent in 2021 and a further 3¾ per cent in 2022. Scientific progress, pharmaceutical advances, more effective tracing and isolation, and adjustments in the behaviour of people and firms will help keep the virus in check, allowing restrictions on mobility to be lifted progressively. Importantly, policies to support jobs and firms, in place since the beginning of the pandemic, will enable a faster rebound when restrictions are lifted. Together with reduced uncertainty, these improvements should encourage the use of accumulated savings to fuel consumption and investment. The exceptional fiscal relief provided throughout 2020 - and needed beyond - will pay off handsomely. The rebound will be stronger and faster as more and more activities re-open, limiting the aggregate income loss from the crisis.

We project the recovery will be uneven across countries, potentially leading to lasting changes in the world economy. The countries and regions with effective test, track and isolate systems, where vaccination will be deployed rapidly, are likely to perform relatively well, though the overall weakness of global demand will hold them back. China, which started recovering earlier, is projected to grow strongly, accounting for over one-third of world economic growth in 2021. OECD economies will rebound, growing at 3.3% in 2021, but recovering only partially from the deep 2020 recession. The contribution of Europe and North America to global growth will remain smaller than their weight in the world economy.

The outlook continues to be exceptionally uncertain, with both upside and downside risks. On the upside, efficient vaccination campaigns and better co-operation between countries could accelerate the distribution of the vaccine worldwide. Conversely, the current resurgence of the virus in many places reminds us that governments may be forced again to tighten restrictions on economic activity, especially if the distribution of effective vaccines progresses slowly. And confidence would take a hit if vaccine distribution or secondary effects proved disappointing. The toll on the economy could be severe, in turn raising the risk of financial turmoil from fragile sovereigns and corporates, with global spillovers.

Despite the huge policy band-aid, and even in an upside scenario, the pandemic will have damaged the socio-economic fabric of countries worldwide. Output is projected to remain around 5% below pre-crisis expectations in many countries in 2022, raising the spectre of substantial permanent costs from the pandemic. The most vulnerable will continue to suffer disproportionately. Smaller firms and entrepreneurs are more likely to go out of business. Many low wage earners have lost their jobs and are only covered by unemployment insurance, at best, with poor prospects of finding new jobs soon. People living in poverty and usually less well covered by social safety nets have seen their situation deteriorate even further. Children and youth from less well-off backgrounds, and less qualified adult workers have struggled to learn and work from home, with potentially long lasting damage.

Governments will have to continue using their policy instruments actively, with better targeting to help those hardest hit by the pandemic. The fact that vaccines are in sight suggests that this is not the time to reduce support, as was done too early in the aftermath of the Global Financial Crisis. Rather it confirms health and economic policies must work hand in hand. Public health measures have to double down to limit the impact of renewed virus outbreaks and the associated restrictions. It is also crucial that policymakers ensure continuous fiscal support to keep sectors, firms and the associated jobs alive. The lessons from the past nine months are that such policy action was and remains appropriate. Monetary and fiscal policies will need to continue working vigorously in the same direction, at least as long as the health crisis threatens otherwise viable economic activities and employment.

Heightened policy activism need not be a concern if deployed to deliver higher and fairer growth. Extensive fiscal support is pushing public debt levels to record highs, but the cost of debt is at record lows. A striking feature of the outlook is the absence of correlation between the extent of fiscal support and the resulting economic performance, suggesting not all measures have been used wisely. Unprecedented monetary and fiscal support cannot be wasted, it must be funnelled into stronger and better economic growth. There are at least three priorities for policymakers. First, investing in essential goods and services such as education, health, physical and digital infrastructure. Second, decisive actions to reverse durably the rise in poverty and income inequality. Third, international cooperation: the world cannot solve a global crisis through single-country and inward-looking actions.

Redirecting public spending towards essential goods and services would signal that governments have learnt lessons from the crisis. The need for enhanced resilience should drive public and private investment in health, education and infrastructure. Better health resilience is not just about vaccine distribution and beds in intensive care units, it is also about prevention and affordable access to healthcare for all. Enhanced resilience is also about investing in skills, ensuring better education and labour market outcomes, and ultimately higher trend growth and wellbeing. This starts with more and better-targeted resources for the early years of education, better paid and trained education staff, as well as better lifelong training support, especially for vulnerable groups including parents in difficulties. Too often previous crises have resulted in lower investment and lasting infrastructure gaps, including in digital and decarbonised energy. This needs to change.

Support for the most vulnerable, especially children, youth and the less-skilled, who have not been fully sheltered from the crisis, will have to intensify. Education systems can improve in many countries, leveraging on lessons drawn from the crisis. Governments must invest to ensure all households, teachers and pupils can access good quality broadband and are equipped for digital education, especially for those in deprived environments. The crisis has shown the urgency of improving digital skills. It has also revealed shortfalls in social support systems. Fiscal policy should be better directed to vulnerable groups outside the usual welfare system who have not been eligible for the additional help provided so far, for their own benefit and the benefit of society as a whole.

Finally, international cooperation has faltered in recent years, just when it was needed more than ever. The "Global" Financial Crisis was mostly a crisis of a few advanced economies, but triggered an unprecedented cooperative response. The pandemic is the first fully global crisis since World War II: it has been answered by massive national responses, but closed borders and little cooperation. Protectionism and shutting frontiers are not the answer: they prevent the distribution of essential goods throughout the world and penalise economies that rely on their participation in global value chains to catch up. This must be reversed. Wide, rapid and generous production and distribution of effective medical treatments and vaccines must be organised for all countries. Multilateral fora must enhance action on debt transparency and a moratorium where needed, while supervisors need to pay high attention to the indebtedness of firms. The world must avoid the health and economic crisis also becoming a financial one.

When asked what the post-COVID-19 world will look like, let's hope the answer will be: "perhaps mostly the same, but a little bit better".

1st December 2020

Laurence Boone
OECD Chief Economist

1. General assessment of the macroeconomic situation

Introduction

The COVID-19 pandemic continues to exert a substantial toll on economies and societies. Prospects for an eventual path out of the crisis have improved, with encouraging news about progress in developing an effective vaccine, but the near-term outlook remains very uncertain. Renewed virus outbreaks in many economies, and the containment measures being introduced, have checked the pace of the global rebound from the output collapse in the first half of 2020, and are likely to result in further near-term output declines, particularly in many European economies. This pattern is likely to persist for some time, given the significant development and logistical challenges in deploying a vaccine widely around the world. Living with the virus for at least another six to nine months will prove challenging. Local outbreaks are likely to continue and will have to be addressed with targeted containment measures if possible, or full economy-wide lockdowns if necessary, which will hold down growth. Some businesses in the sectors most exposed to these continued containment measures may not be able to survive for an extended period without additional support, raising the risk of further job losses and insolvencies that hit demand throughout the economy.

On the assumption that renewed virus outbreaks remain contained, and that the prospect of a widely available vaccine towards the end of 2021 helps to support confidence, a gradual but uneven recovery in the global economy should occur in the next two years (Table 1.1). After a strong decline this year, global GDP is projected to rise by around 4¼ per cent in 2021, and a further 3¾ per cent in 2022. Overall, by the end of 2021, global GDP would be at pre-crisis levels, helped by the strong recovery in China, but performance would differ markedly across the main economies. Output is projected to remain around 5% below pre-crisis expectations in many countries in 2022, raising the risk of substantial permanent costs from the pandemic. Countries and regions with effective test, track and isolate systems are likely to perform relatively well, as they have done since the onset of the pandemic, but will still be held back by the overall weakness of global demand. These output prospects would allow only gradual declines in unemployment, and damp near-term incentives for companies to invest. Persistent slack would also temper increases in wage and price inflation.

The outlook would be brighter if faster progress towards developing and distributing an effective vaccine reduces uncertainty and the need for precautionary saving. This would point the way towards a stronger recovery, especially in 2022, and a more sustained pick-up in investment and consumer spending. On the downside, growth would be weaker if virus outbreaks were to intensify more widely, as is already the case in Europe, or if the challenges in ensuring widespread deployment of a vaccine proved to be greater than currently expected. This would imply an extended period in which containment measures were deployed to control the spread of the virus, and weaken growth prospects substantially. Confidence is still fragile, and further setbacks could remove any GDP growth in large parts of the world through 2021 or longer, deepening the already inflicted scars from the crisis.

Policies can play a pivotal role in supporting the economy while the health crisis persists and in easing the adjustment to a post-COVID-19 environment and governments need to react further if the recovery falters. Effective and well-resourced healthcare policies, as well as supportive and flexible macroeconomic and structural measures, are essential both to contain the impact of the virus and to minimise the potential long-run costs of the pandemic on living standards.

- The current accommodative monetary policy stance needs to be continued, as planned, by key central banks in the advanced economies. Central banks should also continue to provide a backstop to credit markets, and ensure that low and stable interest rates are maintained. If economic weakness deepens, or appears likely to persist for longer than expected, the remaining limited scope to ease monetary conditions should be used.

Table 1.1. A gradual but uneven global recovery

OECD area, unless noted otherwise

	Average 2013-2019	2019	2020	2021	2022	2020 Q4	2021 Q4	2022 Q4
			Per cent					
Real GDP growth[1]								
World[2]	3.3	2.7	-4.2	4.2	3.7	-3.0	3.8	3.8
G20[2]	3.5	2.9	-3.8	4.7	3.7	-2.3	3.6	3.9
OECD[2]	2.2	1.6	-5.5	3.3	3.2	-5.1	3.7	2.9
United States	2.5	2.2	-3.7	3.2	3.5	-3.2	3.4	2.9
Euro area	1.8	1.3	-7.5	3.6	3.3	-7.3	4.7	2.9
Japan	0.9	0.7	-5.3	2.3	1.5	-3.2	2.0	1.5
Non-OECD[2]	4.3	3.6	-3.0	5.1	4.2	-1.2	3.8	4.5
China	6.8	6.1	1.8	8.0	4.9	5.4	4.1	5.4
India[3]	6.8	4.2	-9.9	7.9	4.8			
Brazil	-0.5	1.1	-6.0	2.6	2.2			
Unemployment rate[4]	6.5	5.4	7.2	7.4	6.9	7.2	7.3	6.6
Inflation[1,5]	1.7	1.9	1.5	1.4	1.6	1.2	1.5	1.7
Fiscal balance[6]	-3.2	-3.0	-11.5	-8.4	-5.7			
World real trade growth[1]	3.3	1.0	-10.3	3.9	4.4	-9.9	5.1	4.1

1. Percentage changes; last three columns show the change over a year earlier.
2. Moving nominal GDP weights, using purchasing power parities.
3. Fiscal year.
4. Per cent of labour force.
5. Private consumption deflator.
6. Per cent of GDP.
Source: OECD Economic Outlook 108 database.

StatLink https://doi.org/10.1787/888934216867

- Fiscal policy support needs to be pursued as long as containment measures limit economic activity, and also subsequently to help restore sustainable economic growth. Additional fiscal measures are required in some countries to avoid an imminent fiscal cliff when time-limited emergency measures expire. The aim for all countries should be to avoid a premature and abrupt removal of stimulus whilst economies are still fragile and growth remains hampered by containment measures. Public debt is set to rise substantially, from already high pre-crisis levels in some countries, requiring spending to be targeted effectively. Ensuring debt sustainability will be a priority only once the recovery is well advanced, although planning for the steps that may be needed should start now.

- Exceptional crisis-related policies need to be increasingly focused on supporting viable companies, and accompanied by structural reforms that help to raise opportunities for displaced workers and vulnerable people, strengthen economic dynamism and mitigate climate change. Together, these can help to foster the reallocation of labour and capital resources towards sectors and activities with sustainable growth potential, raising living standards for everyone.

Many emerging-market economies and developing countries have been particularly hard hit by the pandemic. In some cases, extensive borrowing abroad to cushion the blow has added to existing challenges from high sovereign or corporate debt prior to the crisis. Debt restructuring for some of these borrowers is likely in the coming years. This process would be facilitated by increased transparency about the full extent of indebtedness, including contingent liabilities, and a more developed framework on how to deal with sovereign bankruptcy that includes all major creditors.

Stronger international co-operation remains necessary to help end the pandemic more quickly, speed up the global economic recovery, and build on the G20 efforts to address debt problems of emerging-market economies and developing countries. The sharing of knowledge, medical and financial resources, and reductions in harmful bans to trade, especially in healthcare products, are essential to address the challenges brought by the pandemic. International co-operation to ensure that a vaccine is available for everyone is necessary to ensure a faster rebound in global activity from the effects of the pandemic. Such preparation should also start now.

The global recovery remains partial and uneven

The economic outlook remains very uncertain, with the recovery in activity becoming increasingly hesitant. After the unprecedented sudden shock in the first half of the year, with global GDP in the second quarter of 2020 10% lower than at the end of 2019, output picked up sharply in the third quarter as containment measures became less stringent, businesses reopened and household spending resumed (Figure 1.1). Despite the welcome upturn, output in the advanced economies remained around 4½ per cent below pre-pandemic levels in the third quarter, close to the peak decline in output experienced during the global financial crisis. Without the prompt and effective policy support introduced in all economies to cushion the impact of the shock on household incomes and companies, output and employment would have been substantially weaker.

Figure 1.1. Output rebounded in the third quarter of 2020 after the sharp contraction in the first half of the year

Per cent change from 2019Q4

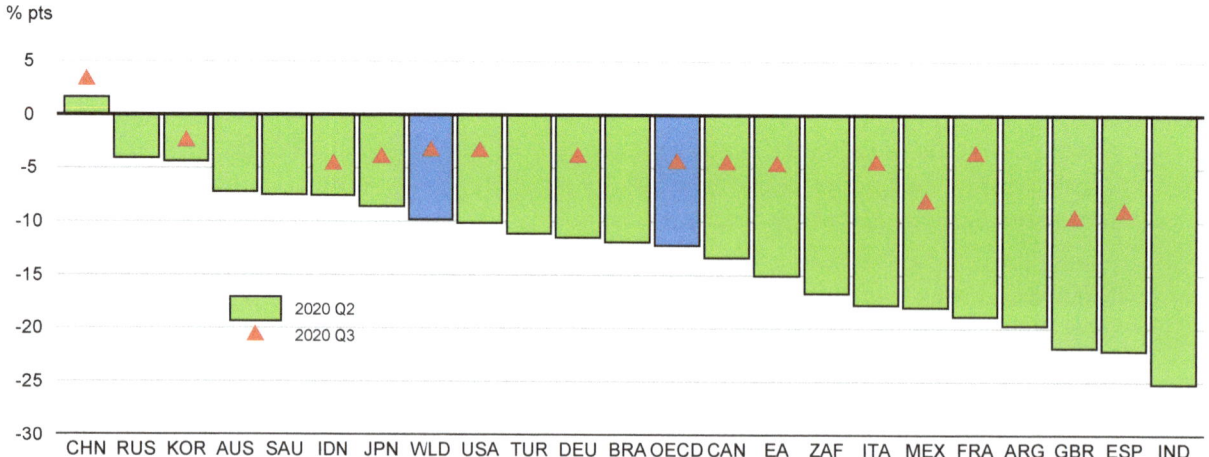

Note: Global GDP and OECD GDP are PPP-weighted aggregates.
Source: OECD Economic Outlook 108 database.

StatLink ᴹˢᴾ https://doi.org/10.1787/888934216886

After the initial bounce-back in many activities following the easing of confinement measures, the pace of the recovery has eased recently, especially in Europe where output may now be declining again. Daily measures of mobility remain below pre-pandemic levels, and have begun to turn down again in the advanced economies (Figure 1.3, Panel A), with more stringent containment measures being implemented to address renewed virus surges. Search-based Google Trends indicators up to mid-November also suggest that GDP growth in the fourth quarter of 2020 may be negative in many European countries where the stringency of containment measures has been tightened recently (Chapter 2, Issue Note 1). As seen in the second quarter of 2020, more stringent containment measures, and lower mobility are associated with weaker activity outcomes (Box 1.1). The initial rebound in some business surveys has also weakened, particularly in services. Amongst the countries with monthly economy-wide estimates of economic activity, just over two-thirds of the decline in output between January and April had been restored by September (Figure 1.3, Panel B), but with marked differences across sectors (Box 1.2).

- Some categories of spending bounced back relatively quickly as economies reopened, particularly household retail spending (Figure 1.3, Panel C). Household spending on services, especially ones requiring close proximity between producers and customers or international travel, remains more subdued. In the United States and Japan, two economies with monthly estimates of total consumers' expenditure, aggregate spending remains around 4% below immediate pre-pandemic levels.

- Household saving rates rose by between 10 to 20 percentage points in most advanced economies in the second quarter, with government emergency measures supporting incomes, higher precautionary saving, and restrictions on consumer spending. Household bank deposit holdings also soared in many economies (Box 1.3). While this provides scope to finance additional spending, survey evidence suggests that precautionary saving could remain elevated while confidence is subdued and uncertainty persists about the evolution of the virus and labour market developments (Bank of Canada, 2020).

- A significant proportion of the additional saving has accrued to higher-income households with a lower marginal propensity to consume (Bounie et al., 2020; Chetty et al., 2020), reflecting the extent to which the pandemic has added to existing income inequalities. Reductions in hours worked during the pandemic have been concentrated amongst lower-skilled occupations and lower-paid workers (see below). Containment measures may have also constrained the spending of higher-income households to a greater extent, reflecting a relatively high share of spending on service activities such as international travel, dining-out and cultural events.

- Global industrial production has also recovered, helped by strong growth in China (Figure 1.3, Panel D). However, shortfalls from pre-pandemic levels remain in many advanced economies, with demand for specialised capital goods being much weaker than for consumer goods, particularly in Japan and Germany. Investment intentions have weakened in several countries, and expectations that virus-related uncertainty will persist for some time (Figure 1.6) will keep business investment at low levels.

- Global trade volumes contracted sharply in the first half of 2020, with merchandise trade falling by 16% from its pre-pandemic level, and international travel and tourism being largely curtailed (Figure 1.7, Panel A). The pick-up in activity during reopening has been reflected in trade and container port traffic, especially in China, Korea and a number of smaller Asian economies such as Vietnam, helped by the rise in global demand for masks and other personal protective equipment, and teleworking-related goods, including IT equipment. The recovery in industrial production in China has also boosted demand for many raw materials in commodity exporting economies, particularly metals. Survey measures of global export orders have recovered from their trough in April, but remain soft. Air passenger traffic and travel also remain exceptionally weak (Figure 1.7, Panel B), hitting export revenues in tourism-dependent economies.

Box 1.1. Explaining cross-country differences in growth performance in the second quarter of 2020

In the second quarter of 2020, output and consumer spending declined sharply in many advanced and emerging-market economies (Figure 1.2). However, the extent of the contraction differed significantly across countries, with GDP and private consumption falling by over 15% in some countries, and by 5% or less in others. This box highlights the strong cross-country association between activity, the strictness of containment measures and changes in mobility, complementing the detailed analysis of the relationship between mobility and containment policy measures (Chapter 2, Issue Note 4).

Containment measures are captured using the aggregate stringency index produced by the Oxford Blavatnik School of Government (Hale et al., 2020), and mobility by the Google indicator of retail and recreational mobility. Changes in containment measures are associated with changes in mobility, but mobility measures may also pick up other factors, such as voluntary physical distancing, or a reluctance to leave the home when concerns about the pandemic are high.

Figure 1.2. Growth outcomes in the second quarter of 2020 are associated with differences in national containment measures and mobility

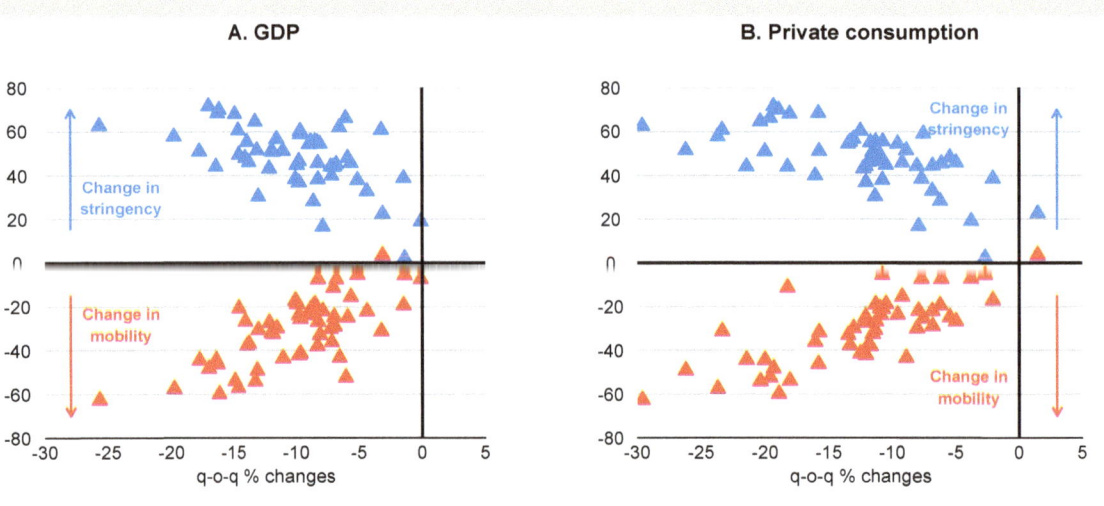

Note: The panels show OECD countries and non-OECD advanced and emerging-market economies from Asia, Latin America and Africa for which data are available (China is excluded). The country coverage differs between the two panels. The vertical axes show changes in the quarterly averages of the Oxford stringency index and the Google mobility index for the retail and recreation sector.
Source: OECD Economic Outlook 108 database; Google LLC, *Google COVID-19 Community Mobility Reports*, https://www.google.com/covid19/mobility; Oxford Coronavirus government response tracker; and OECD calculations.

StatLink ⬛ᴵˢᴸ https://doi.org/10.1787/888934216905

Empirical investigation

Both mobility and the stringency of containment measures are strongly correlated across countries with GDP growth and private consumption growth (Figure 1.2). The relative importance of these indicators can also be assessed econometrically using cross-country equations for quarterly changes in real GDP and private consumption in the second quarter of 2020. Two separate equations are estimated to allow for the possibility of differences in the extent to which mobility and stringency affect different activity indicators. For instance, cross-country variation in GDP growth stems in part from factors that may be less directly affected by domestic containment measures, such as government consumption and exports.[1] Both explanatory variables are expressed as the change in quarterly average values.[2] The equations are estimated for a group of advanced and emerging-market economies for which data are available, and exclude large outliers (leaving a sample of 43 economies for private consumption and 49 for GDP).[3]

Key findings include:

- Both mobility and stringency are found to have been significantly associated with cross-country differences in growth outcomes in the second quarter of 2020.

- The results imply that a tightening of the average Oxford stringency index by 10 points is associated with a reduction of around 1 percentage point in quarterly GDP growth, for a given level of mobility, with a decline of 10 points in the Google community mobility indicator associated with a reduction of around 1.7 percentage points in quarterly GDP growth. For real private consumption growth, the respective numbers are 0.6 and 2.8 percentage points. The larger impact of the mobility indicator on consumption growth than on GDP growth may reflect the fact that retail and recreational mobility is more relevant for household consumption than for other economic activities.

- The estimated equations explain roughly 60% of the cross-country variation in GDP growth and around 75% of the cross-country variation in private consumption growth.

- For both GDP and private consumption equations, the residuals tend to be on average positive in Asia, where containment measures have been relatively mild in some countries, but negative in Europe, where more-restrictive measures were applied. This may point to some potential non-linearities in the aggregate relationships between growth, mobility and containment measures, or it may indicate that some particular types of containment measures, such as full shutdowns, have stronger effects than others.

It is too early to know whether the cross-sectional relationships found for the second quarter of 2020 can be used to help track output growth through the pandemic. However, early flash estimates for GDP growth in the third quarter of 2020 have continued to be correlated with quarter-on-quarter changes in mobility across countries. The estimated relationships for the second quarter of 2020 also provide a guide for potential developments in the fourth quarter of 2020, suggesting that growth may again turn negative in countries that are tightening confinement measures substantially and experiencing marked declines in mobility indicators. However, the relation may be slightly weaker as some sectors have not reopened, or their activity remains subdued. There may also have been a growing shift to on-line sales of goods and services.

_____

1. International comparison is further complicated by different statistical approaches to measuring output volumes of the public sector during lockdowns (see fiscal policy section).

2. In both equations, the two indicators are significant at least at a 2% significance level. The significance is robust to exclusion of the country outliers.

3. The group covers most OECD economies and several non-OECD economies from Asia, Latin America and Africa. The sample for private consumption is smaller given fewer emerging-market economies with quarterly data for private consumption.

Figure 1.3. The pace of the recovery has slowed

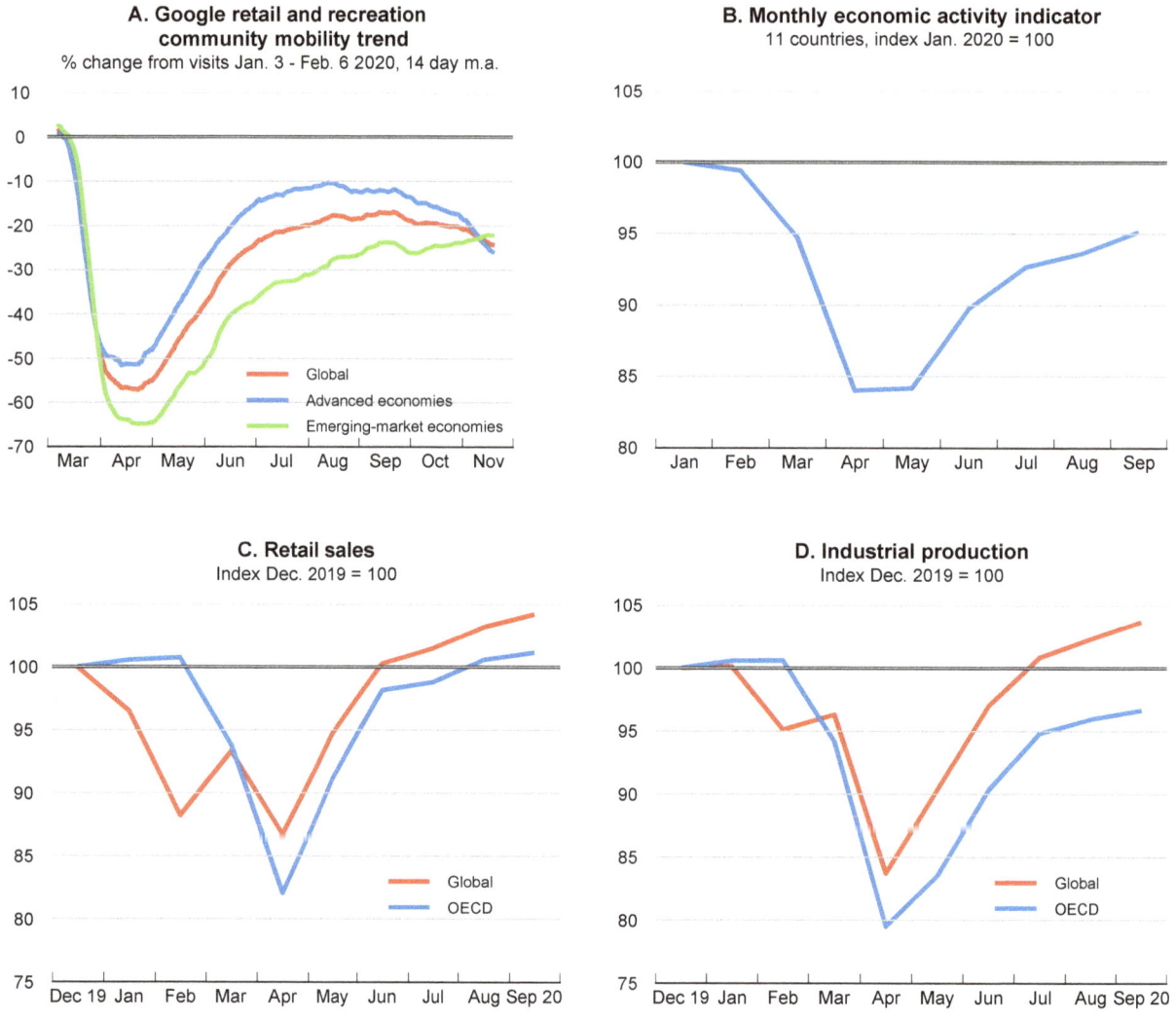

A. Google retail and recreation community mobility trend
% change from visits Jan. 3 - Feb. 6 2020, 14 day m.a.

Global
Advanced economies
Emerging-market economies

B. Monthly economic activity indicator
11 countries, index Jan. 2020 = 100

C. Retail sales
Index Dec. 2019 = 100

Global
OECD

D. Industrial production
Index Dec. 2019 = 100

Global
OECD

Note: Panel A and Panel B are PPP-weighted averages. Data for China are not available for Panel A. Countries included in Panel B are Argentina, Brazil, Canada, Chile, Colombia, Finland, Japan, Korea, Mexico, Norway and the United Kingdom. Data in Panel C are for retail sales in the majority of countries, but monthly household consumption is used for the United States and the monthly synthetic consumption indicator is used for Japan.
Source: Google LLC, *Google COVID-19 Community Mobility Reports*, https://www.google.com/covid19/mobility; OECD Main Economic Indicators database; Refinitiv; and OECD calculations.

StatLink https://doi.org/10.1787/888934216924

Box 1.2. The sectoral impact of the pandemic

As anticipated at the start of the pandemic, the economic impact has varied across sectors. Monthly output data and special business surveys being undertaken in some countries provide a timely indication of the different impact of the pandemic across businesses, both in the early stages of the crisis and subsequently. Differences across countries in the containment measures used in response to the pandemic, and changes in consumer behaviour, often beginning before containment measures took effect, have both had a significant impact on activity, particularly in service sectors.

The initial decline in output was especially marked in countries such as the United Kingdom and France, where full economy-wide confinement was required for an extended period (Figure 1.4, Panel A). In contrast, other countries, particularly in Asia, used regional or sector-specific containment measures, and relied more extensively on an effective test, trace and isolate system to control the virus.

- In the first two-three months of the pandemic, output fell particularly sharply in service activities requiring close proximity between consumers and producers, or large crowds, or travel (Figure 1.4, Panel A), declining by 60-80% in several countries.
- Output in many other parts of the economy, including manufacturing, construction and most other market-based services also tumbled, although the extent of the decline was more varied, possibly reflecting the mix of containment measures being imposed and differences in specialisation. Declines in these sectors were typically somewhat larger in Canada, France and the United Kingdom than in Japan or Norway.

As the recovery has progressed, with many containment measures relaxed until recently, output has gradually picked up in most sectors (Figure 1.4, Panel B).

- Output in the service sectors most affected initially has remained weak, raising the likelihood of persistent costs from the pandemic. Activity in accommodation, food services, events and recreation, and transportation, particularly air travel services, all continue to be impacted by physical distancing requirements and border closures.
- The recovery has also been slow in administrative and support services, a category of output that includes travel agencies, where demand is extremely weak. Professional and technical services activity has been less affected, but the rebound since April has also been muted, likely reflecting general demand weakness.
- In contrast, wholesale and retail trade output has largely returned to the immediate pre-pandemic level, helped by the strong rebound in retail sales.

The special business surveys being undertaken by some national statistics offices and central banks provide additional insight into the effects of the pandemic across sectors, including on workforce arrangements, the extent to which government support schemes are being used, investment plans, and corporate finances (OECD, 2020a). A common pattern across countries for which data are available is the extent to which future investment plans have been revised down in all sectors.

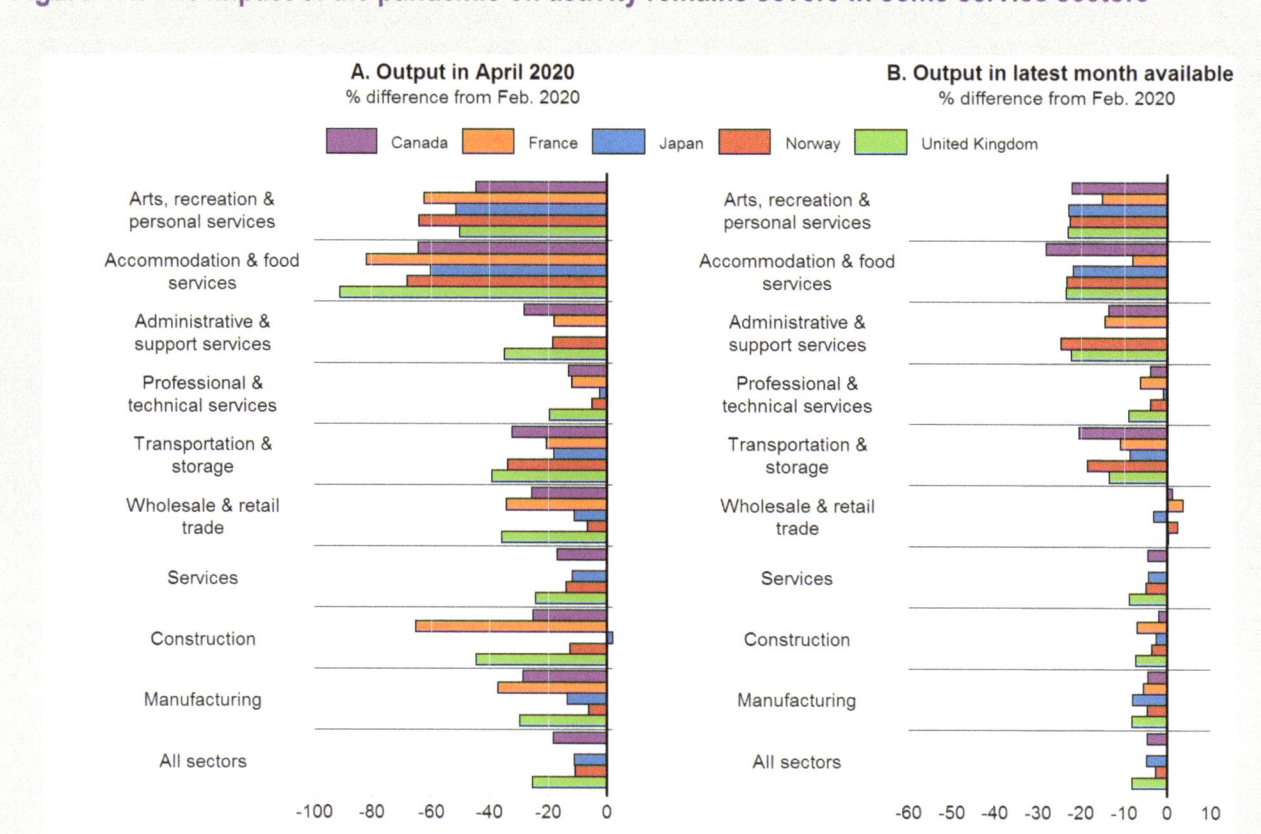

Figure 1.4. The impact of the pandemic on activity remains severe in some service sectors

A. Output in April 2020
% difference from Feb. 2020

B. Output in latest month available
% difference from Feb. 2020

Canada · France · Japan · Norway · United Kingdom

Note: Monthly GDP in Canada, Norway and the United Kingdom, monthly output in Japan and France. Data based on national industrial classifications. The latest available official data are for September in Japan, Norway and the United Kingdom, and August in Canada. For France, data for manufacturing and construction are for September, data in other sectors are for August. Data on all sector output and total service sector output are not available for France. Service sector output in Japan is output in the tertiary sector, which includes utilities. Transportation data for Norway exclude ocean transport.

Source: Office of National Statistics; Ministry of Economy, Trade and Industry, Japan; Insee; Statistics Canada; Statistics Norway; and OECD calculations.

StatLink https://doi.org/10.1787/888934216943

Information on financial status and operating costs highlights the pressures that some firms continue to face, especially in the hardest-hit service sectors.

- In Belgium, around one-fifth of responding firms indicated that they could not meet their financial liabilities for more than three months without receiving additional equity or credit (Figure 1.5, Panel A). An additional sizeable share of firms indicated that financial liabilities could only be met for between three and six months.

- Financial pressures are strongest in the events and recreation sector, and the accommodation and food services sector, with around 40% and 30% of firms respectively indicating that financial labilities cannot be met for more than three months.

- In the United Kingdom, around one-fifth of responding firms reported that their operating costs were currently exceeding turnover, with the excess being over 50% in half of these cases (Figure 1.5, Panel B). A further one-fifth indicated that operating costs were equal to turnover.

- Financial fragilities again appear to be greater in the hardest hit sectors. Around three-fifths of firms in the arts, recreation and entertainment sector, and two-fifths of firms in accommodation and food services, reported that operating costs currently exceeded turnover.

- Answers to separate questions on perceived bankruptcy risk provide a similar picture for businesses who continue to trade. For instance, in the United Kingdom, around 18% of all firms report moderate or severe bankruptcy risks at the end of September; in accommodation and food services, the share was 38%.

Figure 1.5. There are signs of financial fragilities in some service sectors

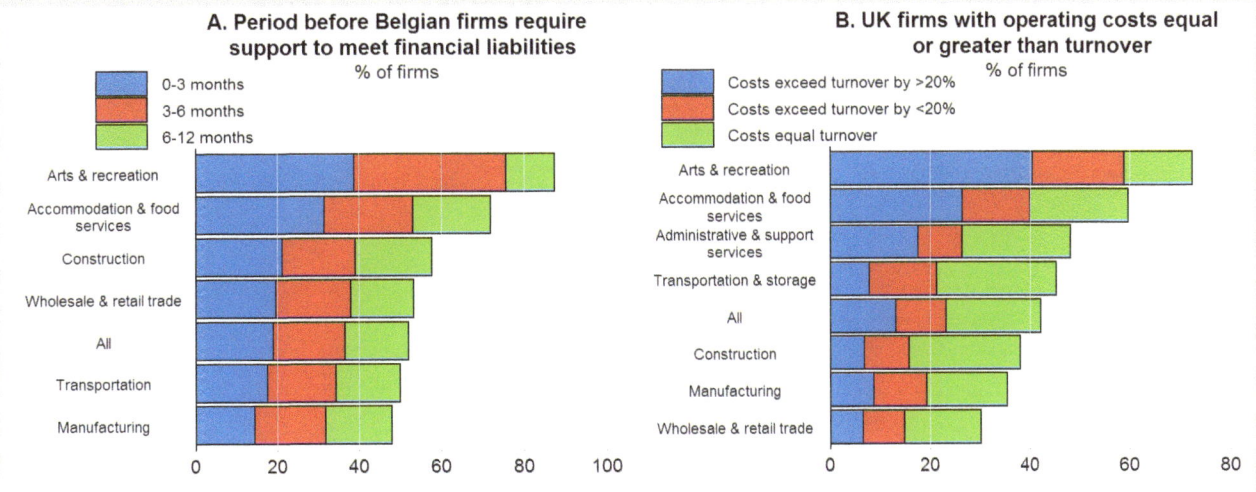

Note: Data in Panel A are responses in September to the question "How long can you still meet your current financial obligations without having to rely on additional equity or credit?", weighted by the number of responding firms. Data in Panel B are responses weighted by turnover to the question "In the last two weeks, how did your business's turnover compare to its operating costs?", and refer to the period September 21 to October 4. Firms replying not sure are excluded from the calculations.

Source: National Bank of Belgium; Office for National Statistics; and OECD calculations.

StatLink 🔗 https://doi.org/10.1787/888934216962

Figure 1.6. Uncertainty about the pandemic is expected to persist for some time

Expected end date for COVID-19-related uncertainty, per cent of responding firms

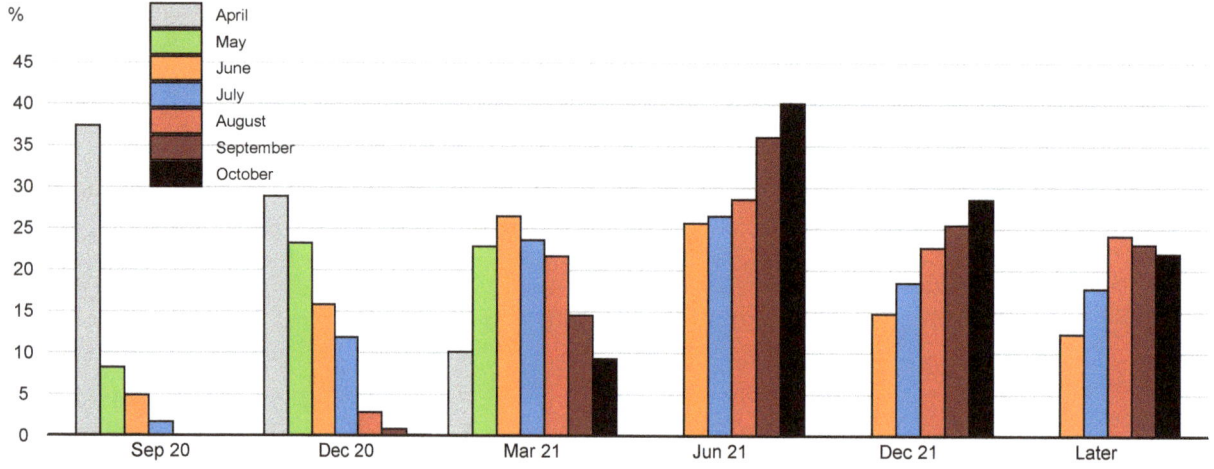

Note: Data are based on responses by UK firms to the question: "When do you think it is most likely that the coronavirus-related uncertainty facing your business will be resolved?".
Source: Bank of England Decision Maker Panel.

StatLink 🖳 https://doi.org/10.1787/888934216981

Figure 1.7. Global trade is slowly recovering, but international travel remains at very low levels

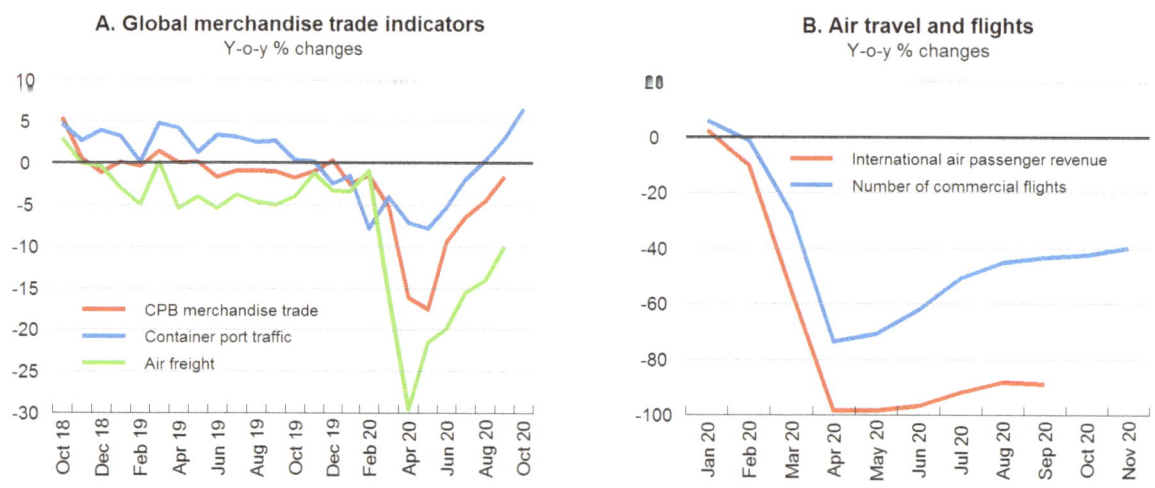

Source: CPB; IATA; RWI/ISL Container Throughput Index; flightradar24.com; and OECD calculations.

StatLink 🖳 https://doi.org/10.1787/888934217000

Box 1.3. The increase in bank deposits during the COVID-19 crisis: Possible drivers and implications

Unprecedented increase in bank deposits

Since end-2019, the bank deposits of non-financial corporations (NFCs) have increased rapidly in Japan, the United States and many European countries,[1] far above the average growth rates over the same period in the past five years (Figure 1.8, Panel A). In contrast, in the global financial crisis, corporate deposits declined amid the credit crunch and, in some cases, a delayed policy response.[2] Deposits of households have also increased but to a smaller extent; though still, in many countries, at a faster rate than in the previous years or at the beginning of the global financial crisis (Figure 1.8, Panel B).

Possible explanations

Several factors could explain the observed surge in deposits:

- Containment measures made some household purchases impossible (Boxes 1.1 and 1.2) at a time when incomes were maintained by government support, thus increasing saving and bank deposits. This effect should be temporary and dissipate as containment measures are lifted gradually and pent-up demand is satisfied. Indeed, so far, growth in deposits was concentrated in the March-May period, when strict lockdown was in force in many countries. In the following months, until the recent reintroduction of containment measures, the rate of growth in deposits of both households and NFCs slowed in most countries, though it remained above the average rate over the same period in the past five years.

- Containment measures are likely to have particularly affected consumption of some high-ticket services by high-income households, stimulating aggregate savings. High-income households tend to spend a higher share of their income on services that are heavily affected by containment measures, such as international travel, restaurants and cultural events. As the restrictions are likely to persist, so does this motive for saving.

- High uncertainty about the pandemic and future economic prospects has strengthened motives for precautionary saving, discouraging investment and purchases of durable goods.[3] These effects are likely to be more persistent.

- Amid disruptions to revenues, NFCs' preferences for holding cash have increased with the aim of raising their buffers and avoiding liquidity shortfalls. Cash hoarding was facilitated by drawing on loan facilities (e.g. revolving credit lines), issuance of corporate bonds by large firms (Goel and Serena, 2020), and by government sponsored loan programmes.[4] NFCs could have also reduced riskier financial investments (e.g. in money market funds).

- Crisis-related tax deferral measures have helped households and NFCs to increase liquidity and could have persistent effects, as money could be kept aside to meet postponed tax obligations. Tax deferrals are officially estimated to be high in some countries, exceeding, for example, 13% of GDP in Italy and close to 5% of GDP in Japan.

Possible implications

A reversal in any of the above factors may result in additional investment and consumption, boosting aggregate demand and accelerating the economic recovery. Back-of-the-envelope calculations show that "excess" deposits are large relative to pre-crisis business investment, potentially indicating a sizeable future impact on investment (Figure 1.8, Panel C). For households, "excess" deposits are relatively small relative to private consumption (Figure 1.8, Panel C), but both household deposits and consumption are much larger relative to GDP (Figure 1.8, Panels E and F), potentially implying a bigger aggregate impact.

Figure 1.8. Selected indicators about bank deposits

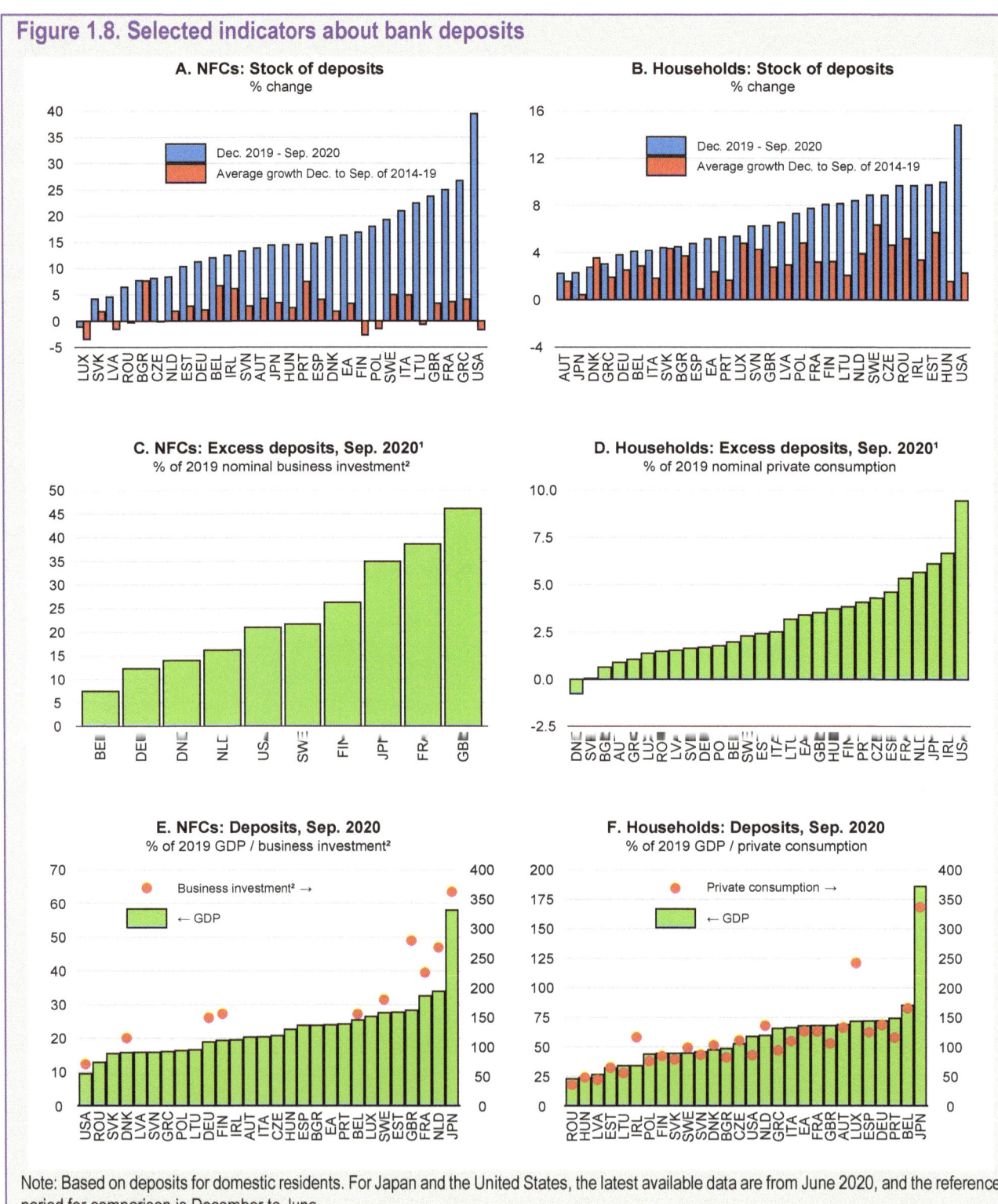

Note: Based on deposits for domestic residents. For Japan and the United States, the latest available data are from June 2020, and the reference period for comparison is December to June.
1. Excess deposits are calculated as a difference between the September 2020 level of deposits and the level implied by the average percentage change over the past five years (December to September) applied to the December 2019 level.
2. Business investment data are available only for the countries shown.
Source: OECD Economic Outlook 108 database; Bank of Japan; European Central Bank; US Federal Reserve; and OECD calculations.

StatLink 📊 https://doi.org/10.1787/888934217019

However, there are several reasons why these excess savings may not boost aggregate private demand beyond negative confidence effects. For example, the distribution of deposits may be skewed. If the increase in NFCs' deposits has been driven by a few large firms that benefitted from the crisis, particularly in the technology sector, excess deposits are unlikely to stimulate future economy-wide investment. Similarly, if the increase in household deposits were mostly driven by high-income households with a relative low marginal propensity to consume, then a reduction in uncertainty and containment measures would not necessarily lead to a broad-based strengthening of consumption. Moreover, firms could use excess deposits to settle payments due to other companies, creditors or tax authorities.

---

1. Country coverage is determined by the availability of data for non-financial corporations and households.
2. The growth rate of bank deposits is computed over nine months from the start of the global financial crisis (2008Q4 for European countries and Japan, and 2008Q3 for the United States) to ensure comparability with the data available for the COVID-19 crisis.
3. For example, Mody et al. (2012) show that the change in the unemployment rate – a proxy for variation in economic uncertainty – boosts precautionary savings.
4. In November, the size of the resources made available to the economy through government-sponsored loan programmes (loans and guarantees) was above 10% of 2019 GDP in Canada, France, Germany, Italy, Japan, Spain and the United Kingdom.

High-frequency data suggest that the recent resurgence of the COVID-19 pandemic, and the containment measures implemented in response, are again weakening activity and mobility in affected countries, particularly in Europe. Most governments initially resorted to targeted localised restrictions on specific regions or activities, but these have not sufficiently checked the upturn in new COVID-19 cases, especially in countries that lack an effective track, trace and isolate system and in which compliance with quarantine restrictions is patchy. New cases were initially concentrated amongst younger people, but hospitalisations are now also rising sharply, as older people catch the virus. As a result, some governments have now imposed significant nationwide restrictions once again, including the closure of many businesses. Mobility indicators related to retail and recreational activities have turned down since the start of September in the major European economies (Figure 1.9, Panel A), though to a smaller extent than seen last April. In Israel, where a second nationwide lockdown was implemented from mid-September to mid-October, credit card spending plummeted almost as sharply as in the first full lockdown (Figure 1.9, Panel B), especially on already hard-hit service activities, raising the risks of higher unemployment and bankruptcies. This indicates the extent to which renewed nationwide or widespread lockdowns could have powerful negative effects on activity, as in the first wave (Box 1.1).

Figure 1.9. The resurgence of the virus is hitting activity in affected countries

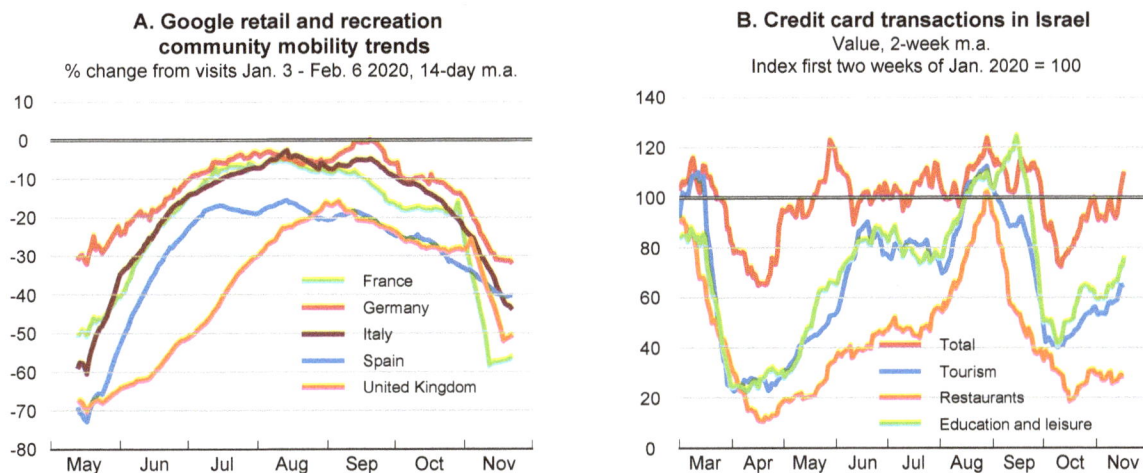

Source: Google LLC, *Google COVID-19 Community Mobility Reports*, https://www.google.com/covid19/mobility; Bank of Israel; and OECD calculations.

StatLink 🔢 https://doi.org/10.1787/888934217038

Additional containment measures are likely to place further pressure on labour markets. Hours worked fell sharply at the height of the pandemic and have recovered slowly since then (Figure 1.10, Panel A). Job prospects and hours worked continue to diverge across sectors, remaining especially weak in some of the service sectors most affected by containment measures and restrictions on international travel. The divergence in outcomes across sectors has also been reflected in differences in labour demand by types of occupation and by earnings levels (Figure 1.11). Total hours worked have fallen particularly sharply for lower-skilled workers and for workers at the bottom end of the earnings distribution in many countries, adding to the high level of inequality that existed prior to the pandemic.

In the median OECD economy, the unemployment rate in September was around 1¼ percentage points higher than immediately prior to the pandemic, but this masked considerable differences across economies. Unemployment has edged up only mildly in Japan and in many European economies, largely due to job retention measures such as short-time work and wage subsidies, but has risen sharply in the United States and Canada, as well as in some emerging-market economies hard hit by the pandemic.[1] Younger people have been especially affected, with the youth unemployment rate rising by over 3 percentage points in the median OECD economy since February this year. High-frequency indicators of hiring rates and new job postings have begun to recover after falling sharply at the height of the pandemic, particularly in services (Figure 1.10, Panel B).

Figure 1.10. Labour market conditions are recovering slowly

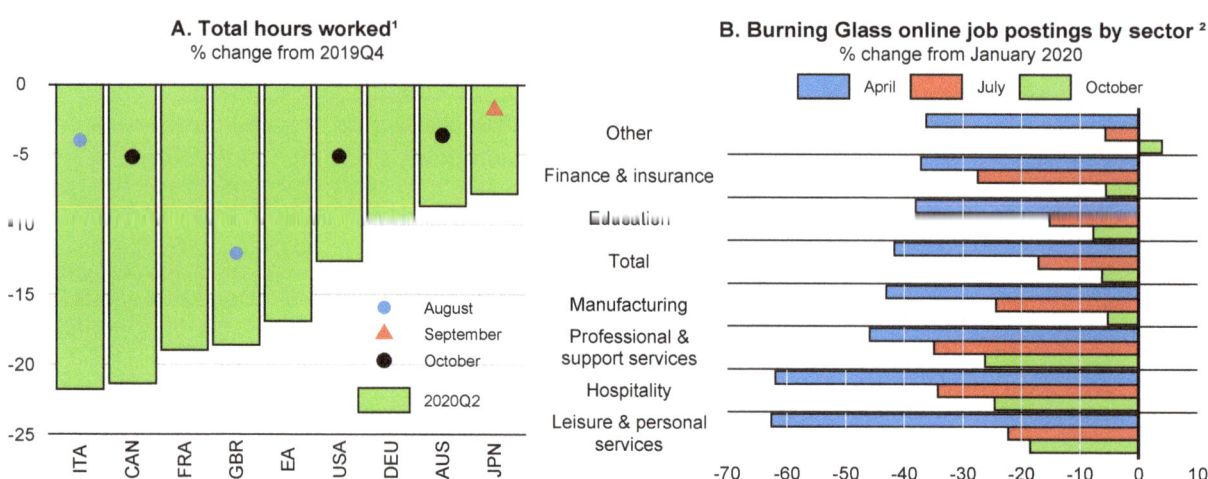

1. Economy-wide data for hours worked in all economies apart from the United States, where the data refer to total hours worked by private non-farm employees. For Japan, estimates are based on total employment and average monthly hours worked by employed persons. August estimates for Italy based on firms with more than 500 employees in industry and services.
2. Based on online job postings in Australia, Canada, New Zealand, Singapore, the United Kingdom and the United States. The occupational group "professional and support services" includes professional, scientific and administrative support services.
Source: Bureau of Economic Analysis; Statistics Canada; Australian Bureau of Statistics; Statistics Bureau, Japan; Eurostat; Office for National Statistics; Burning Glass Technologies; and OECD calculations.

StatLink ᘯᔕᒲ https://doi.org/10.1787/888934217057

---

[1] Differences in the statistical treatment of furloughed workers hamper direct comparisons between the United States and Canada, and other countries. In the former, they are classified as unemployed rather than as employed.

Figure 1.11. Lower-skilled and low-wage workers have been particularly affected

Note: Data for Australia refer to the three months ending in the month shown. Community services refers to community and personal service workers.
Source: Australian Bureau of Statistics; Statistics Canada; and OECD calculations.

StatLink https://doi.org/10.1787/888934217076

In spite of a highly uncertain outlook, financial conditions have largely normalised since the peak of the crisis following rapid and sweeping responses by central banks. The fast spread of the pandemic and strict containment measures triggered historical declines in financial asset prices and a general spike in volatility in March and April, with some markets ceasing to function properly. Since then, equity prices have rebounded across the board, and volatility indicators have reverted to historical standards, despite their recent fluctuations in some economic areas (Figure 1.12, Panel A). Long-term government bond yields have remained low in many advanced economies, after having reached historical lows amid the massive monetary policy easing, a general flight to safety and the subdued outlook (Figure 1.12, Panel B). With a few exceptions, currencies have also bounced back against the US dollar in key advanced and emerging-market economies, reflecting both improving global risk sentiment and concerns about a worsening of the COVID-19 crisis in the United States.

Importantly, financial stability concerns have abated in the more fragile segments of the market. Capital flows to emerging-market economies have quickly rebounded after the March sell-off, alleviating the funding pressures faced by many sovereign borrowers with massive fiscal needs. Tensions have also eased in the corporate sector in both advanced and emerging-market economies, with large firms successfully tapping markets to raise cash and/or build buffers, and corporate bond spreads reverting to their pre-crisis level for investment-grade borrowers. However, a number of lower-rated corporate and sovereign borrowers still face high borrowing costs and/or have delayed new issuances.[2] While downgrades of corporates – which have been concentrated amongst weaker debtors – have slowed and so far remained below the peaks during the global financial crisis, negative outlooks are at unprecedented highs (IMF, 2020; Standard and Poor's, 2020). So far, banks in the main advanced economies have remained resilient thanks to robust capital and liquidity buffers (Bank of Japan, 2020; Lagarde, 2020a; Quarles, 2020). However, banks' equity prices have remained significantly below pre-crisis levels, profitability has declined and lending standards have generally tightened, with banks continuing to suffer losses if economic activity in specific sectors remains subdued or contracts further. Money market funds and investment funds have also experienced significant liquidity stress.

---

[2] For instance, Sub-Saharan countries have not issued new debt since March.

Figure 1.12. Financial market conditions have partly normalised

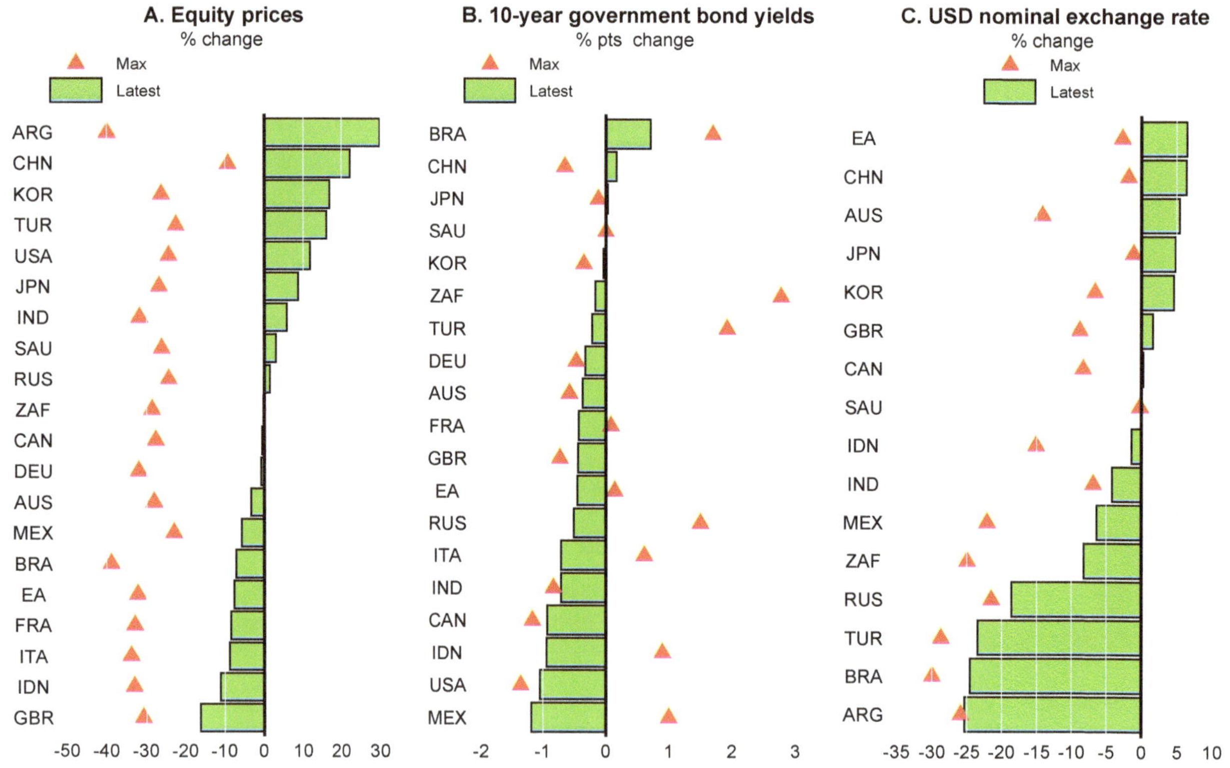

A. Equity prices
% change

B. 10-year government bond yields
% pts change

C. USD nominal exchange rate
% change

Note: "Latest" refers to the change between end-2019 and the latest available data up to 26 November. "Max" refers to the maximum change since end 2010. Based on a 10 day average of daily observations.

Source: Refinitiv; and OECD calculations.

StatLink ㎰🖘 https://doi.org/10.1787/888934217095

Financial stability concerns are likely to re-emerge. Although immediate liquidity pressures have disappeared, the continued rapid debt build-up in the sovereign and non-financial sectors will lead to solvency concerns in a large number of economies (Chapter 2, Issue Note 2). For instance, speculative-grade corporate default rates in the United States and Europe are projected to double by mid-2021 on some estimates, with hard-hit sectors such as airlines, hotels and the auto industry likely to be particularly affected (Standard and Poor's, 2020). Bankruptcies of small and medium-sized enterprises (SMEs), especially in the hard-pressed accommodation, food and entertainment sectors, are also projected to increase (IMF, 2020; Box 1.2). In the United States, the high level of corporate debt and elevated valuations in commercial real estate prior to the crisis could also lead to higher-than-expected losses on loans to some of these businesses (Quarles, 2020).

Challenges might be particularly acute in some emerging-market economies, where policy options are more limited (see below) and there is greater exposure to global demand shocks. Countries relying extensively on the most severely affected sectors – such as tourism and hospitality – and commodity exporters are particularly affected. Although some commodity prices (such as food and metals) have recovered from their trough in April, helped by strong demand from China, the prices of other key exports remain subdued. The prospect of a rebound in tourism also remains very bleak in the short term, with consumers' fears of contagion and international travel restrictions likely to persist well into 2021.

A gradual recovery amidst persisting uncertainty

Moderate growth is set to continue provided the pandemic can be contained effectively

The near-term global outlook remains highly uncertain. Growth prospects depend on many factors, including the magnitude, duration and frequency of new COVID-19 outbreaks, the degree to which these can be effectively contained, the time until an effective vaccine can be widely deployed, and the extent to which significant fiscal and monetary policy actions continue to support demand. Recent developments point to a rising possibility that effective vaccines will be widely deployed towards the end of 2021, improving the prospects for a durable recovery. However, time will be needed to manufacture and distribute the vaccine around the world and ensure it reaches those most at risk. Until then, sporadic and potentially sizeable outbreaks of the virus are likely to continue, as currently being experienced in many Northern Hemisphere economies, necessitating continued containment measures and strategies that differ across countries. Targeted restrictions on mobility and activity will need to be used to address any new outbreaks, accompanied by reinforced personal hygiene measures. Limits on personal interactions are assumed to persist, such as physical distancing requirements and restrictions on the size of gatherings. Restrictions on people crossing national borders are also expected to remain in force, at least partially. Voluntary physical distancing may also continue to restrain household spending.

Living with the virus for at least another six to nine months is likely to prove challenging. The impact of renewed periods of tighter containment measures on activity and confidence will differ across economies, depending on the effectiveness of testing, contact tracing and quarantine arrangements, and the availability of sufficient hospital capacity. However, even where outbreaks are more easily controlled, some of the service sectors most affected by restrictions may be disrupted. With these sectors accounting for a sizeable share of total activity and employment in many economies, adverse spillovers from job losses and bankruptcies into demand in other parts of the economy are likely. Persistent unemployment would also worsen the risk of poverty and deprivation for millions of informal workers. Pre-existing vulnerabilities that have been heightened by the pandemic, such as high corporate and sovereign debt in many countries, and trade tensions between the major economies, could also slow the pace of the recovery if there are prolonged outbreaks of the virus.

Based on the assumptions set out above, a gradual but uneven recovery in the global economy is projected to continue in the next two years following a temporary interruption at the end of the current year. After a decline of 4¼ per cent in 2020, global GDP is projected to pick up by 4¼ per cent in 2021, and a further 3¾ per cent in 2022 (Table 1.1; Figure 1.13, Panel A). OECD GDP is projected to rise by around 3¼ per cent per annum in 2021 and 2022, after dropping by around 5½ per cent in 2020. By the end of 2021, the level of global output is projected to have returned to that at the end of 2019 (Figure 1.13, Panel C), although this is not the case in all countries.

Output is set to remain persistently weaker than projected prior to the pandemic (Figure 1.13, Panel D), suggesting that the risk of long-lasting costs from the pandemic is high. Such shortfalls are projected to be relatively low in China, Korea, Japan and some Northern European economies, at between 1-2 per cent in 2022. The median advanced and emerging-market economy could have lost the equivalent of 4 to 5 years of per capita real income growth by 2022. Initial estimates of potential output growth in the aftermath of the pandemic also highlight the likelihood of permanent costs from the outbreak, with potential output growth in the OECD economies projected to slow to just over 1¼ per cent per annum in 2021-22, some ½ percentage point weaker than immediately prior to the crisis.

Figure 1.13. Growth is projected to remain moderate with long-lasting costs

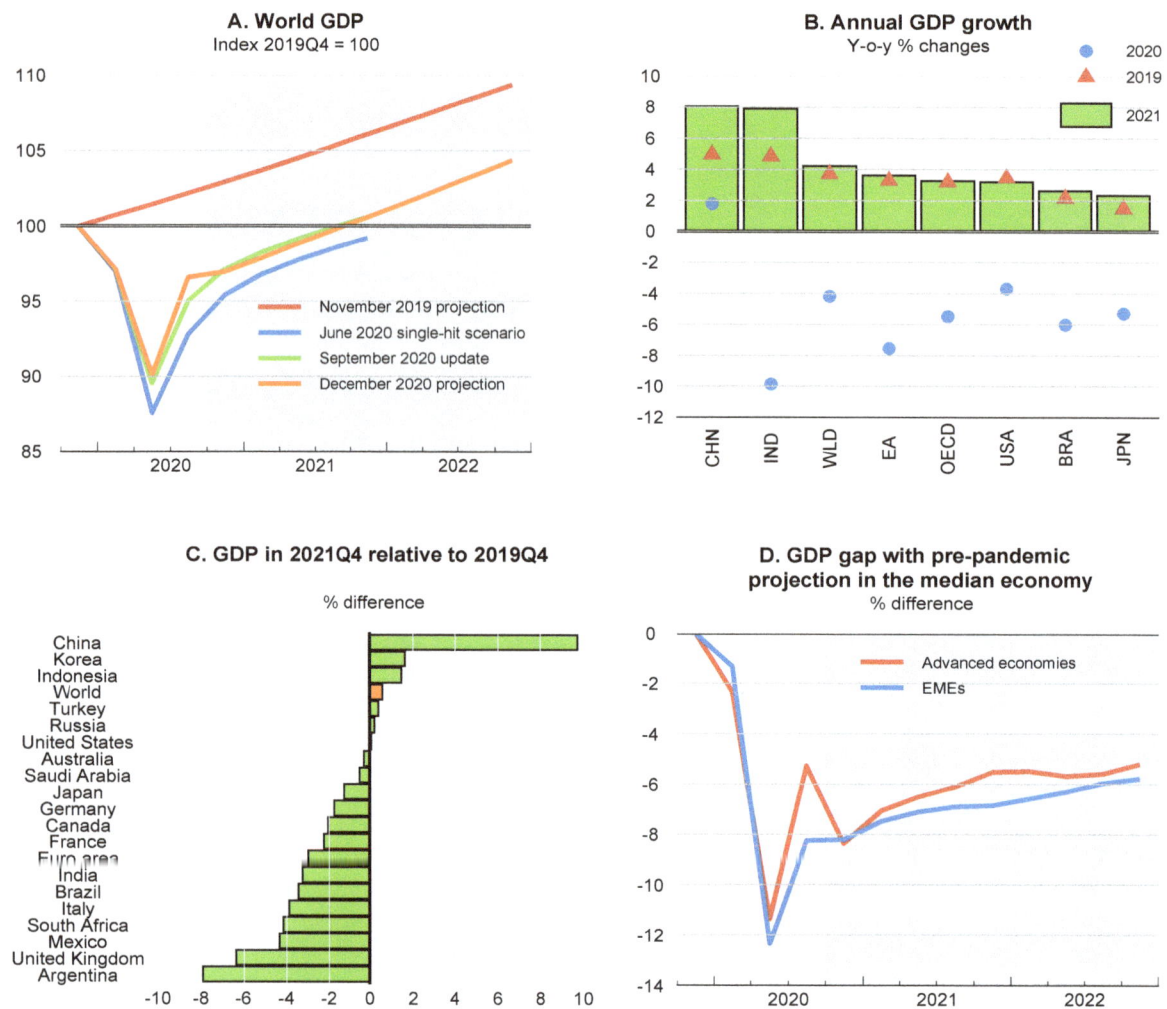

Note: The November 2019 OECD Economic Outlook projections are extended into 2022 using the November 2019 estimates of the potential output growth rate for each economy in 2021.
Source: OECD Economic Outlook 108 database; OECD Economic Outlook 107 database; OECD Economic Outlook 106 database; OECD Interim Economic Outlook 108 database; and OECD calculations.

StatLink https://doi.org/10.1787/888934217114

Considerable heterogeneity in developments in the major economies is set to persist, both between advanced and emerging-market economies, and between regions (Figure 1.13, Panel B). The economic impact of the pandemic and its aftermath has been relatively well contained in many Asia-Pacific and Northern European economies, reflecting effective containment measures, including well-resourced test, track and isolate systems, and familiarity with precautionary measures to protect against risks from transmissible diseases. In contrast, the measures required to control virus outbreaks in other parts of Europe and other emerging-market economies have been prolonged and involved much deeper declines in output.

- In the United States, GDP growth is projected to be between 3¼-3½ per cent over the next two years, after an output decline of 3¾ per cent in 2020. High uncertainty, elevated unemployment, and further localised virus outbreaks are likely to restrain the pace of the recovery, particularly in the near term, but an assumed additional fiscal package early in 2021 should help to support household incomes and spending, and accommodative monetary policy will continue to boost activity, particularly in the housing market.

- A gradual recovery is underway in Japan, with GDP growth projected to be around 2¼ per cent in 2021 and 1½ per cent in 2022, following an output decline of 5¼ per cent in 2020. Improving external demand will help exports strengthen further, but weak real income growth is likely to hold back private consumption. Strong fiscal measures have helped to cushion activity this year but a tighter fiscal stance in 2021, despite the new supplementary budget announced in November, will slow the pace of the recovery.

- In the euro area, GDP has declined by 7½ per cent this year, and near-term prospects are weak. Output is projected to drop by close to 3% in the fourth quarter of 2020, reflecting the recent reintroduction of stringent containment measures in most countries. Provided virus outbreaks can be effectively contained in the near term, and confidence restored, a moderate recovery is projected in 2021-22. However, area-wide pre-pandemic output levels may not be fully regained until after 2022. After sizeable support this year, fiscal policy is set to be broadly neutral in 2021 and mildly restrictive in 2022 despite the modest outlook, but Next Generation EU grants should help support investment in the hardest-hit economies during the projection period.

- A solid recovery is expected to continue in China, with GDP growth projected to be around 8% in 2021 and 5% in 2022. Monetary stimulus is now being withdrawn but fiscal policy is set to remain supportive. Strong investment in real estate and infrastructure, helped by policy stimulus and stronger credit growth, and improved export performance are driving the pick-up, and helping to boost external demand in many commodity-producing economies and key supply-chain partners in Asia. Progress in rebalancing the economy has however slowed, and significant financial risks remain from shadow banking and elevated corporate sector debt.

- The impact of the pandemic in many other emerging-market economies has been prolonged relative to that in China, reflecting difficulties in getting the pandemic under control, high poverty and informality levels, declining tourist inflows, and limited scope for policy support. Gradual recoveries are now starting in most economies, but the shortfalls from expectations prior to the pandemic are likely to remain sizeable.

- Output in India is projected to rise by 8% in FY 2021-22 provided confidence improves, after having declined by 10% in FY 2020-21. Further reductions in policy interest rates should help to support demand, if the current upturn in inflation subsides, but there is limited scope for additional fiscal measures, and pressures on corporate balance sheets and banking sector bad loans are also likely to restrain the pace of the upturn.

- A gradual recovery is projected to continue in Brazil, with GDP rising by 2½ per cent in 2021 and 2¼ per cent in 2022, after contracting by 6% this year. Strong fiscal and monetary support have helped to protect incomes and prevent a larger output decline this year. High unemployment and the planned withdrawal of some crisis-related fiscal measures will temper household spending in 2021, but historically low real interest rates and favourable credit conditions should help investment to strengthen.

Fiscal support is helping to underpin demand in the near term, with job retention schemes and business support measures continuing in many countries, but this is unlikely to be able to prevent rising business failures and attendant job losses in the service sectors most affected by ongoing containment measures until an effective vaccine is widely deployed. In the median OECD economy, using conventional but uncertain estimates of the fiscal stance based on changes in the underlying primary balance, a mild fiscal tightening of 0.7% of GDP is expected in 2021, after easing of 4.2% of GDP in 2020. The exceptional additional monetary and financial policy measures introduced since the start of the pandemic are important for economic stabilisation, helping to ensure financial stability and limit debt service burdens. However, their impact on consumer spending and business investment will depend on the extent to which confidence recovers and firms lower their hurdle rates for investment.

High uncertainty, subdued confidence and employment are likely to keep precautionary saving elevated for a while, although this should fade slowly during 2021-22. The increasing concentration of saving amongst higher-income households with a lower marginal propensity to consume, and likely declines in the incomes of lower-income households, will also check the rebound in consumer spending in some countries (Box 1.3). In the advanced economies, private consumption is projected to rise by 3½ per cent per annum in 2021-22 after declining by over 6% this year, with household saving rates remaining above pre-pandemic levels throughout the projection period.

Soft demand growth and considerable uncertainty are likely to hold back investment for an extended period, particularly by companies with high debt. In the major economies, business investment is projected to be around 1¾ per cent higher in 2021 than this year on average, but with the level remaining well below that prior to the pandemic. A stronger pick up is projected in 2022, with business investment rising by over 4%. The recovery in housing investment is projected to be a little quicker, helped by the sensitivity of demand to lower mortgage rates, rising by 4% in the advanced economies in 2021. In spite of the recovery in gross investment, net productive investment appears set to weaken further. An extended period of weak investment adds to the risks of low output growth becoming persistent, and contributes to the estimated moderation of potential output growth in the aftermath of the pandemic. In the median OECD economy, net productive investment (business plus government) is projected to average 3¼ per cent of GDP over 2020-22, down from 4½ per cent of GDP over 2015-19.

Labour market conditions are projected to remain subdued. The unemployment rate in the OECD economies is expected to moderate only by around ¾ percentage point over the next two years, from around 7¼ per cent in the fourth quarter of 2020 (Figure 1.14, Panel A). Employment growth is projected to be only modest, with temporary wage and employment support schemes due to fade out in some countries. Continued uncertainty for much of 2021 may also mean that many companies initially choose to meet improved demand by expanding hours worked per employee, rather than the overall size of their workforce, particularly if they are retaining staff with assistance from job retention schemes. Many discouraged workers and those experiencing longer spells of unemployment may leave the labour force, damping participation, and some older workers may decide to retire earlier than expected. Employment and participation rates are projected to remain below their pre-pandemic levels (Figure 1.14, Panel B), contributing to the longer-term costs of the pandemic. Persisting slack in labour markets is in turn likely to check the growth of wages and incomes.

Figure 1.14. Labour market conditions are expected to remain subdued

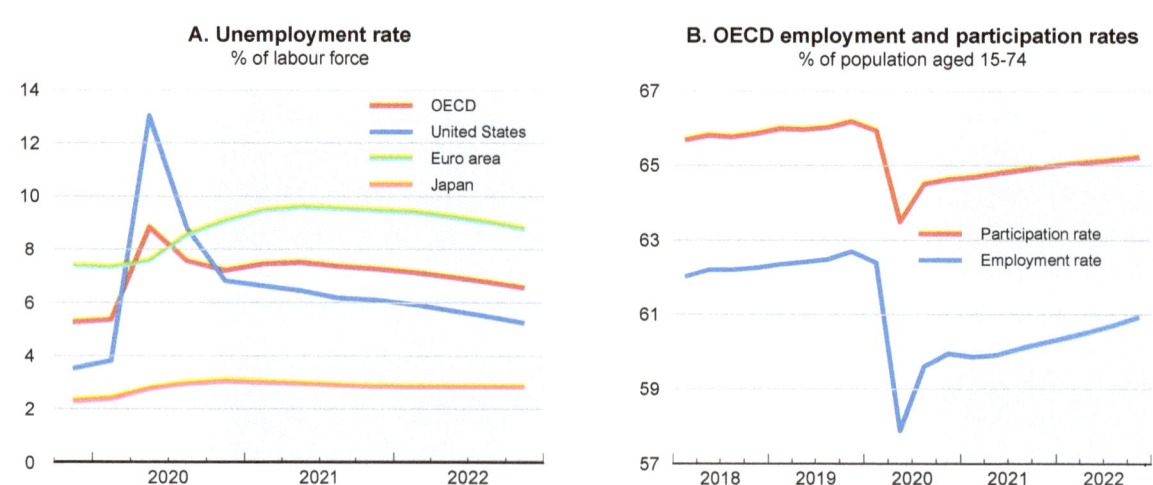

Source: OECD Economic Outlook 108 database; and OECD calculations.

StatLink ⬛🖳 https://doi.org/10.1787/888934217133

World trade is projected to continue recovering slowly, rising on average by around 4¼ per cent per annum over 2021-22, after declining by 10¼ per cent in 2020. The weak recovery in investment – a trade-intensive component of demand – and the likelihood that containment measures will continue to weigh on international travel and tourism both contribute to the modest rebound in overall trade.[3] The trade decline in 2020 is broadly similar to that seen during the global financial crisis, despite the much greater fall in activity during the pandemic. In part, this reflects the sharp fall in consumer demand in services where trade intensity is low.

Inflation rates in advanced economies have rebounded since the trough in early/mid-2020, especially in the United States, but generally remain below pre-pandemic levels. This trend is projected to persist in the short term, with inflation being subdued in 2021 and converging slowly to pre-crisis levels only by the end of 2022 in most countries (Figure 1.15, Panel A). Inflation in most emerging-market economies is also expected to remain moderate, or even decline, over the next two years (Figure 1.15, Panel B). Although supply disruptions – such as non-tariff trade barriers or unexpected bottlenecks in global production and distribution – could accelerate the return to trend inflation, the forces currently weighing on aggregate demand around the world – contagion fears, high unemployment, and rising precautionary saving – clearly dominate the inflation outlook. As a result, inflation should remain well below central banks' targets in the coming two years, especially in advanced economies. However, in emerging-market economies, inflation could be higher than projected if domestic currencies depreciate again.

Figure 1.15. Inflation is projected to remain low

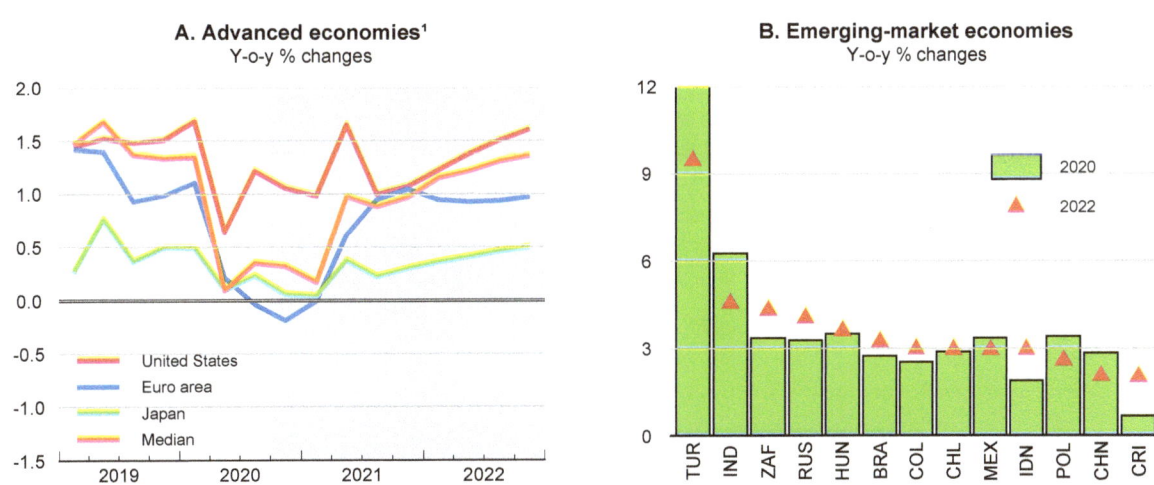

Note: Panels show the overall harmonised consumer price index for EU countries; the overall consumer price deflator for the United States; and the overall consumer price index for the remaining countries.
1. Advanced economies include OECD countries except Chile, Colombia, Hungary, Mexico, Poland and Turkey.
Source: OECD Economic Outlook 108 database; and OECD calculations.

StatLink https://doi.org/10.1787/888934217152

[3] For the year 2020, the UN World Tourism Organisation estimates a 1 billion drop in tourist arrivals and a loss of USD 1 trillion in export revenues from tourism. Around 100 million of tourism jobs are estimated to be directly at risk.

A considerable amount of uncertainty still surrounds inflation dynamics. Since the onset of the COVID-19 pandemic, many services have not been provided due to strict containment measures and many individual prices have had to be extrapolated by statistical offices (Bureau of Labor Statistics, 2020; Eurostat, 2020). This is expected to continue with the renewal of containment measures in some countries. In addition, the COVID-19 pandemic has affected the way consumers allocate spending, potentially leading to an understatement of actual inflation (Cavallo, 2020). Available estimates of the changes in spending patterns caused by COVID-19 point to an increase in the weight of food at home in US consumption baskets, at the expense of transportation services, recreation and restaurants. Since food prices (transport prices) have generally risen (decreased) faster than other items, official inflation statistics based on pre-COVID-19 weights could understate the level of inflation faced by consumers. The inflation outlook also remains highly uncertain, given the special nature of the COVID-19 crisis, which affects both supply and demand and in very heterogeneous ways across individual items and countries. The balance of risks in the longer term, however, remains tilted to the downside given the influence of both cyclical and structural downward pressure on prices in most countries (Chapter 2, Issue Note 3).

Key risks to the projections

Uncertainty remains about the time before a vaccine can be widely deployed, and the impact it would have

The baseline projections are conditional on the evolution of the pandemic, the judgements about the actions taken to contain the spread of the virus and their economic impact, and the assumption that improving prospects for the successful deployment of a vaccine sustain consumer and business confidence. A wide range of outcomes could occur over the next two years. Two scenarios set out below use the NiGEM global macroeconomic model to illustrate the potential implications of alternative assumptions.

- On the upside, a faster deployment than assumed of a vaccine could provide a greater boost to confidence and a stronger pick-up in spending than in the baseline projections. This would boost GDP growth, especially in 2022, and strengthen the impact of the monetary policy easing implemented since the start of the pandemic.

- On the downside, if the challenges involved in producing and deploying an effective vaccine were to prove greater than expected, prolonging the period in which continued containment measures were required to limit COVID-19 outbreaks, confidence would remain weak for longer, and uncertainty deepen. This would further raise the risk of bankruptcies and job losses, particularly in sectors in which activity would be severely restricted again. Precautionary saving by consumers would increase, business investment would weaken, with capital being scrapped in some sectors, and substantial repricing could occur in financial markets, reflecting greater risk aversion. This would weaken global growth, particularly in 2021.

The upside scenario: a resurgence in confidence

The upside scenario considers the impact of a stronger boost to the confidence of consumers and companies, raising the prospects of a stronger rebound in spending and output. To illustrate this, an endogenous reduction in household saving rates is applied starting from the latter half of 2021 in all economies, with this shock fading slowly through 2022. Policy interest rates are assumed to remain at their baseline levels, implying an increasingly accommodative monetary policy stance as demand strengthens. The automatic fiscal stabilisers are allowed to operate fully in all countries, so that the fiscal balance improves as activity picks up.

Key features of the results are as follows:

- Overall, the level of world GDP is raised by around 2½ per cent (relative to baseline) at the peak of the shock, with global GDP growth raised by ¾ percentage point in 2021 and 1¾ percentage point in 2022 (Figure 16, Panel A). This would bring global GDP growth to around 5% and 5½ per cent in 2021 and 2022 respectively.

- Output returns to pre-pandemic levels more quickly in all regions (Figure 16, Panel B), and the gap between baseline activity and pre-crisis expectations is halved. World trade growth is also strengthened substantially, rising by around 3¾ percentage point (relative to baseline) in 2022, boosting exports in all economies.

- The initial decline in the saving rate, higher household incomes as activity picks up and a 1 percentage point decline in the unemployment rate result in a substantial boost to spending, with private consumption over 3% higher in the advanced economies. Business investment is also stimulated by stronger demand, rising by 2¾ per cent (relative to baseline) in the median advanced economy. This boosts the capital stock and the prospects for a sustained recovery.

- Stronger growth also helps to ease government debt burdens, with the government debt-to-GDP ratio declining by around 4 percentage points in the median advanced economy in 2022.

The downside scenario: heightened uncertainty and additional costs

The shocks considered in the downside scenario are as follows:

- Consumer confidence is assumed to decline as prospects for an early deployment of the vaccine recede, reducing household spending and pushing up household saving rates by around 2 percentage points in the median advanced economy.

- Heightened uncertainty and a longer period of weak demand are assumed to result in the further closure of businesses and the scrapping of capital through 2021. The shocks imply an ex-ante reduction of 1% in the business capital stock by the latter half of 2021, with additional reductions occurring endogenously as the collective impact of the shocks applied is felt on output and investment.[4]

- Higher uncertainty and shortfalls in output developments relative to expectations are also assumed to result in weaker risk appetite and repricing in financial markets. This is captured by an increase of 50 basis points in the risk premia on corporate bonds and equities that persists throughout 2021, and declines of 15% and 10% respectively in global equity prices and non-food commodity prices.

All these shocks are assumed to fade gradually through 2022. Their impact is partly cushioned by policy responses. Monetary policy is allowed to be endogenous, with policy interest rates lowered (relative to baseline), but for illustrative purposes there is assumed to be a binding zero lower bound. Thus, policy interest rates either cannot become negative or remain unchanged where they are already negative. The automatic fiscal stabilisers are also allowed to operate fully in all countries, implying that governments do not react to the shock by attempting to maintain a previously announced budget path.

These shocks would have substantial adverse economic effects. Global activity could come to a virtual standstill through much of 2021 before recovering gradually through 2022, remaining well below the projected baseline path and further adding to the costs of the pandemic (Figure 1.16, Panel A). Global output would recover to pre-pandemic levels only at the end of 2022, a year later than in the baseline projection.

---

[4] The level of detail differs across the models for each country or region in NiGEM. In the smaller country models, proportionate shocks to domestic demand and potential output are applied in place of specific shocks to consumer spending and the capital stock.

- The level of world GDP is reduced by close to 4.5% (relative to baseline) at the peak of the shock, with the full-year impact lowering global GDP growth in 2021 and 2022 by 2¾ percentage points and 1½ percentage points respectively. Broadly similar effects occur in most major economies and regions in 2021, with Europe and North America hit more heavily than the Asia-Pacific economies (Figure 1.16, Panel B). Relatively strong output declines occur in small open economies with a high trade intensity, and in those countries where there are relatively few policy offsets, due to limited monetary policy space, or weak levels of social protection or automatic budgetary stabilisers.

- Global trade is also affected significantly by the drop in demand, with trade growth declining by over 7 percentage points in 2021, relative to the baseline.

- Higher household saving, greater uncertainty and tighter financial conditions result in substantial cutbacks in private demand and higher unemployment. Business investment declines by around 12% in the median advanced economy in 2021, and the unemployment rate rises by 1.7 percentage points by the end of the year.

- The overall impact of lower commodity prices is broadly neutral. Commodity exporters are hit by lower export revenues, but commodity-importing economies benefit from lower prices.

- The net effects of the combined shocks are deflationary, with consumer price inflation in the advanced economies pushed down by over 1¼ percentage point in 2021.

- Reductions in policy interest rates in the economies that have policy space help to cushion the negative effects on domestic activity and provide support for an eventual recovery. Policy interest rates are lowered by 2 percentage points or more in several large emerging-market economies, and by 25 basis points in the United States and Canada.

- In the median advanced economy, the government debt-to-GDP ratio is increased by over 7½ percentage points by 2022.

Figure 1.10. There is considerable uncertainty around the baseline projection

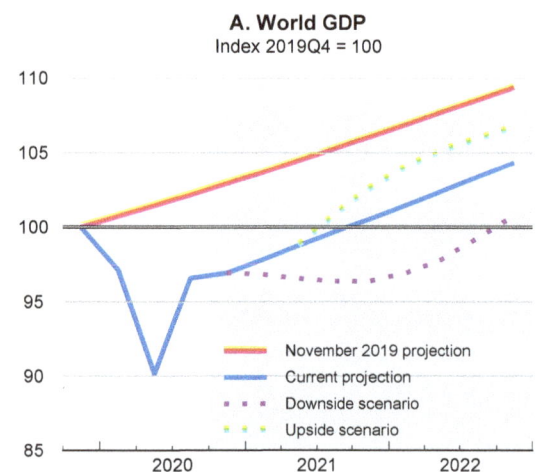

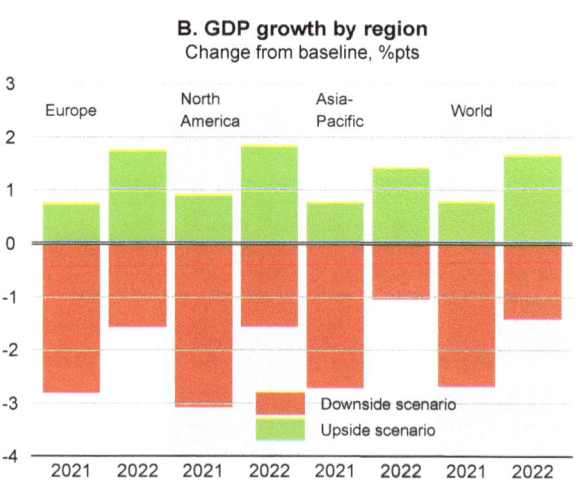

Note: See text for description of the scenarios. Regional estimates in Panel B are PPP-weighted aggregates. The Asia-Pacific regional aggregate includes Australia, China, Japan Korea, New Zealand and the Dynamic Asian economies. Europe comprises the euro area economies, the Czech Republic, Denmark, Hungary, Norway, Poland, Sweden, Switzerland and the United Kingdom.
Source: OECD calculations using the NiGEM macroeconomic model.

StatLink 🔗 https://doi.org/10.1787/888934217171

In the scenario set out above, all shocks are assumed to occur in all countries. It is possible that the direct impact of further and stronger COVID-19 outbreaks on consumer spending and investment could be limited in some countries, particularly those in the Asia-Pacific region with effective test, track and isolate schemes and strictly observed containment measures. Nonetheless, in an interconnected world, such economies remain fully exposed to external shocks, from weaker global demand, restrictions on cross-border travel, and fluctuations in global financial and commodity markets. Removing the domestic demand shocks in the major Asia-Pacific economies would lower the overall impact on global GDP by around one-quarter, but still leave global activity well below the baseline in 2021 and 2022.

Additional timely and well-targeted discretionary macroeconomic policy responses could also help to offset downside shocks, the resulting disruptions to the economy, and heightened financial market volatility. Fiscal actions may be needed, including prolonged support for indebted companies and continuations of job protection and income support schemes. Monetary and financial policy programmes will need to be scaled up or extended, particularly liquidity and lending support, and further steps taken to increase monetary policy accommodation. Options include expanded asset purchase programmes, or forward guidance to help interest rates stay low for longer. An expansion of government transfers by 2% of GDP for two years could offset around one-fifth of the overall shock, reducing the hit to global GDP growth (relative to baseline) by around 0.4 percentage point per annum on average in these two years. Effects from higher transfers might be stronger still if they could be targeted fully on low-income households with a high marginal propensity to consume.

The lingering risk that the downside scenario materialises is a particular concern, as a downside surprise (relative to the projections) would be more likely to induce repricing in financial markets and possible discontinuities from higher corporate bankruptcies. Monetary policy may also face increasing constraints in reacting to such a shock, particularly in countries in which policy rates are close to an effective lower bound.

The outlook for trade remains uncertain

Many longstanding downside risks are still affecting the global trade outlook. However, the US-China Phase I agreement[5] signed early this year, recent free trade agreements between the EU and some Asian partners and Mercosur,[6] and a recent noticeable increase in trade-facilitating measures (Figure 1.17) show that some progress has been made in easing restraints on international trade. This has been further demonstrated by the trade pact recently agreed between members of the Regional Comprehensive Economic Partnership (RCEP) - China, Japan, Korea, Australia, the ASEAN countries and New Zealand - which reduces tariffs on trade for goods, expands market access for some services and unifies rules of origin within the block. Even so, some of the distortionary barriers to trade introduced around the world over the past two years are still in place. Tariff and non-tariff barriers remain high, and continue to limit global trade.

---

[5] The agreement commits China to purchase a cumulative additional USD 200 billion of American goods and services in 2020-21 (on top of a baseline of USD 180 billion imports in 2017). At present, China has imported less than one-third of the total goods covered by the agreement, with the exception of high-tech products like US semiconductors and chip-making equipment, which China imported for an amount above the agreed target. However, US export controls on the semiconductor supply chain, initially imposed on Huawei and recently extended to foreign manufactures supplying Huawei, might generate large future falls in China's total purchases.

[6] The EU-Japan Economic Partnership Agreement came into force on 1 February 2019. Free trade agreements with Singapore and Vietnam entered into force in November 2019 and August 2020 respectively. A trade agreement with Mercosur (Argentina, Brazil, Paraguay and Uruguay) was in principle reached on 28 June 2019.

Figure 1.17. Non-COVID-19-related import-restrictive measures continue to rise

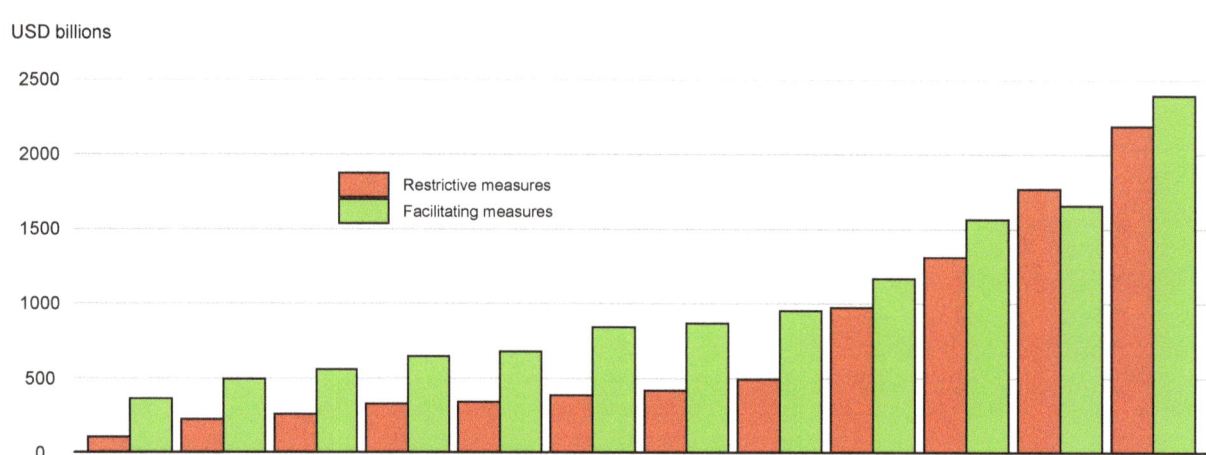

Note: These figures are estimates and represent the cumulative coverage of the trade measures (i.e. annual imports of the products concerned from economies affected by the measures). Liberalisation associated with the 2015 Expansion of the WTO's Information Technology Agreement is not included in the figures. COVID-19 trade and trade-related measures are not included.
Source: World Trade Organization (2020), "Report on G-20 Trade Measures", 30 October.

StatLink 〽️ https://doi.org/10.1787/888934217190

Uncertainty surrounding Brexit is also continuing to weigh on growth prospects. The transitional period agreed in the UK–EU Withdrawal Agreement will expire on 31 December 2020. If a deal is not ratified, the United Kingdom could end the transition period without any trade agreement, with particularly high risks of rising trade barriers, reduced labour mobility and lower foreign direct investment. Recent scenario analyses suggest that a no-deal exit of the United Kingdom from the EU Single Market would hit activity in the near term and continue to have strong negative effects in the medium term. It would entail physical and financial disruptions of different magnitudes across sectors, with exports falling by more than 30% in a few manufacturing sectors (notably the motor vehicle and transport, meat and textile sectors) and by almost 20% in the financial and insurance sector (OECD, 2020b).

A further source of uncertainty at the global level is that the World Trade Organization's Appellate Body has ceased to function while waiting for the appointment of a new members' board, fuelling concerns about the capacity to fulfil its mandate of settling trade disputes and enforcing international rules.[7]

On top of this gloomy trade environment, the COVID-19 outbreak is creating additional downside risks. Many countries reacted in the early phase of the pandemic by tightening trade restrictions (for example on medical supplies) – particularly in Europe and North America. Even though many of these restrictions proved temporary, and were lifted quickly, they added to growing uncertainty. In the event of a substantial weakening in the recovery, with a new surge in global demand for medical supplies, a risk is that such restrictions could be reintroduced.

---

[7] The Multi-Party Interim Appeal Arbitration Arrangement (MPIA), notified to the World Trade Organization (WTO) on 30 April, 2020, was signed by the European Union and a subset of WTO members to overcome the paralysis of the WTO's dispute settlement process. However, it provides only an interim solution and has limited reach given that only 22 of the WTO's 164 members have so far joined.

In addition, disruptions and shortages for a few but essential products have revived discussions about the costs of the international fragmentation of production. Reductions in trade dependency, including repatriating production, are seen as a potential way of reducing risk, but could also impose substantial efficiency costs. Besides, attempts to relocate production can weaken diversification, which reduces the scope for adjusting to shocks. Instead, since trade plays an important stabilising role, governments can strengthen resilience for most goods and services by taking actions to facilitate free movement. For some goods considered as "essential", policymakers can also improve risk preparedness by monitoring the concentration of supply sources and increasing stockpiles.

Policy requirements

With the virus continuing to spread in many regions of the world, and many countries experiencing a resurgence of cases, well-targeted public health measures and supportive macroeconomic and structural policies are required to preserve confidence and reduce uncertainty until an effective vaccine can be widely deployed. Governments need to use containment measures that control the virus without unduly burdening the economy (Chapter 2, Issue Note 4). Faced with the challenge of fostering the recovery while containment measures remain in place and some sectors undergo structural transformations, crisis-related support policies should be flexible and state-contingent, evolving as the recovery progresses to support workers and ensure assistance is focused on viable companies. Exceptional crisis-related policies need to be accompanied by the structural reforms most likely to raise opportunities for displaced workers and improve economic dynamism, fostering the reallocation of labour and capital resources towards sectors and activities that strengthen growth, enhance resilience and contribute to environmental sustainability. National policy efforts need to be accompanied by enhanced global co-operation to help mitigate and supress the virus, speed up the economic recovery, and keep trade and investment flowing freely.

Comprehensive public health interventions remain necessary

Comprehensive public health interventions remain necessary to limit and mitigate new COVID-19 outbreaks until vaccination becomes widespread. A key requirement is that healthcare systems can deal effectively with any resurgence of infections without unduly delaying necessary interventions for other patients. Governments need to maintain sufficient resources to allow large-scale test, track, trace and isolate programmes to operate effectively and limit further sharp rises in infection numbers, as has been achieved in several Asia-Pacific countries, and ensure adequate healthcare capacity and stocks of personal protective equipment. Mitigation measures, such as physical distancing and the widespread use of masks, also help to limit the spread of the virus (Chapter 2, Issue Note 4). Such steps would allow timely and targeted localised measures to be used to deal with new outbreaks, rather than renewed economy-wide confinement measures, limiting the overall economic and social costs. Nonetheless, new restrictions may still sap confidence and slow the pace of the economic recovery until a vaccine is deployed successfully.

Global co-operation and co-ordination remain essential to tackle the global health challenge. No country is able to obtain the range of products necessary to combat COVID-19 purely from domestic resources. Greater funding and multilateral efforts are needed to ensure efficient production of medical products and help affordable vaccines and treatments to be available swiftly everywhere. Decisions about stockpiling and health-emergency assistance in advanced economies should be designed in an inclusive way, taking into account the needs of the most vulnerable emerging-market economies and developing countries, where healthcare capacity is limited and resources are not available for significant investment.

Monetary policy needs to remain supportive

Advanced economies swiftly and markedly eased monetary and financial policies in response to the pandemic in the first half of the year. This involved interest rate cuts, renewed asset purchases, expansion of US dollar swap lines, and easing of bank prudential regulations (OECD, 2020c; Figure 1.18; Table 1.2). Since then, few new measures have been announced.[8] This is warranted given some stabilisation in financial markets (see above) and the fact that many programmes are still being implemented. The main central banks continue to purchase government and private debt instruments, keeping interest rates low. Moreover, some announced liquidity and lending support measures have not yet been fully used (Table 1.3). The monetary authorities have committed to sustain credit support well until the crisis phase is over, and to act further if the outlook deteriorates, which is appropriate (Brainard, 2020; Kuroda, 2020; Lagarde, 2020b).

During the on-going crisis, giving strong support to demand, providing a backstop to key credit markets and ensuring financial stability should remain key objectives of monetary policy. The current numerous monetary and financial policy programmes offer flexibility to deal with sporadic virus outbreaks and associated disruptions to the economy and heightened financial market volatility. Buffers still exist within the current programmes, in particular regarding emergency lending and support to bank lending, which can be extended if needed (Table 1.3). While several programmes in the United States are about to expire by the end of 2020, they could be prolonged or reinstated.[9] Also, asset purchases can be increased to ease general financial conditions. Any further easing of prudential regulation should be conditional on transparent disclosures of financial exposures and restrictions on dividend payments and bonuses.

If there are unexpected hurdles in deploying an effective vaccine, denting confidence and requiring further containment measures, with a renewed decline in economic activity, additional accommodation will be needed. While the scope to reduce policy rates in the main economic areas is limited,[10] central banks have effective tools to maintain low government bond yields and thus pricing of credit in other segments of financial markets. The tools to control longer-term interest rates involve forward guidance on interest rates and larger net government bond purchases. To maintain low yields at longer maturities, central banks could also opt for yield curve control, similar to that pursued by the Bank of Japan.[11] This framework helps to control the price of longer-term government bonds directly, in contrast to standard quantitative easing which focusses on the quantity of assets purchased.

---

[8] In September, the ECB relaxed the leverage ratio, freeing up to EUR 73 billion of capital to support lending. In October, the Reserve Bank of Australia cut policy interest rates by 10 basis points and announced purchases of government bonds over the next six months of AUD 100 billion (5% of GDP in 2019). In November, the Bank of England increased the target stock of purchased government bonds by GBP 150 billion (7% of GDP in 2019).

[9] The programmes set to close down are the Primary Market Corporate Credit Facility, the Secondary Market Corporate Credit Facility, the Municipal Liquidity Facility, and the Main Street Lending Program. The Commercial Paper Funding Facility, the Money Market Mutual Fund Liquidity Facility, the Primary Dealer Credit Facility and the Paycheck Protection Program Liquidity Facility have been extended for an additional 90 days.

[10] Policy rates are already negative in the euro area and Japan and only marginally positive in the United States. The marginal positive effects of even more negative interest rates may decline and risks could increase (Brunnermeier and Koby, 2016; Borio and Gambacorta, 2017; Eggertsson et al., 2019). In the United States, the side effects of negative interest rates could be more pervasive than in Europe and Japan, given the greater importance of money market funds in the financial system.

[11] Japan has been targeting 10-year government bond yields for more than four years already; the Reserve Bank of Australia started targeting 3-year government bond yields in March 2020; and the idea has been mooted as an option in the United States, although it is not yet deemed warranted in the current environment (Clarida, 2020).

Figure 1.18. The global monetary policy stance was eased substantially in the first half of 2020

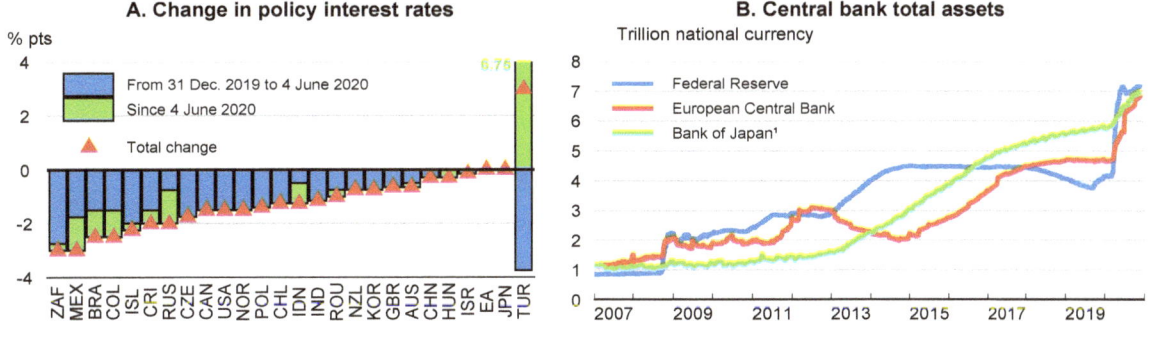

A. Change in policy interest rates

B. Central bank total assets

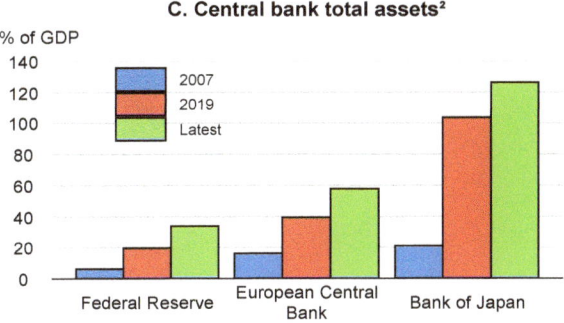

C. Central bank total assets²

1. Hundred trillion yen.
2. The latest observation is expressed in per cent of GDP in 2019.
Source: OECD Economic Outlook 108 database; Refinitiv; and OECD calculations.

StatLink 🔗 https://doi.org/10.1787/888934217209

Table 1.2. Asset purchases and lending/liquidity support measures by key central banks since early-2020

	Asset purchases	Lending support measures	Liquidity support measures
Bank of Japan	- Government bonds and Treasury bills to maintain stability in the bond market and stabilise the entire yield curve at a low level. - Commercial paper and corporate bonds (temporarily JPY 20 tr in total) to ensure smooth financing of firms and maintaining stability in financial markets. - Exchange-traded funds (annual pace of temporarily JPY 12 tr) and Japan real estate investment trusts (annual pace of temporarily JPY 0.18 tr) to lower risk premia of asset prices.	- Special Funds-Supplying Operations to Facilitate Financing in Response to the COVID-19 (fund-provisioning against private debt pledged as collateral and eligible loans, such as interest-free and unsecured loans made by eligible counterparties based on the government's emergency economic measures: JPY 120 tr) with a view to firmly supporting financial institutions to fulfil their function for a wide range of private sectors.	- Provision of ample yen liquidity using market operations with long maturities against pooled collateral. - Provision of ample US dollar liquidity through the US dollar funds-supplying operations. - Temporary increase in the number of issues of Japanese government securities (JGSs) offered in the Securities Lending Facility and offers of sales of JGSs with repurchase agreements to stabilise the repo market.
ECB	- Pandemic Emergency Purchase Programme (EUR 1.35 tr – public and private securities) to lower borrowing costs and increase lending. - Temporary addition to the Asset Purchases Programme (EUR 120 bn) to ease financial conditions over the yield curve.	- Easing of parameters of targeted longer-term refinancing operations (TLTROs), including lower interest rate, higher borrowing allowance, and lower lending performance thresholds, to support bank lending. - Temporary broadening of the collateral base, reduction in valuation haircuts and removal of credit quality requirements of collateral to support access to credit for firms and households.	- Pandemic Emergency Longer-Term Refinancing Operations, benefiting from the collateral easing measures, and a series of LTROs designed to bridge liquidity needs to support to the euro area financial system and the smooth functioning of money markets.

	Asset purchases	Lending support measures	Liquidity support measures
Federal Reserve	- Treasury securities, agency mortgage-backed securities and agency commercial mortgage-backed securities to smooth functioning of credit markets.	- Primary and Secondary Market Corporate Credit Facilities and Term Asset-Backed Securities Loan Facility (USD 850 bn in total) to support credit to employers. - Municipal Liquidity Facility (USD 500 bn) to help state and local governments manage cash-flow. - Main Street Lending Programs (USD 600 bn) to support lending to small and medium-sized businesses. - Acceptance of loans made under the Small Business Administration's Paycheck Protection Program as eligible collateral to support access to credit for small businesses. - Modification of the Liquidity Coverage Ratio rule to support participation in the Money Market Mutual Fund Liquidity Facility and the Paycheck Protection Program Liquidity Facility to support credit to households and businesses.	- Expansion of overnight and term repurchase agreement operations to support effective policy implementation and the smooth functioning of short-term US dollar funding markets.

Note: Lending support measures refer to programmes explicitly supporting lending to the private sector by banks and other creditors. Liquidity support measures generally refer to liquidity support for financial institutions aiming to improve functioning of money markets.
Source: Bank of Japan; European Central Bank; and Federal Reserve.

Table 1.3. The use of selected lending and liquidity support programmes

Central bank	Programme name	Announced envelope	Latest amount	
			bn/tr NC	% of GDP
Bank of Japan	Special Funds-Supplying Operations to Facilitate Financing in Response to the COVID-19	120	51.5	9.3
	Purchases of CP	9.5	4.3	0.8
	Purchases of corporate bonds	10.5	6.2	1.1
ECB	Pandemic Emergency Purchase Programme (PEPP)	1,350	661	5.7
	Pandemic Emergency Longer-Term Refinancing Operations (PELTROs)	unlimited	25	0.2
	Targeted Longer-Term Refinancing Operations (TLTRO III)	2,900 ¹	1,699	14.3
Federal Reserve	Main Street Lending Programs (MSLP)	600	43	0.2
	Municipal Liquidity Facility (MLF)	500	17	0.1
	Corporate Credit Facilities (CCF)	750	46	0.2
	Commercial Paper Funding Facility (CPFF)	unlimited	9	0.0
	Term Asset-Backed Securities Loan Facility (TALF)	100	12	0.1
	Money Market Mutual Fund Liquidity Facility (MMLF)	unlimited	5	0.0
	Primary Dealer Credit Facility (PDCF)	unlimited	0.3	0.0
	Paycheck Protection Program Liquidity Facility (PPPLF)	unlimited	57	0.3

1. Approximate estimate by OECD.
Note: Amounts are in trillions of yen for the Bank of Japan and billions of national currency for the ECB and the Federal Reserve, and in per cent of GDP in 2019.
Source: Bank of Japan; European Central Bank; Federal Reserve; and OECD calculations.

In the longer term, the main challenge for monetary policy will be how to achieve sustainably higher inflation. Central banks already faced this challenge before the COVID-19 crisis, in the context of a secular decline in growth, inflation and estimates of the neutral interest rate. This has prompted reviews of the monetary policy frameworks by the main central banks (Chapter 2, Issue Note 3). In the United States, the review has resulted in the adoption of a flexible form of average inflation targeting, which is expected to help boost inflation. However, in advanced economies, a combination of structural changes over recent decades related to the production and distribution of goods and services, firms' business models, and demand structure, may complicate the achieving of higher inflation, leading to a prolonged period of low interest rates. This would benefit fiscal sustainability (see below), but may result in excessive risk-taking in financial markets, in the absence of effective macro-prudential measures; reduced profitability of pension funds, insurance companies and banks; and perceptions that central banks contribute to rising inequality.

Fiscal policy support needs to be maintained in the short term

In many advanced economies, governments announced big support programmes at the beginning of the pandemic. Since then, the measures have been extended in some countries. While they vary in size and composition, the support to individuals and businesses has included primarily expanded short-time work schemes, extended unemployment benefits, extra sick and childcare leave, reductions in, or deferrals of, taxes and social security contributions, moratoria on private liabilities (such as rents, electricity bills and debt payments), loans, recapitalisations and loan guarantees. While not all of the budgeted allocations will be used (for instance, due to a low take-up) or reflected in budget balances according to national accounting conventions (for instance, some loan guarantees, tax deferrals and moratoria on private liabilities), fiscal support in 2020 is estimated to be massive in many OECD economies.[12]

- Discretionary fiscal easing, as approximated by the change in the underlying primary balance, is estimated to be 4.2% of potential GDP in the median OECD economy in 2020, but with considerable cross-country differences (Figure 1.19, Panel A). This is nearly twice as much as in 2008 and 2009. However, changes in estimated underlying primary balances should be treated with caution, as the standard cyclical adjustment framework may be less reliable in the current environment.[13]

- Public consumption is estimated to add on average around 0.4 percentage point to real GDP growth in 2020, and more than 1 percentage point in a few countries (Figure 1.20, Panel A). The average contribution is more than twice as large as during the global financial crisis.[14]

- Social transfers are estimated to have helped offset some of the decline in household market income, resulting in a much smaller decline in disposable income or even an increase in a few cases (Figure 1.20, Panel B).[15] The average support for household disposable income from social transfers in 2020 is about 30% larger than in 2009 once differences in the market income loss in these years are taken into account.

The working of automatic stabilisers and new support measures are set to result in large budget deficits in 2020, around 8¼ per cent of GDP on average across OECD countries and over 15% of GDP in Canada, the United Kingdom and the United States (Figure 1.21, Panel A).

---

[12] According to official estimates, the effective take-up of credit guarantees as a percentage of outstanding commitments is 4% in Australia (as of end-August), 6% in Germany (as of end-September), and 80.5% in Spain, 41.7% in France, 22.2% in the United Kingdom and 24% in Italy (as of end October).

[13] This reflects the large size of the COVID-19 shock, its effect on potential output and the special nature of some fiscal measures, in particular job retention schemes, which affect the elasticities of revenue and spending with respect to the output gap.

[14] Some of the differences in government consumption growth across countries reflect different statistical approaches to account for the lockdown in measuring output volumes of the public sector. For instance, during the lockdowns in the first half of 2020, France and the United Kingdom recorded a drop in employment in non-health public sector employment due to the closure of schools and other public services (or reduced working time), and thus in output, while public employees were still paid salaries. In contrast, statistical agencies in other countries, including Germany, did not assume a similar drop in employment and output.

[15] In most countries, the percentage change in household disposable income is estimated to be very similar to the percentage change in the sum of market income and social transfers.

Figure 1.19. Changes in the discretionary fiscal stance vary across countries

Change in the underlying primary balance, in per cent of potential GDP

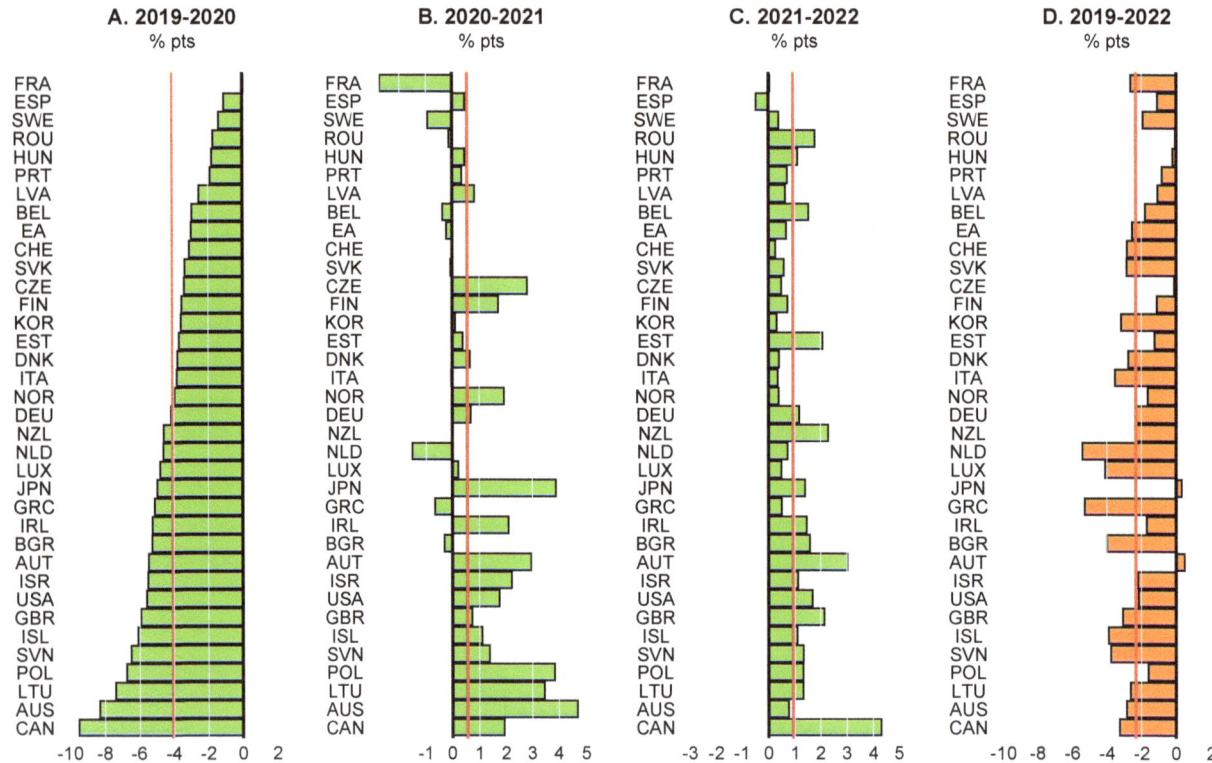

Note: Vertical lines indicate the medians.
Source: OECD Economic Outlook 108 database; and OECD calculations.

StatLink 🔛 https://doi.org/10.1787/888934217228

Strong and timely fiscal support was necessary given the unprecedented scale of the negative shock and a high degree of uncertainty. Without the decisive fiscal response, the loss of economic activity, income and employment, and the associated increase in income inequality, would have been larger in the short term and longer-lasting.

Fiscal support still needs to be maintained over the next few years but its size and nature should adapt to the changing situation. Given large fiscal needs, government support measures should be spent well and be cost effective. The initial broad support to the whole economy will need to evolve gradually towards more targeted support to the hardest-hit sectors, facilitating labour and capital reallocation from sectors facing a structural demand weakness (see below). Opting for a full and early expiry of special programmes in 2021 should be avoided, or offset with other more targeted measures. Consolidation could undermine growth excessively, and may not bring fiscal savings given that it could result in higher cyclical social spending and lower cyclical revenues. In the event of renewed economic weakness, the automatic stabilisers should be allowed to operate fully and current special support measures maintained or extended.

Figure 1.20. Fiscal policy is providing considerable support to growth

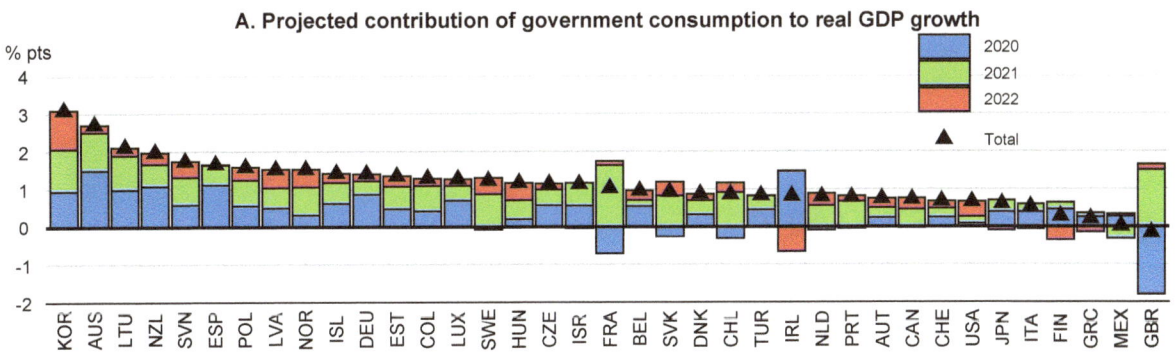

A. Projected contribution of government consumption to real GDP growth

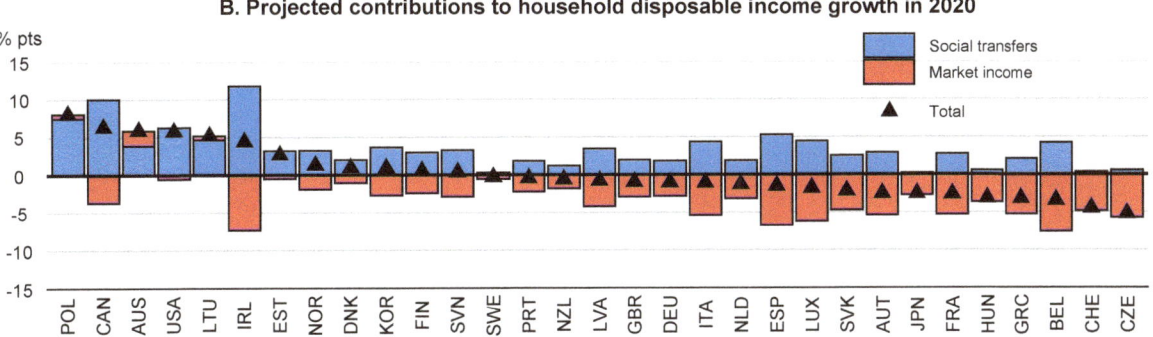

B. Projected contributions to household disposable income growth in 2020

Source: OECD Economic Outlook 108 database; and OECD calculations.

StatLink [STATLINK icon] https://doi.org/10.1787/888934217247

The current projections assume that some support measures will expire based on existing legislation (Annex 1.A). Thus, in many OECD countries, a discretionary fiscal tightening is projected in 2021-22, though not fully offsetting the earlier easing in most cases, as appropriate given the economic outlook. (Figure 1.19, Panels B-D). This, together with some cyclical improvement, should reduce budget deficits by 2022. In all OECD economies, budget balances will remain below 2019 levels, on average by around 4% of GDP, and in some countries will remain high by historical standards (Figure 1.21, Panel A). The projected large budget deficits and the fall in output level will lead to a sizeable increase in government debt-to-GDP ratios (Figure 1.21, Panel B). By the end of 2022, they will be nearly 20% of GDP higher than in 2019 in the median OECD economy, and over 40% of GDP higher in Canada and the United Kingdom. In many economies, government debt as a share of GDP will reach the highest level, at least, in the past four to five decades. Notwithstanding the increase in public debt in most economies, ensuring debt sustainability should be a priority only once the recovery is well advanced, due to persistently low interest rates, although planning for the steps that may be needed should start now.

Figure 1.21. Government budget deficits and debt will widen

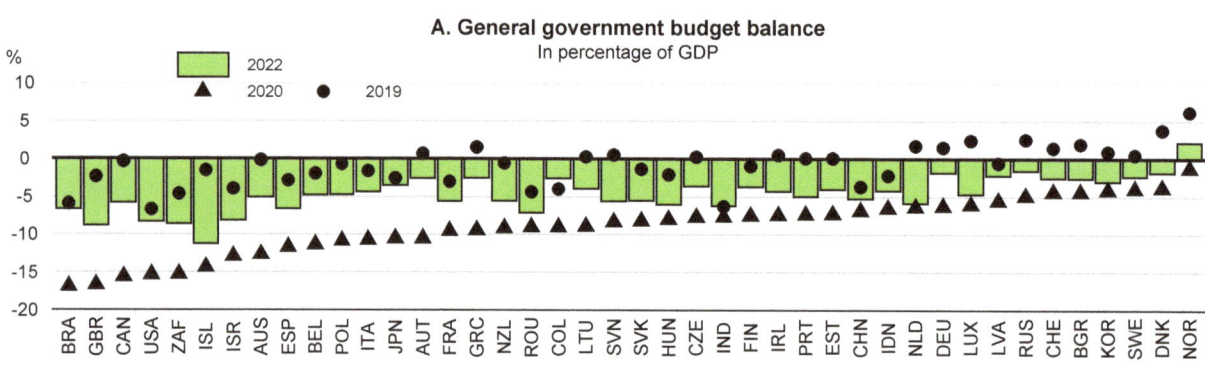

A. General government budget balance
In percentage of GDP

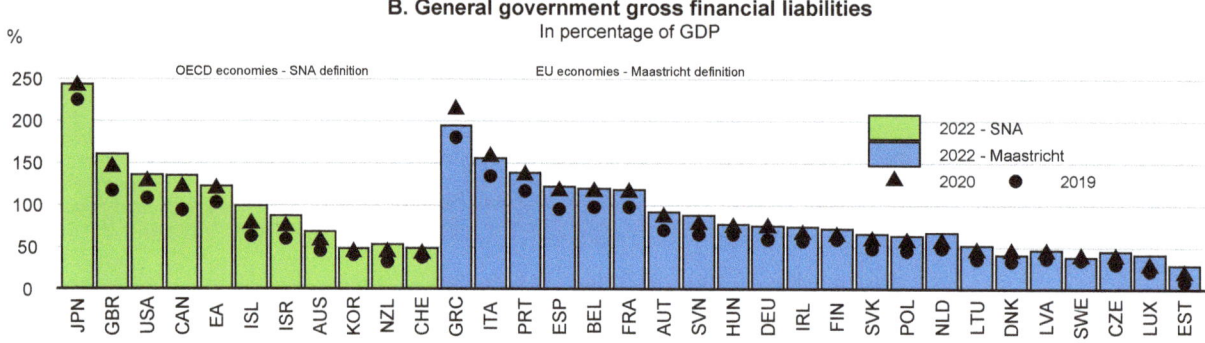

B. General government gross financial liabilities
In percentage of GDP

Source: OECD Economic Outlook 108 database; and OECD calculations.

StatLink ⛓️ https://doi.org/10.1787/888934217266

Policy challenges in emerging-market economies and developing countries

Many emerging-market economies entered the COVID-19 pandemic with a combination of high (private and public) debt, limited fiscal space and – at least for some countries – a significant exposure to debt denominated in foreign currency (OECD, 2020c; Figure 1.22).[16] Exposure to foreign-currency-denominated debt has imposed an additional constraint on the monetary authorities in some countries, since monetary easing can amplify financial stability risks, via currency depreciations, and de-anchor inflation expectations. Foreign ownership of corporate bonds had also increased in some emerging-market economies and developing countries, potentially exposing them to rollover risks in the event that domestic currencies depreciate and revenues drop.

---

[16] Since the global financial crisis, debt has increased steadily in many economies as share of GDP, reaching historical highs by emerging-market standards in Brazil, Chile and China. Countries such Argentina, Chile, Mexico and Turkey have also accumulated a significant share of corporate loans and debt securities denominated in foreign currencies (primarily in US dollars). Foreign currency debt statistics in Chile in Figure 1.22, panel B, are inflated by intra-company loans (without a direct currency risk exposure) and foreign currency bonds and loans financing companies which are hedged.

Figure 1.22. Vulnerabilities in emerging-market economies

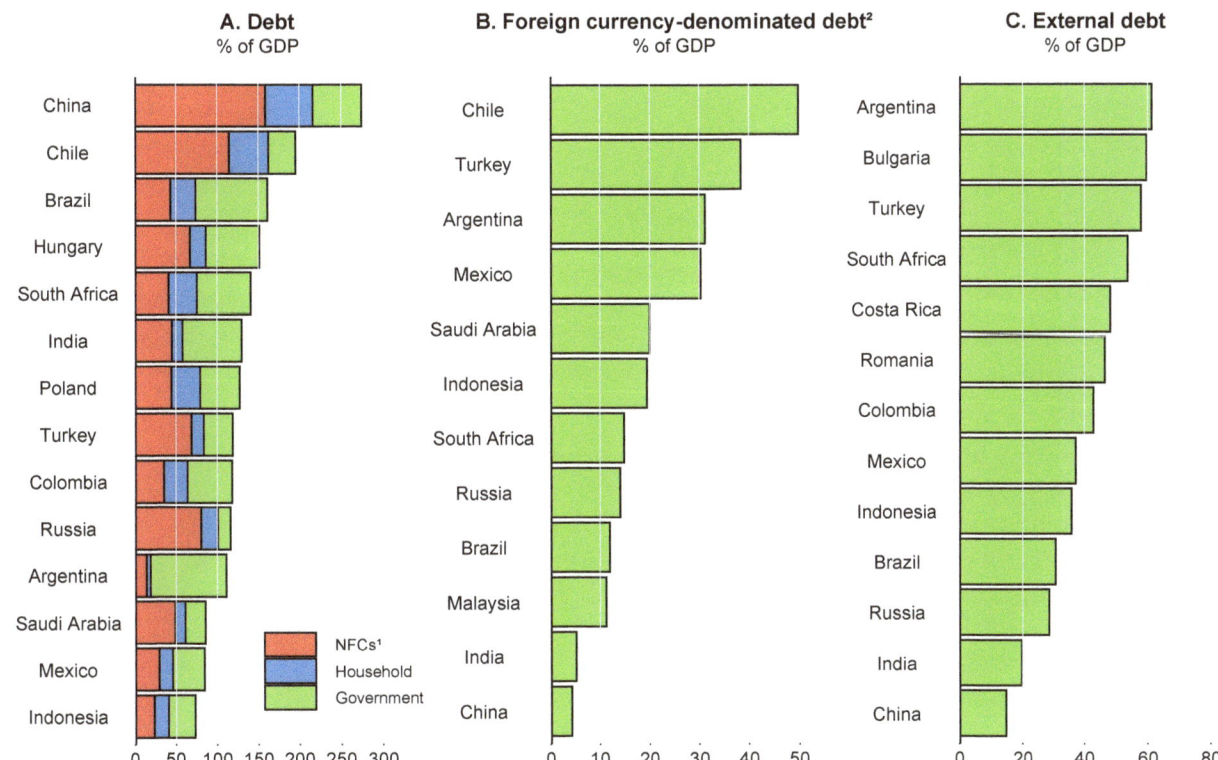

Note: Data as of 2020Q1 (except Panel C where data refer to 2019).
1. 'NFCs' refers to non-financial corporations.
2. Sum of cross-border and locally issued loans and debt securities denominated in US dollars, euros and Japanese yen borrowed by the domestic non-bank sector.
Source: OECD Economic Outlook 108 database; Bank for International Settlements; Joint External Debt Hub (World Bank databank); and OECD calculations.

StatLink ᴹˢᴾ https://doi.org/10.1787/888934217285

Governments in the major emerging-market economies, as well as some smaller economies, have been able to issue debt at relatively low rates over the past few months (IMF, 2020).[17] A similar picture emerges for corporates, with firms in emerging-market economies – especially large and higher-rated firms – stepping up their bond issuance and increasing borrowing from banks to deal with the drop in revenues, refinance their debt, and/or build precautionary cash buffers. However, sovereign debt sustainability concerns are likely to re-emerge as the crisis lingers. These challenges are also likely to be aggravated by fragilities in the corporate and banking sectors.[18]

---

[17] Local currency government bond issuance has picked up pace and several emerging-market economies, such as Chile, Colombia, and Thailand, have already managed to fund most of their projected deficits for 2020–21. The current year has also been a record year for sovereign issuance in hard currencies. Further new issuance is expected in 2020Q4 in a number of key emerging-market economies. Hard-currency bond spreads for investment-grade issuers have also returned to (or close to) their pre-crisis level.

[18] Market access and contingent liabilities of over-indebted State-Owned Enterprises (SOEs) represent a growing concern in several emerging-market economies, where they account for a significant portion of the debt securities issued externally. These firms, which are typically overexposed to global demand shocks and commodity price drops, benefit from both explicit and implicit guarantees from their sovereigns (IMF, 2019). A weak tail of banks, which could

Many emerging-market economies eased their monetary policy stance and expanded fiscal support in the wake of the COVID-19 crisis, which was facilitated by policy easing in advanced economies (Figure 1.18). This swift and strong policy response succeeded in preventing a sharper economic contraction, eased liquidity pressures on private agents and relieved stress in key segments of the funding market. Discretionary fiscal support also cushioned the impact of the shock on household jobs and incomes, especially at the lower end of the distribution.[19] The latter development has been particularly welcome in emerging-market economies, as – in many of them – remittances collapsed and automatic stabilisers are generally weaker because of high levels of informality.

Whenever possible, emerging-market economies should continue policy support to avoid unnecessary long-term damage to the economy. The duration and strength of any additional policy response, however, will have to be tailored to domestic and external conditions.[20] More importantly, as the crisis lingers and additional policy support becomes costlier, policymakers might need to move away from full-fledged support and prioritise more targeted policies.

- *Monetary and financial policies*: Countries with a credible macroeconomic policy framework, flexible exchange rate arrangements and manageable exposures to foreign-currency-denominated debt, have room to accommodate the shock further. For the economies with inflation rates close to target and anchored inflation expectations, this could involve further reductions in policy interest rates and looking through any temporary increases in inflation due to temporary depreciations of domestic currencies. In countries where low real interest rates make further monetary policy easing difficult and/or foreign currency debt is high, central banks might favour targeted liquidity support, rather than outright monetary easing.[21] Countries could also ease capital inflow restrictions imposed on foreign currency operations by domestic financial institutions, including via reducing foreign-currency reserve requirements (OECD, 2020d).

- *Fiscal policy*: the automatic stabilisers could still be allowed to operate fully and some further temporary fiscal stimulus might be considered if debt sustainability is not at risk. Where trade-offs between fiscal support and sustainability are important, fiscal measures should be targeted at initiatives that can boost potential output (such as health, education and infrastructure) and have long-lasting benefits. Improving the general efficiency of spending and enhancing transparency and accountability should be encouraged, including via reporting all foreign liabilities and all fiscal and quasi-fiscal activities, particularly spending on COVID-19-related healthcare support and financial transfers. This would limit the risk of mismanagement of funds, corruption and money laundering.

---

see their capital buffers depleted in an adverse scenario, has also been recently identified in emerging-market economies (IMF, 2020).

[19] For instance, the temporary emergency cash transfer programme implemented in Brazil benefitted over 67 million – most low-income – individuals, limiting the immediate impact of the shock on poverty.

[20] Important dimensions include the duration and magnitude of financial market stress, the level of commodity prices, the strength of negative international demand spillovers, the intensity of domestic disruptions due to the pandemic and the policy space currently available to mitigate the negative shocks.

[21] For instance, where in place, reserve requirements could be lowered as a counter-cyclical policy instrument (Cordella et al., 2014). Regulatory forbearance – potentially targeted at financial institutions with a high share of fragile borrowers on their balance sheets – could also be deployed but not to address broader solvency issues caused by bad bank governance or excessive risk-taking prior the crisis.

Structural reforms and better targeted support for companies and workers are needed ensure a sustainable and inclusive recovery

The disruption resulting from the pandemic could leave long-lasting scars. Living standards are below earlier expectations, investment is set to remain weak for some time, and longer unemployment spells may result in higher structural unemployment or withdrawal from the labour force, particularly by vulnerable groups. Adjusting to the lasting impact of the crisis is likely to require labour and capital reallocation, although the extent of such reallocation is uncertain. Many sectors most affected by physical distancing requirements and associated changes in consumer preferences may be permanently smaller after the crisis. A lasting shift to remote working and the increasing digital delivery of services, including e-commerce, could also change the mix of jobs available and the location of many workplaces. These shifts magnify longstanding pre-pandemic problems from the extended period of weak growth in the aftermath of the global financial crisis, widening inequalities in outcomes and access to opportunities, and the need to adjust to digitalisation and climate change.

The policies put in place to foster the recovery from COVID-19 are an opportunity to address these old and new challenges if economic stimulus measures and recovery plans combine an emphasis on restoring growth and creating jobs with the achievement of environmental goals. Measures put in place at the height of the pandemic to support jobs, incomes and companies need to be flexible and agile, increasingly focusing on workers rather than jobs, and on companies expected to be viable as the recovery progresses, and be accompanied by structural policy reforms that will help to accelerate the recovery. The long-lasting scars from the recession are likely to be smaller in countries in which product and labour markets can accommodate the necessary reallocations in the aftermath of the shock (Caldera Sánchez et al., 2017; Ollivaud and Turner, 2014).

Support for workers

The sectors most affected by physical distancing requirements and associated changes in consumer behaviour are employment-intensive, accounting for up to 20% of total employment (Figure 1.23).[22] Some of these sectors, particularly hospitality and leisure services, have been important sources of overall job growth over the past decade, especially for women. Low-paid workers, young people, and workers in non-standard jobs and the informal economy are also comparatively exposed to the risk of job losses and long-term unemployment in the aftermath of the pandemic. For younger workers, labour market entry during a recession can impart scarring effects on earnings for many years.

The extent to which output in heavily affected sectors will be able to return to pre-pandemic levels is unclear. A key challenge is to broaden the focus of emergency job and income schemes to ensure sufficient support for workers who may need to move to new positions in other sectors or locations.

- Job retention schemes, such as short-time work programmes or wage subsidies, are effective in preserving existing jobs but may hinder desirable adjustment across sectors, especially if the recovery is slower than expected. Over time, their focus needs to be adjusted gradually to support workers rather than jobs (OECD, 2020e), as is being done in some countries. Increasing the cost of unworked hours in these schemes for employers, and reassessing the eligibility of companies claiming support, could help to identify businesses who expect to remain viable for an extended period and encourage companies to increase working hours as soon as possible. Greater flexibility may also be required to allow differentiated support for companies, with resources increasingly targeted on sectors and companies most affected by ongoing containment measures. Steps to refocus support may need to be paused in the event of a widespread renewed downturn in activity.

---

[22] Two of the most heavily affected sectors by the border closures and the decline in tourism are air travel services and travel agencies. These sectors are a relatively small part of total activity and employment, accounting for around 0.4-0.5% of total employment in many OECD economies.

Figure 1.23. Many of the sectors heavily affected by the pandemic are employment-intensive

Share of total employment, per cent

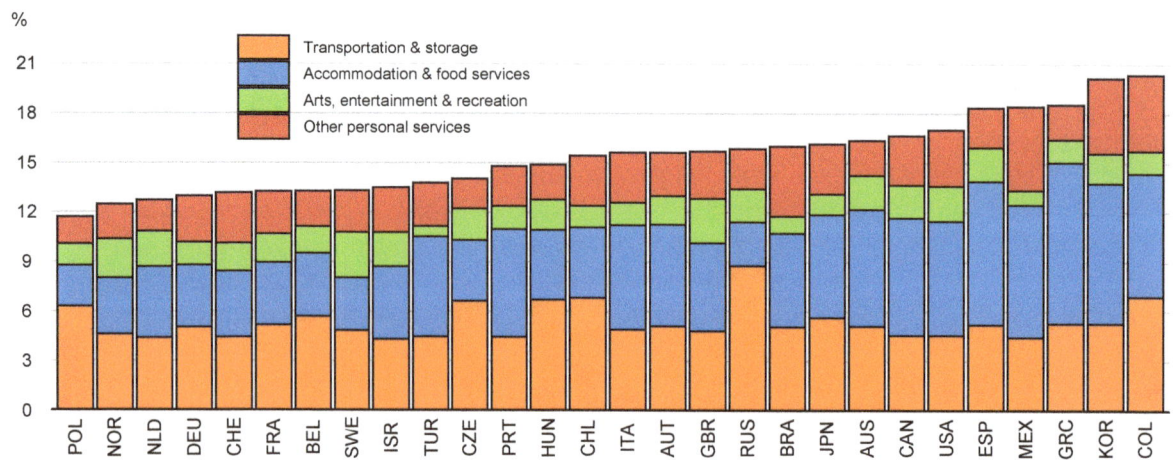

Note: Data for 2019 for all countries apart from Australia and the United States (2018) and Canada (2016).
Source: OECD Annual Labour Force Statistics; OECD STAN database; OECD Annual National Accounts; and OECD calculations.

StatLink 🛢️🖜 https://doi.org/10.1787/888934217304

- In countries where unemployment benefits were raised to support incomes at the height of the pandemic, such as the United States, there is less risk of preserving non-viable jobs, but more risk of income losses. Some pre-crisis job matches that become viable again as activity recovers might also not be restored

Alongside this, substantial additional investments in active labour market programmes, including employment services to help jobseekers find a job (Andrews and Saia, 2017), and enhanced vocational education and training are needed to create new opportunities for displaced workers, lower-skilled workers, and those on reduced working hours.[23] Reforms to reduce barriers to labour mobility, such as occupational licensing restrictions and housing market rigidities, would also help to facilitate job reallocation and reduce the chances of persistent scarring effects (Hermansen, 2019; Bambalaite et al., 2020; Causa and Pichelmann, 2020). Enhanced childcare provision and adequate income protection for vulnerable groups also need to be an integral part of well-designed policy packages to enhance participation, and make the labour market more inclusive (OECD, 2019a). A package of measures of this kind would help to improve opportunities and foster reallocation, whilst maintaining support for demand in the near term.

Income support for workers and households has been enhanced since the onset of the pandemic, by extending existing benefits and seeking to fill gaps in social protection systems by providing new assistance to temporary workers, the self-employed and informal workers in emerging-market economies (OECD, 2020f). Some countries have also made specific one-off payments to vulnerable groups, such as cash transfers to low-income single parents in Japan. However, some vulnerable people, such as temporary migrant workers, remain excluded from benefits such as paid sick leave (OECD, 2020g). Access to financial support and paid sick leave will need to be maintained for the duration of the pandemic to sustain incomes and allow newly infected workers to quarantine quickly. Longer-lasting improvements in social safety nets may also be needed to prevent inequalities of income and opportunities from widening further.

---

[23] Active labour market policies can be particularly useful for addressing unemployment problems for specific sectors and groups at risk of marginalisation (low-skilled, old or migrant workers) when aggregate stabilisation policies do not ensure sectoral employment stabilisation (Andersen, 2016).

At the same time, steps will have to be taken to move gradually from unconditional support to more targeted assistance that helps to preserve incentives for work and job search. For instance, the gap between short-time work benefits and regular unemployment benefits may need to be better aligned in advanced economies with job retention schemes, especially in countries with particularly generous short-term work benefits (OECD, 2020e). Setting clear state-contingent criteria for adjustments, such as linking changes to benefits or benefit durations to the unemployment rate, could help to increase the timeliness and predictability of changes.

Participation in training while on reduced working hours can help workers improve the viability of their current job or improve the prospect of finding a new job. The COVID-19 crisis has added to the long-standing need to provide more effective vocational education and training to help workers cope with challenges from the risk of automation and digital advances. Many of the workers most in need of training often find it hard to obtain (Figure 1.24, Panel A). On average in the OECD economies, about 40% of adults participate regularly in formal and non-formal job-related training, and they are disproportionately high-skilled (OECD, 2019b). However, only around one-fifth of low-skilled workers, some of whom work in sectors heavily affected by the pandemic, such as hospitality services, typically benefit from adult learning opportunities. Prior to the pandemic, improvements to vocational education and training were identified a key priority for future reforms in over half of the countries included in *Going for Growth* (OECD, 2019a) (Figure 1.24, Panel B).

Figure 1.24. Further reforms are required to help all workers acquire new skills

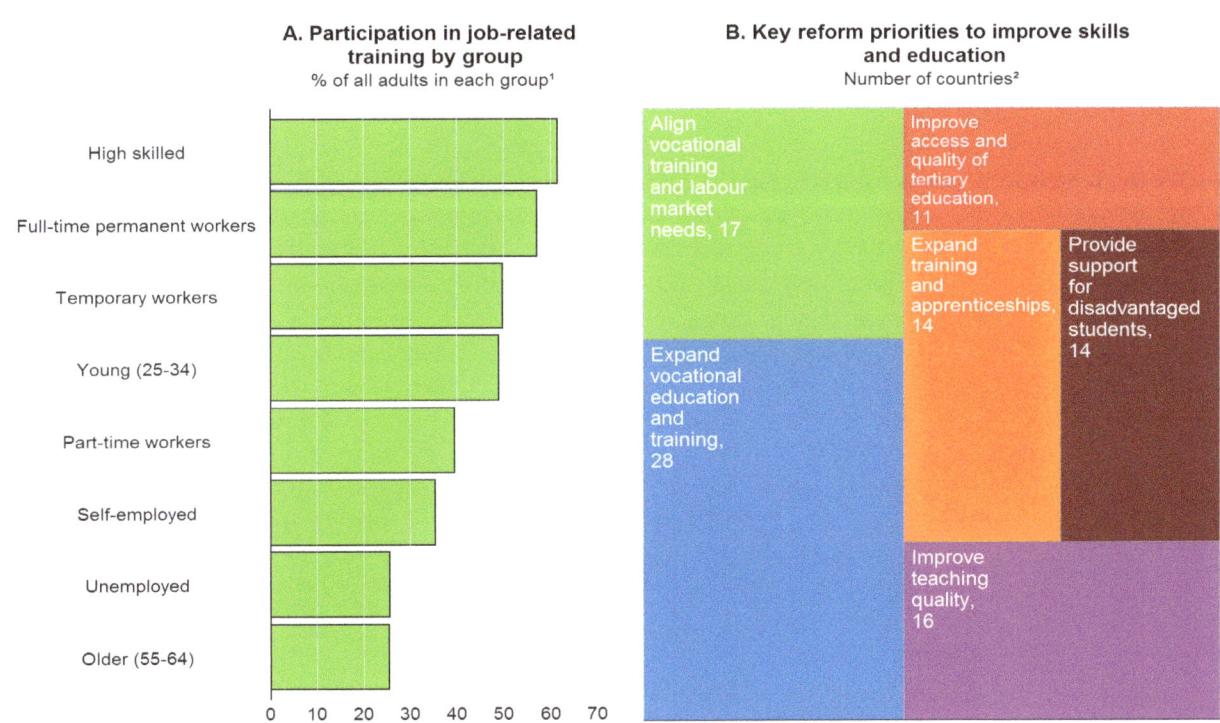

1. Share of adults aged 16-65 in each group who participated in formal or non-formal job-related training over the previous 12 months, based on an unweighted average of OECD countries participating in the Survey for Adult Skills (PIAAC) in 2012 and 2015. Low (high) skilled refers to adults who score at level 1 or below (levels 4 or 5) on the PIAAC literacy scale. Temporary workers are those on fixed term or temporary work agency contracts. Part-time workers are adults who work less than 30 hours per week. Full-time permanent workers are adults in full-time jobs with an indefinite work contract. Unemployed refers to all unemployed who have not been dismissed for economic reasons in their last job.
2. Number of economies for which the measure was a key structural reform priority in 2019. Going for Growth contains structural reform recommendations for 45 countries, plus the European Union.
Source: OECD (2019), *Employment Outlook*, OECD Publishing, Paris; and OECD (2019), *Going for Growth*, OECD Publishing, Paris.

StatLink 🔍 https://doi.org/10.1787/888934217323

- A key challenge is to organise training for those most in need in ways that allow it to be combined with part-time work and irregular work schedules. This is easier when training is targeted at individuals rather than groups, delivered in a flexible manner through online teaching tools and modular courses, and the duration is relatively short, with appropriate testing and recognition of the knowledge acquired (OECD, 2019b; OECD 2020h). The crisis provides an opportunity to promote participation in training for displaced workers and those on reduced hours, and has already seen a substantial increase in online learning by adults, with successful examples including the rapid training of new contact tracers for test, track and trace systems and care workers.

- On-line learning provides one way of helping to overcome barriers to participation in training (OECD, 2020i), by allowing participants greater choice in the time at which training is undertaken, and access to flexible online learning courses. Many countries could take additional steps to encourage training during short-time work by requiring participating firms and workers to undertake training, and providing financial incentives if necessary.[24] Ensuring adequate internet access, and introducing individually targeted programmes for low-wage and low-skilled workers and vulnerable groups, particularly those with lower digital skills, would also encourage the participation in training of those individuals in need.

Support for companies

Minimising long-term scarring, and paving the way for productivity growth after the crisis, also requires a gradual reallocation of capital towards sustainable sectors and activities with growing productive potential. Government support for companies through wage subsidies, tax deferrals and guarantees will need to be phased out gradually as the recovery progresses to ensure that unviable firms are not supported for an extended period. To the extent that support measures encourage firms to take on additional debt, there is a risk that higher leverage ratios and debt-service burdens will reduce the internal resources available to finance new investment and employment (Chapter 2, Issue Note 2). Possible approaches could include extending the maturity of loan guarantees, or converting pandemic-related public support into public equity stakes, although care should be taken to ensure this does not distort competition and that there are transparent and clearly defined recovery plans and conditional exit strategies for such investments (OECD, 2020j). Some assistance could also be made state-contingent, with repayments (or deferred payments) beginning only once profits are returned. A further useful option to meet the funding needs of SMEs, an important source of new job growth, would be to convert government (crisis-related) loans into grants, conditional on the funding being used to cover operating expenses.

---

[24] In some countries, such as Hungary and the Netherlands, participation in training is a requirement for receiving short-time work subsidies. Since June this year, the Netherlands has required employers applying to job retention schemes to declare that they actively encourage training, and taken additional measures to make on-line training and development courses freely available.

Past patterns suggest that company insolvencies are likely to rise the longer the crisis continues (Chapter 2, Issue Note 2; Deutsche Bundesbank, 2020). The dispensations from normal insolvency and banking regulations used by many countries to limit corporate bankruptcies this year will also have to be phased out gradually as the recovery progresses. Survey evidence shows that many firms presently continue to make operating losses and perceive significant bankruptcy risks, particularly in sectors most heavily affected by the crisis (Box 1.2). To avoid undue delay in insolvency proceedings, reforms to streamline insolvency procedures and ensure that bankruptcy laws do not overly penalise failure may be needed in some countries to spur future productivity-enhancing capital reallocation (Adalet McGowan et al., 2017).

Reforms to spur business dynamism by strengthening competition and opening up product markets are also essential to take account of the structural changes arising from digitalisation, spur productivity-enhancing reallocation, encourage new entrants, and help reduce the longstanding gaps between the best performing firms and others (Figure 1.25). Key reforms in some countries include streamlining permits and licensing barriers, ensuring that product markets are open to foreign producers and investors (via trade and foreign investment), and lower regulatory barriers in services and network sectors (OECD, 2019a).

Figure 1.25. Labour productivity gaps between frontier firms and others remain wide

Value added per worker

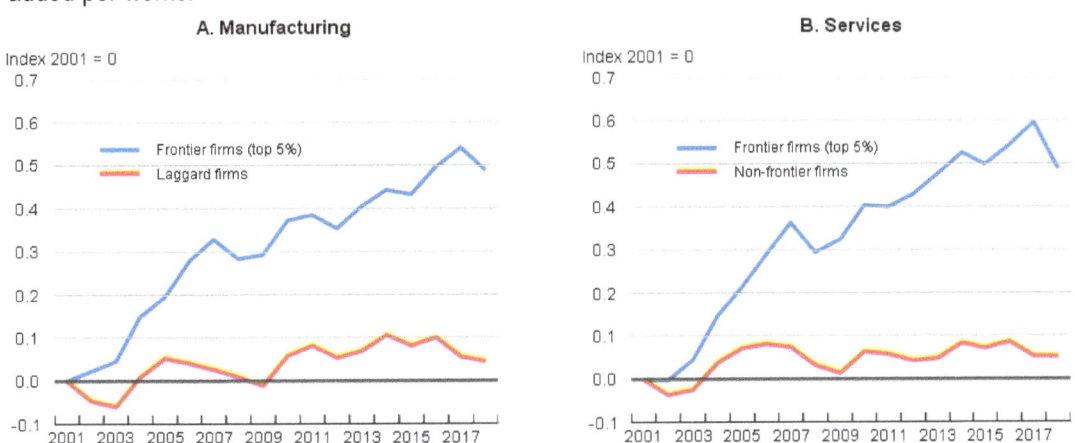

Note: The global frontier is the average of log labour productivity for the top 5% of firms with the highest productivity levels within each 2-digit industry in 21 countries. Laggards capture the average log productivity of all the other firms. Unweighted averages across 2-digit industries are shown, normalised to zero in the starting year. The vertical axes represent log-differences from the starting year: for instance, the frontier in manufacturing has a value of about 0.5 in 2018, which corresponds to approximately 50% higher productivity than in 2001. Services refer to non-financial business sector services.
Source: The Orbis database of Bureau van Dijk, updated following the methodology in Andrews, D., C. Criscuolo and P. Gal (2016), "The Best versus the Rest: The Global Productivity Slowdown, Divergence across Firms and the Role of Public Policy", *OECD Productivity Working Papers*, No. 5, OECD Publishing, Paris.

StatLink ⬛ https://doi.org/10.1787/888934217342

Mitigating climate change

Government efforts to support the economic recovery also need to take advantage of the opportunity to incorporate the necessary actions required to foster the shift from fossil fuels to renewables and limit the long-term threat from climate change. Many governments have included "green" recovery measures in their fiscal stimulus and investment programmes in response to the COVID-19 crisis, but these typically account only for a small share of the overall support provided, and the balance between green and non-green spending is relatively unfavourable (OECD, 2020k). Some actions, such as reductions or waivers of environmental taxes, fees and charges, or financial support for emissions-intensive companies such as airlines, are likely to have a direct or indirect negative impact on environmental outcomes unless accompanied by decarbonisation conditions.

Sector-specific financial support measures should be conditional on environmental improvements where possible, such as stronger environmental commitments and performance in pollution-intensive sectors that are particularly affected by the crisis. The potential for an extended period of substantially lower fossil-fuel prices than expected a year ago further raises the urgent need to introduce effective incentives for firms to invest in energy-efficient technologies. Better alignment of long-term price signals with environmental and climate policy objectives, including through carbon pricing, would lower environmental policy uncertainty and improve the prospects for the funding of longer-term investments in clean technologies, although compensating measures will be essential to mitigate the adverse distributional impact on poorer households and small businesses. Opportunities also exist to signal support for behavioural changes that may help a low-carbon transition, such as facilitating teleworking, and ensuring widespread availability of high-speed broadband.

Governments can also help directly by implementing well-designed large infrastructure investment projects, including expanded and modernised electricity grids and spending on renewables, as well as projects with shorter payback periods, such as more energy-efficient buildings and appliances (IEA, 2020a). Such investments, in conjunction with measures to ensure competitive markets, can be a source of new employment opportunities, particularly in sectors such as construction and waste management, and help to preserve existing jobs at a time when final demand is soft.

A surge in energy investment is required if sustainable energy objectives are to be achieved in full, including the Paris Agreement (IEA, 2020b). On average over the next two decades, average annual energy investment may need to be around 25% higher to achieve this than projected under current policy settings, with gradual changes in the composition of spending towards energy efficiency and renewables (Figure 1.26).

Figure 1.26. Changes in the composition of energy investment are need to meet environmental objectives

Share of total energy investment, per cent

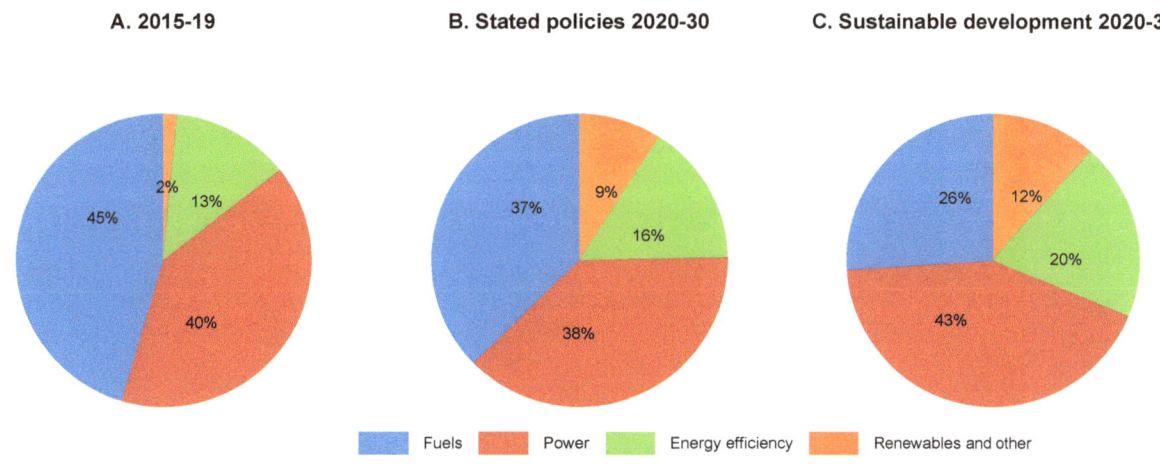

Note: Shares of average annual investment in the period shown. Power investments include spending on power generation, electricity networks and battery storage. The proportions are rounded and may not always sum to 100.
Source: IEA (2020), *World Energy Outlook 2020*, OECD Publishing, Paris; and OECD calculations.

StatLink 🔢 https://doi.org/10.1787/888934217361

Bibliography

Adalet McGowan, M., D. Andrews and V. Millot (2017), "Insolvency Regimes, Zombie Firms and Capital Reallocation", *OECD Economics Department Working Paper*, no. 1399, OECD Publishing, Paris

Andersen, T.M. (2016), "Automatic stabilizers – The intersection of labour market and fiscal policies", *IZA Journal of European Labour Studies*, 5:11.

Andrews, D. and A. Saia (2017), "Coping with Creative Destruction: Reducing the Costs of Firm Exit", *OECD Economics Department Working Paper*, no. 1353, OECD Publishing, Paris

Bambalaite, I., G. Nicoletti and V. Rueden (2020), "Occupational Entry Regulations and their Effects on Productivity in Services: Firm-level Evidence", *OECD Economics Department Working Papers*, No. 1605, OECD Publishing, Paris.

Bank of Canada (2020), *Canadian Survey of Consumer Expectations, Third Quarter of 2020*, Bank of Canada, Ottawa.

Bank of Japan (2020), *Financial System Report*, 22 October.

Borio, C. and L. Gambacorta (2017), "Monetary policy and bank lending in a low interest rate environment: Diminishing effectiveness?", *BIS Working Papers*, No.612, February, Basel.

Bounie, D., Y. Camara, E. Fize, J. Galbraith, C. Landais, C. Lavest, T. Pazem and B. Savatier (2020), "Consumption Dynamics in the Crisis: Real-Time Insights from French Data", *Conseil d'Analyse Économique Focus Note*, no. 049-2020.

Brainard, L. (2020), "Achieving a Broad-Based and Inclusive Recovery", remarks at the "Post-COVID-Policy Challenges for the Global Economy", Society of Professional Economists Annual Online Conference, 21 October.

Brunnermeier, M.K. and Y. Koby, (2016), "The "Reversal Interest Rate": An Effective Lower Bound on Monetary Policy", *IMES Discussion Paper*, No. 2019-E-6, Bank of Japan.

Bureau of Labor Statistics (2020), "Effects of COVID-19 Pandemic on BLS Price Indexes", April 7.

Caldera Sánchez, A. et al. (2017), "Strengthening economic resilience: Insights from the post-1970 record of severe recessions and financial crises", *OECD Economic Policy Papers*, No. 20, OECD Publishing, Paris.

Causa, O. and J. Pichelmann (2020), "Should I Stay or Should I Go? Housing and Residential Mobility Across OECD Countries", *OECD Economics Department Working Papers*, No. 1626, OECD Publishing, Paris.

Cavallo, A. (2020), "Inflation with Covid Consumption Baskets", *Harvard Business School BGIE Unit Working Paper*, No. 20-124, May.

Chetty, R., J. Friedman, N. Hendren and M. Stepner (2020), "The Economic Impact of COVID-19: Evidence from a New Public Database Built From Private Sector Data", *Opportunity Insights Working Paper*, October.

Clarida, R.H. (2020), "The Federal Reserve's New Monetary Policy Framework: A Robust Evolution", speech at the Peterson Institute for International Economics, Washington, D.C., 31 August.

Cordella, T., P. Federico, C. Vegh and G. Vuletin (2014), "Reserve Requirements in the Brave New Macroprudential World", *World Bank Studies,* Washington, DC: World Bank.

Deutsche Bundesbank (2020), *Financial Stability Review.*

Eggertsson, G. B., R. E. Juelsrud, L. H. Summers and E. G. Wold (2019), "Negative Nominal Interest Rates and the Bank Lending Channel", *NBER Working Paper Series*, No. 25416.

Eurostat (2020), "Guidance on the Compilation of the HICP in the Context of the COVID-19 Crisis", Methodological Note, Directorate O, Unit O4, April 0.

Goel, T. and J.M. Serena (2020), "Bonds and syndicated loans during the Covid-19 crisis: Decoupled again?", *BIS Bulletin*, No. 29.

Hermansen, M. (2019), "Occupational Licensing and Job Mobility in the United States", *OECD Economics Department Working Papers*, No. 1585, OECD Publishing, Paris.

IEA (2020a), *Sustainable Recovery*, World Energy Outlook Special Report, International Energy Agency, Paris.

IEA (2020b), *World Energy Outlook 2020*, International Energy Agency, Paris.

IMF (2019), *Global Financial Stability Report: Lower for Longer*, October, International Monetary Fund.

IMF (2020), *Global Financial Stability Report: Bridge to Recovery*, October, International Monetary Fund.

Kuroda, H. (2020), "Japan's Economy and Monetary Policy", speech at a Meeting with Business Leaders in Osaka, 23 September.

Lagarde, C. (2020a), "IMFC Statement", at the forty-second meeting of the International Monetary and Financial Committee, 15 October.

Lagarde, C. (2020b), "Written interview with Harvard International Review", 7 October.

Mody, A., F. Ohnsorge and D. Sandri (2012), "Precautionary Savings in the Great Recession", *IMF Working Papers*, No. 42, International Monetary Fund.

OECD (2019a), *Going for Growth*, OECD Publishing, Paris.

OECD (2019b), *Employment Outlook*, OECD Publishing, Paris.

OECD (2020a), "Issue Note 1: Evaluating the impact of COVID-19 containment measures on activity and spending", in *OECD Economic Outlook*, Volume 2020, Issue 1, OECD Publishing, Paris.

OECD (2020b), *OECD Economic Surveys: United Kingdom 2020*, OECD Publishing, Paris.

OECD (2020c), *OECD Economic Outlook*, Volume 2020, Issue 1, OECD Publishing, Paris.

OECD (2020d), "COVID-19 and Global Capital Flows", *Tackling Coronavirus Series*, June, OECD Publishing, Paris.

OECD (2020e), "Job Retention Schemes during the COVID19 Crisis and Beyond", *OECD Policy Responses to Coronavirus (COVID-19)*, OECD Publishing, Paris.

OECD (2020f), "Supporting Livelihoods During the COVID-19 Crisis: Closing the Gaps in Safety Nets", *OECD Policy Responses to Coronavirus (COVID-19)*, OECD Publishing, Paris

OECD (2020g), "Paid Sick Leave to Protect Income, Health and Jobs Through the COVID-19 Crisis", *OECD Policy Responses to Coronavirus (COVID-19)*, OECD Publishing, Paris

OECD (2020h), "Skill Measures to Mobilise the Workforce During the COVID-19 Crisis", *OECD Policy Responses to Coronavirus (COVID-19)*, OECD Publishing, Paris.

OECD (2020i), "The Potential of Online Learning for Adults: Early Lessons from the COVID-19 crisis", *OECD Policy Responses to Coronavirus (COVID-19)*, OECD Publishing, Paris.

OECD (2020j), "The COVID-19 Crisis and State Ownership in the Economy: Issues and Policy Considerations", *OECD Policy Responses to Coronavirus (COVID-19)*, OECD Publishing, Paris.

OECD (2020k), "Making the Green Recovery Work for Jobs, Income and Growth", OECD Policy Responses to Coronavirus (COVID-19), OECD Publishing, Paris.

Ollivaud, P. and D. Turner (2014), "The Effect of the Global Financial Crisis on OECD Potential Output", *OECD Economics Department Working Papers*, No. 1166, OECD Publishing, Paris.

Quarles, R. K. (2020), "Remarks at the Hoover Institution", Stanford, California, 14 October.

Standard and Poor's (2020), "Global Credit Conditions: The K-Shaped Recovery", *COVID-19 Impact Article Series*, 6 October.

World Trade Organization (2020), "Report on G-20 Trade Measures", 30 October.

Annex 1.A. Policy and other assumptions underlying the projections

Fiscal policy settings for 2020-22 are based as closely as possible on legislated tax and spending provisions and are consistent with the growth, inflation and wage projections. Where government plans have been announced but not legislated, they are incorporated if it is deemed clear that they will be implemented in a shape close to that announced. Where there is insufficient information to determine budget outcomes, underlying primary balances are kept unchanged in relation to potential GDP, implying no discretionary change in the fiscal stance.

Regarding monetary policy, the assumed path of policy interest rates and unconventional measures represents the most likely outcome, conditional upon the OECD projections of activity and inflation, which may differ from the stated path of the monetary authorities.

The projections assume unchanged exchange rates from those prevailing on 3 November 2020: one US dollar equals JPY 104.8, EUR 0.85 (or equivalently one euro equals USD 1.17) and 6.68 renminbi.

The price of a barrel of Brent crude oil is assumed to remain constant at USD 40 throughout the projection period. Non-oil commodity prices are assumed to be constant over the projection period at their average levels from October 2020.

The projections for the United Kingdom are based on an assumption that a basic free trade agreement for goods with the European Union comes into force from the start of 2021.

The cut-off date for information used in the projections is 27 November 2020.

OECD quarterly projections are on a seasonal and working-day-adjusted basis for selected key variables. This implies that differences between adjusted and unadjusted annual data may occur, though these in general are quite small. In some countries, official forecasts of annual figures do not include working-day adjustments. Even when official forecasts do adjust for working days, the size of the adjustment may in some cases differ from that used by the OECD.

2. Issues notes on current policy challenges

Issue Note 1. The OECD Weekly Tracker of activity based on Google Trends[1]

A pre-requisite for good macroeconomic policymaking is timely information on the current state of the economy, particularly when economic activity is changing rapidly. Given that GDP is usually only available on a quarterly basis (with first estimates typically published four weeks or later after the end of the quarter), policymakers and forecasters have long made use of more timely higher frequency data, such as survey-based indicators like Purchasing Managers' Indices (PMIs). However, both the current crisis and the earlier ones have shown that the underlying relationship with survey-based indicators can become unreliable when changes in economic activity are abrupt and massive (Vermeulen, 2012).This problem has prompted a search for alternative high-frequency indicators of economic activity. This issue note discusses one such indicator based on Google Trends, which are used to construct a Weekly Tracker that provides real-time estimates of GDP growth in 46 economies covering G20, OECD and OECD partner countries.

The COVID-19 crisis called for the use of high-frequency indicators

The 2020 crisis is unique in its magnitude and speed, and highlights the caveats of standard indicators. Leading indicators most commonly used by policymakers fall in two categories: "hard" and "soft" (Table 2.1). Hard indicators are collected by national administrations or statistical agencies and are published with delays ranging from one to three months, which is a major constraint for policymakers facing rapid fluctuations in activity. Soft indicators are timelier, but can become less informative about GDP during recessions. PMIs and confidence surveys are often based on averages of qualitative answers based on the net balance of respondents' optimism or pessimism, which limits their ability to quantify the magnitude of an ongoing crisis.

Table 2.1. Standard indicators were outpaced by the crisis

Indicator	Type	Frequency	Release	Relationship to GDP
GDP	Hard	Quarterly (monthly for GBR, CAN and SWE)	Usually 1-2 months after the end of the quarter	
Industrial production	Hard	Monthly	Around 30-55 days after the end of the month	Linear
Retail sales	Hard	Monthly	Around 8-10 weeks after the end of the month	Linear
PMIs	Soft	Monthly	Around start of the next month	Linear in normal times, non-linear around crises
Consumer confidence	Soft	Monthly	Around start of the next month	Linear in normal times, non-linear around crises
Google Mobility	High-frequency	Daily	With a 7-day delay	Difficult to calibrate as historical data start mid-February 2020
Google Trends	High-frequency	Daily, weekly or monthly	With a 5-day delay	Model-based relationship

Source: OECD.

---

[1] The GDP growth real-time tracker based on Google Trends discussed in this note is described in Woloszko (2020).

As a specific example, the information provided by standard indicators to French policymakers when they implemented the lockdown in mid-March illustrates the limitations of the traditional gauges at a time of crisis. The first indicator releases after the lockdown was implemented on 17 March were the flash PMIs on 24 March. They sent mixed signals reflecting the uneven nature of the shock as the manufacturing PMI fell moderately (to 42.9), while the services PMI fell to an all-time low (29.0). On 27 March, consumer confidence readings for February edged down marginally (to 103 from 104), well above market expectations (of 92), consistent with the unexpectedly high business confidence released one day before. The flash GDP release for the first quarter of 2020 came out on 30 April, showing a decline of 5.8% compared with the previous quarter. The release did not provide specific information about activity in March as the GDP figure is a quarterly average. The first traditional hard indicators to provide information about activity in March were household consumption (-17.9% month-on-month) and industrial production (-16.2% month-on-month), but these were only published on 30 April and 7 May, respectively, over six weeks after the start of the lockdown.

The past few years have seen the emergence of new types of high-frequency indicators. These include flight departures, restaurant bookings, mobility reports based on anonymised personal data from Google and Apple, air quality indices, news-based indicators such as the Economic Policy Uncertainty Index (Baker et al., 2016), electricity consumption, and credit card transactions. These new indicators are often available on a daily or real-time basis and for a range of countries. Policy institutions and national statistical agencies across the world have turned to such alternative data, including the ECB (Benatti et al., 2020), the Bank of England (Bank of England, 2020), INSEE (INSEE, 2020a), the Federal Reserve Bank of St. Louis (Kliesen, 2020), the Federal Reserve Bank of Cleveland (Knotek et al., 2020), and the IMF (Chen et al., 2020). Relatedly, the Harvard-based project on Opportunity Insights gathered a large number of high-frequency data on the US economy from private companies. The OECD has used a number of high-frequency indicators (OECD, 2020a), including Google Mobility reports (based on the locations of Google Maps users). This note focuses on Google Trends data, which provides aggregate information from Google Search.

Google Trends data for economic nowcasting

What makes Google Trends a powerful tool for economic predictions is its coverage of a large number of aspects of economic activity.[2] Data about search behaviour can be informative about consumption (e.g. related to searches for "vehicles", "households appliances"), labour markets (e.g. "unemployment benefits"), housing (e.g. "real estate agency", "mortgage"), business services (e.g. "venture capital", "bankruptcy"), industrial activity (e.g. "maritime transport", "agricultural equipment") as well as economic sentiment (e.g. "recession") and poverty (e.g. "food bank"). Signals about multiple facets of the economy can be aggregated to infer a timely picture of the macro economy. Using many variables also reduces the risk related to structural breaks in specific series, which was highlighted by the failure of the "Google Flu" experiment.[3]

---

[2] This works builds on a growing literature using Google Trends data for "nowcasting" the current state of the economy (Varian and Choi, 2009; Carrière-Swallow and Labbé, 2010; D'Amuri et al., 2012; Combes and Clément, 2016; Narita and Yin, 2018; Ferrara and Simoni, 2019; OECD, 2020c; Morgavi, 2020; Gonzales et al., 2020; OECD, 2020d; Cournède et al., 2020) as well as more recent work assessing the impact of the COVID-19 crisis (Abay et al., 2020; Doerr and Gambacorta, 2020).

[3] In 2009, Google started tracking influenza epidemics based on searches for "influenza" or related symptoms (Ginsberg et al., 2009). In 2013, the experiment was shown to be limited by media coverage of influenza epidemics during major outbreaks that were causing surges in Google searches unrelated to the virus propagation (Butler, 2013).

Google Trends provides aggregated information on relative search intensities for specific keywords or categories of keywords. Search volume indices are based on the volume of searches for a given query divided by the total number of searches at a given time and location. Google has classified searches into 1200 categories that each include up to thousands of keywords across languages. For instance, the category "Autos & Vehicles" aggregates together all searches related to cars such as *"voitures"*, "car", or any car brand name. Search indices based on search categories are thus comparable across countries. The panel of observations covers 46 economies that include G20, OECD and OECD partner countries. It is available since 2004 at a weekly frequency and released in real time with only a 5-day lag and without subsequent historical revisions. This note describes how the wide country-coverage, timeliness and high frequency of Google Trends data has been exploited to model their complex relationship with GDP, using machine learning methods, in order to derive a "Weekly Tracker" of economic activity.

A model of GDP growth based on Google Trends

The Weekly Tracker uses a two-step model to nowcast weekly GDP growth based on Google Trends. First, a quarterly model of GDP growth is estimated based on Google Trends search intensities at a quarterly frequency using a panel model of 46 countries:[4]

$$y_{iq} = f\left(d\, svi_{c,q}, cfe_i \right) + \sigma_i \tag{1}$$

where the year-on-year growth rate of GDP (y_{iq})[5] is modelled as a non-linear function f of the year-on-year log-difference of quarterly averages of search volume indices ($d\, svi_{c,q}$) for categories (indexed by c) and country dummies (cfe_i), plus white noise (σ_i). Second, the function $\hat{f}$, estimated from the quarterly model, is applied to the weekly Google Trends series, assuming that this relationship is frequency-neutral, in order to yield a weekly tracker:

$$\widehat{y_{iw}} = \hat{f}\left(d\, svi_{c,w}, cfe_i \right) \tag{2}$$

The OECD Weekly Tracker can thus be interpreted as an estimate of the year-on-year growth rate of "weekly GDP" (the same week compared to the previous year).

High-frequency and big data have limitations because their production can be less structured than national accounts data as scientific analysis is usually not the original purpose of their collection. These caveats call for specific attention and statistical pre-processing. As a large number of Google Trends variables are judged irrelevant for economic analysis, only 215 categories are selected from 1 200 available categories. Strong seasonal patterns need to be addressed for quarterly and weekly series. The latter are only available for the past five years, which constrains the range of possible seasonal adjustment methods. Selected categories are thus simply transformed to year-on-year growth rates. Breaks occurring in January 2011 and January 2016 caused by changes in the data collection process are addressed by smoothing the year-on-year growth rates. Finally, as the Google Search user base has increased dramatically since 2004, the relative search intensities of most search categories decrease over time. This long-term trend is filtered out using a methodology described in Woloszko (2020).

The relationship between Google Trends variables and GDP growth is fitted using a machine learning algorithm ("neural network", see Csáji, 2001). Google Trends "big" data make it possible to use such algorithms that are powerful but require large samples. The algorithm captures non-linearities that are likely to be key when there are extreme movements in GDP, but which are difficult to estimate with more

---

[4] China and Saudi Arabia are excluded from the sample as the relationship between economic activity and searches on Google seem more heterogeneous than in other countries.

[5] For the United Kingdom and Canada, monthly GDP series are available and were used along with monthly log-differences of Google Trends series.

conventional econometric approaches. Cross-country differences related to Google Search's market penetration or institutional settings are flexibly captured as the neural network allows for all possible interactions between Google Trends variables and country dummies.

Using modern machine learning interpretability tools, the neural network can be exploited to derive insights about non-linear patterns captured by the model. For instance, the OECD Weekly Tracker algorithm captures the fact that searches for "unemployment benefits" start signalling a fall in activity only past a given threshold, as labour markets are dominated by hiring in normal times and firing in bad times. Machine learning tools also identify those Google Trends variables with the best macroeconomic predictive power (including "bankruptcies", "economic crisis", "investment", "luggage", "recruitment", "economic crisis" and "mortgage"), as well as a number of consumption items that consumers may search for on Google. These retail-related variables can also highlight shifts in consumption patterns underlying model predictions.

The quarterly model of year-on-year GDP growth based on Google Trends performs well in out-of-sample nowcast simulations. On average across 46 countries, it has a Root Mean Squared Error (RMSE) that is 17% lower than an autoregressive model that just uses lags of year-on-year GDP growth.[6] The model captures a sizeable share of business cycle variations, including around the global financial crisis (when the available data for training the algorithm was much smaller) and the euro area sovereign debt crisis (Figure 2.1). Its RMSE is on average 8% lower than an autoregressive model in 2008-10 and 41% lower in 2020. The timing of the downturn and subsequent rebound is well captured by the model, although the full magnitude of the negative shock in the second quarter of 2020 is typically under-estimated, given its unprecedented scale. The mean absolute error in predicting year-on-year GDP growth in the first (second) quarter was 2.42 (3.86) percentage points, compared with actual falls in GDP for the median country of 0.12% (10.4%). The tracker thus provides a useful tool for real-time narrative analysis on a weekly basis, although it does not on average outperform models based on more standard variables, once these are eventually released.

---

[6] For the G7 countries, the improvement in the RMSE relative to the use of an autoregressive model is even larger, at 26%.

Figure 2.1. Quarterly model: out-of-sample simulations

Pseudo-real time simulations, nowcasting GDP in growth rate compared to the same quarter of the previous year, seasonally adjusted, from the third quarter of 2006 to the second quarter of 2020

A. United States

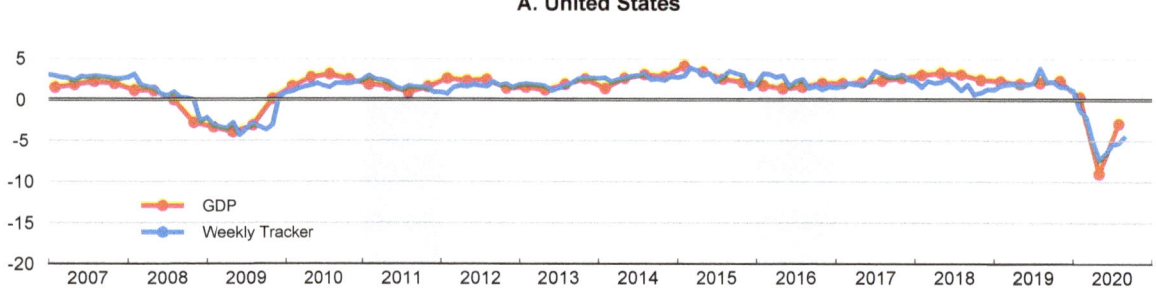

B. France

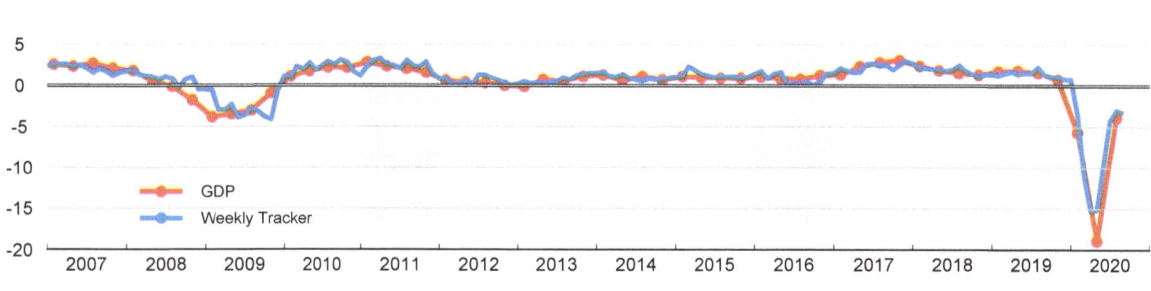

C. Italy

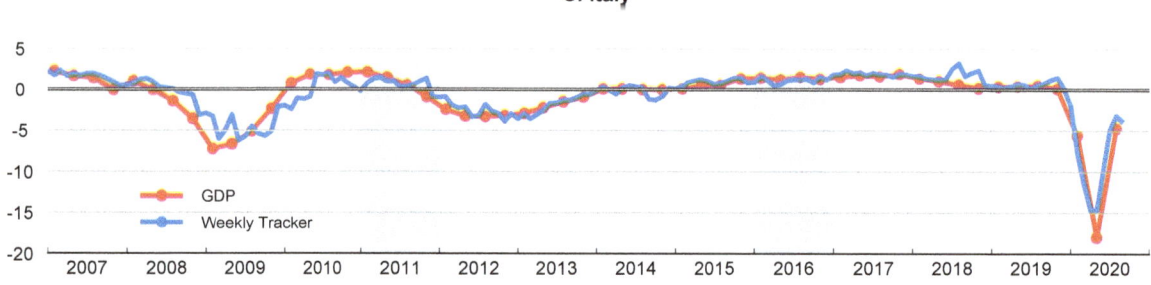

Note: The quarterly model is applied to 3-month moving averages of Google Trends series and yields monthly estimates that can be compared to quarterly GDP growth for February (Q1), May (Q2), August (Q3) and November (Q4). Shaded areas in 2011 and 2016 are years when the tracker is unavailable due to structural breaks in Google Trends data preventing the calculation of year-on-year growth rates in search intensities. Simulations are based on the latest GDP data, not the real-time vintages. For each quarter, the forecast is made five days after the end of the month, so 3-7 weeks before the GDP is published.

Source: Google Trends (https://www.google.com/trends); OECD Quarterly National Accounts; and OECD calculations.

StatLink https://doi.org/10.1787/888934217380

Insights from the OECD Weekly Tracker

The COVID-19 crisis: A week-by-week analysis

The OECD Weekly Tracker provides early and timely indications about economic activity during the COVID-19 crisis and the subsequent recovery (Figures 2.2 to 2.4) and is further validated by a close correlation with weekly movements in mobility (Woloszko, 2020). The magnitude of the shock to economic activity in March was extreme, as confirmed by GDP figures for the second quarter of 2020. The Tracker suggests that in a number of countries there was a rebound in April and May, with impetus slowing from June.

Figure 2.2. The OECD Weekly Tracker: United States

Weekly Tracker of GDP growth based on Google Trends

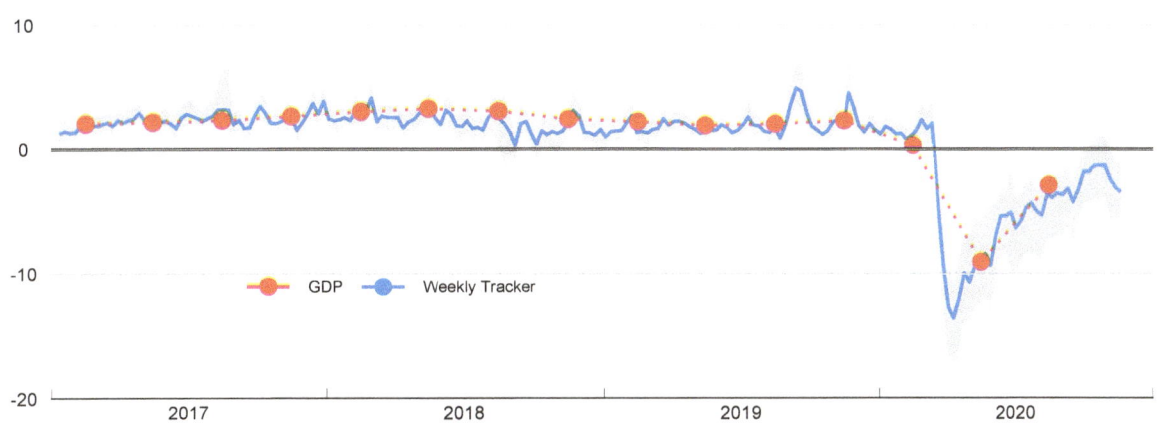

Note: The confidence band shows 95% confidence intervals.
Source: OECD Economic Outlook 108 database; and OECD Weekly Tracker.

StatLink 🖳 https://doi.org/10.1787/888934217399

The OECD Weekly Tracker suggests that this crisis caused major fluctuations in economic activity which were too abrupt to be captured by monthly indicators. Between 2017 and 2019, a high-frequency proxy of GDP growth would not have added much useful information (Figure 2.2). However, in 2020, changes in economic activity were more rapid and pronounced, indicating a clear advantage of a weekly GDP proxy. During March 2020, the Weekly Tracker suggests that for the United States, year-on-year GDP growth fell from 2.4% during the first week to -10.2% in the last week, before reaching -14.7% in mid-April. In India, it fell from 1.6% in the second week to -15.3% in the last week of March, declines of a magnitude later corroborated by actual industrial production figures (-16.3% year-on-year in April). The shock was also particularly sudden in many large European economies: for example, in the United Kingdom, the Weekly Tracker suggests that annual GDP growth fell from 0.4% to -20% in the course of March, reaching -24% in mid-April. In contrast, in addition to being subject to longer publication delays, lower-frequency indicators provide a less detailed picture of both the pattern of the downturn and the recovery dynamics, when activity is changing rapidly.

Figure 2.3. The OECD Weekly Tracker: selected advanced G20 economies in 2020

Weekly Tracker of GDP growth based on Google Trends

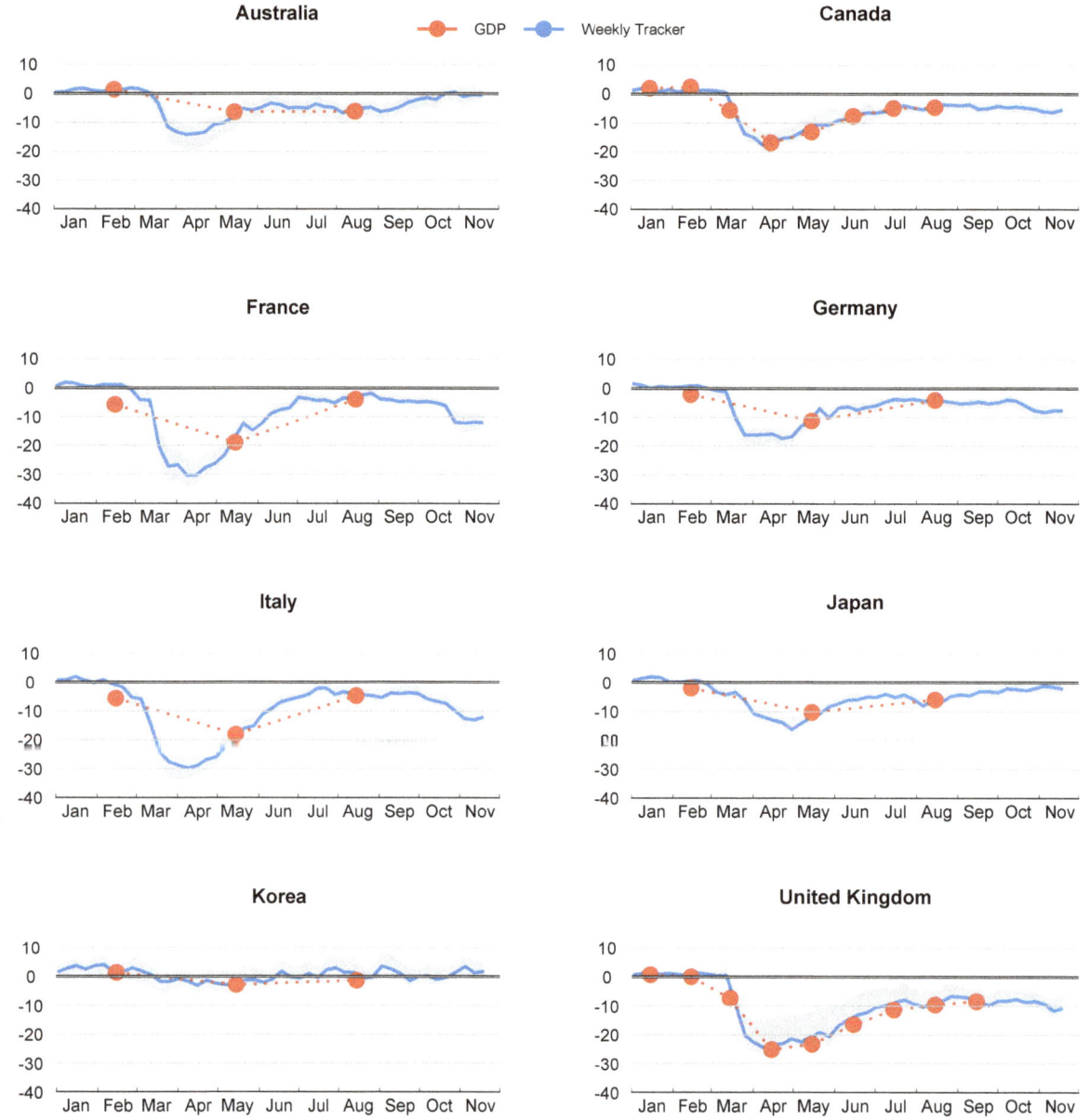

Note: The blue confidence band shows 95% confidence intervals. Red dots representing GDP growth are official outturns except for the third quarter of 2020 for Australia, which is the *Economic Outlook* estimate. Monthly GDP growth series are used when available (for the United Kingdom and Canada).
Source: OECD Economic Outlook 108 database; OECD Weekly Tracker; UK Office for National Statistics; and StatCan.

StatLink https://doi.org/10.1787/888934217418

The OECD Weekly Tracker suggests that the immediate impact on GDP of the global pandemic was particularly heterogeneous across advanced economies (Figure 2.3). In France and Italy, where especially stringent lockdowns were implemented, activity is estimated to have fallen suddenly by around 29% below its 2019 level by early April (which is broadly consistent with GDP outturns for the second quarter). In countries where the lockdowns were less stringent, activity is estimated to have fallen slightly less abruptly:

by 25% in the United Kingdom and by around 13-17% in Germany, Japan, Canada and Australia (again broadly consistent with GDP outturns for the second quarter). Korea, where epidemic control relied more on track-and-test than lockdown policies, had the lowest short-term drop, with the proxy measure of weekly GDP only falling by 4% below a year earlier in the worst week of April. While there is a clear impact from exiting lockdowns, the Weekly Tracker suggests the recovery in economic activity was much more gradual than following the initial impositions.

Figure 2.4. The OECD Weekly Tracker: emerging G20 economies in 2020

Weekly Tracker of GDP growth based on Google Trends

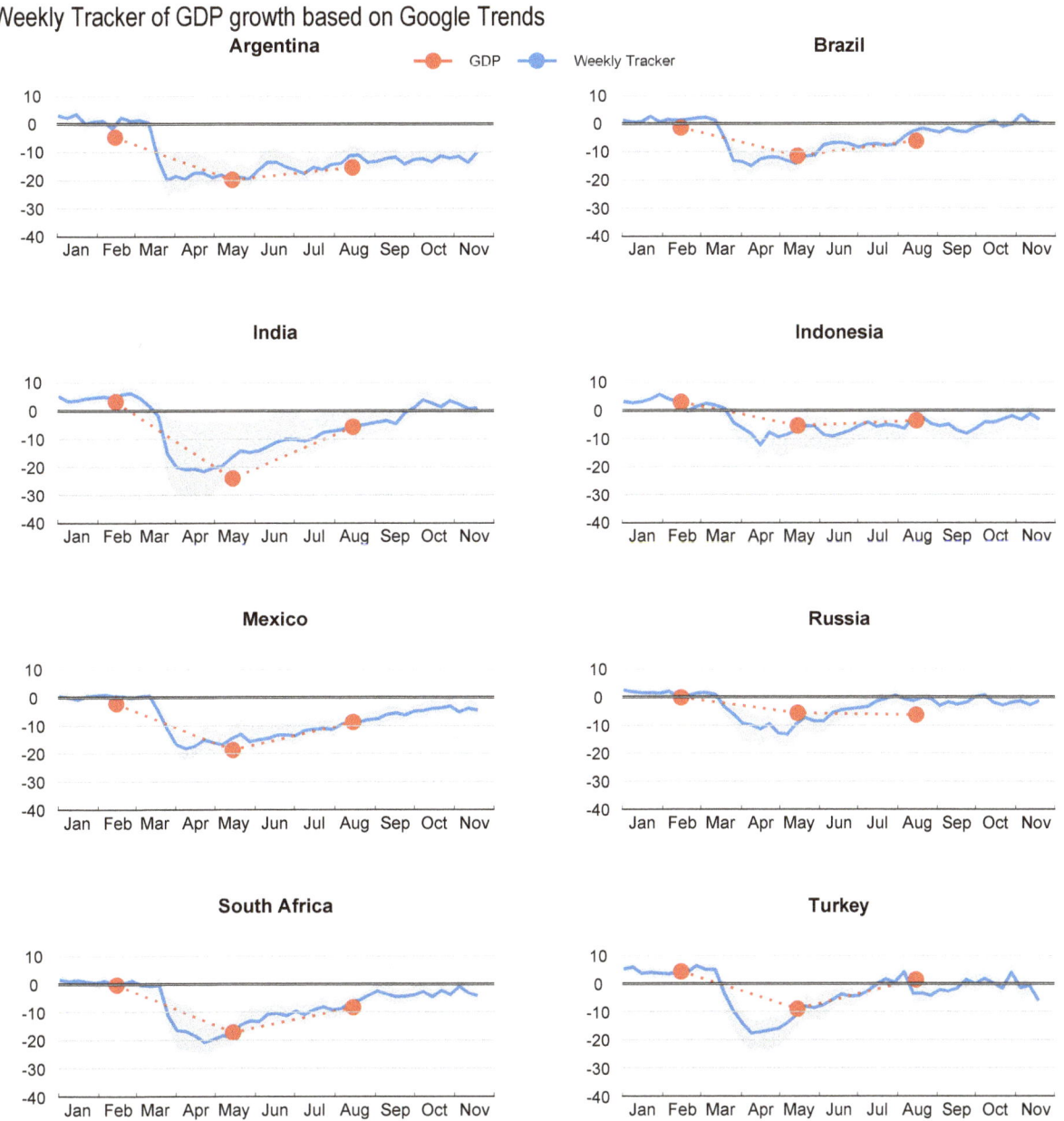

Note: The confidence band shows 95% confidence intervals. Red dots representing GDP growth are official statistics except for the third quarter of 2020 where they are either *Economic Outlook* projections or the outturns when the latter are available (for Indonesia and Mexico).
Source: OECD Economic Outlook 108 database; and OECD Weekly Tracker.

StatLink ᴹˢᴾ https://doi.org/10.1787/888934217437

Many emerging-market economies exhibit a similar sudden fall in activity based on the Weekly Tracker, although the rebound differs widely across countries (Figure 2.4). The initial shock to activity is estimated to be particularly strong in India (-20%), Mexico (-19%), South Africa (-19%), Argentina (-18%), Turkey (-15%) and Brazil (-13%) with regards to the same weeks of 2019. Russia and Indonesia were hit less hard, as the Weekly Tracker suggests that activity at the trough was around 11% lower than in 2019. The fall in activity was particularly swift in Argentina and India, which implemented very stringent confinement policies.

Latest insights from the Weekly Tracker: A stalling recovery below 2019 levels

The OECD Weekly Tracker indicates that the rebound started to slow in June, with the most recent estimates implying that activity stagnated in the third quarter of 2020 well below 2019 levels for most countries (Figure 2.5, Panel A). The out-of-sample performance of the Weekly Tracker for the third quarter appears credible when compared to available GDP outturns for the quarter, given the very volatile environment. Across the 28 countries where GDP growth for the third quarter had been released at the time of finalising this note, the mean absolute error in predicting year-on-year GDP growth was around one percentage point with no evidence of systematic bias, compared with actual falls in GDP for the median country of nearly 5% and variation in quarter-on-quarter growth of between 2% and 18% across countries. On the basis of the Weekly Tracker, the rebound was particularly weak in Argentina, where activity in the third quarter is estimated to be around 15% lower than its 2019 level, as well as Mexico, the United Kingdom, Colombia and Spain, with activity estimated around 8-10% lower than 2019 levels.

The OECD Weekly Tracker up to the second week of November also provides some insight as to which countries have the strongest momentum in activity in the fourth quarter of 2020 (Figure 2.5, Panel B). The tracker suggests that many non-European G20 countries will have positive growth, at least over the first half of the quarter, reflecting some loosening of lockdown stringency, especially in Chile, Argentina, Brazil, India and South Africa, or maintenance of a low level of lockdown stringency. In some countries, including Chile, India, Brazil and Korea, this rebound is predicted to result in the level of GDP in mid-November being higher than a year earlier. In contrast, the Tracker suggests that quarterly growth will be negative in many European countries, where the stringency of lockdown measures has recently been tightened.

Figure 2.5. Most recent predictions of the OECD Weekly Tracker

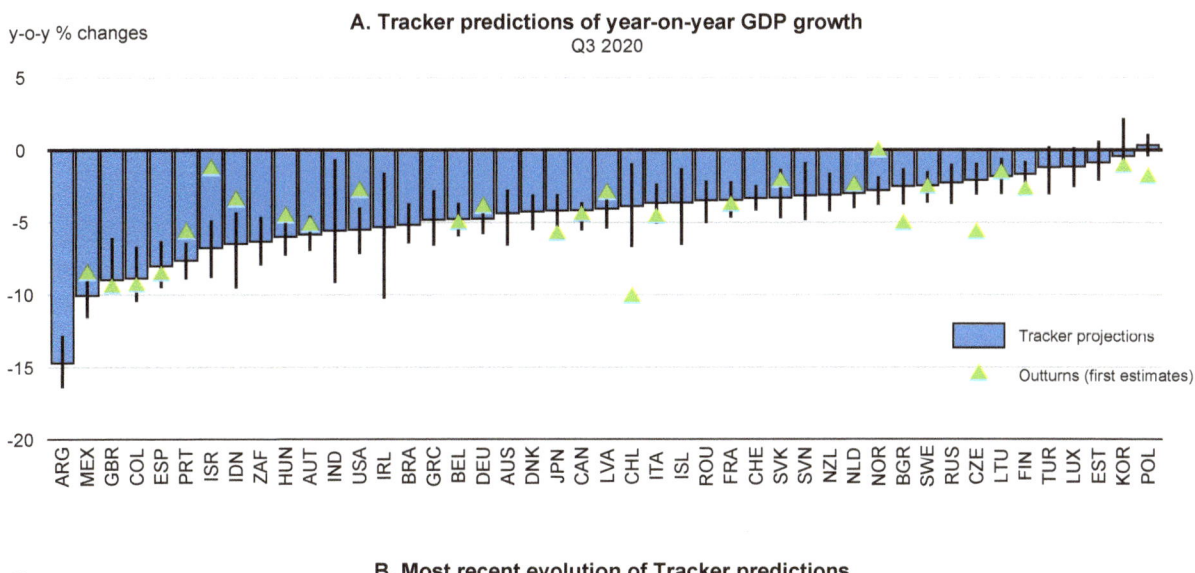

A. Tracker predictions of year-on-year GDP growth
Q3 2020

y-o-y % changes

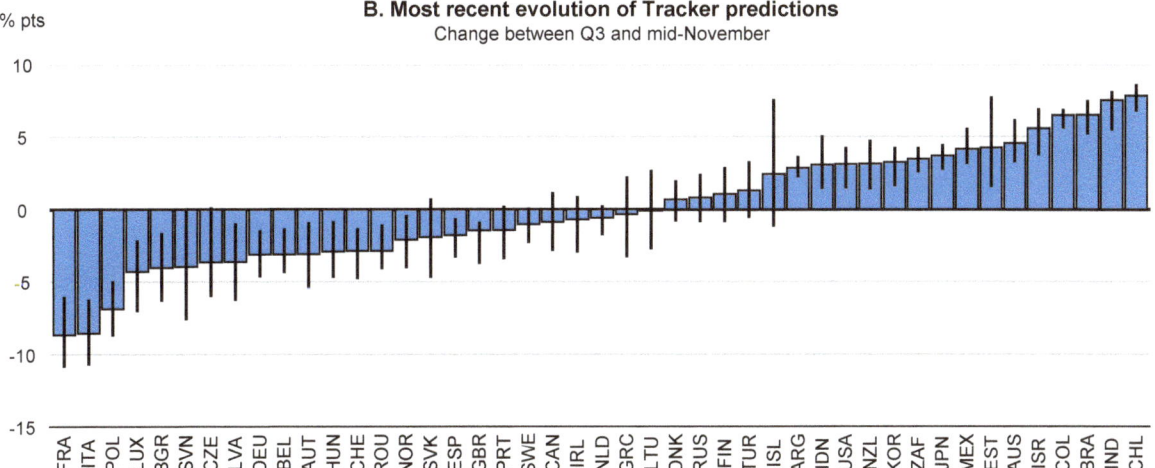

B. Most recent evolution of Tracker predictions
Change between Q3 and mid-November

% pts

Note: In Panel A, the blue bars represent out-of-sample model projections of year-on-year GDP growth based on Google Trends and the black lines represent 95% confidence intervals around them. The triangles are GDP outturns for the third quarter. In panel B, the blue bars represent the difference between the average Tracker value over the first two weeks of November and the third quarter (Q3), while the black lines represent 95% confidence around them.

Source: OECD Economic Outlook 108 database; Google Trends (https://www.google.com/trends); and OECD Weekly Tracker.

StatLink ᵃᵢₛ𝟙 https://doi.org/10.1787/888934217456

Shifting consumption patterns

The Weekly Tracker model also provides insights into the main channels of weaker activity and at a more detailed level than national accounts. Figure 2.6 highlights the role of the fall of consumption of certain services in explaining the overall weakness in activity in France and Argentina, where the rebounds were particularly strong and weak respectively. In the second quarter of 2020, both countries experienced a strong shift in consumption patterns whereby search interest for interaction-based services (including events, performing arts, travel, hotels, sports and restaurants) decreased by around 30% while searches for food and drinks, household appliances and health-related issues increased by around 20%. Lower services consumption was only partially replaced by additional goods consumption resulting in lower overall spending, helping to explain negative model-estimates of year-on-year GDP growth. This pattern partly fades away in France in the third quarter, but not in Argentina, consistent with the different pace at which containment measures were relaxed. The potentially lasting effects of the virus circulation and mobility restrictions may thus explain part of the much weaker rebound in Argentina.

Figure 2.6. Google search intensities per spending categories

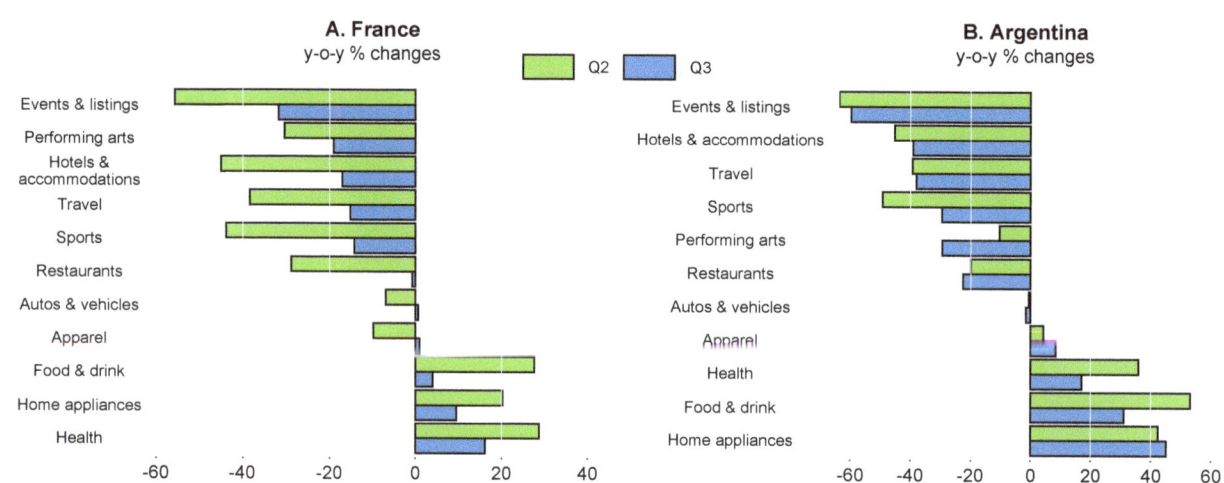

Note: Year-on-year growth rates in search intensities for selected search categories corresponding to spending categories (median over G20 and OECD countries).
Source: Google Trends (https://www.google.com/trends); and OECD calculations.

StatLink https://doi.org/10.1787/888934217475

Bibliography

Abay, K., K. Tafere and A. Woldemichael (2020), "Winners and Losers from COVID-19: Global Evidence from Google Search", *World Bank Policy Research Working Paper*, No. 9268, World Bank, Washngton D.C., https://papers.ssrn.com/abstract=3617347 (accessed on 1 September 2020).

Baker, S. R., N. Bloom and S. J. Davis (2016), "Measuring Economic Policy Uncertainty", *Quarterly Journal of Economics*, 131(4), 1593-1636.

Bank of England (2020), *How are we monitoring the economy during the Covid-19 pandemic?*, https://www.bankofengland.co.uk/bank-overground/2020/how-are-we-monitoring-the-economy-during-the-covid-19-pandemic (accessed on 16 October 2020).

Benatti, N. et al. (2020), "High-frequency data developments in the euro area labour market", ECB Economic Bulletin, 5/2020, https://www.ecb.europa.eu/pub/economic-bulletin/focus/2020/html/ecb.ebbox202005_06~a8d6c566d3.en.html (accessed on 16 October 2020).

Butler, D. (2013), *When Google got flu wrong*, http://dx.doi.org/10.1038/494155a.

Carrière-Swallow, Y. and F. Labbé (2010), *Nowcasting With Google Trends in an Emerging Market*, https://ideas.repec.org/p/chb/bcchwp/588.html.

Chen, S. et al. (2020), "Tracking the Economic Impact of COVID-19 and Mitigation Policies in Europe and the United States", *IMF Research*, IMF.

Combes, S., and B. Clément (2016), "Nowcasting with Google Trends, the more is not always the better", http://dx.doi.org/10.4995/CARMA2016.2016.4226.

Cournède, B., V. Ziemann and F. De Pace (2020), *Housing amid Covid-19: Policy responses and challenges*, OECD Policy Responses to Coronavirus (COVID-19), OECD, Paris.

Csáji, B. (2001), *Approximation with Artificial Neural Networks*, Faculty of Sciences, Etvs Lornd University, Hungary.

D'Amuri, F. et al. (2012), "The Predictive Power of Google Searches in Forecasting Unemployment", Bank of Italy Temi di Discussione (Working Paper), No. 891.

Doerr, S. and L. Gambacorta (2020), "Identifying Regions at Risk with Google Trends: The Impact of Covid-19 on US Labour Markets", *BIS Bulletins*, https://ideas.repec.org/p/bis/bisblt/8.html (accessed on 1 September 2020).

Ferrara, L. and A. Simoni (2019), "When Are Google Data Useful to Nowcast GDP? An Approach Via Pre-Selection and Shrinkage", *SSRN Electronic Journal*, http://dx.doi.org/10.2139/ssrn.3370917.

Ginsberg, J. et al. (2009), "Detecting Influenza Epidemics Using Search Engine Query Data", *Nature*, Vol. 457/7232, 1012-1014, http://dx.doi.org/10.1038/nature07634.

Gonzales, F., A. Jaax and A. Mourougane (2020), "Nowcasting aggregate services trade. A pilot approach to providing insights into monthly balance of payments data", OECD, Paris.

INSEE (2020a), *Les données « haute fréquence » sont surtout utiles à la prévision économique en période de crise brutale – Points de conjoncture 2020*, Insee, Note de Conjoncture, https://www.insee.fr/fr/statistiques/4513034?sommaire=4473296 (accessed on 16 October 2020).

INSEE (2020b), *Points de conjoncture 2020, Note de Conjoncture du 23 Avril 2020*, https://www.insee.fr/fr/statistiques/4481458.

Kliesen, K. (2020), "Tracking the U.S. Economy and Financial Markets During the COVID-19 Outbreak", The FRED Blog, https://fredblog.stlouisfed.org/2020/03/tracking-the-u-s-economy-and-financial-markets-during-the-covid-19-outbreak/ (accessed on 16 October 2020).

Knotek, E. et al. (2020), "Consumers and COVID-19: A Real-Time Survey", *Economic Commentary (Federal Reserve Bank of Cleveland)*, 1-6, http://dx.doi.org/10.26509/frbc-ec-202008.

Morgavi, H. (2020), "A GARCH Model to Now-cast Private Consumption Using Google Trends Data", forthcoming, *OECD Economics Department Working Papers*, forthcoming, OECD, Paris.

Narita, F. and R. Yin (2018), "In Search of Information: Use of Google Trends' Data to Narrow Information Gaps for Low-income Developing Countries", *IMF Working Papers*, No. 18/286, IMF, Washington DC.

OECD (2020a), *OECD Economic Outlook, Interim Report September 2020*, OECD Publishing, Paris, https://dx.doi.org/10.1787/34ffc900-en.

OECD (2020b), "Evaluating the Initial Impact of COVID-19 Containment Measures on Economic Activity", *OECD Policy Responses to Coronavirus (COVID-19)*, https://www.oecd.org/coronavirus/policy-responses/evaluating-the-initial-impact-of-covid-19-containment-measures-on-economic-activity-b1f6b68b/

OECD (2020c), "Issue Note 5: Flattening the unemployment curve? Policies to support workers' income and promote a speedy labour market recovery", *OECD Economic Outlook*, June, OECD Publishing, Paris, https://dx.doi.org/10.1787/1a9ce64a-en.

OECD (2020d), "Digital platforms and the COVID-19 crisis", *OECD Policy Responses to Coronavirus (COVID-19)*, OECD, Paris.

Varian, H. and H. Choi (2009), "Predicting the Present with Google Trends", *SSRN Electronic Journal*, http://dx.doi.org/10.2139/ssrn.1659302.

Vermeulen, P. (2012), "Quantifying the Qualitative Responses of the Output Purchasing Managers Index in the US and the Euro Area", *ECB Working Paper*, No. 1417, ECB, Frankfurt am Main, http://www.ecb.europa.euFax+496913446000http://www.ecb.europa.eu/pub/scientific/wps/date/html/index.en.html (accessed on 16 October 2020).

Woloszko, N. (2020), "A Weekly Tracker of activity based on machine learning and Google Trends", *OECD Economics Department Working Papers*, No. 1634, OECD, Paris.

Issue Note 2. Insolvency and debt overhang following the COVID-19 outbreak: Assessment of risks and policy responses

This note investigates the likelihood of corporate insolvency and the potential implications of debt overhang for non-financial corporations associated with the Coronavirus (COVID-19) outbreak. Based on simple accounting exercises, it evaluates the extent to which firms may deplete their equity buffers and increase their leverage ratios in the course of the crisis. Next, relying on regression analysis and looking at the historical relationship between firms' leverage and investment, it examines the potential impact of higher debt levels on investment during the recovery. Against this background, the note outlines a number of policy options to flatten the curve of crisis-related insolvencies, which could potentially affect otherwise viable firms, and to lessen the risk of debt-overhang, which could otherwise slow down the speed of recovery.

Introduction

A swift and decisive response of policymakers across OECD countries has helped businesses to bridge short-term liquidity shortfalls due to the economic shock following the COVID-19 outbreak, avoiding immediate and widespread insolvency crises. However, following the post-lockdown period, many countries have now entered a second wave of the health crisis. With a shock of such unprecedented scale, firms are forced to deplete their cash and equity buffers as well as to raise new financing; the situation is likely to translate into an enduring risk of a wave of corporate insolvencies and in a significant increase in leverage, depressing investment and job creation for a long time.

Building on earlier work (OECD, 2020a), which focused on the short-term risk of a liquidity crisis, this note assesses two key medium and long-term risks:[1]

- *Widespread distress and rising leverage.* The number of non-financial corporations in distress, i.e. firms that are anticipated to have a negative book value of equity and therefore a high risk of insolvency, is increasing worldwide. An accounting exercise is performed based on a sample of almost one million firms located in 14 European countries to assess the decline of net profit over a one year period, the associated decline in equity and the increase in leverage ratios.
- *The negative effect of debt overhang on investment.* Higher levels of corporate debt require businesses to reduce investment in the aftermath of economic crises, thereby slowing the speed of the recovery. Relying on regression analysis and looking at the historical relationship between investment and the financial leverage ratio at the firm level as well as this relationship during the global financial crisis (GFC), a calculation is made of the potential implications of the projected increase in leverage for investment ratios in the recovery from the COVID-19 crisis.

---

[1] A more detailed version of this note (OECD, 2020b) is available in the OECD Covid Hub.

Against these risks, the note discusses options for policymakers to prevent widespread insolvencies and support firms without further increasing debt and leverage across firms. The exceptional magnitude of the crisis and the high levels of uncertainty that firms still face are likely to make the distinction between viable and non-viable firms more difficult. The risk of supporting potentially non-viable firms needs to be balanced against the risk of forcing viable and productive firms into premature liquidation. This is because insolvency frameworks tend to become less efficient during a crisis, especially when courts are congested, potentially leading to liquidation of a higher number of viable firms than desirable, with adverse effects on growth (Iverson, 2018).

To get around the necessity of identifying non-viable firms at an early stage, policy support needs to preserve optionality, i.e. helping firms weather the COVID-19 crisis but regularly re-assessing their viability. More broadly, one potential strategy for governments would be to adopt a multidimensional cascading approach. At first, policymakers could aim at "flattening the curve of insolvencies" by providing additional resources and restoring the equity of distressed firms. Next, if those additional resources are not sufficient, they could encourage timely debt restructuring to allow distressed firms to continue operating smoothly. These two steps should reduce the number of viable firms that would be otherwise liquidated. Finally, to deal with firms that would still be non-viable despite public support and debt restructuring, governments could improve the efficiency of liquidation procedures to unlock potentially productive resources. Over time, policymakers will acquire new information on what the "post-pandemic" normal will look like and policy may need to facilitate the "necessary" reallocations implied by the COVID-19 crisis.

Equity, leverage and debt overhang: An empirical assessment

Evaluating the impact of the pandemic on firm financial conditions

Using a simple accounting exercise, as in Carletti et al. (2020), the impact of the pandemic on firms' long-term viability is evaluated quantitatively. The economic shock is modelled as a change in firms' operating profits, resulting from a sharp reversal in sales and from firms' inability to fully adjust their operating expenses. After calculating the decline in profits, taking into consideration governments job support schemes implemented during the first phase of the crisis, the model predicts the evolution of financial conditions along two dimensions.[2] First, it calculates the new hypothetical value of net equity (i.e. the difference between the book value of assets and liabilities) one year after the implementation of containment measures. Firms whose net equity is predicted to be negative are classified in this framework as distressed, and thus at risk of being insolvent. This exercise provides information about the amount of equity that would be needed to restore firms' pre-crisis financial structure. Second, the model quantifies the increase in firms' leverage ratios caused by the reduction in equity relative to a "No-COVID-19" scenario.

[2] Job support schemes are modelled as conditional on the size and length of the shock -- for more details, see Box 2 in OECD (2020b). However, calculations do not include support schemes based on loans and loan guarantees as, while critical in addressing liquidity needs, they do not directly contribute to firms' profitability.

To proxy the magnitude of the sectoral drop in sales, the analysis relies on the first-round demand and supply shocks computed at a detailed sectoral level by del Rio-Chanona et al. (2020), who account for the large heterogeneity in the ability to telework across sectors.[3] With respect to the duration of the shock, the model presents two alternative scenarios. An "upside scenario", which foresees a sharp drop in activity lasting two months (equivalent to the average duration of the shock most countries experienced in the second quarter of 2020), followed by a progressive but not complete recovery in the remaining part of the year. A "downside" scenario, which initially overlaps with the "upside" scenario, but then has a slower recovery due to more widespread further outbreaks of the virus accompanied by stricter mobility restrictions.

The analysis of firms' financial vulnerabilities relies on financial statements of non-financial corporations from the latest vintage of the Orbis database. After applying cleaning procedures, the final sample consists of 872 648 unique firms, operating in both manufacturing and non-financial business services industries, for 14 European countries.[4] Importantly, as the objective of the exercise is to investigate the extent to which solvent firms may become distressed due to the COVID-19 shock, the sample excludes firms that would have been distressed (e.g. firms with negative book value of equity at the end of 2018) and would have experienced negative profits even in normal times. It follows that the findings show an incremental – rather than total – effect following the COVID-19 shock.

The sharp decline in profits reduces equity buffers

The estimated decline in profits is sizeable, on average between 40% and 50% of normal-time profits (depending on the scenario considered). Following this sharp reduction, 7.3% (9.1%) of otherwise viable companies would become distressed in the upside (downside) scenario (Figure 2.7) and, accordingly, 6.2% (7.7%) of previously "safe jobs" would be endangered. The highlighted incremental effect following the COVID-19 shock implies that the total number of distressed firms would double compared with "normal times", as approximately 8% of firms are estimated to already be endangered in a No-COVID-19 scenario.

---

[3] The authors classify industries as essential or non-essential and construct a Remote Labour Index, which measures the ability of different occupations to work from home: the supply shock is not binding for essential industries, while inversely proportional to the capacity to telework for non-essential ones. To quantify the demand shock, they exploit a study of the potential impact of a severe influenza epidemic developed by the US Congressional Budget Office.

[4] Reflecting data availability, countries included in the sample are: Belgium, Denmark, Finland, France, Germany, Hungary, Ireland, Italy, Poland, Portugal, Romania, Spain, Sweden and the United Kingdom. At present, Orbis is the largest cross-country firm-level dataset available and accessible for economic and financial research. However, it does not cover the universe of firms, and the extent of the coverage varies considerably across countries. To deal with those limitations, the note purposely avoids in-depth cross-country comparisons, as well as the provision of absolute numbers on the aggregate level of the shortfall.

The results differ across sectors and type of firms. The share of otherwise viable companies becoming distressed reaches 26% (32% in the downside scenario) in the "Accommodation and food service activities" sector, while it is almost zero in the "Information and communication" and "Professional services" sectors (Figure 2.7). The "Transports", "Wholesale and retail trade", as well as "Arts, entertainment and recreation" and "Other services activities" sectors are also severely hit by the crisis.[5] The share of distressed firms in manufacturing is below average. More broadly, and consistent with the diverse ability of firms to use innovative technologies and teleworking arrangements, tangible investment-intensive sectors are relatively more affected than intangible investment-intensive ones (Figure 2.8, Panel A). Similarly, more productive companies are relatively less impacted than low-productivity firms; yet, the estimated percentage of firms in the top quartile of the productivity distribution becoming distressed is not negligible (Figure 2.8, Panel B). In addition, old and large firms are better positioned to face the shock compared to their younger and smaller counterparts (Figure 2.8, Panels C and D).

Figure 2.7. A substantial portion of otherwise viable firms is predicted to become distressed

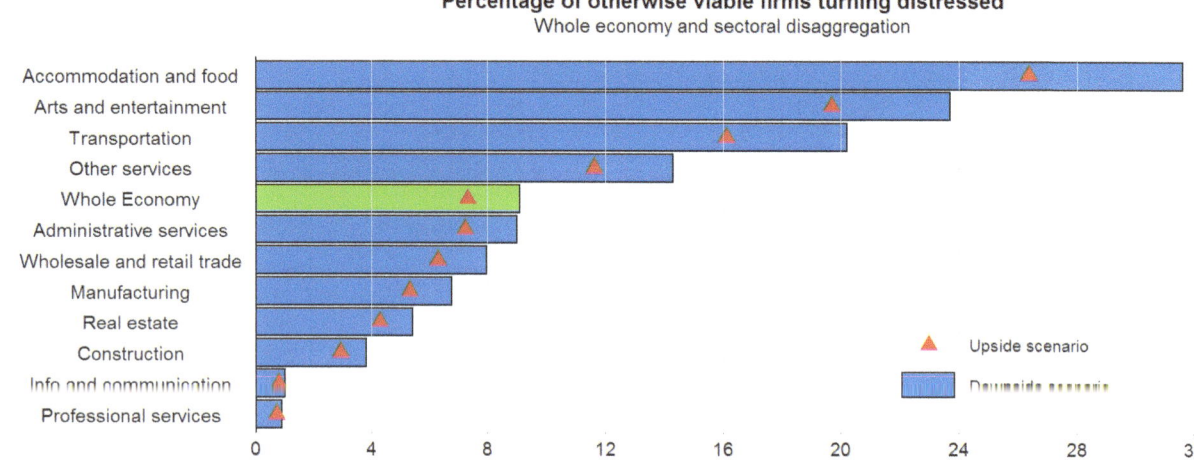

Percentage of otherwise viable firms turning distressed
Whole economy and sectoral disaggregation

Note: The figure shows the percentage of distressed firms in the upside (red triangles) and downside (green and blue bars) scenarios for the whole economy and at the sector level (1-Digit NACE Rev2 classification). Firms are defined as distressed if their book value of equity is predicted to be negative one year after the implementation of containment measures. The sample is restricted ex-ante to firms having both positive profits and book value of equity in the 2018 reference year.
Source: OECD calculations based on Orbis® data.

StatLink 𝗦 https://doi.org/10.1787/888934217494

---

[5] Consistently, the percentage of jobs at risk reaches 20% (24%) in the "Accommodation and food service activities" sector in the upside (downside) scenario; it is around 16% (20%) for the "Transports" and "Arts, entertainment and recreation", and almost zero in the least affected sectors.

Figure 2.8. The impact of the shock is heterogeneous across types of sectors and firms

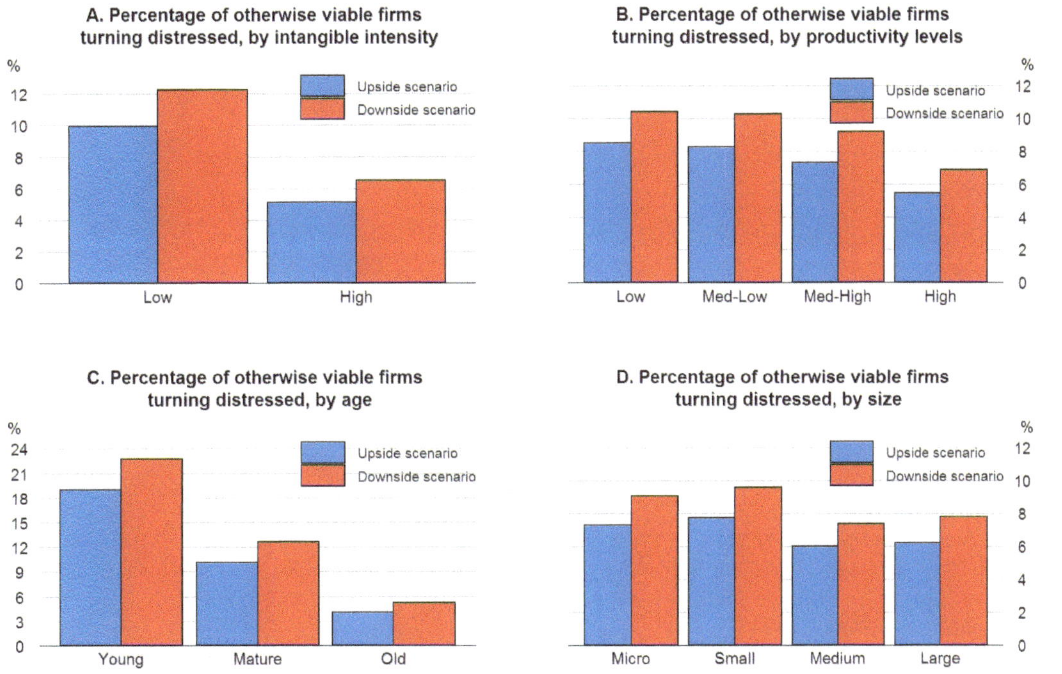

A. Percentage of otherwise viable firms turning distressed, by intangible intensity

B. Percentage of otherwise viable firms turning distressed, by productivity levels

C. Percentage of otherwise viable firms turning distressed, by age

D. Percentage of otherwise viable firms turning distressed, by size

Note: The figure shows the percentage of distressed firms in the upside (blue bars) and downside (red bars) scenarios: by sectoral intangible intensity (Panel A); by productivity levels (Panel B); by firms' age (Panel C); by firms' size (Panel D). Details on the construction of the intangible intensity, productivity, age and size variables are in OECD (2020b). Firms are defined as distressed if their book value of equity is predicted to be negative one year after the implementation of containment measures. The sample is restricted ex-ante to firms having both positive profits and book value of equity in the 2018 reference year. For the sake of exposition, the vertical-axis scale varies among panels.
Source: OECD calculations based on Orbis® data.

StatLink https://doi.org/10.1787/888934217513

The crisis will leave firms highly indebted and with a lower ability to service debt

The reduction in equity relative to normal times has immediate consequences on firms' leverage ratios: the ratio of total liabilities to total assets would increase by 6.7 percentage points in the upside scenario and 8 percentage points in the downside scenario for the median firm in the sample (Figure 2.9, Panel A). Importantly, while leverage ratios are estimated to substantially increase due to the COVID-19 shock over the whole range of the pre-crisis distribution, the new distribution of firms according to their leverage ratio shows a larger portion of firms with very high leverage ratios, underlying the likelihood of large-scale over-indebtedness (Figure 2.9, Panel B).

Similarly, the sizeable decline in profits relative to the business-as-usual scenario may impair firms' ability to service their debt. Figure 2.10 shows that, despite assuming no increase in interest payments compared to normal times, 30% (36%) of the companies are not profitable enough to cover their interest expenses in the upside scenario (downside scenario) – i.e. they have an interest coverage ratio lower than unity. In line with this, the interest coverage ratio is estimated to be approximately halved due the COVID-19 outbreak for the median firm. Figure 2.10 also disaggregates results at the sector level, showing once again large heterogeneity across sectors and that a consistent portion of firms in the "Accommodation and food service activities", the "Arts, entertainment and recreation" and "Transport" sectors will find it difficult to service their debt. Unsurprisingly, young, small and less productive companies are also predicted to be hit more severely by the crisis according to this metric.

Figure 2.9. Firms' leverage is expected to increase in the aftermath of the crisis

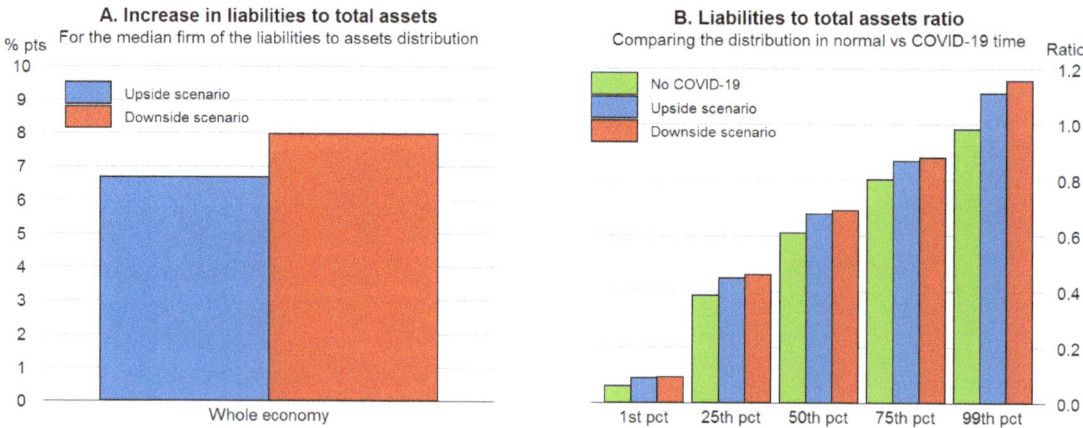

A. Increase in liabilities to total assets
For the median firm of the liabilities to assets distribution

B. Liabilities to total assets ratio
Comparing the distribution in normal vs COVID-19 time

Note: Panel A shows the percentage points increase in the liabilities-to-total assets ratio for the median firm of the leverage distribution following the COVID-19 outbreak in the upside (blue bar) and downside (red bar) scenarios. Panel B shows the levels of the liabilities-to-total assets ratio in the no-COVID (green bars), upside (blue bars) and downside (red bars) scenarios at different points of the leverage distribution. The sample is restricted ex-ante to firms having both positive profits and book value of equity in the 2018 reference year. Further details are in OECD (2020b).
Source: OECD calculations based on Orbis® data.

StatLink https://doi.org/10.1787/888934217532

Figure 2.10. A large portion of otherwise viable firms will find it hard to service their debt

Percentage of otherwise viable firms not covering interest expenses
Whole economy and sectoral disaggregation

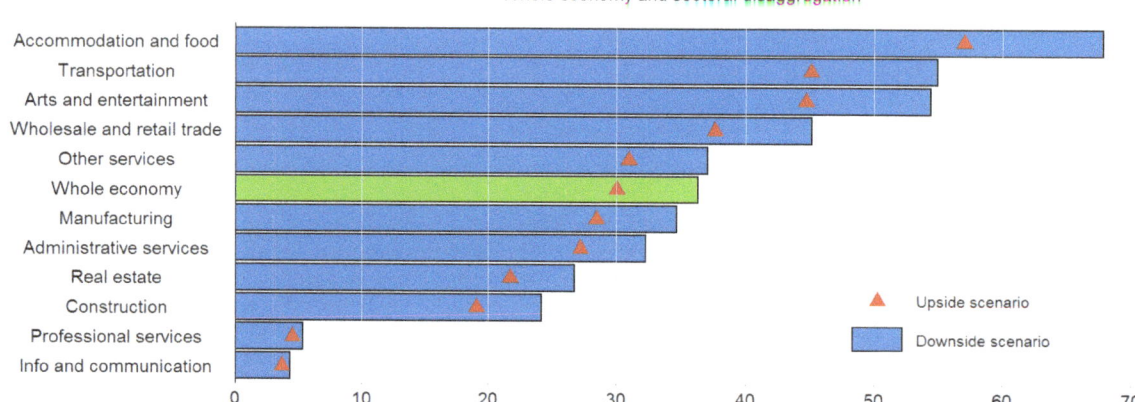

Note: The figure shows the percentage of firms whose interest coverage ratio falls below unity due to the COVID-19 outbreak in the upside (red triangles) and downside (green and blue bars) scenarios, both for the whole economy and at the sector level (1-Digit NACE Rev2 classification). The sample is restricted ex-ante to firms having both positive profits and book value of equity in the 2018 reference year.
Source: OECD calculations based on Orbis® data.

StatLink https://doi.org/10.1787/888934217551

A high level of debt combined with a high risk of default could undermine recovery

The increase in the level of indebtedness and the risk of default can push firms towards the so-called "debt overhang" risk. When a firm has a high outstanding debt with a high likelihood of default, the reduced ability to invest and limited access to new credit generate pressure to deleverage by cutting costs and downsizing, even in companies with profitable investment opportunities, potentially slowing down the recovery. As shown in the early part of the crisis, a combination of negative pressure on sales, high uncertainty about future sales and profits, and growing debt burdens has increased the risk of default, have led to downgrades of corporate credit ratings. For example, in March 2020, 389 non-financial corporations across OECD countries saw a decrease in their credit rating, compared to 61 downgrades in March 2019. In turn, the deterioration in the quality of loans may impair banks' balance sheets, reducing lending towards firms with good growth opportunities.

To assess formally how the rising tide of debt associated with the COVID-19 outbreak would affect investment and the potential magnitude of the effect, two separate empirical exercises are undertaken:[6]

- A panel data analysis, similar in spirit to Barbiero et al. (2020), examines the historical relationship between indebtedness and investment over the 1995-2018 period. Results suggest that an increase in the ratio of debt to total assets comparable to the one predicted by the accounting model would imply a decline in the ratio of investment to fixed assets of 2 percentage points (2.3 percentage points) in the upside (downside) scenario (Figure 2.11, Panel A).
- A cross-sectional analysis similar in spirit to Kalemli-Ozcan et al. (2019) examines the specific features characterising this relationship during the GFC. The results strengthen the previous findings, showing that the relationship holds also in the presence of a large shock such as the GFC and that the effect of a change in debt on investment is heterogeneous across firms. Firms that entered the GFC with a higher financial leverage ratio experienced a sharper decline in investment. In contrast, an increase in debt could foster investment in firms with very low initial indebtedness levels (Figure 2.11, Panel B).

Overall, the analysis confirms that a debt overhang could hamper investment and impede a fast recovery following the COVID-19 outbreak, given the record-high debt levels at the beginning of 2020 and the ongoing and expected rise in corporate debt due to the economic consequences of the pandemic.

---

[6] Details on the estimation strategy are reported in Box 3 in OECD (2020b).

Figure 2.11. High financial leverage decreases investment

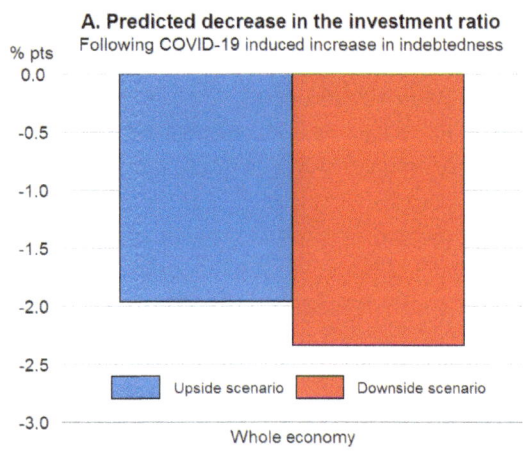

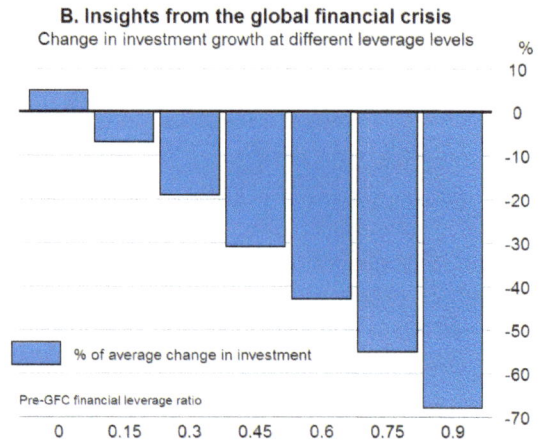

Note: Panel A shows the predicted decrease in the investment-to-fixed assets ratios under the hypothetical increase in the debt-to-total asset ratios shown in Figure 2.9 (Panel A) for the median firm. Estimates on the correlation between debt and investment ratios are based on column (7) of Table A.3 in OECD (2020b). Panel B shows the predicted percentage growth in the change in the ratio of investment to fixed assets following a one-standard deviation increase in the (post- minus pre-GFC) change in financial leverage, at different pre-crisis indebtedness levels. To interpret the size of the effect, the vertical-axis is scaled by the absolute value of the mean of the change in the investment ratio, hence obtaining the effect of a one standard deviation increase in the explanatory variable of interest on the average value of the dependent variable. Estimates are based on specification 2 of Table A.4 in OECD (2020b).
Source: OECD calculations based on Orbis® data.

StatLink 🔗 https://doi.org/10.1787/888934217570

Policy options

The empirical analysis stresses that the rise of corporate debt could threaten the recovery, suggesting that governments should be careful when designing support packages. In the initial phase of the COVID-19 crisis, temporary deferral or repayments of loans either by private agents (e.g. banks in the Netherlands) or public sources (e.g. loans by the Ministry of Tourism in Spain) played a key role in relieving financially distressed businesses and preventing early insolvency. Loan guarantees also helped distressed firms to meet their immediate financial commitments, avoiding widespread defaults (e.g. the Überbrückungskredite – loan guarantees for short-term credits – processed by specialised Austrian banks). However, such support may not address the issue of their long-term viability due to the associated rise in indebtedness. The rest of this note sheds light on various policy options to support distressed firms without compromising their ability to invest. First, it focuses explicitly on the design of crisis-related measures and on the necessity of favouring equity-type financing over debt to recapitalise distressed firms. Second, it considers the potential role of debt resolution mechanisms in mitigating debt overhang and in sorting out viable and non-viable firms.

Flattening the curve of insolvency while reducing the debt overhang risk

Increasing equity capital provides a way to support viable businesses without raising corporate debt. Relative to increases in debt, additional equity improves leverage ratios and reduces interest coverage ratios, thereby reducing corporate refinancing costs and helping a potential recovery. In times of high uncertainty over future sales growth, equity financing may also be desirable from the viewpoint of entrepreneurs, given that equity acts like an automatic stabiliser. Governments have various policy options to expand equity financing to support viable businesses.

Favouring equity and quasi-equity type of public financing

Equity injections can help viable firms, which suffer from financial difficulties solely due to the COVID-19 pandemic but are likely to return to profitability afterwards, to raise much-needed cash to finance their working capital while keeping assets free for raising debt in the future. Hybrid instruments like preferred equity appear particularly well-adapted as they provide a senior claim to dividends and assets in case of liquidation while they entail no voting rights and hence do not require governments to be involved in management. However, the authorities need to ensure that losses for taxpayers are minimised, competition in markets is not overly distorted and that equity injections do not crowd out other investors (OECD, 2020h). It is hence important to ensure that such support is state-contingent and includes mechanisms to incentivise all parties to wind down support when economic conditions improve (OECD, 2020c; OECD, 2020d). Temporary forms of preferred equity, e.g. retractable preferred equity, would also help to formulate an exit strategy in advance.

Supporting the financing needs of SMEs and start-ups may require a different and more comprehensive approach, as equity markets for small and medium-sized, as well as young, firms are thinner and often lacking altogether.[7] This makes the valuation of equity capital and thus the design of the injection more difficult. Besides direct equity injections, policymakers could revert to indirect measures. For instance, loan repayments could be linked to businesses' returns: firms that recover most robustly would pay back more, in the form of future taxes, while those that struggle longer would pay back less. Such support would have several advantages. It could help to flatten the curve of bankruptcies. In addition, agreements to pay higher taxes in the future against guaranteed credits would be easier to monitor than a potentially large number of equity injections in a large number of single entities.

While subject to the existence of sufficient fiscal space, another useful measure to address SME funding needs without raising debt consists of converting government (crisis-related) loans into grants. For instance, in the United States, loans obtained through the "Paycheck Protection Program" could be turned into grants conditional on the recipient firm spending at least three-quarters of the loan on payroll expenses and the rest on rent and utility bills. Similarly, the German government launched the "Immediate Assistance Programme" (Soforthilfeprogramm) to provide grants to small businesses, the self-employed and freelancers, conditional on using the funds to mainly cover rental and leasing expenses; applications should be filed directly with regional governments, and the maximum amount of the grant is set proportional to firm's size.

Stimulating the uptake and provision of equity capital

One way for policymakers to leverage on the need for equity in the post-COVID-19 world would be to grant an allowance for corporate equity (ACE). Such an allowance would partially or totally offset the tax benefits of using debt financing and make equity financing more attractive. Their design should however ensure that multinationals do not exploit ACE for tax-planning and that their fiscal cost is acceptable, for instance by granting them to new equity capital only. In the OECD area, a few countries (such as Italy and Belgium) have already introduced ACE or experimented with it in the past and their experience can serve as an example (Zangari, 2014; Hebous and Ruf, 2017). Moreover, deductions on income taxes and reliefs on the taxation of capital gains for eligible investments can foster the provision of private equity capital. Such tax incentives are often used to stimulate investment in high-risk, early-stage businesses, e.g. as in the UK's Enterprise Investment and Seed Enterprise Investment scheme, but could potentially also be extended to a wider set of firms, such as smaller companies facing tight financing frictions.

---

[7] For a recent discussion on start-ups during the COVID-19 crisis see OECD (2020g).

Debt-equity swaps constitute a further tool to address high leverage. They involve the conversion of outstanding debt that cannot be repaid into equity of an otherwise viable company. Debt-equity swaps may appear attractive in theory, but raise some implementation issues. A debt-equity swap requires the estimation of the market value of debt and equity, and an agreement between shareholders and debtholders about the exchange ratio. The lack of equity markets for SMEs, in particular smaller ones, impedes a cost-efficient estimation of the market value of equity. Consequently, debt-equity swaps appear more appropriate to address elevated leverage in circumstances where agreements on underlying terms are more likely to be reached, such as subsidiaries of a large firm, than as a more general policy tool.

Besides immediate short-term measures aimed at dealing with the economic consequences of the COVID-19 pandemic, there are options to ensure that equity markets continue to develop, including by widening access to equity markets for smaller firms by e.g. reducing costs and streamlining listing requirements (Kaousar Nassr and Wehinger, 2016). For instance, COVID-19-related equity programmes could speed up the implementation of the Capital Market Union in EU countries, which in turn could help to address intra-EU segmentation along national boundaries. Similarly, policymakers can improve the development and attractiveness of equity markets by using financial literacy as a tool to boost stock market participation and the financial knowledge of entrepreneurs.

Ensuring the restructuring of viable firms in temporary distress and liquidation of unviable ones

Equity and quasi-equity injections might prove insufficient to allow firms to operate normally if leverage ratios and the risk of default remain high. For those firms, reducing the debt burden through debt restructuring can change both the timing of a potential default and their possibility of investing (Frantz and Instefjord, 2019). Most countries have already modified their insolvency framework to give insolvent firms a chance to survive in the short run, for instance by relaxing the obligation for directors to file for bankruptcy once insolvent (e.g. France, Germany, Luxembourg, Portugal and Spain) or by relaxing creditors' right to initiate insolvency proceedings, as done in Italy, Spain, Switzerland and Turkey (OECD, 2020e; INSOL International-World Bank Group, 2020). However, more structural changes to features of insolvency regimes, which can be a barrier to successful restructuring, could help to coordinate creditors' claims in a manner that is consistent with preserving the viability of the firm. The crisis can provide an opportunity for such reforms.

Favouring new financing

Continuity of firm operations during restructuring increases the chances of a successful restructuring but often requires firms to have access to bridge financing. However, access to new funds may be difficult when debt levels are already high and the risk of default is significant, leading to debt overhang. Across the OECD, new financing can have either no priority at all over existing creditors or priority over only unsecured creditors or else priority over both secured and unsecured creditors. In normal times, insolvency regimes have to balance incentives for debtors to invest and take risks with incentives for creditors to supply funds. Therefore, new financing should be granted priority ahead of unsecured creditors but not over existing secured creditors since this would adversely affect the long-term availability of credit and legal certainty (Adalet McGowan and Andrews, 2018). Yet, several OECD countries currently do not offer any priority to new financing, so granting it over unsecured creditors would be beneficial. Further, in the context of the current crisis and assuming that the extensive guarantees and liquidity injections reach the right firms, the blocking of the "credit channel" might not be the main concern. An alternative but more controversial option to improve access to new financing is to temporarily suspend the priority enjoyed by secured creditors in favour of new investors when they invest in distressed firms (Gurrea-Martínez, 2020).

OECD ECONOMIC OUTLOOK, VOLUME 2020 ISSUE 2 © OECD 2020

Promoting pre-insolvency frameworks

Efficient pre-insolvency frameworks and debt restructuring could help to address debt overhang by lowering the negative impact of deleveraging on GDP growth and speeding up the resolution of non-performing loans (Carcea et al., 2015; Bricongne et al., 2016). While a majority of OECD countries have some type of pre-insolvency legislation, until recently they were generally missing in non-European OECD countries (Adalet McGowan and Andrews, 2018). A number of countries have strengthened out-of-court procedures in recent years. For example, in 2018, Belgium granted the courts the ability to endorse a settlement between a debtor and two or more of its creditors to make it enforceable. Lithuania overhauled the insolvency regime in 2020, accelerating timely initiation and resolution of personal and corporate insolvency proceedings and increasing returns for creditors, bringing them among the countries with the most efficient insolvency regimes according to the OECD indicator (OECD, forthcoming). In addition, several countries have encouraged lenders to reach out-of-court agreements with debtors materially affected by the COVID-19 crisis, especially when these agreements just involve a deferral of loan repayments (Australia, China, India, Malaysia and Singapore). More generally, introducing preventative restructuring or pre-insolvency frameworks, for instance as in the EU Directive on Preventive Restructuring Frameworks and Second Chance, could be accompanied by other incentives for private creditors to restructure debt, such as tax incentives (e.g. tax exemption for creditors who forgive part of debt). Effective design of such policies can be based on existing guidelines, such as the World Bank's "Toolkit for Out-of-Court Restructuring" (World Bank, 2016).

Establishing specific procedures for SMEs

SMEs may warrant different treatment from other firms in a debt restructuring strategy, as complex, lengthy and rigid procedures, necessary expertise and the high costs of insolvency can be demanding for this category of firms. Indeed, SMEs are more likely to be liquidated than restructured, since they have to bear costs that are disproportionately higher than those faced by larger enterprises. In the current juncture with a high risk of insolvency among SMEs, the social cost of inefficient debt restructuring for SMEs could be very large.

Against this background, formal procedures can be simplified for SMEs and informal procedures, which typically avoid the procedural complexities and timelines of court proceedings and are often associated with better outcomes for SMEs, can be adopted relatively quickly (World Bank, 2020). A number of countries have taken measures to simplify insolvency procedures for SMEs in response to the COVID-19 pandemic. The new COVID-19 moratorium in Switzerland provides SMEs with a simple procedure to obtain a temporary stay of their payment obligations. Brazil has proposed to implement simplified insolvency rules for SMEs (during judicial restructuring plans, they can be allowed to pay debt in up to 60 monthly instalments instead of 36 months, as is currently the case). In the United States, the threshold required to access the simplified insolvency rules of the Small Business Reorganisation Act of 2019 has been increased to allow more companies access to simplified proceedings. Introduction of such simplified rules and flexibility with payment plans could increase the likelihood that non-viable SMEs exit and viable ones in temporary distress are restructured immediately.

Dealing with systemic debt restructuring of large companies

In-court debt restructuring for large firms appears broadly efficient in normal times, but during systemic crises case-by-case restructuring can become difficult, availability of private capital is limited and co-ordination problems become more serious. In these conditions, court-supervised restructuring can be too time-consuming. Against this background, government agencies could prioritise out-of-court renegotiations whenever possible, a strategy that proved to be successful after the GFC (Bernstein et al., 2019; Hotchkiss et al., 2012). When out-of-court restructuring is difficult due to too many creditors, a centralised out-of-court approach might be desirable; such as the centralised out-of-court debt restructuring approach (the so-called "London approach") developed by the Bank of England in the 1990s or the "super Chapter 11" developed in the United States designed to deal with systemic crises.

Strengthening the efficiency of the liquidation framework to improve resource allocation

Providing equity support for distressed firms and ensuring debt restructuring should reduce a build-up of undesirable bankruptcies, but some firms will still remain non-viable in the post-COVID-19 world (e.g. due to their business model, their financial situation or their product specialisation). Against this risk, policymakers need to address several challenges to ensure that the liquidation process of such firms is efficient.

- *Ensuring the highest possible recovery rate for creditors.* When the number of distressed firms is too large, the courts become overwhelmed, standard insolvency procedures work less effectively, and the recovery rates for creditors can be reduced, potentially at fire-sale prices. Any reforms that can simplify and speed up in-court processes would help in this respect. In the short term, increasing resources for the court system, for instance by adding new temporary judges on insolvency procedures or reallocating judges depending on the busiest jurisdictions, would improve the recovery rate of creditors.

- *Ensuring that liquidation is established by an independent broker.* Public agencies such as public development banks in charge of loan guarantees may not be well placed to negotiate liquidation given their own exposed balance sheets (Bertay et al., 2015).Therefore, one challenge for policymakers is to establish an independent organisation to ensure that decisions with respect to liquidation and debt restructuring are not distorted (Hege, 2020).

- *Reducing specific barriers to market exit for small firms.* The corporate versus personal distinction in assets and liabilities is often blurred for small firms. In that context, the type of personal insolvency regime matters for reducing the scars from the crisis, in particular by enabling a post-insolvency second chance for entrepreneurs and the availability of a "fresh start" – i.e. the exemption of future earnings from obligations to repay past debt due to liquidation bankruptcy. Many countries are already lowering time to discharge to three years to be in line with the EU Directive on Insolvency and Second Chance (e.g. Germany), but they could try to expedite this part of the reform, which can facilitate reallocation (e.g. Spain is considering this option).

Bibliography

Adalet McGowan, M., and D. Andrews (2018), "Design of Insolvency Regimes Across Countries", *OECD Economics Department Working Papers*, No. 1504, OECD Publishing, Paris.

Barbiero, F., A. Popov and M. Wolski (2020), "Debt Overhang, Global Growth Opportunities, and Investment", *Journal of Banking and Finance*, 120, Article 105950.

Bernstein, S., J. Lerner and F. Mezzanotti (2019). "Private Equity and Financial Fragility During the Crisis", *Review of Financial Studies*, 32(4), 1309–1373.

Bertay, A., A. Demirguc-Kunt and H. Huizinga (2015), "Bank Ownership and Credit over the Business Cycle: Is Lending by State Banks less Procyclical?", *Journal of Banking and Finance,* 50(3), 326-339.

Bricongne, J.C, M. Demertzis, P. Pontuch and A. Turrini (2016). "Macroeconomic Relevance of Insolvency Frameworks in a High-Debt Context: An EU Perspective", European Economy - Discussion Papers, No.2015-032, Directorate General Economic and Financial Affairs, European Commission.

Carcea, M., D. Ciriaci, C. Cuerpo, D. Lorenzani and P. Pontuch (2015), "The Economic Impact of Rescue and Recovery Frameworks in the EU", *EU Discussion Papers*, No. 004.

Carletti, E., T. Oliviero, M. Pagano, L. Pelizzon and M. G. Subrahmanyam (2020), "The COVID-19 Shock and Equity Shortfall: Firm-level Evidence from Italy", *CEPR Discussion Paper*, No. 14831.

del Rio-Chanona, R. M., P. Mealy, A. Pichler, F. Lafond and J. D. Farmer (2020), "Supply and Demand

Shocks in the COVID-19 Pandemic: An Industry and Occupation Perspective", *COVID Economics: Vetted and Real-Time Papers*, Issue 6.

Frantz, P., and N. Instefjord (2019), "Debt Overhang and Non-distressed Debt Restructuring", *Journal of Financial Intermediation*, Vol. 37(C), 75-88.

Gurrea-Martínez, A. (2020), "Insolvency Law in Times of COVID-19", *Ibero-American Institute for Law and Finance Working Paper*, No. 2

Hebous, S., and M. Ruf (2017),"Evaluating the Effects of ACE Systems on Multinational Debt Financing and Investment", *Journal of Public Economics*, 156, 131-149.

Hege, U. (2020), "Corporate Debt Threatens to Derail Recovery", *TSE Mag #20*.

Hotchkiss, E.S., P. Stromberg and D. Smith (2012), "Private Equity and the Resolution of Financial Distress", AFA 2012 Chicago Meetings Paper, *ECGI - Finance Working Paper*, No. 331.

Iverson, B. (2018), "Get in Line: Chapter 11 Restructuring in Crowded Bankruptcy Courts", *Management Science*, 64(11), 5370-5394.

INSOL International-World Bank Group (2020), *Global Guide Corporate Insolvency: Responses in Times of Covid-191: Report*, Washington D.C.

Kalemli-Ozcan, S., L.A. Laeven and D. Moreno (2019), "Debt Overhang, Rollover Risk, and Corporate Investment: Evidence from the European Crisis", *ECB Working Paper*, No. 2241.

Kaousar Nassr, I. and G. Wehinger (2016), "Opportunities and limitations of public equity markets for SMEs", *OECD Journal: Financial Market Trends*, 2015/1.

OECD (2020a), "Corporate Sector Vulnerabilities During the COVID-19 Outbreak: Assessment and Policy Responses", *Tackling Coronavirus Series*, OECD Publishing, Paris.

OECD (2020b), "Insolvency and Debt Overhang Following the COVID-19 Outbreak: Assessment of Risks and Policy Responses", *Tackling Coronavirus Series*, OECD Publishing, Paris.

OECD (2020c), "The COVID-19 Crisis and State Ownership in the Economy: Issues and Policy Considerations", *Tackling Coronavirus Series*, OECD Publishing, Paris.

OECD (2020d), "Supporting Businesses in Financial Distress to Avoid Insolvency During the COVID-19 Crisis", *Tackling Coronavirus Series*, OECD Publishing, Paris.

OECD (2020e), "National Corporate Governance Related Initiatives During the COVID-19 Crisis: A Survey of 37 Jurisdictions", *Tackling Coronavirus Series*, OECD Publishing, Paris.

OECD (2020g), "Start-ups in the Time of COVID-19: Facing the Challenges, Seizing the Opportunities", *Tackling Coronavirus Series*, OECD Publishing, Paris.

OECD (2020h),"COVID-19 Government Financing Support Programmes for Businesses", OECD Publishing, Paris.

World Bank (2016), *Principles for Effective Insolvency and Creditor/Debtor Regimes*, World Bank Group, Washington D.C.

World Bank (2017), *Report on the Treatment of MSME Insolvency*, World Bank Group, Washington D.C.

World Bank (2018), *Saving Entrepreneurs, Saving Enterprises: Proposals on the Treatment of MSME Insolvency*, World Bank Group, Washington D.C.

Zangari, E. (2014), "Addressing the Debt Bias: A Comparison Between the Belgian and the Italian ACE Systems", *Taxation Papers – Working Paper*, No. 44, European Commission.

Issue Note 3. Post-financial-crisis changes to monetary policy frameworks: Driving factors and remaining challenges

Several central banks in advanced economies have embarked on monetary policy reviews in the context of persistently low inflation, interest rates and potential GDP growth in past decades and increasing use of unconventional tools since the global financial crisis. These reviews are welcome as they allow central banks to rethink openly their targets, tools and communication in the context of a changing economic environment. The engagement with the public on these issues can strengthen their legitimacy and credibility.

Recently implemented and discussed changes to monetary policy frameworks, which depend crucially on the inflation expectations channel via committing to achieve higher inflation in the future and "lower for longer" interest rates, give hopes for improving the effectiveness of monetary policy and achieving stable higher inflation. However, as argued in this note, challenges with controlling inflation expectations, their uncertain demand effects and continued structural changes that hold down inflation all point to caution. Thus, future – ideally regular – reviews could focus more on longer-term determinants of inflation.

Monetary policy frameworks and their reviews

Monetary policy frameworks define the legal environment in which the monetary authority operates and provide operational guidance for the conduct of monetary policy. This includes an institutional structure (e.g. a governance mechanism and a decision-making process within the central bank), as well as a set of goals, operational targets, instruments, procedures and communications. Although some differences exist in the way monetary policy is conducted across jurisdictions, monetary policy frameworks have broadly converged across countries in terms of mandates (price stability), operational targets (around a 2% inflation rate over the medium term), and instruments (both conventional and unconventional tools) over the past 20 years (Table 2.2).

Table 2.2. Monetary policy frameworks in selected economies

	Mandate	Operational Targets	Instruments	Press conference and minutes release	Publication of forecasts
US Federal Reserve	Price stability, maximum employment & moderate long-term interest rates	2% inflation target on average, measured by the PCE	Conventional tools QE Forward guidance	Following FOMC meetings (8 times a year), the Federal Reserve holds a press conference and releases minutes	Staff and FOMC's projections, including interest rate path
European Central Bank	Price stability	Inflation below but close to 2% over the medium term, measured by the HICP	Conventional tools QE Forward guidance Negative interest rate policy	Following Governing Council meetings (every 6 weeks), the ECB holds a press conference and releases accounts of the meetings	Staff's projections
Bank of England	Price stability	2% inflation target at all times, measured by headline CPI	Conventional tools QE Forward guidance	Following MPC meetings (8 times a year), the BoE holds a press conference and releases minutes	Staff's and MPC's projections, including interest rate path
Bank of Japan	Price stability	2% inflation target with overshooting commitment, at "the earliest possible time", measured by CPI (all items less fresh food)	Conventional tools QE Forward guidance Negative interest rate policy Yield curve control	Following MPMs (8 times a year), the BoJ holds a press conference and releases minutes	Policy Board's projections
Bank of Canada	Price stability	2% inflation target with a band (+/- 1%) over the medium term, measured by headline CPI	Conventional tools QE Forward Guidance	Following policy decisions (8 times a year), the BoC holds a press conference. No minutes are released	Staff's projections, including interest rate path
Sveriges Riksbank	Price stability	2% inflation target with a band (+/- 1%), within 2 years, measured by the CPIF	Conventional tools QE Forward guidance	Following monetary policy meetings (5 times a year), the Riksbank holds a press conference and releases minutes	Staff's projections, including interest rate path
Swiss National Bank	Price stability	Inflation range between 0% and 2% over the medium term, measured by headline CPI	Conventional tools QE FX interventions	Following monetary policy assessment (quarterly), the SNB holds a press conference (twice a year). No minutes are released	Staff's projections

Note: QE refers to quantitative easing measures (asset purchases by central banks); PCE refers to the Personal Consumption Expenditure deflator; CPI is a consumer price index; CPIF is a consumer price index with a fixed interest rate; and HICP is a harmonised index of consumer prices. FOMC refers to the Federal Open Market Committee, MPC to the Monetary Policy Committee and MPMs to monetary policy meetings.
Source: Samarina, A. and N. Apokoritis (2020), "Evolution of Monetary Policy Frameworks in the Post-crisis Environment", *DNB Working Paper*, No. 664; Bank for International Settlements (2019), "Monetary Policy Frameworks and Central Bank Market Operations", MC Compendium; and central bank websites.

In contrast, no standardised approach to reviewing monetary policy frameworks exists. With the exception of the Bank of Canada, which has been conducting reviews every five years,[1] most countries have done so on an *ad-hoc* basis and with varying scope. The number of such *ad-hoc* reviews, however, has increased significantly over the past few years and some have led to several substantial changes, in particular to the frameworks of the Bank of Japan and the US Federal Reserve (Box 2.1). Other monetary authorities have also recently announced their intentions to conduct thorough reviews in the coming years.[2] More generally, central banks have indicated their willingness to make reviews both public and recurrent to improve the transparency and accountability of monetary policy and ensure that monetary policy strategies are adapted to the economic environment, which is a welcome development.

Changes to monetary policy frameworks since the global financial crisis

A combination of deep structural changes and unexpected shocks has challenged the way monetary policy is conducted in many advanced countries. The secular decline in productivity growth and inflation, along with the reduction in neutral interest rates estimates, have significantly increased the risk that policy rates hit the zero lower bound (ZLB). The observed flattening of the Phillips curve, which has complicated the extraction of meaningful signals from labour market outcomes, also suggests that, other things being constant, monetary policy needs to be more aggressive to achieve a given change in inflation, with risks to central banks' credibility.[3] The global financial crisis and the COVID-19 pandemic, both of which prompted very accommodative policy and an enlargement of monetary policy tools, including purchases of public and private assets, forward guidance and negative policy interest rates, further highlighted the limits of conventional monetary policy measures. Both shocks also underscored the importance of financial stability issues when designing monetary policy.

Against this background, major central banks have not waited for formal reviews to amend, implicitly or explicitly, their monetary policy frameworks over the past decade to help reaching their targets (Samarina and Apokoritis, 2020). Although key building blocks (such as governance mechanisms and mandates) have generally been unchanged, tools and communication strategies have been significantly modified. The use of unconventional monetary policy tools, in particular quantitative easing (QE) and forward guidance, has become pervasive. This trend recently culminated in the issuance of a new statement on "Longer-Run Goals and Monetary Policy Strategy" by the US Federal Reserve in August 2020, which ended a review

---

[1] The unique Canadian review process is the legacy of introducing the inflation targeting regime in 1991, which was initially based on a short-term agreement between the government of Canada and the Bank of Canada that specified the inflation target and required a formal review process (Amano et al., 2020). The review and renewal process has been deliberate, in-depth, research-driven and transparent, involving consultation with relevant stakeholders, and contributed to increased independence and transparency consistent with good governance and enhanced political legitimacy of the framework.

[2] In January 2020, the ECB President announced a framework review, focusing primarily on medium-term policy objectives (definition of the inflation target, time to reach it, etc.) as well as on issues regarding financial stability, interactions between monetary and fiscal policies, employment and environmental sustainability. The results are expected to be released in 2021. The Bank of England has also launched an internal research programme about its policy framework, expected to be finalised in early 2021.

[3] When the Phillips curve is relatively flat, central banks need to move interest rates and aggregate demand significantly to offset a given shock and bring inflation back to target, other things being equal. The flattening can also raise problems of credibility and political feasibility (Beaudry et al., 2020). When inflation is high, lowering inflation is costly in terms of output and employment, unless inflation expectations remain well anchored on the official target. In contrast, when inflation is low, monetary policy could be constrained by the zero lower bound in stimulating demand sufficiently.

process that started in 2018.[4] The new statement formalised many of the changes that had been made, *de facto*, to the US monetary policy framework to address the challenges posed by the "new normal" (Box 2.1).

Box 2.1. What is new in the US monetary policy framework?

On 27 August, the US Federal Open Market Committee issued a new statement on "Longer-Run Goals and Monetary Policy Strategy", effectively modifying its monetary policy framework for the first time since 2012 in three important dimensions. First, the Federal Reserve moved to a flexible form of average inflation targeting (FAIT) and will now "seek to achieve inflation that averages 2% over time". Although no formal metric was provided, the statement indicates that an inflation "moderately over 2% for some time" would be tolerated after periods of low inflation. Second, the statement reiterated the importance of its (full) employment mandate and indicated that monetary policy would now react to "shortfalls in" rather than "deviations from" the broad-based and inclusive maximum employment goal. In practice, this modification implies that improvements in the labour market, based on a set of indicators rather than estimated NAIRUs, would trigger a tightening only if they come with significant price pressures. Third, the statement made clear that financial stability concerns would play a role in shaping monetary policy decisions.

In some respects, these announcements represent small deviations from the existing framework. The general mandate of the Federal Reserve, which is decided by Congress, remains unchanged and focused on promoting maximum employment, stable prices, and moderate long-term interest rates. No major announcement was made with regard to either the Federal Reserve's policy tools or communications practices. Moreover, while the statement consolidates the "flexible" way in which the Federal Reserve has been operating to achieve its objectives, it does not define how the target of 2% average inflation will be calculated.

These modifications, however, still represent a significant shift in the way the Federal Reserve carries out its mission. From an institutional perspective, the statement concludes the first-ever public review of the monetary policy framework, and generally signals the willingness of the monetary authorities to remain transparent and accountable in the future.[1] On a conceptual level, those revisions also acknowledge the "new normal" environment in which the Federal Reserve operates and the constraints it puts on policy. On the inflation side, the accommodative stance implied by the new statement – which now allows for a temporary overshooting of the symmetric 2% long-run target – clearly highlights the risks associated with running persistently low levels of realised inflation (in particular a de-anchoring of inflation expectations), and the constraints imposed by the zero lower bound in such a scenario. On the real side, the shift away from "pre-emptive striking" reflects the difficulty in pinning down the equilibrium unemployment rate and, more generally, the uncertainty surrounding the link between labour market outcomes and inflation.

---

1. The process, which started in 2018, incorporated feedbacks from public "Fed Listens" events, academia, and the FOMC internal discussions. According to the statement, this review process will now take place every five years.

---

[4] The ECB President signaled that the ECB could mimic the Federal Reserve's approach and allow inflation to exceed the target temporarily (Lagarde, 2020). This would also represent an important change to the ECB framework.

Although the revised frameworks all signal a strong commitment to push inflation higher, they have generally fallen short of the more radical and comprehensive alternatives discussed in both academic and policy circles, but which are based on the same premises. The alternatives include raising the inflation target and one of the so-called make-up strategies, like targeting an explicit price (or nominal GDP) level, where past misses of the target should be compensated in the future (Blanchard et al., 2010; Bean, 2013; Ball, 2014; Baker et al., 2017; Amano et al., 2020; Arias et al., 2020).[5,6] However, some frameworks can be now considered "soft" forms of these alternative options. For instance, the Bank of Japan's "inflation-overshooting commitment" announced in September 2016 can be regarded as a form of a make-up strategy. Similarly, the switch to a flexible form of average inflation targeting (FAIT) will take the US Federal Reserve closer to a price-level targeting, since the FOMC will de facto aim to make up for past inflation misses.

Old challenges

Monetary policy has been successful in influencing financial markets, the first stage of monetary policy pass-through to demand (in particular investment) and inflation. However, over the past two decades, core inflation in advanced economies has rarely risen above (implicit or explicit) targets.[7] New policy frameworks based on make-up strategies give hope to overcome the low-inflation challenge. However, there are reasons for caution. Their efficacy crucially hinges on the population's understanding of, and reaction to, monetary policy commitments and strong effects of demand-supply imbalances on inflation – i.e. a steep Phillips curve (Hebden et al., 2020). As argued below, controlling inflation expectations to affect demand is difficult in practice and several structural factors have likely reduced the sensitivity of inflation to demand pressures.

Persistently low inflation

In the workhorse model used by central banks, inflation is determined by inflation expectations and the strength of demand relative to productive capacities (the so-called output gap). Assuming households and firms behave rationally, higher expected inflation can stimulate today's household spending by lowering perceptions of real interest rates and encouraging firms to increase prices in order to prevent a fall in relative prices. Similarly, when demand persistently exceeds the supply of goods and services, producers will be encouraged to increase prices. However, when interest rates are low and close to the ZLB, the scope to stimulate demand through yield curve changes, and in turn inflation, is limited. In this case, inflation expectations become the main available channel to boost inflation, as assumed by the many make-up strategies discussed above (Svensson, 2003; Yellen, 2016; Bernanke, 2020).

---

[5] One exception is the increase in the inflation target from 1% to a 2% by the Bank of Japan in January 2013. Before this change, "price stability goal in the medium to long term" was in a positive range of 2% or lower in terms of the year-on-year rate of change in the CPI and was set at 1%.

[6] Pros and cons of these various alternatives are discussed in Box 1.2 in OECD (2018). Arias et al. (2020) undertake simulation-based comparisons of some of these alternatives, including average inflation targeting (AIT) over eight years, asymmetric and temporary AIT and temporary price-level targeting. They find that make-up strategies generally improve macroeconomic stability compared with traditional inflation targeting, but the size of these gains is moderate across the models and strategies considered, with longer make-up windows yielding somewhat larger gains.

[7] Between 2000 and 2019, core inflation (i.e. inflation excluding prices of food and energy) exceeded 2% only 26% of the time (quarters) in the United States, 6% in the euro area and never in Japan (excluding the effects of the consumption tax increase in the second quarter of 2014 to the first quarter of 2015). For headline inflation, the corresponding figures are 40%, 48% and 1%. In the euro area, though, headline inflation at constant taxes was above 2% only 18% of the time.

Inflation expectations

Well-anchored inflation expectations are considered to be the primary factor behind the low and stable inflation observed over the past three decades (Yellen, 2016; Williams, 2020). By anchoring expectations around the target, central banks prevent temporary shocks to inflation from feeding into the wage and price formation processes. Some evidence suggests that higher inflation expectations can boost consumption and investment.[8] However, three challenges may reduce the effectiveness of inflation expectations as a practical policy channel as intended by central banks (Mavroeidis et al., 2014; Bachmann et al., 2015; Coibion et al., 2020b).

First, although firms set prices of most goods and services, little is known about their inflation expectations. Surveys of firms' aggregate inflation expectations are rare and of limited quality, in contrast to surveys of households' expectations (Coibion et al., 2020a). According to theoretical predictions, inflation expectations of firms and households are key for consumption, investment and wage-price setting decisions, as opposed to inflation expectations of financial market participants and professional forecasters.[9]

Second, both households and businesses are generally poorly informed about realised and expected inflation, or inflation targets, and their expectations have been persistently above targets. They are also rather inattentive to monetary policy changes. This general lack of knowledge about inflation is not surprising in a low-inflation environment, where the (costly) process of gathering information about prices might not be worth pursuing. Inferring about inflation from personal experience is also complex. As a result, households tend to form their views about aggregate inflation from few frequently purchased items, like gasoline, electricity and processed food (Shioji, 2015; Coeuré, 2019; Coibion et al., 2020a), resulting in "perceived" inflation at much higher levels than actual inflation (Figure 2.12), and with views varying widely across individuals.[10] Recent evidence also shows that households have a rather limited understanding of monetary policy announcements and that expectations of neither households nor firms seem to respond much to such communications (Coibion et al., 2020a; Coibion et al., 2020b).

---

[8] For example, households with higher inflation expectations tend to be more positive towards spending, especially on durables (D'Acunto et al., 2016; Duca et al., 2018). Also, higher expected inflation was also positively correlated with Italian firms' willingness to invest in 2012-16, operating through the standard interest channel (Grasso and Ropele, 2018).

[9] Central banks tend to focus more on inflation expectations derived from financial instruments and professional forecasts. This could be justified by a wider and timelier availability of such indicators as well as the focus on monetary policy transmission to market interest rates as a first step to influence demand and inflation.

[10] Based on a survey of German consumers in 2015, Dräger and Nghiem (2020) found that approximately 50% of respondents believed that inflation over the previous 12 months had been 5% or above (against 0.3% for actual inflation). In 2002, Mankiw et al. (2003) found significant disagreement in consumer expectations over the following year, with 5% of the population expecting deflation and 10% expecting inflation of at least 10%. In Japan, 70% of individuals surveyed from August to September 2020 perceived that annual inflation was positive, when realised inflation was zero, and average expected inflation per year over the next five years was 4.1% (the median was 2%) (Bank of Japan, 2020a).

Figure 2.12. Household inflation expectations tend to exceed realised inflation and targets

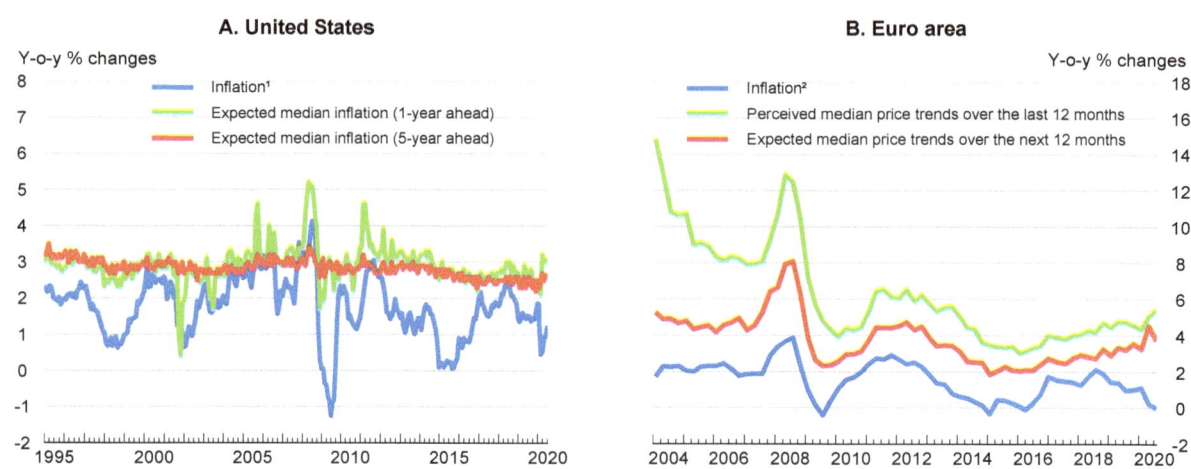

1. Personal consumption expenditure deflator, including food and energy prices.
2. Harmonised index of consumer prices, including food and energy prices.
Source: Bureau of Economic Analysis; Eurostat; European Commission; Refinitiv; and OECD calculations.

StatLink ⏤ https://doi.org/10.1787/888934217589

Third, evidence is mixed about the impact of inflation expectations on households' consumption (Bachmann et al., 2015). Under some circumstances, households' expectations about future price changes can have a powerful impact on their consumption decisions. This is for instance the case with VAT rate increases, when their announcements tend to boost consumers' purchases prior to the tax change (Kueng, 2011; D'Acunto et al., 2010).[11] However, a durable boost to household consumption due to monetary policy forward-guidance, even when well understood by consumers, may be less powerful. Higher expected inflation may not stimulate aggregate consumption durably if real income is expected to decline or stagnate. With constant nominal income, higher inflation could just shift demand from non-essential goods and services to necessities. Higher inflation may also increase perceived uncertainty and result in higher household saving. Indeed, according to psychological studies, most people resent inflation and associate it with bad times for buying and having negative effects on their finances (Katona, 1974; Ranyard et al., 2008). Moreover, the effects of monetary policy are uncertain and refer to a distant future, which may be discounted by households and businesses in their consumption and investment decisions.

Structural shifts in supply and demand

Over the past three decades, a combination of structural changes in advanced economies, related to the production and distribution of goods and services, firms' business models and demand structure, have limited pressures on aggregate inflation and led to persistent and large relative price changes of certain categories of goods and services (Figure 2.13). The persistence of such forces, which are largely beyond monetary policy decisions and communications, have aggravated the challenge for central banks in attaining their inflation targets.

---

[11] However, tax increases are generally one-off and widely-anticipated events in a near future, and they have usually produced short-lived positive effects, with offsets in subsequent periods. For instance, in Japan, consumption tax increases in 2014 and 2019 led to front-loaded purchases ahead of the expected increase in prices, but were followed by a consumption decline (Bank of Japan, 2020b).

Figure 2.13. Persistent deflation has taken place for some categories of goods and services

Average annual percentage change between the first eight months in 2000 and 2020

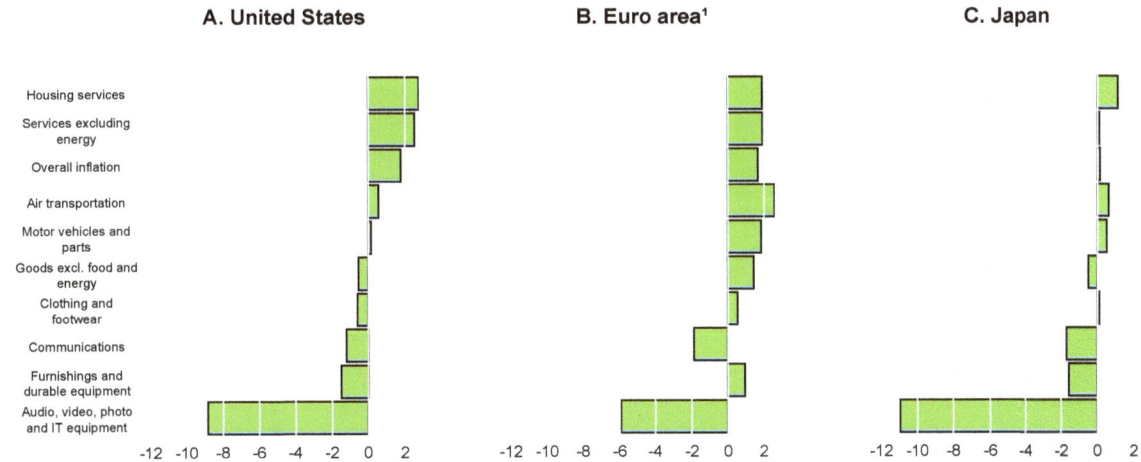

Note: The selected categories are not exactly identical across the three economic areas.
1. For the euro area, services and goods inflation include prices of food and energy.
Source: Eurostat; Ministry of Internal Affairs and Communications, Japan; US Bureau of Economic Analysis; and OECD calculations.

StatLink https://doi.org/10.1787/888934217608

- ***Globalisation, technological progress and market concentration***: The integration of low-wage emerging-market economies, in particular China, into global value chains (GVCs) combined with trade liberalisation over the past three decades has led to a substantial decline in production costs, expanded supply massively and increased import competition, putting a downward pressure on domestic producer goods prices (Autor et al., 2013; Andrews et al., 2018). Globalisation has also coincided with a rapid technological progress in production of many goods or their components, including electronics, adding to downward price pressures. These two powerful structural changes have been associated with increased market concentration in manufacturing (Autor et al., 2020). Stronger import competition and rising market concentration can reduce the pass-through from wages to prices in goods-producing sectors, partly explaining the lack of higher goods inflation and thus overall inflation in the recent expansions in the United States (Heise et al., 2020).

- ***Retail sector and network industries***: There has been increasing interest in the role of gradual structural changes in the retail sector for determining goods inflation. In the United States, over the past three decades, the retail sector has changed from one with many small firms to one dominated by large firms, with large retailers increasingly sourcing from China (Smith, 2019). Direct sourcing from low-cost countries has helped to eliminate substantial mark-ups of intermediaries (Ganapati, 2018), contributing to the closure of small shops (Smith, 2019). The rise of general merchandisers selling goods from different industries could have led to reduced margins on some goods to attract clients as profits are maximised at the chain level and not for individual goods.[12] Low retail margins have also been possible due to weak wage growth in the sector.[13] The past decades have also witnessed a rise of e-commerce, which could have damped prices by increasing price transparency

---

[12] For instance, Bonomo et al. (2020) find that a typical retail multi-product store in Israel synchronises its regular price changes around occasional "peak" days, once or twice per month.

[13] For instance, in the United States, the median hourly wage in sales and related occupations has grown by only slightly more than headline inflation over the past ten years (2.2% vs 1.5% on average per year).

and eroding profit margins, notably in some traditionally face-to-face businesses. Indeed, online inflation for some categories of goods and services is found to be lower than inflation measured by the official consumer price index (Goolsbee and Klenow, 2018), but e-commerce is estimated to explain only a small part of the recent low inflation (Ciccarelli and Osbat, 2017). A growing importance of network industries in services (like communication, TV and music streaming services, air transport) has also likely contributed to muted inflation developments. These sectors are characterised by high fixed costs, low marginal costs of extra supply (enabled by technological progress), and strong competition. Maximisation of their profits depends on market share gains, limiting possibilities to increase prices persistently.

- *Weakening demand and large supply*: Limited price pressures resulting from globalisation and technological progress may have been weakened further by relative saturation of demand for many durable goods compared with ample production capacities. This mechanism is based on the premise that when a new product is developed, demand for it grows very fast and income elasticity of demand is high. This stimulates production capacity and technological progress, leading over time to lower prices. At the same time, the income elasticity of demand falls with rising ownership of the product by households and higher population income (Matsuyama, 2002; Yoshikawa, 2003; Bessen, 2018). Ultimately, when the desired level of possession of the product has been attained, "new demand" for buying the good for the first time vanishes and demand is driven by replacement or renewal motives only (Komiyama, 2014). As this phenomenon may affect many durable household products in advanced economies (cars, home appliances, etc.), the scope to increase prices for such goods, that still account for a considerable part of the consumption basket, may be limited by the fear of a fall in demand. The saturation of demand could be accelerated by the fall in prices (Bessen, 2018) and population aging, which tend to decrease per-capita consumption growth (Fujita and Fujiwara, 2016) – the two phenomena observed in many advanced economies in the past decades.

If the above structural trends persist in advanced economies, central banks may continue to struggle to achieve persistently higher inflation in the future. There is, however, large uncertainty about future structural developments, partly related to uncertain long-term impacts of the COVID-19 crisis. In the absence of protectionist policies or a large-scale reshoring of manufacturing production motivated by strategic considerations, globalisation forces are likely to continue limiting upward pressures on prices in advanced economies. The COVID-19 experience may encourage reshoring though. Changes more amenable to policy interventions – such as a quick catch-up of wages in low-cost-production countries or market regulation – are not likely to materialise in the medium term. Also, deeper forces – such as technological progress and population ageing – are unlikely to alleviate the "saturated" demand problem in the medium to long term. In contrast to the experience of past decades, inflationary pressures and inflation volatility could result from disruptive climate changes. Disruption to production, shipping and migration patterns induced by exogenous climate events, for instance, could all increase the costs of production and distribution around the world, in particular for food. Policies to address climate changes, such as the implementation of a carbon tax or the suspension of fossil fuel subsidies, could also push up prices.

Bibliography

Amano, R., T. J. Carter and L. L. Schembri (2020), "Strengthening Inflation Targeting: Review and Renewal Processes in Canada and Other Advanced Jurisdictions," *Staff Discussion Paper*, No. 2020-7, Bank of Canada.

Andrews, D., P. Gal and W. Witheridge (2018), "A Genie in a Bottle? Globalisation, Competition and Inflation," *OECD Economics Department Working Papers*, No. 1462, OECD Publishing, Paris.

Arias, J., M. Bodenstein, H. Chung, T. Drautzburg and A. Raffo (2020), "Alternative Strategies: How Do They Work? How Might They Help?," *Finance and Economics Discussion Series*, No. 2020-068, Board of Governors of the Federal Reserve System.

Autor, D. H., D. Dorn and G. H. Hanson (2013), "The China Syndrome: Local Labor Market Effects of Import Competition in the United States," *American Economic Review*, 103(6), 2121–68.

Autor, D., D. Dorn, L. F. Katz, C. Patterson, and J. Van Reenen (2020): "The Fall of the Labor Share and the Rise of Superstar Firms," *The Quarterly Journal of Economics*, 135(2), 645–709.

Bachmann, R., T. O. Berg and E. R. Sims (2015), "Inflation Expectations and Readiness to Spend: Cross-Sectional Evidence", *American Economic Journal: Economic Policy*, 7(1), 1-35.

Baker, D. et al. (2017), "Prominent Economists Question Fed Inflation Target", letter to the Federal Reserve Board of Governors, The Center for Popular Democracy, 8 June.

Ball, L. (2014), "The Case for a Long-Run Inflation Target of Four Percent", *IMF Working Papers*, No 14/92.

Bank for International Settlements (2019), "Monetary Policy Frameworks and Central Bank Market Operations", MC Compendium, October.

Bank of Japan (2020a), *Results of the 83rd Opinion Survey on the General Public's Views and Behavior (September 2020 Survey)*, October.

Bank of Japan (2020b), "Developments in Household Spending after the Consumption Tax Hike", Box 4 in *Outlook for Economic Activity and Prices*, January.

Bean, C. (2013), "Nominal Income Targets – An Old Wine in a New Bottle", speech at the Institute for Economic Affairs Conference on the State of the Economy, London, 27 February.

Beaudry, P., C. Hou and F. Portier (2020), "Monetary Policy when the Phillips Curve is Locally Quite Flat", *CEPR Discussion Papers*, No. 15184.

Bernanke, B. S. (2020), "The New Tools of Monetary Policy. American Economic Association Presidential Address", January 4.

Bessen, J. (2018), "AI and Jobs: the Role of Demand", *NBER Working Paper Series*, No. 24235.

Blanchard, O., G. Dell'Ariccia and P. Mauro (2010), "Rethinking Macroeconomic Policy", *Journal of Money, Credit and Banking*, 42(1), 199-215.

Bonomo, M., C. Carvalho, O. Kryvtsov, S. Ribon and R. Rigato (2020), "Multi-Product Pricing: Theory and Evidence from Large Retailers in Israel", *Bank of Canada Staff Working Papers*, No. 2020-12, 7 April.

Ciccarelli, M. and C. Osbat (eds) (2017), "Low Inflation in the Euro Area: Causes and Consequences", *Occasional Paper Series*, No. 181, European Central Bank.

Coeuré, B. (2019), "Inflation Expectations and the Conduct of Monetary Policy", speech at an event organised by the SAFE Policy Center, Frankfurt am Main, 11 July.

Coibion, O., Y. Gorodnichenko, E. S. Knotek II and R. Schoenle (2020a), "Average Inflation Targeting and Household Expectations", *Federal Reserve Bank of Cleveland Working Paper*, 20-26.

Coibion, O., Y. Gorodnichenko, S. Kumar and M. Pedemonte (2020b), "Inflation Expectations as a Policy Tool?", *Journal of International Economics*, 124.

D'Acunto, F., D. Hoang and M. Weber (2016), "Unconventional Fiscal Policy, Inflation Expectations, and

Consumption Expenditure", *CESifo Working Paper Series*, No. 5793.

Dräger, L. and G. Nghiem (2020), "Are Consumers' Spending Decisions in Line with an Euler Equation?", *Review of Economics and Statistics*, forthcoming.

Duca, I., G. Kenny and A. Reuter (2018), "Inflation Expectation, Consumption and the Lower Bound: Micro Evidence from a Large Euro Area Survey", *ECB Working Paper Series*, No. 2196.

Fujita, S. and I. Fujiwara (2016), "Declining Trends in the Real Interest Rate and Inflation: The Role of Aging", *Federal Reserve Bank of Philadelphia Working Paper*, No. 16-29.

Ganapati, S. (2018), "The Modern Wholesaler: Global Sourcing, Domestic Distribution, and Scale Economies", *CES Working Papers*, No. 18-49, Center for Economic Studies, U.S. Census Bureau.

Goolsbee, A. D. and P. J. Klenow (2018), "Internet Rising, Prices Falling: Measuring Inflation in a World of E-Commerce", *AEA Papers and Proceedings*, 108, 488-92.

Grasso, A. and T. Ropele (2018), "Firms' Inflation Expectations and Investment Plans," *Temi di discussione (Economic Working Papers)*, No. 1203, Bank of Italy, Economic Research and International Relations Area.

Hebden, J., E. P. Herbst, J. Tang, G. Topa and F. Winkler (2020), "How Robust Are Makeup Strategies to Key Alternative Assumptions?", *Finance and Economics Discussion Series*, No. 2020-069, Board of Governors of the Federal Reserve System.

Heise, S., F. Karahan and A. Şahin (2020), "The Missing Inflation Puzzle: The Role of the Wage-Price Pass-Through", *NBER Working Paper Series*, No. 27663.

Katona, G. (1974), "Psychology and Consumer Economics", *Journal of Consumer Research*, 1(1), 1-8.

Komiyama, H. (2014), "'Diffusive Demand' and 'Creative Demand — Overcoming Product Saturation with Demand for Innovation'", In: *Beyond the Limits to Growth. Science for Sustainable Societies*. Springer, Tokyo.

Kueng, L. (2014), "Tax News: The Response of Households Spending to Changes in Expected Taxes", *NBER Working Paper Series*, No. 20437.

Lagarde, C. (2020), "The monetary policy strategy review: some prelimnary considerations", Speech at the "ECB and Its Watchers XXI" conference, 30 September.

Mankiw, N. G., R. Reis and J. Wolfers (2003), "Disagreement about Inflation Expectations", *NBER Macroeconomics Annual*, 209-248.

Matsuyama, K. (2002), "The Rise of Mass Consumption Societies", *Journal of political Economy*, 110(5), 1035-1070.

Mavroeidis, S., M. Plagborg-Møller and J. H. Stock (2014), "Empirical Evidence on Inflation Expectations in the New Keynesian Phillips Curve", *Journal of Economic Literature*, 52(1), 124-88.

OECD (2018), *OECD Economic Outlook*, Volume 2018, Issue 1, OECD Publishing, Paris.

Ranyard, R., F. Del Missier, N. Bonini, D. Duxbury and B. Summers (2008), "Perceptions and Expectations of Price Changes and Inflation: A Review and Conceptual Framework", *Journal of Economic Psychology*, 29, 378-400.

Samarina, A. and N. Apokoritis (2020), "Evolution of Monetary Policy Frameworks in the Post-crisis Environment", *DNB Working Paper*, No. 664, De Nederlandsche Bank.

Shioji, E. (2015), "Time Varying Pass-through: Will the Yen Depreciation Help Japan Hit the Inflation Target?", *Journal of the Japanese and International Economies*, 37, 43-58.

Smith, D. (2019), "Concentration and Foreign Sourcing in the U.S. Retail Sector", *2019 Meeting Papers*, 1258, Society for Economic Dynamics.

Svensson, L. E. O. (2003), "Escaping from a Liquidity Trap and Deflation: The Foolproof Way and Others", *Journal of Economic Perspectives*, 17 (4):145-166.

Williams, J. C. (2020), "Inflation Targeting - Securing the Anchor", remarks at the Bank of England Research Workshop on "The Future of Inflation Targeting", London, 9 January.

Yellen, J. L. (2016), "Macroeconomic Research After the Crisis", speech at "The Elusive 'Great' Recovery: Causes and Implications for Future Business Cycle Dynamics", 60th annual economic conference sponsored by the Federal Reserve Bank of Boston, Boston, Massachusetts, 14 October.

Yoshikawa, H. (2003), "The Role of Demand in Macroeconomics", *Japanese Economic Review*, 54(1), 1-27.

Issue Note 4. Walking the tightrope: Avoiding a lockdown while containing the virus

Recent optimistic news about the availability of a number of vaccines against the coronavirus needs to be tempered by the realisation that, even in the countries that are in the vanguard, it is likely to be the middle of next year before a large share of the population has been vaccinated. In the meantime, governments around the world are trying to calibrate policy interventions so as to keep the spread of the disease under control without crippling economic activity, in many cases with limited success as virus transmission has recently picked up again in several countries. This study uses country experience during the first phase of the pandemic to estimate the impact of different government interventions on both the reproduction rate of the virus, R, and on mobility, as a proxy for economic activity. The empirical results then inform a number of scenarios where the epidemic/economic trade-off of different policy packages is assessed.[1]

Explaining mobility as a proxy for economic activity

The containment policies implemented by governments to reduce the spread of the virus come at an economic cost, proxied here in terms of their effect on mobility. Data on mobility are made available by Google, based on the movement of people with Android-based smartphones and with "location history".

Figure 2.14. Link between mobility and GDP forecast revisions at a quarterly frequency for the first and second quarters of 2020

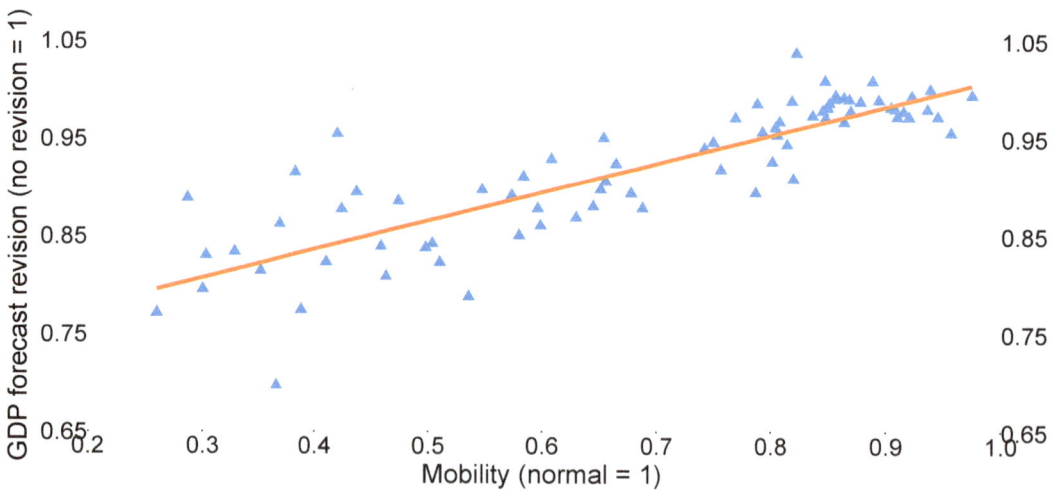

Note: The vertical axis is the ratio of the latest GDP estimate (or official outturn) to the projected level for the corresponding quarter in the December 2019 *OECD Economic Outlook*. Each dot represents a country/quarter combination. The chart covers OECD and BRIICS countries.
Source: Google LLC, *Google COVID-19 Community Mobility Reports*, https://www.google.com/covid19/mobility; OECD Economic Outlook No. 106 and 108 databases; and OECD calculations.

StatLink ⟦⟧ https://doi.org/10.1787/888934217627

---

[1] Further details of the estimation methodology, results and underlying data can be found in OECD (2020).

The effect on mobility of containment policies

To represent government containment policies, the empirical analysis here relies on a set of variables maintained by the Oxford Blavatnik School of Government (Hale et al., 2020) distinguishing eight types of policy, which in their original form are scored according to the degree of stringency or comprehensiveness with which they are applied (Table 2.3, Figure 2.15).[2, 3]

Table 2.3. Scoring of different stringency levels of containment policies

Containment measure	Scoring of degree of stringency
School closures	1: Recommend closing
	2: Require closing (only some levels or categories, eg just high school, or just public schools)
	3: Require closing all levels
Workplace closures	1: Recommend closing (or work from home)
	2: Require closing (or work from home) for some sectors or categories of workers
	3: Require closing (or work from home) all-but-essential workplaces (e.g. grocery stores, doctors)
Cancel public events	1: Recommend cancelling
	2: Require cancelling
Restrictions on gatherings	1: Restrictions on very large gatherings (above 1000 people)
	2: Restrictions on gatherings between 101-1000 people
	3: Restrictions on gatherings between 11-100 people
	4: Restrictions on gatherings of 10 people or less
Close public transport	1: Recommend closing (or significantly reduce volume/route/means of transport available)
	2: Require closing (or prohibit most citizens from using it)
Stay at home requirements	1: Recommend not leaving house
	2: Require not leaving house with exceptions for daily exercise, grocery shopping, and 'essential' trips
	3: Require not leaving house with minimal exceptions (e.g. only once a week, or one person at a time)
Restrictions on internal movement	1: Recommend not to travel between regions/cities
	2: Internal movement restrictions in place
International travel controls	1: Screening
	2: Quarantine arrivals from high-risk regions
	3: Ban on arrivals from some regions
	4: Ban on all regions or total border closure

Note: Scoring scheme used by the Oxford Covid-19 Government Response Tracker. Not shown in the table, but "No measures" or "No restrictions" are always scored 0.
Source: Hale, T., et al. (2020), "Oxford COVID-19 Government Response Tracker", Blavatnik School of Government, Oxford University.

Empirical estimation suggests that seven of the eight types of containment policies have a negative effect on mobility (Figure 2.16).[4] Also, the more stringent application of a particular policy tends to reduce mobility by more: for example, the most severe form of workplace closure (score of 3) has 9 times the effect on mobility of the mildest form (score of 1). Three forms of containment policies stand out as having a particularly large effect on mobility, namely workplace closures, stay-at-home requirements and school closures: the most stringent application of just these three policies is estimated to reduce mobility by more than 40%. Other policies such as the cancellation of public events and travel restrictions, have a significant but smaller effect on mobility, although in some cases the most limited application of a policy has no significant effect on mobility.

---

[2] For the purposes of estimation, the cardinal value of these scores are ignored (as there is no reason, for example, to expect a policy with a stringency value of 3 to have treble the effect of a policy with a value of 1) and instead the same policy at different levels of stringency are included as distinct dummy variables (taking the value of zero or one). Subsequently, if the estimation does not deliver the expected ordinal ranking in coefficients (so that a more stringent application of a policy has a greater effect), the same coefficient may be imposed across different levels of stringency by combining policy variables.

[3] The Oxford measures are highly aggregative and so do not allow a distinction to be drawn regarding the effect of more detailed measures, such as the effect of specifically closing bars and restaurant or retail outlets. However, as more observational data become available or there is greater efficacy in tracking and reporting systems, it may be possible to recommend better targeted restrictions, see for example Haug et al. (2020) and Magnusson et al. (2020).

[4] The failure to detect any effect from restrictions on gatherings is likely related to its close correlation with the policy to cancel public events.

Figure 2.15. Percentage of countries at different stringency levels for containment policies

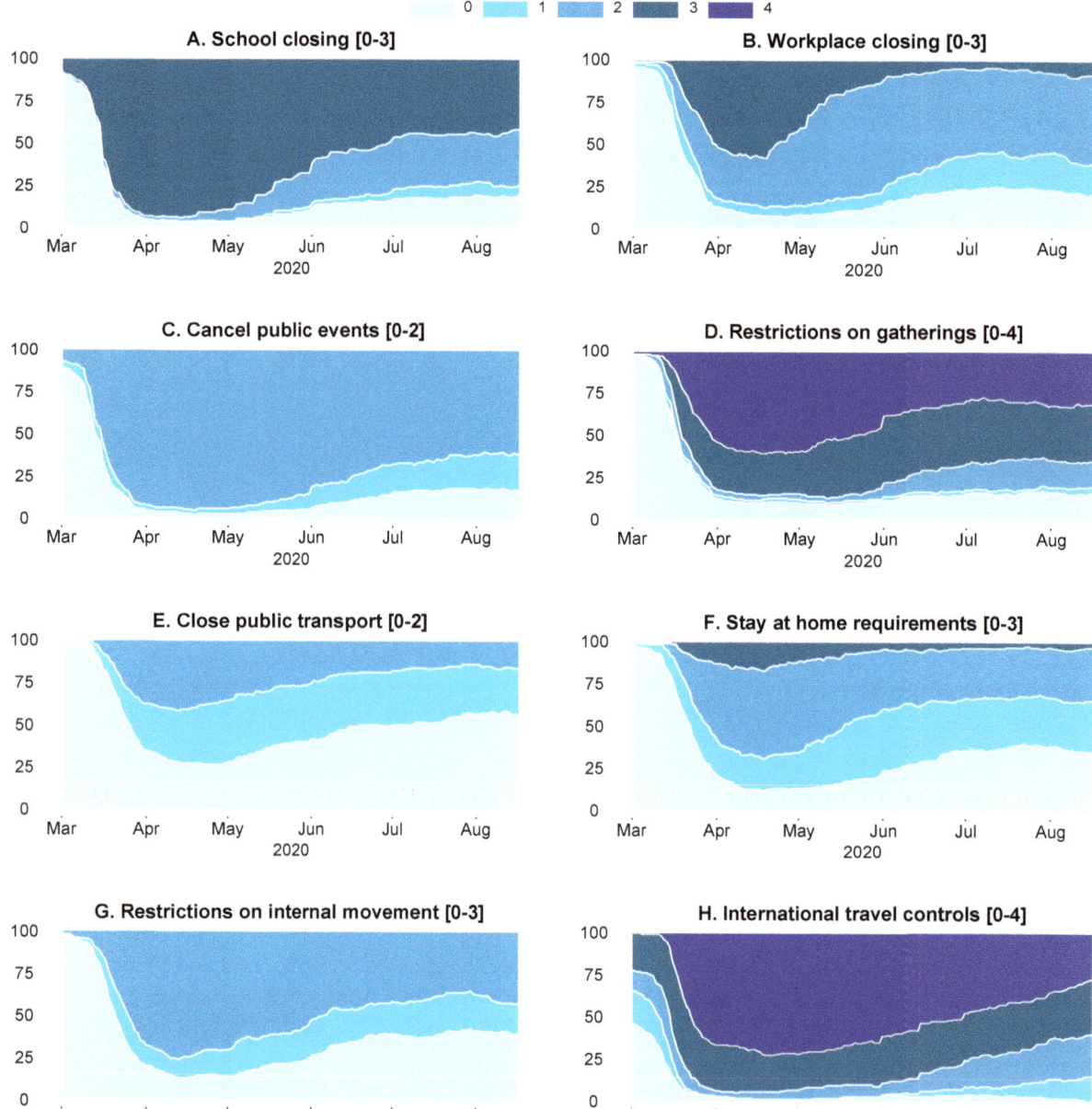

Note: Based on the Oxford Covid-19 Government Response Tracker. Stringency is evaluated as an ordinal index, with a higher number representing greater stringency. Each panel subtitle indicates the range for that category in square brackets. The charts are based on the source's full country coverage for a given date, at most 185 countries.

Source: OECD calculations based on Hale, T., et al. (2020), "Oxford COVID-19 Government Response Tracker", Blavatnik School of Government, Oxford University.

StatLink 🔢 https://doi.org/10.1787/888934217646

Figure 2.16. The estimated effect of containment policies and natural caution on mobility

Effect on mobility (in the absence of the virus and containment measures, 'normal' mobility is indexed at 1.0)

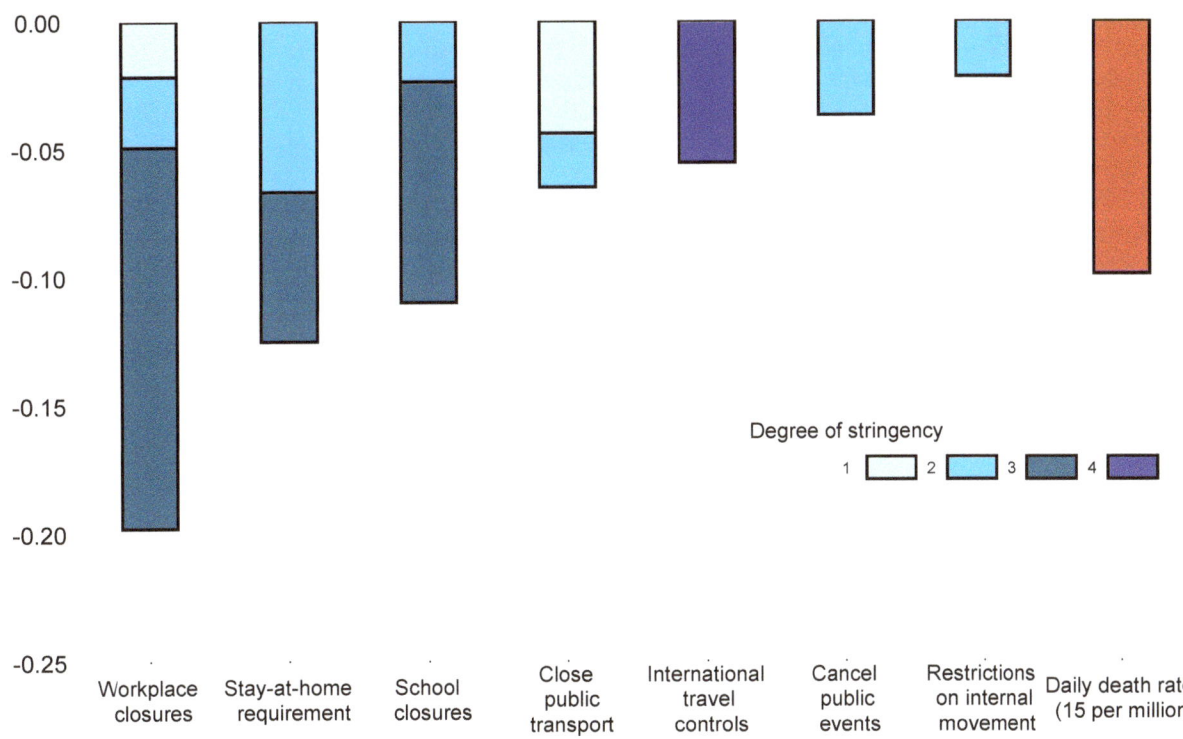

Note: The chart shows the estimated effect on mobility of different containment policies at varying degrees of stringency, as well as the effect of increased natural caution, proxied by the daily death rate. If a particular degree of policy stringency is not shown in the bar chart, then it either means there is no significant effect on mobility (this being the case when bar segments at a higher level of stringency are shown), or that it has the same effect as the policy at the previous level of stringency (when bar segments at a lower level of stringency are shown).
Source: OECD calculations based on estimations reported in OECD (2020), "Walking the tightrope: avoiding a lockdown while containing the virus", *OECD Policy Responses to Coronavirus (COVID-19)*, OECD Publishing, Paris.

StatLink 🔢 https://doi.org/10.1787/888934217665

The effect on mobility of more cautious behaviour

The virus is likely to have an impact on reducing mobility as general awareness increases natural caution and so increases voluntary physical distancing, independently of government policies. This effect is proxied in the empirical analysis by the inclusion of the national daily death rate from the virus. A national daily death rate running at around 15 per million – similar to the rate experienced by some major OECD countries going into the lockdown in March – is estimated to reduce mobility by 10%, independently of any government-mandated polices.

Explaining the reproductive rate

The effective reproductive number (R) of a communicable disease is the average number of secondary cases per infectious case. As is now widely understood, to eliminate the virus, R has to be maintained consistently below unity. The median R estimate for a worldwide sample of approximately 70 countries fell from around 3 in February to around 1 in early May and has remained stable since (Figure 2.17, Panel A).[5] This, however, hides considerable cross-country variation, with R nearing 1.5 in October in European countries, before a further set of major lockdown measures was implemented (Figure 2.17, Panel B). In order to explain this profile three categories of variables are used in the empirical analysis: containment policies which enforce physical distancing, as described above; other public health policies, including testing and tracing; and variables which proxy more cautious social behaviour of the general population as well as the effect of an increasing share of the population having been infected and so possibly being less likely to spread the virus in future.

An important feature of the estimated equation explaining R is that the preferred functional form for the dependent variable is logarithmic implying that any policy intervention will have a larger effect when R is initially high than when it is low, and underlines the merit of early policy interventions.

Figure 2.17. Median and interquartile range for the effective reproduction rate (R)

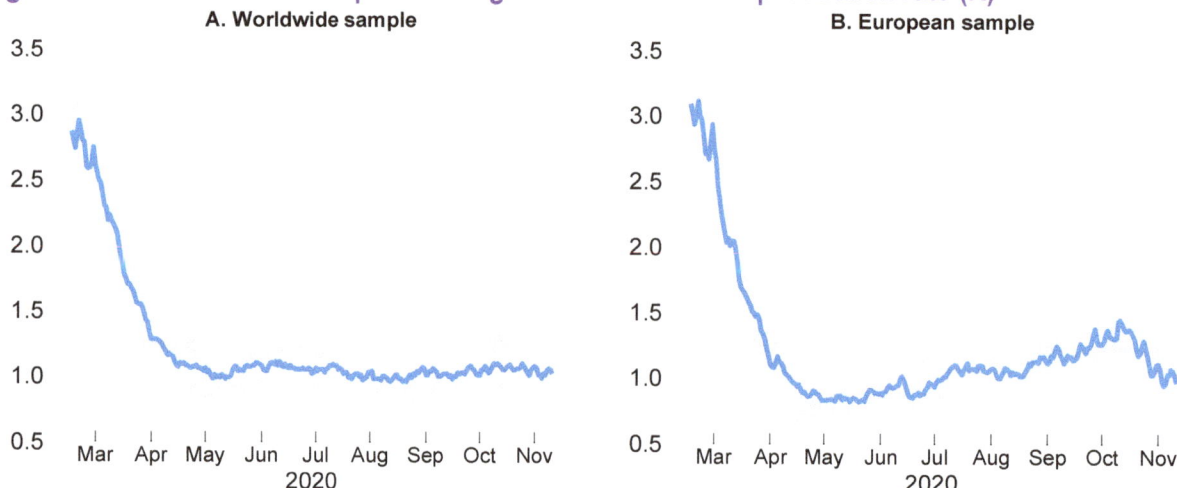

Source: OECD calculations of R for individual countries are derived from data on deaths and infections, see OECD (2020) for details. The chart summarises trends in R for a selection of worldwide (Panel A) or European (Panel B) countries for which R can be computed over the full sample period.

StatLink ᵐˢ⁴ https://doi.org/10.1787/888934217684

---

[5] Estimates of the reproduction number, R, for each country have been constructed specifically for this work using an approach adapted from the epidemiological literature and daily series on confirmed infections and deaths from the European Centre for Disease Prevention and Control (ECDC) (for a detailed explanation see OECD, 2020).

The effect of containment policies on R

In estimation, the coefficients on five containment policies -- workplace closures, restrictions on gatherings, stay-at-home requirements, international travel controls and school closures -- are found to have a significant effect in reducing R (Figure 2.18). The coefficient on school closures has the largest effect of any containment policies, but there is a degree of collinearity between school closures, stay-at-home requirements and workplace closures arising because such containment policies have often been imposed at the same time. Further testing suggests that while the sum of the coefficients on these three containment variables is a robust indication of the effect of a combined package, the coefficient on any one of them is less reliable as it is sensitive to the exclusion of the other variables. Similarly, the absence of any role for the closure of public events in the equation is likely related to its overlap with restrictions on the size of gatherings, which is included. The combined effect of applying all containment polices suggests that from an initial R0 value of about 3, a complete package of containment measures would nearly halve the effective reproduction number.[6]

A feature of these results with potentially important policy implications is that the full R reduction is often achieved well before the maximum level of stringency is reached: for example, a stringency score of 2 on the workplace closure variable ("*for some sectors*") reduces R, but it is not possible to detect any additional effect on R from a further increase in the degree of stringency ("*closure for all-but-essential workplaces*").

The effect of public health policies on R

Test and trace policies

To capture the effect of test-and-trace policies, the policy indicators from the Blavatnik School of Government at the University of Oxford (Hale et al., 2020) are used, which in their original form are scored according to the comprehensiveness of the policy (Table 2.4). They suggest there was a substantial improvement in the number of countries increasing the extent of their test and trace policies in the 2-3 months from March, but further increases since then have been modest (Figure 2.19).[7] An additional variable, constructed by the OECD, considers the importance of specific testing in care homes (Table 2.5). However, an important limitation of these indicators is that none cover issues of timing, which can be key to a successful strategy: tests need to be done quickly and with a minimum delay before the results are available and then contacts need to be traced quickly. On the other hand, many issues relating to testing, including timing, may be easier when the level of infections is lower, and this can be readily tested in the empirical framework.

---

[6] Note that given the log specification of R the effectiveness of policies in terms of their absolute effect on R is non-linear and weakens at lower initial values of R. In addition, as described in the scenario analysis below, the effect on R from a full package of lockdown measures is likely to be enhanced by greater caution from the general population.

[7] For the modelling work used here, the cardinal values of these scores are again ignored and instead different dummy variables are used to represent test-and-trace variables at different degrees of comprehensiveness.

Figure 2.18. Effect of containment policies and public health policies on (logged) R

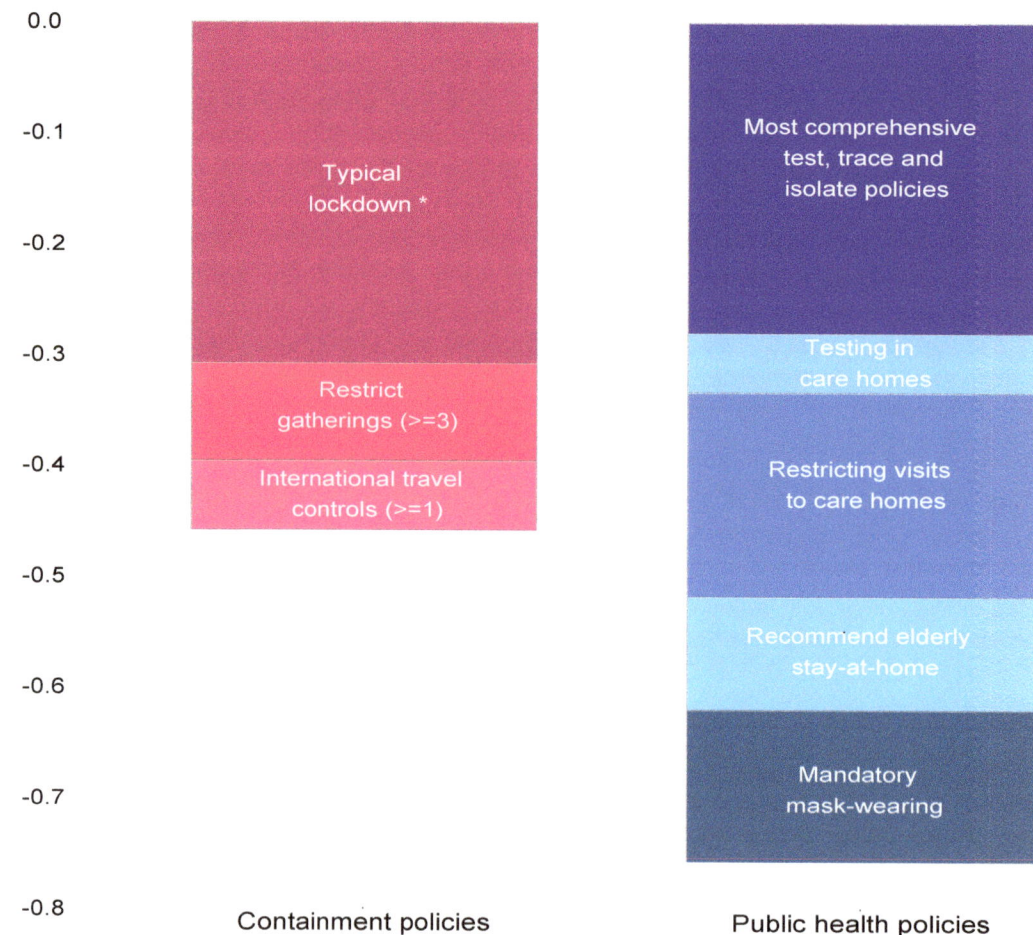

Note: This chart decomposes the effect on (logged) R from the different containment policies (left hand side red bars) and public health policies (right hand side blue bars) according to an estimated equation. The log specification means that the absolute effect of a policy on R is greater the larger the initial value of R: from an initial R value of 3.0 (1.5) the effect of a 'Typical lockdown', which reduces logged R by 0.3 in both cases, is to reduce R in absolute terms by 0.8 (0.4). The maximum effect of the containment policies is shown in the chart, corresponding to a degree of stringency greater or equal to n, denoted by the number (>=n) shown in brackets next to the relevant segment of the bar chart.

* The effects of school closures (>=2), stay-at-home requirements (>=1) and workplace closures (>=2) have been combined into one segment labelled 'Typical lockdown', this is both because such policies have often been imposed at the same time and, as discussed in the main text, because multicollinearity means that the sum of the coefficients on these three containment variables are more reliable than any of the individual coefficients.

Source: OECD calculations based on an equation estimated for a worldwide sample of countries reported in OECD (2020), "Walking the tightrope: avoiding a lockdown while containing the virus", *OECD Policy Responses to Coronavirus (COVID-19)*, OECD Publishing, Paris.

StatLink 🔊🖼️ https://doi.org/10.1787/888934217703

Table 2.4. Oxford Covid-19 Government Response Tracker: Scoring of testing and contact tracing variables

H2 Testing policy[1]: Who can be tested?
0: No testing policy
1: Only those who both (a) have symptoms AND (b) meet specific criteria (e.g. key workers, admiitted to hospital, came into contact with a known case, returned from overseas)
2: Testing of anyone showing COVID-19 symptoms
3: Open public testing (e.g. "drive through" testing available to asymptomatic people).

H3 Contact tracing: Are governments doing contact tracing?
0: No contact tracing
1: Limited contact tracing - not done for all cases
2: Comprehensive contact tracing - done for all identified cases.

Note: Scoring scheme used by the Oxford Covid-19 Government Response Tracker. (1): Testing variable relates to policies testing for infection (PCR test), not to policies testing for immunity (antibody tests).
Source: Hale, T., et al. (2020), "Oxford COVID-19 Government Response Tracker", Blavatnik School of Government, Oxford University.

Empirical results suggest that test and trace policies can reduce the spread of the virus, although the most comprehensive form of test and trace policies are more than 2½ times as effective in reducing R than more limited forms. Test and trace polices are most effective when the infection rate is not too high (which in estimation is taken to be less than 10 new daily cases per million population, a rate which was well exceeded by many countries in March and April). A rather unsurprising finding, given the difficulties of tracking all contact persons in a timely manner if the system is overwhelmed with new cases. Overall, the effect of the most effective test and trace regime in an environment of low daily infection, is estimated to have a greater effect on reducing R than any other public health interventions and is 2-3 times more effective than most individual containment measures (Figure 2.19).

Figure 2.19. Percentage of countries at different stringency levels for testing and contact tracing

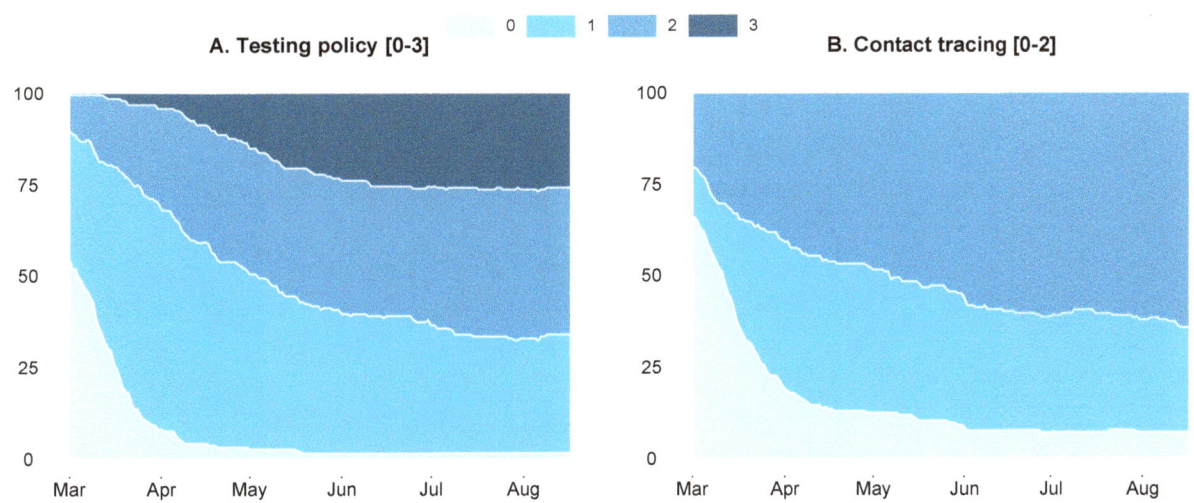

Note: Based on the Oxford Covid-19 Government Response Tracker.
Source: OECD calculations based on Hale, T., et al. (2020), "Oxford COVID-19 Government Response Tracker", Blavatnik School of Government, Oxford University.

StatLink ᠁ https://doi.org/10.1787/888934217722

Shielding the elderly

The elderly population is especially vulnerable to COVID-19 with much higher mortality rates than other demographic groups. A particular concern is that mortality rates have been very high in care homes in some OECD countries (ECDC, 2020; Gandal et al. 2020). The current empirical work tests for the effectiveness of three types of government policies targeted at the elderly or care homes using variables constructed by the OECD (Table 2.5): firstly, recommendations to persuade the elderly to stay at home; secondly, restricting visits to care homes; and thirdly, testing of residents and/or staff of care homes. Measures to specifically protect the elderly were relatively rare in mid-March, but have become more common across countries since then.[8]

The empirical analysis provides evidence that each of these policies can play a role in shielding the elderly population. The combined effect of these polices on reducing R is estimated to exceed the effect of most individual containment measures (Figure 2.18).

Mandating mask-wearing

Evidence from both clinical trials (Raina et al., 2020) and empirical analysis of public policy pronouncements at the regional or country-level (Leffler et al., 2020; Hatzius et al., 2020; Mitze et al., 2020), increasingly suggests that face masks can provide protection against the transmission of the coronavirus. This is especially true in closed and densely packed spaces and because a considerable share of infected people show no symptoms but have a high viral load. In the current study, mask wearing is investigated using variables constructed by the OECD, which denote whether there is an obligation to wear masks in shops, public transport or more generally in closed spaces (Table 2.5). While few countries had mandatory mask-wearing in closed public spaces in mid-March, a majority of OECD countries had adopted such measures by end-July.

The empirical analysis suggests a negative effect on R from the introduction of mandatory mask wearing in all closed public spaces (Figure 2.18), although other results (not reported) suggest that extending mask wearing obligations to the outdoors does not appear to add much to reducing the reproduction rate.

Table 2.5. OECD scoring of additional public health measures

Public health measure	Scoring of degree of stringency
Protection of the elderly	
Testing in care homes	1: Testing of residents and/or staff in care homes, regional level
	2: Testing of residents and/or staff in care homes, national level
Restricting visits to care homes	1: Ban on visits, regional level
	2: Ban on visits, national level
Keeping the elderly at home	1: Government recommendation to stay at home
Mask wearing	
Compulsory mask wearing indoors	1: Mandatory at the local level
	2: Mandatory nationwide

Source: Constructed by the OECD using text search in three COVID-19-related databases.

---

[8] These variables as well as the mask wearing variable are constructed using text search in three COVID-19-related databases: the COVID-19 Government Measures Dataset, run by the Assessment Capacities Project (ACAPS); a database on government responses to the coronavirus compiled by the CoronaNet Research Project; and the CCCSL dataset of the Complexity Science Hub Vienna. For further details see OECD (2020).

The effect on R of more cautious behaviour and moving towards herd immunity

In addition to the variables representing policy responses, the estimation also includes different measures of the death rate from the virus as explanatory variables. Both the national and global daily death rates are included to proxy for general awareness of the virus prompting more cautious behaviour, for example voluntary physical distancing and increased hand-washing. The importance of these variables is that they proxy for changes in behaviour that are likely regardless of government-mandated restrictions.

Total national deaths attributed to the virus expressed as a share of the population are also separately included as a proxy for the share of the population that has been infected, with the expectation of a negative coefficient; as the share of the population that has been infected rises (and presumably becomes immune, though for an uncertain period), the speed with which the virus spreads should be reduced.

These variables are all statistically significant with the expected negative sign and their magnitudes imply they play an important role in the evolution of R.

- The global daily death rate has fluctuated around 0.5 per million during the period considered which, from an initial value of R0 of 3, would be expected to reduce R by about 0.6.
- The national daily death rate varies substantially, both across countries and over time, but for some OECD countries it was running at around 15 per million going into the lockdown in March, and this would reduce R by a further 0.6.
- The total national death rate also varies substantially across countries and has been increasing relentlessly in most countries. It is used here to proxy the profile of the number of people that have already been infected (and so are subsequently immune), so helping to reduce R. In a number of major OECD countries (including the United Kingdom, Spain, Italy and France) the total death rate currently exceeds 400 per million, at which level R would be reduced from 3 to 2.5.

Scenario analysis

In order to draw out the policy implications of the estimation results described above, they are used to construct a number of stylised scenarios to follow the evolution of R and mobility from the first outbreak of the virus, through full lockdown measures, followed by a number of alternative containment strategies (Table 2.6, Figure 2.20).

At the first outbreak of the virus, for the typical country, the initial reproduction number R is estimated to be about 3 and, before the impact of the virus is felt on the economy, mobility is normal (represented by the red triangle at the top right-hand-side corner of Figure 2.20). Even before the implementation of government-mandated measures, awareness of the seriousness of the virus (represented by the daily death rate) is likely to reduce mobility and foster more cautious behaviour, leading to a fall in R, although it remains well above 1 (the red triangle-labelled "Pre-lockdown + natural caution" in Figure 2.20 which is calibrated on the daily death rates of a number of major OECD economies just prior to the lockdown).

Once the number of daily infections is high (here proxied by the high national daily death rate), the implementation of a wide range of containment measures will be essential to contain the spread of the virus. In the scenarios considered here, the implementation of full lockdown (FLD) measures, accompanied by a limited test-and-trace regime, reduces R to close to 1, but at the cost of a sharp fall in mobility (represented by the blue squares in Figure 2.20). The degree of stringency with which lockdown measures are applied will determine the extent of the fall in mobility, with two scenarios considered here: the first assumes that containment policies are applied with a degree of stringency which is typical of that followed by countries in March/April (calibrated on the response of the median country); the second assumes all containment policies to be applied to their maximum possible degree of stringency. Mobility falls by more than 40% in the former case and by more than 60% in the latter; however, the estimation results suggest there is little additional benefit in terms of lowering R from maximising the degree of stringency of containment policies (particularly with regard to workplace closures or stay-at-home requirements).

Even in the absence of further policy changes, R will evolve during a lockdown as the number of infections/deaths change. The fall in the daily death rate may tend to lower natural caution and so lead to some increase in R and mobility; on the other hand, as the total number of individuals that have already been infected and are immune rises, then this will tend to lower R. The estimation results and particular calibrations used in constructing these scenarios suggest these two effects roughly cancel each other out.

A number of strategies for avoiding or exiting full lockdowns are considered (represented by the green circles in Figure 2.20). The basic issue facing policymakers is how to prevent the need for a full set of containment policies while bringing or keeping R under control. The estimation results explaining R, summarised in Table 2.6, suggest that the implementation of a comprehensive test and trace policy together with a package of other public health measures can more than compensate for the removal of lockdown policies, so that their successful implementation would see a return to near normality of mobility, with R remaining below 1 (as represented by the green circle labelled "*No LD + full health measures*" in Figure 2.20).

A larger reduction in R would be achieved, if comprehensive public health measures were accompanied by maintaining some limited containment policies. Bearing in mind their impact on mobility, the containment policies which appear the most obvious candidates for being extended are:

- Restrictions on international travel, including obligations to quarantine all arrivals from selected countries, which would reduce R significantly and may have only a small effect on mobility (although this may be because the mobility measure does not capture international mobility accurately).

- Restrictions on gatherings has a substantial effect on reducing R, whereas the cancellation of public events (which would seem to be inevitably linked) has a relatively small effect on mobility. Such policies may be particularly effective because such large public gatherings may otherwise represent a risk of being so-called "superspreader" events.

Such a package of measures would generate a more decisive reduction in R below 1, although it would come at some cost to mobility (*Partial LD + full health measures*" in Figure 2.20).

In practice, implementing a full range of public health policies and a comprehensive test, trace and isolate regime may be difficult, especially if the daily infection rate begins to rise. Variant scenarios with "*limited health measures*" assume only a limited test-and-trace regime together with mandating mask-wearing in indoor public places, but no other public health policies targeted at the elderly or care homes. Such a combination of policies accompanied by a full relaxation of lockdown measures might see mobility initially return to just below normal levels (assuming the daily death rate has previously been reduced by the lockdown), but R will likely increase well above 1 (represented by the scenario labelled "*No LD + limited health measures*" in Figure 2.20). However, this situation would not represent a stable equilibrium, as with R above 1 there would be a subsequent pick-up in infections and deaths, which in turn would further reduce mobility, regardless of any further government action.

A limited set of health measures accompanied by maintaining the same limited containment policies, would come at a more immediate cost to mobility, but bring R down by more, although in the scenario considered here it would still remain above 1 ("*Partial LD + limited health measures*"), and so would not represent a sustainable situation.

Figure 2.20. Stylised scenarios: from the first outbreak of the virus, through lockdown and exit

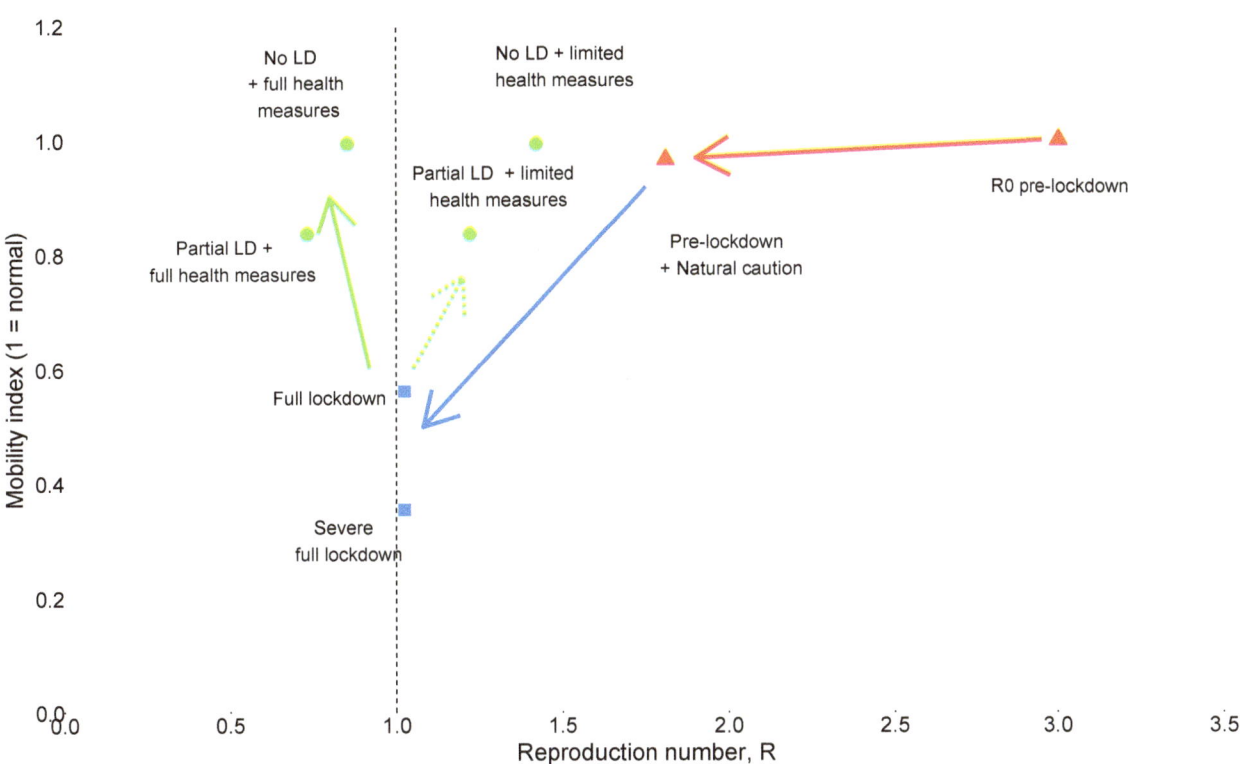

Note: The points represent scenarios, each of which are generated from consistent combinations of the equations for R and mobility using assumptions for the explanatory variables that are summarised in Table 2.6. The red triangles denote the situation at the start of the virus outbreak, blue squares the situation following full lock-down policies, and the green circles represent various exit scenarios.

Table 2.6. Scenario assumptions and outcomes for R and mobility

Scenario	Containment measures	Testing,tracing & isolation		Other public health policies				Daily national deaths	Daily global deaths	Total national deaths	R	Mobility index (1.00 = normal)
		Extensive	Limited	Mask-wearing	Testing in care homes	Elderly stay at home	Ban care home visits	per million of population				
Pre-lockdown												
R0	None	-	-	-	-	-	-	0	0	0	3.00	1.00
Natural caution	None	-	-	-	-	-	-	5.0	0.8	50	1.81	0.97
Lockdown												
Full lockdown (FLD)	Comprehensive	-	√	-	-	-	-	5.0	0.8	50	1.02	0.56
Severe FLD	Comprehensive & severe	-	√	-	-	-	-	5.0	0.8	50	1.02	0.35
Exit from lockdown												
Partial LD & full health measures	Ban large public events, restrict gatherings, quarantine international travellers	√	-	√	√	√	√	1.0	0.7	300	0.73	0.84
Partial LD & limited health measures	Ban large public events, restrict gatherings, quarantine international travellers	-	√	√	-	-	-	1.0	0.7	300	1.22	0.84
No LD & full health measures	None	√	-	√	√	√	√	1.0	0.7	300	0.85	0.99
No LD & limited health measures	None	-	√	√	-	-	-	1.0	0.7	300	1.42	0.99

Note: The assumptions here correspond to the scenarios illustrated in Figure 2.20.

StatLink ᫿ᔿ🖎 https://doi.org/10.1787/888934217741

Bibliography

ECDC (2020), "Surveillance of Covid-19 at long-term care facilities in the EU/EEA", European Centre for Disease Prevention and Control Technical Report, 19 May.

Gandal, N., et al. (2020), "Long-term care facilities as a risk factor in death from Covid-19", 13 July, published on *VOX, CEPR Policy Portal* (https://voxeu.org).

Hale, T., et al. (2020), "Oxford COVID-19 Government Response Tracker", Blavatnik School of Government, Oxford University.

Hatzius, J., D. Struyven and I. Rosenberg (2020), "Face Masks and GDP", *Goldman Sachs Global Economics Analyst,* 29 June.

Haug, N., et al. (2020), "Ranking the effectiveness of worldwide COVID-19 government interventions", *Nature Human Behaviour.*

Leffler, G., et al. (2020), "Association of country-wide coronavirus mortality with demographics, testing, lockdowns, and public wearing of masks", mimeo.

Magnusson, K., et al. (2020), "Occupational risk of COVID-19 in the 1st vs 2nd wave of infection", medRxiv, 3 November.

Mitze, T., et al. (2020), "Face Masks Considerably Reduce Covid-19 Cases in Germany: A Synthetic Control Method Approach", *Covid Economics*, No. 27, 9 June.

OECD (2020), "Walking the tightrope: avoiding a lockdown while containing the virus", *OECD Policy Responses to Coronavirus (COVID-19),* OECD Publishing, Paris.

Raina, M., et al. (2020), "Human coronavirus data from four clinical trials of masks and respirators", *International Journal of Infectious Diseases*, 96, 631-633.

3. Developments in individual OECD and selected non-member economies

Argentina

After falling sharply this year, GDP is projected to expand by 3.7% in 2021. Rising macroeconomic imbalances and prolonged lockdown measures weigh on domestic demand and limit the pace of the recovery, despite a successful restructuring of public debt with private creditors. Employment has fallen strongly. Monetary financing of the high fiscal deficit is putting further pressure on inflation and the gap between the official and the parallel exchange rate. A gradual lifting of confinement measures will allow some recovery of private consumption, but investment will remain weak until imbalances are addressed.

Bold and timely measures have been taken to contain the pandemic and support households and firms, but they have raised the already high fiscal deficit. Reducing macroeconomic imbalances will require prudent fiscal policies and changes to monetary and exchange rate policies. Efficiency gains in public spending and revenue raising, including through a review of special regimes, exemptions and loopholes in the tax system, would improve the fiscal position. Expanding conditional cash transfers is key to reduce poverty and support incomes, including for informal workers.

Containment measures have recently been relaxed in the capital region

Despite a long lockdown in place 20 March, daily infection cases and deaths are still high, in particular in low-income urban neighbourhoods. In most provinces outside of the capital, the lockdown was replaced by physical distancing measures as of late April, until rising case numbers in provincial urban areas in August triggered renewed tightening of confinement measures. The Greater Buenos Aires area saw a decrease in daily case numbers and a lifting of confinement measures in late October. Nationwide containment measures have now been replaced by region-specific restrictions and schools are allowed to reopen on a case by case basis.

Argentina

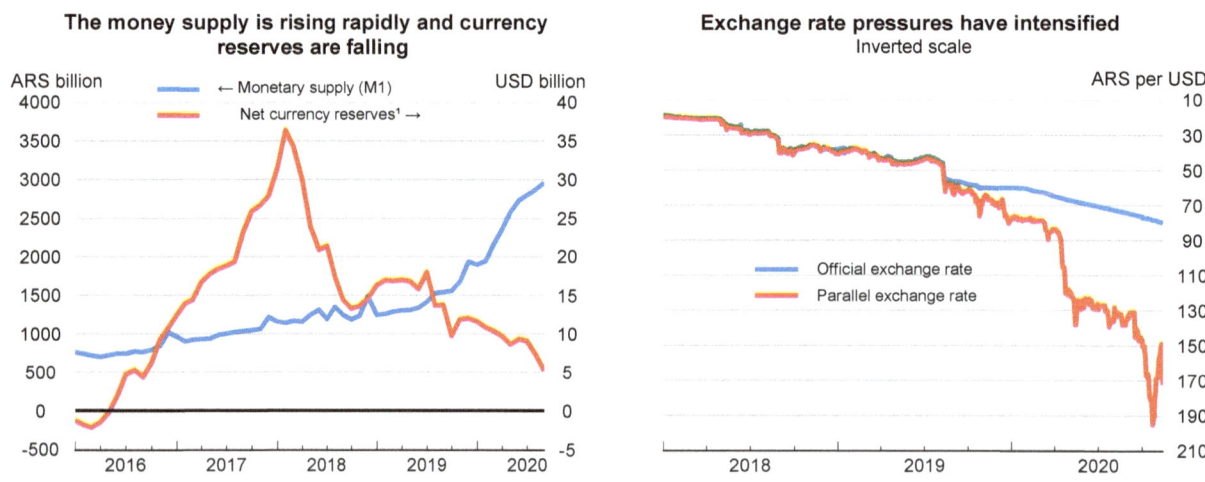

1. Net currency reserves are calculated as official reserve assets held by the central bank minus predetermined short-term net drains on these assets.
Source: Refinitiv; Ámbito.com and OECD Economic Outlook 108 database.

StatLink ⫘ https://doi.org/10.1787/888934217760

Argentina: Demand, output and prices

Argentina	2017	2018	2019	2020	2021	2022
	Current prices ARS billion	Percentage changes, volume (2004 prices)				
GDP at market prices	10 660.2	-2.6	-2.1	-12.9	3.7	4.6
Private consumption	7 114.6	-2.2	-6.6	-15.7	2.4	6.1
Government consumption	1 886.5	-1.7	-1.0	-3.2	6.2	-0.9
Gross fixed capital formation	1 616.3	-6.0	-16.0	-29.8	-2.0	4.5
Final domestic demand	10 617.4	-2.7	-7.1	-15.7	2.6	4.6
Stockbuilding[1]	325.2	-0.9	-2.0	-0.6	0.4	0.0
Total domestic demand	10 942.6	-3.7	-8.7	-15.8	2.7	4.5
Exports of goods and services	1 206.8	0.5	9.0	-11.2	4.3	6.8
Imports of goods and services	1 489.2	-4.5	-19.0	-23.5	-0.2	6.9
Net exports[1]	- 282.4	0.7	4.5	1.6	0.8	0.3
Memorandum items						
GDP deflator	–	40.0	50.6	38.9	38.5	40.0
Current account balance (% of GDP)	–	-4.8	-0.7	2.3	2.6	2.4

1. Contributions to changes in real GDP, actual amount in the first column.
Source: OECD Economic Outlook 108 database.

StatLink https://doi.org/10.1787/888934217779

Long and strict lockdown measures have taken their toll

The long lockdown has severely affected labour-intensive tourism, leisure, health, social and personal services. Employment has decreased markedly, particularly among low-skilled and informal workers. This weighs on household incomes and holds back private consumption, despite some recent improvements, including in spending on durable goods. The limited reopening that began in late April allowed a rebound of manufacturing and construction activity. Argentina successfully restructured its foreign and domestic law public debt in September and has initiated debt talks with multilateral lenders, but investor confidence and access to capital markets are still limited by significant macroeconomic imbalances. Inflation started to rise in August, despite weak domestic demand and strict price controls, and the spread between the official and the parallel exchange rate surpassed 100% in mid-October. Net currency reserves of the central bank are declining rapidly. Tighter currency restrictions have weighed on imports, while solid commodity demand from China and an ongoing recovery in Brazil have buoyed exports.

Policies have so far protected household incomes and firms

Fiscal policy has supported poor and vulnerable households through one-off bonuses, in-kind payments and reinforced unemployment benefits (1.5% of GDP). Wage subsidies and lower payroll tax liabilities have helped some firms, partially compensating for the costs of a generalised ban on dismissals for 240 days. The crisis response has exacerbated the high fiscal deficit, which has been financed through transfers from the central bank, and the money supply has risen significantly. Recent policy announcements suggest more efforts to tap into domestic capital markets and less reliance on monetary financing going forward. Reserve requirements and provisioning needs have been eased, bank holdings of central bank paper limited, and lending incentives strengthened.

Growing macroeconomic imbalances delay the recovery

Investment and consumer confidence are unlikely to pick up before macroeconomic uncertainties are resolved and the pandemic subsides. The recent easing of confinement measures will support a recovery in some services sectors, but physical distancing measures and sporadic local outbreaks will damp prospects for a quick recovery. Bankruptcies and job losses will rise once the current wage subsidies for formal sector workers and the ban on dismissals expire. This will further add to high unemployment and weaken domestic demand. Inflationary pressures will intensify once strict price controls are relaxed and domestic demand recovers.

GDP is projected to fall by just below 13% in 2020, before starting to recover by 3.7% and 4.6% in 2021 and 2022, respectively. Risks to this outlook include a spike in inflation, as money demand may not absorb recent increases in supply or future treasury financing needs may rise. Moreover, low international reserves entail risks of a disorderly devaluation, which would add to inflationary pressures. An increase in infection cases could lead to a renewed lockdown. On the upside, a swifter recovery in neighbouring Brazil, stronger commodity demand as well as a more competitive exchange rate could support exports.

Reducing imbalances and facilitating structural change are key for the recovery

A country-wide tracing, testing and isolation strategy should accompany the gradual lifting of confinement measures to avoid setbacks in the fight against COVID-19. A credible medium-term fiscal strategy centred on improvements in public spending efficiency, and cutting back regressive tax exemptions and special regimes, could pave the way to reduce macroeconomic imbalances. A stronger and more inclusive recovery will require more policy action to foster formal job creation and lower labour market duality. Social protection could be strengthened by building on existing cash transfer schemes, while simultaneously reducing the cost of creating formal jobs. This would also support the necessary structural adjustment post-crisis. Strengthening the trust in public institutions, including an independent judiciary and central bank, would further help to rebuild much needed confidence.

Australia

Australia has been hit by the coronavirus pandemic less severely than other countries, although the state of Victoria experienced a significant surge in cases in the third quarter with corresponding lockdown orders. Real GDP is expected to contract by 3.8% in 2020, but is projected to grow by 3.2% in 2021 and 3.1% in 2022. The unemployment rate will rise initially as job retention schemes taper off in 2021 and will slowly decline thereafter. Household saving will gradually decrease and support private consumption. A risk is that the recovery in business and consumer sentiment is hampered by a rise in business insolvencies and renewed labour market weakness as policy support is scaled back in 2021.

Fiscal policy support will be reduced in 2021, but the impact will be offset by the recovery in private sector activity as containment restrictions ease further. Monetary policy will remain accommodative given below-target inflation and significant labour market slack. Fiscal and monetary support should be maintained until the economic recovery is firmly entrenched. At the same time, replacing real-estate stamp duty with a recurrent land tax would boost labour mobility and economic growth. Similarly, reducing interstate differences in education, training programmes and occupational licensing would enhance the potential for labour reallocation.

Strict containment measures were reimposed in Victoria

Most states have successfully sustained a very low number of active COVID-19 cases since containment measures were relaxed in May and June. However, Victoria, the second most populous state, experienced a significant re-emergence of infections that prompted the reimposition of strict state-wide containment measures for over three months. So far, Victoria has accounted for around 90% of Australia's pandemic-related deaths. After peaking in early August, the number of new infections in the state gradually declined and the state government began easing containment measures in mid-October. Interstate travel has been heavily curtailed since the onset of the pandemic, with some states only recently reopening their borders.

Australia

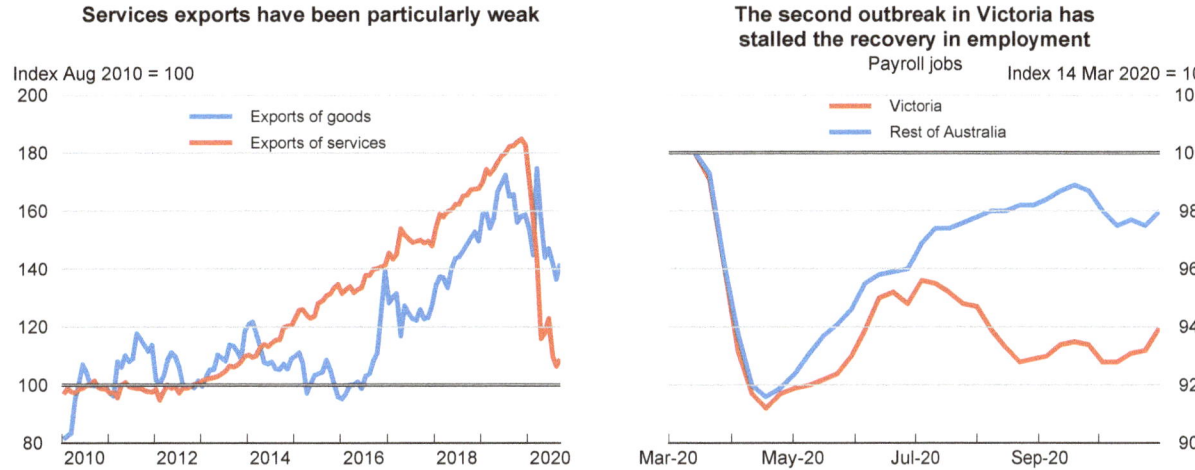

Services exports have been particularly weak

The second outbreak in Victoria has stalled the recovery in employment

Source: Refinitiv; and Australian Bureau of Statistics.

StatLink https://doi.org/10.1787/888934217798

Australia: Demand, output and prices

Australia	2017	2018	2019	2020	2021	2022
	Current prices AUD billion	Percentage changes, volume (2017/2018 prices)				
GDP at market prices	1 808.3	2.8	1.8	-3.8	3.2	3.1
Private consumption	1 020.8	2.6	1.4	-7.5	4.7	4.2
Government consumption	336.3	4.0	5.4	7.8	4.7	0.9
Gross fixed capital formation	437.2	2.5	-2.0	-9.7	2.1	3.8
Final domestic demand	1 794.3	2.9	1.4	-5.0	4.1	3.4
Stockbuilding[1]	4.4	0.1	-0.2	0.9	0.4	0.0
Total domestic demand	1 798.7	2.9	1.1	-4.1	4.5	3.4
Exports of goods and services	387.0	5.0	3.2	-9.3	1.0	3.8
Imports of goods and services	377.5	4.2	-1.3	-12.7	6.6	5.7
Net exports[1]	9.5	0.2	1.0	0.4	-1.0	-0.3
Memorandum items						
GDP deflator	_	2.3	3.1	0.3	1.3	1.3
Consumer price index	_	1.9	1.6	0.7	1.6	1.6
Core inflation index[2]	_	1.7	1.6	1.1	1.3	1.6
Unemployment rate (% of labour force)	_	5.3	5.2	6.8	7.9	7.4
Household saving ratio, net (% of disposable income)	_	3.5	3.7	14.4	11.7	8.9
General government financial balance (% of GDP)	_	0.2	-0.2	-12.7	-6.5	-5.1
General government gross debt (% of GDP)	_	43.5	45.8	57.7	64.1	68.8
Current account balance (% of GDP)	_	-2.1	0.6	2.3	1.6	1.4

1. Contributions to changes in real GDP, actual amount in the first column.
2. Consumer price index excluding food and energy.
Source: OECD Economic Outlook 108 database.

StatLink 🔗 https://doi.org/10.1787/888934217817

The recovery has been uneven

The economic recovery has been uneven due to differences in the impact of voluntary and imposed confinement across regions, industries and firms. Continued international border restrictions have hampered the recovery in education and tourism exports. Mobility indicators suggest that retail, recreation, workplace and transit station activity remain below pre-pandemic levels. The second virus outbreak in Victoria led to an interstate divergence in consumer sentiment and labour market outcomes: while employment in Victoria is still 6% below the level in March 2020, the number of employed persons in the Northern Territory, South Australia and Western Australia is back to around pre-pandemic levels. Mining, manufacturing and retail trade payroll jobs have rebounded strongly, but accumulated job losses in vulnerable services industries such as arts, recreation, accommodation and food remain high, at between 13% and 16%. Smaller firms have also experienced larger job losses and declines in sales. The government's temporary wage subsidy, "JobKeeper", has covered nearly one million employers and one-third of all employment, containing the rise in the measured unemployment rate so far.

Macroeconomic policies are shielding incomes and easing borrowing terms

In October, the federal budget included new measures that increased direct fiscal support during the pandemic to 11.2% of GDP. Additional fiscal easing is concentrated in the fourth quarter of 2020 and the first half of 2021. New fiscal support plans include tax relief for households and firms, hiring subsidies, support payments, essential services spending, infrastructure investment and business tax deductions. Public spending will be scaled back during the second half of 2021, as the private sector recovery becomes more firmly entrenched. The government also announced a debtor-friendly and simplified liquidation model for small businesses to come into effect in 2021. Its implementation will be key given the expiry of the moratorium on directors' personal liability for trading while insolvent at end-2020. The central bank has reduced its policy rate and three-year Australian government bond yield target to 0.1%, reoriented its forward guidance from forecast to actual inflation and extended its long-term, low-cost funding to banks to boost business loans. In addition to directly reducing interest rates as part of the yield curve control policy, the central bank has introduced an asset purchase programme targeted at long-term bonds issued by the Commonwealth, as well as states and territories, to ease further financial conditions.

The unwinding of support measures will slow down the recovery

The easing of Victoria's lockdown and strong fiscal support will boost GDP growth in the near term. The infrastructure-led economic recovery in China will help sustain commodity exports and mining investment. In contrast, services exports will recover only slowly due to persistent border restrictions, and higher domestic demand will increase imports, reducing net exports. The unwinding of the strong fiscal support will be a headwind to higher GDP growth in the second half of 2021. Gradual phasing out of job retention programmes and increased labour force participation will cause the unemployment rate to rise further. However, consumption will continue to be supported by households gradually drawing down their increased savings and the further easing of containment measures. Headline inflation will initially decline following the attenuation of the carryover effects from the rise in commodity prices and the removal of the childcare fee waiver in the third quarter of 2020 and will slowly increase thereafter. Underlying inflation will remain subdued as economic slack is only reduced gradually. A key risk to the outlook is a fall in business and consumer confidence, as reduced government support is accompanied by a rise in business liquidations and unemployment. Furthermore, any additional escalation in geopolitical tensions with China may undermine export growth. On the upside, a faster-than-expected phasing out of border restrictions would boost the recovery in services exports.

Sustaining the recovery and enabling labour reallocation are key priorities

Further policy measures should focus on sustaining the economic recovery from the pandemic as well as reducing barriers to labour reallocation. Fiscal and monetary policy support should not be withdrawn before the recovery is well entrenched. At the same time, replacing taxes and fees on property transactions, such as stamp duty, with a recurrent land tax as is being contemplated by the government of several states would achieve a more growth-friendly tax mix and promote labour mobility. Introducing well-designed skills programmes would enable rehiring in sectors such as hospitality and recreation services and may facilitate reallocation of labour from these sectors to manufacturing or digital services, sustaining the economy's growth capacity. Paring back occupational licensing and implementing the government's plans to recognise licenses across jurisdictions automatically would also boost labour mobility. In addition, to mitigate partly rising inequalities caused by the pandemic, the authorities should permanently strengthen the social safety net and support increased investment in social housing.

Austria

GDP is estimated to contract by 8% in 2020 and projected to pick up only gradually over the coming two years, remaining well below its pre-crisis level by the end of 2022. Unemployment has increased significantly, and is projected to remain elevated. Weak tax revenues and a generous support package have resulted in a large budget deficit. Inflation will remain subdued in the near term.

Swift and decisive action has contributed to safeguard jobs and firms in 2020, but the authorities need to ensure that well-intended short-term policy support does not hamper long-run growth. Stricter conditionality of the short-time work scheme would facilitate the reallocation of labour across sectors. Policy makers should consider introducing tax incentives for the provision and uptake of equity capital to avoid a widespread corporate debt overhang.

The surge in new COVID-19 cases has prompted a tightening of sanitary restrictions

The authorities reinstated a strict lockdown in mid-November as a rapid surge in the number of hospitalised patients with COVID-19 has put the country's strong health system at risk of being overwhelmed. The lockdown comprises home-schooling and restrictions on the hospitality sector, most trade businesses and personal services. Only supermarkets, pharmacies and other essential businesses are allowed to remain open. People are instructed to reduce in-person contacts and stay at home for all but a few exceptions such as buying groceries or travelling to work.

Austria

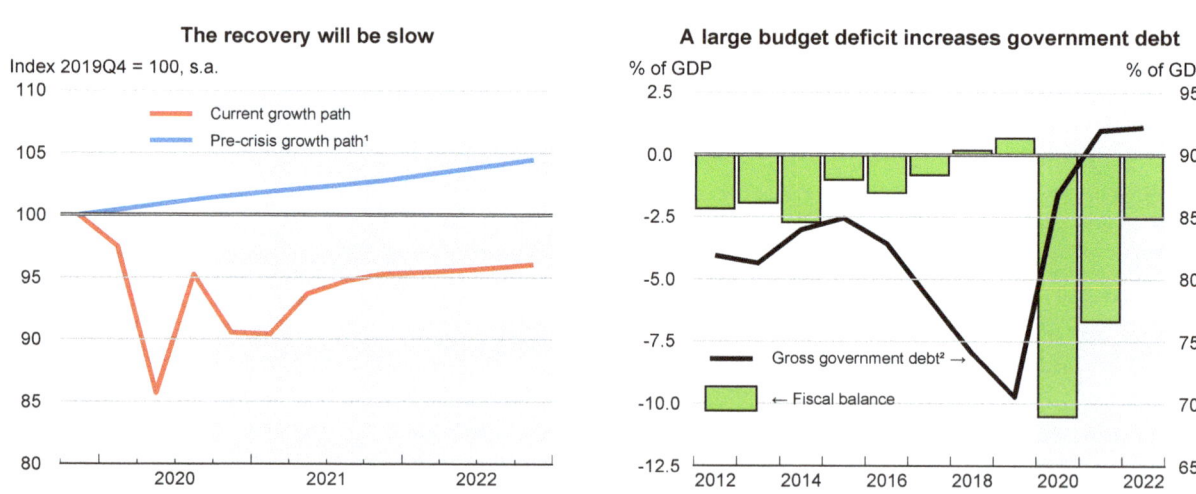

1. The pre-crisis growth path is based on the November 2019 OECD Economic Outlook projection, with linear extrapolation for 2022 based on trend growth in 2021.
2. Maastricht definition.
Source: OECD Economic Outlook 106 and 108 databases.

StatLink 🖲️📊 https://doi.org/10.1787/888934217836

Austria: Demand, output and prices

Austria	2017	2018	2019	2020	2021	2022
	Current prices EUR billion	Percentage changes, volume (2015 prices)				
GDP at market prices*	369.5	2.5	1.4	-8.0	1.4	2.3
Private consumption	193.9	1.1	0.8	-7.9	2.9	2.3
Government consumption	72.0	1.2	1.4	1.2	1.2	1.2
Gross fixed capital formation	87.1	4.0	3.9	-7.0	1.9	3.2
Final domestic demand	353.0	1.8	1.7	-5.8	2.2	2.3
Stockbuilding[1]	4.1	0.4	-0.7	-0.8	-0.3	0.0
Total domestic demand	357.0	2.2	0.9	-6.6	2.0	2.4
Exports of goods and services	201.2	4.9	2.9	-13.3	4.0	4.3
Imports of goods and services	188.7	4.6	2.5	-12.7	3.9	4.5
Net exports[1]	12.5	0.3	0.3	-0.8	0.1	0.0
Memorandum items						
GDP deflator	_	1.7	1.7	0.7	1.1	1.1
Harmonised index of consumer prices	_	2.1	1.5	1.3	1.3	1.6
Harmonised index of core inflation[2]	_	1.8	1.7	1.7	1.2	1.6
Unemployment rate (% of labour force)	_	4.8	4.5	5.6	5.6	5.1
Household saving ratio, net (% of disposable income)	_	7.8	8.2	17.0	15.4	12.6
General government financial balance (% of GDP)	_	0.2	0.7	-10.5	-6.7	-2.6
General government gross debt (% of GDP)	_	96.8	95.0	111.2	116.3	116.6
General government debt, Maastricht definition (% of GDP)	_	74.1	70.6	86.8	91.9	92.2
Current account balance (% of GDP)	_	1.3	2.8	2.9	3.1	3.2

* Based on seasonal and working-day adjusted quarterly data; may differ from official non-working-day adjusted annual data.
1. Contributions to changes in real GDP, actual amount in the first column.
2. Harmonised index of consumer prices excluding food, energy, alcohol and tobacco.
Source: OECD Economic Outlook 108 database.

StatLink ᵐˢ⁴ https://doi.org/10.1787/888934217855

The labour market improved over the summer but the outlook is now uncertain

After a historic output decline in the first half of 2020, economic activity rebounded over the summer. The increase in activity came alongside an improved situation on the labour market. A bit more than 400 000 persons were registered for short-time work in September, compared with over 1.3 million in mid-April, though the actual uptake will only be known later. The number of unemployed workers decreased by around 156 000 from the peak in April. Nevertheless, employment has declined in most sectors since March. The number of tourist overnight stays in summer was more than 30% lower than last year. The hospitality sector and other services sectors requiring close personal contact have been most affected by the pandemic. The renewed lockdown will continue to put a strain on the labour market.

A generous support package has helped to avoid a more severe downturn

A support package amounting to around EUR 38 billion (around 10% of GDP) has been gradually implemented since March. In June, the authorities announced further measures to stimulate the economy. With the June measures, the total support package amounts to around EUR 50 billion (around 13% of GDP), including credit guarantees. The new measures include an extension of the short-time work scheme until March 2021, new expenditure measures on climate protection and digital teaching, additional funds for hardship cases across micro and small firms and for caretaking, research and medical equipment, and tax reliefs and VAT reductions in selected sectors. The June support programme also includes tax incentives for corporate investment, in particular in green and digital technologies, and a retroactive reduction of the income tax rate in the first tax bracket from 25% to 20% should help to accelerate the recovery. Furthermore, the government has announced that it will spend an estimated EUR 3 billion to refund businesses for up to 80% of foregone revenues in November 2020 subject to a ceiling of EUR 800 000.

GDP is projected to recover only gradually

Output is set to decline in the near term as containment measures and voluntary restraints due to health concerns take a toll on private consumption. Disruptions in global value chains and moderate growth in key trading partners are putting downward pressure on exports and investment. As an effective vaccine is implemented, activity will recover over 2021-22, but will still be well below its pre-crisis trend level by the end of 2022. The unemployment rate will remain high through 2021 and only start to edge down in 2022. The generous support package has resulted in a large budget deficit, but it will decrease steadily over the projection period. To the extent that the phasing-out of the fiscal stimulus is not compensated by a decline in the household saving rate, it will weigh on growth in 2021 and 2022. Downside risks to the projection remain high. Many businesses in the tourism sector are family-owned and tend to be highly leveraged. If travel restrictions and recurring lower demand prevail over an extended period, a wave of insolvencies may follow with negative consequences for employment in remote areas and regional cohesion.

Policy makers should take the opportunity to promote the development of markets for equity capital

Options to support businesses while avoiding large increases in corporate debt are limited since markets for equity capital are less developed than elsewhere. The authorities should incentivise the provision and uptake of equity capital, for example by granting a tax allowance on corporate equity or by providing tax incentives for venture capital and private equity investment in small and medium-sized enterprises. They should also continue to strengthen qualifying conditions for the short-time work scheme, for instance regarding training measures related to advanced digital tools and activities, to promote a healthy reallocation of jobs towards more promising sectors and productive firms.

Belgium

Strongly hit by the COVID-19 crisis, GDP is set to contract by 7.5% in 2020 and recover slowly thereafter. The economy is currently affected by strict containment measures adopted in late 2020. While easing from current levels, such measures are expected to continue to fight sporadic virus outbreaks until a vaccine is rolled out. They will weigh on household consumption, with precautionary saving remaining high in the coming two years. Weak and uncertain growth prospects as well as squeezed profit margins are set to constrain business investment.

Until vaccination becomes widespread, the authorities should enhance effective measures against virus outbreaks, such as testing, tracing and isolating, while strengthening the public health system as planned. They should continue fiscal support, targeting firms directly affected by confinement measures, to avoid unnecessary business failures and extension of support to non-viable businesses. As part of the recovery plan, the new government intends to increase public investment, focusing on the digital agenda and energy transition, which is welcome in order to support the recovery while adapting to new challenges.

Belgium

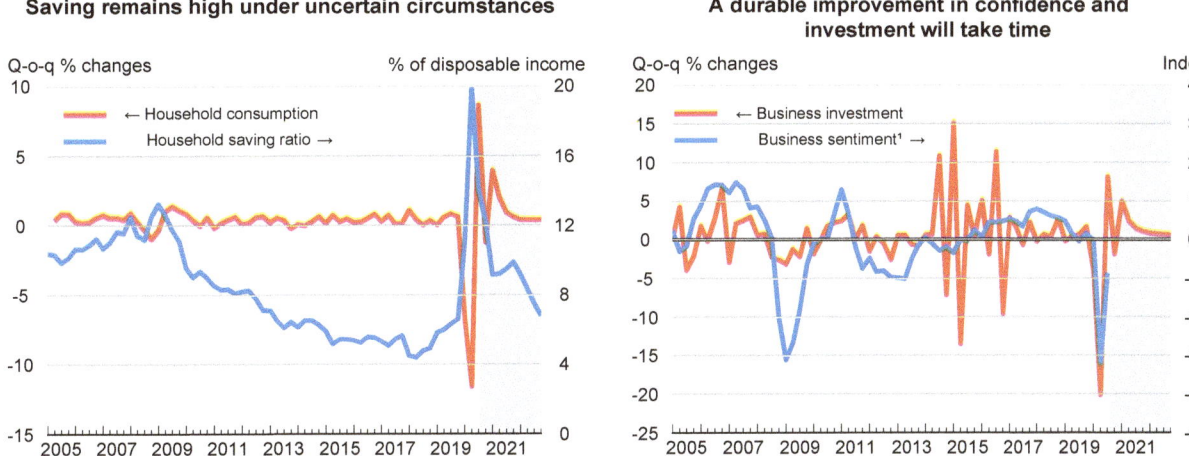

1. The series is based on the quarterly average and is normalised using its long-term average and standard deviation.
Source: OECD Economic Outlook 108 database; and National Bank of Belgium.

StatLink https://doi.org/10.1787/888934217874

Belgium: Demand, output and prices

Belgium	2017	2018	2019	2020	2021	2022
	Current prices EUR billion	Percentage changes, volume (2015 prices)				
GDP at market prices	445.0	1.8	1.7	-7.5	4.7	2.7
Private consumption	229.1	1.9	1.5	-10.6	6.2	2.4
Government consumption	102.4	1.3	1.7	2.4	0.6	1.0
Gross fixed capital formation	103.6	3.4	3.4	-13.5	5.7	3.9
Final domestic demand	435.1	2.1	2.0	-8.3	4.6	2.4
Stockbuilding[1,2]	5.2	0.3	-0.4	0.5	-0.1	0.0
Total domestic demand	440.4	2.4	1.5	-7.7	4.5	2.4
Exports of goods and services	370.2	0.6	1.0	-7.8	5.1	3.9
Imports of goods and services	365.6	1.3	0.8	-8.1	4.9	3.5
Net exports[1]	4.6	-0.5	0.2	0.2	0.2	0.3
Memorandum items						
GDP deflator	–	1.6	1.7	0.6	0.9	0.5
Harmonised index of consumer prices	–	2.3	1.2	0.5	0.7	0.6
Harmonised index of core inflation[3]	–	1.3	1.5	1.3	0.5	0.6
Unemployment rate (% of labour force)	–	6.0	5.4	5.7	7.9	6.8
Household saving ratio, net (% of disposable income)	–	4.7	6.2	14.3	9.5	8.0
General government financial balance (% of GDP)	–	-0.8	-1.9	-11.3	-8.1	-4.8
General government gross debt (% of GDP)	–	118.3	120.9	139.2	141.5	143.0
General government debt, Maastricht definition (% of GDP)	–	99.8	98.1	116.3	118.7	120.2
Current account balance (% of GDP)	–	-0.8	0.3	-1.1	-0.3	0.0

1. Contributions to changes in real GDP, actual amount in the first column.
2. Including statistical discrepancy. Statistical discrepancy contributes to 5.3% in 2019 percentage changes.
3. Harmonised index of consumer prices excluding food, energy, alcohol and tobacco.
Source: OECD Economic Outlook 108 database.

StatLink https://doi.org/10.1787/888934217893

The resurgence of the epidemic has required new restrictions

The epidemic has surged again, with the number of confirmed cases rising to higher levels than during the peak in April. The authorities had removed the generalised lockdown measures beginning from May, with some exceptions such as the ban on mass events, but they have introduced broad-based strict measures since October. These include the closure of bars and restaurants, a night curfew adopted in mid-October, the closure of shops selling non-essential products and the obligation to telework (with some exceptions) for six weeks beginning in early November. The number of hospitalised patients and the occupation of intensive care beds had surpassed their peaks earlier this year at the end of October but began to decline thereafter.

The economy has been severely affected

GDP declined by 14.8% in the first half of 2020, which was only partially offset by the rebound in the third quarter. The negative impact was less severe than initially expected as some sectors, such as professional services, demonstrated resilience. In addition, the policy measures that were adopted swiftly helped to sustain economic activity significantly. The gradual removal of the initial containment measures led to a partial and uneven recovery. Business sentiment has recovered from the trough earlier this year, but remains well below pre-crisis levels. Due to the new strict containment measures, the turnover in private businesses dipped to 17% below normal levels in mid-November. It is particularly subdued in sectors that have been strongly affected by various containment measures for long, such as the arts and entertainment sector as well as the food and accommodation sector (at 77% and 66% below normal levels, respectively), which is likely to extend into next year.

Policy measures have been swiftly deployed

The national authorities have introduced a number of fiscal measures following the generalised lockdown in early 2020, which amount to 3.9% of GDP. Direct income support measures account for a significant part of this amount. They include, among others, emergency measures in the temporary layoff scheme and replacement income for the self-employed, as well as compensations for businesses. These were effective in protecting jobs and businesses and in sustaining economic activity. To address short-term liquidity problems, the authorities made it possible to defer the repayment of credits and introduced a guarantee scheme for new credits and credit lines (which amounts to 10.7% of GDP). These measures, along with the European Central Bank's accommodative monetary policy and prudential policy easing by the National Bank of Belgium, have supported aggregate demand. With the economy on a recovery path, some measures were phased out progressively in early autumn. Notably, the emergency measures in the temporary layoff scheme no longer applied to new applicants except for those firms directly affected by confinement measures, while the benefits for those already on temporary layoff are continuing until the end of 2020. However, the federal government reintroduced the emergency measures following the tightening of containment measures in early November.

The economy is set to continue to recover slowly in an uncertain environment

The recovery will be temporarily disrupted by the new strict containment measures and is expected to continue being hampered by potential restrictions imposed in response to sporadic outbreaks of the pandemic until vaccination against the virus becomes general in late 2021. The recovery in business investment will be slow, due to weakened financial positions of firms and uncertain economic prospects. As the emergency measures in the temporary layoff scheme cannot absorb all employment losses, unemployment is set to rise from the fourth quarter of 2020, which will weigh on wages and prices. Employment losses will hurt private consumption, despite generous unemployment benefits, as job market uncertainty will keep precautionary saving high. In addition, consumption of some goods and services will remain restrained, in particular those related to the sectors directly affected by containment measures. Exports will rise as the global economy recovers.

Policy measures should facilitate a solid recovery

The government plans to give firms a temporary tax exemption on their profits if they use them to buttress their capital. This should help strengthen firms' financial positions. Given the recent tightening of containment measures, fiscal support should be continued. At the same time, the authorities should target these measures, including the temporary layoff scheme, the deferral of loan repayments and public guarantees, strictly to those directly affected by confinement measures to avoid extending support to non-viable businesses. This will also help safeguard fiscal discipline, as public debt in Belgium is already very high. As some jobs will be permanently lost, the authorities should strengthen public employment services to promote upskilling and reskilling of workers.

Brazil

Despite new infections and fatalities remaining high, the economy has started to recover across a wide range of sectors. GDP growth is expected to be 2.6% in 2021 and 2.2% in 2022, but activity will still fall short of pre-pandemic levels by late 2022. Inflation will remain below target and high liquidity provision, including through record-low interest rates, will support investment. Fiscal vulnerabilities have been exacerbated by the necessary policy response and public debt has risen. A failure to continue structural reform progress could hold back investment and future growth.

The strong fiscal and monetary policy response managed to prevent a sharper economic contraction. A temporary emergency benefit has supported over 67 million low-income households, cushioning the impact on household incomes and poverty. As the recovery will take time and some jobs may not return, well-targeted improvements in social protection would be warranted. Reallocating some current expenditures and raising spending efficiency would allow such improvements to be financed, while simultaneously resuming the fiscal adjustment underway before the pandemic. Structural reforms to enhance domestic and external competition and improve the investment climate could raise productivity, while better professional training would allow more people to seize new economic opportunities.

Brazil 1

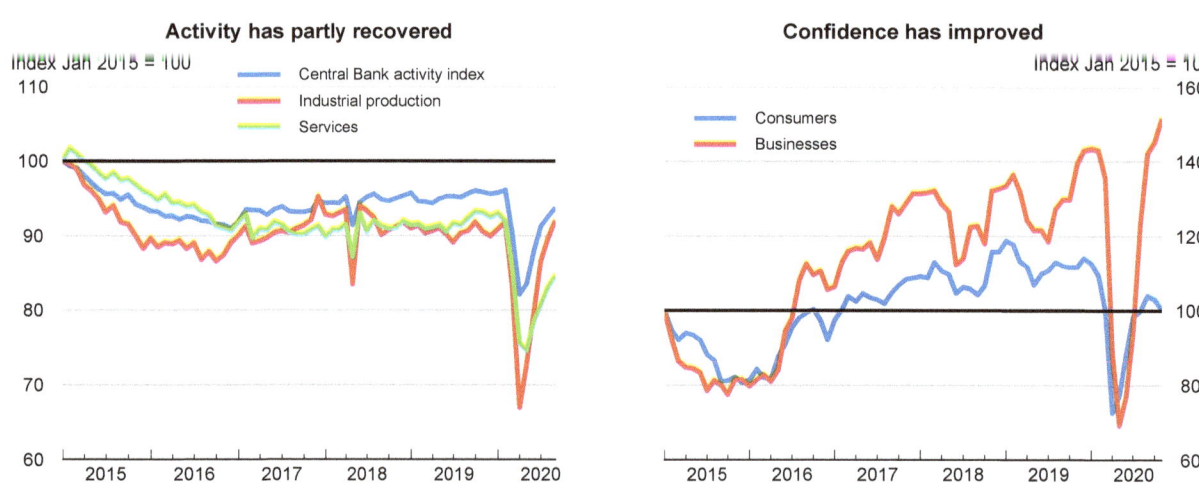

Source: CEIC; Central Bank of Brazil; and Refinitiv.

StatLink https://doi.org/10.1787/888934217912

Brazil: Demand, output and prices

Brazil	2017 Current prices BRL billion	2018	2019	2020	2021	2022
		Percentage changes, volume (2000 prices)				
GDP at market prices	6 583.3	1.2	1.1	-6.0	2.6	2.2
Private consumption	4 245.1	2.1	1.8	-7.0	3.8	2.2
Government consumption	1 327.8	0.4	-0.4	-1.6	-0.1	-0.4
Gross fixed capital formation	958.8	3.7	2.3	-10.2	-0.4	5.6
Final domestic demand	6 531.6	2.0	1.4	-6.4	2.3	2.1
Stockbuilding[1]	4.4	-0.4	0.2	-0.8	0.1	0.0
Total domestic demand	6 536.0	1.6	1.6	-7.2	2.5	2.1
Exports of goods and services	824.4	3.4	-2.5	1.4	5.3	4.0
Imports of goods and services	777.1	7.7	1.1	-6.2	4.3	4.0
Net exports[1]	47.3	-0.5	-0.5	1.1	0.3	0.1
Memorandum items						
GDP deflator	_	3.4	4.2	4.0	2.0	2.9
Consumer price index	_	3.7	3.7	2.7	2.5	3.2
Private consumption deflator	_	2.9	3.8	1.2	1.9	2.9
General government financial balance (% of GDP)	_	-7.1	-5.9	-16.9	-7.6	-6.7
Current account balance (% of GDP)	_	-2.2	-2.7	-1.2	-1.1	-1.0

1. Contributions to changes in real GDP, actual amount in the first column.
Source: OECD Economic Outlook 108 database.

StatLink https://doi.org/10.1787/888934217931

Brazil 2

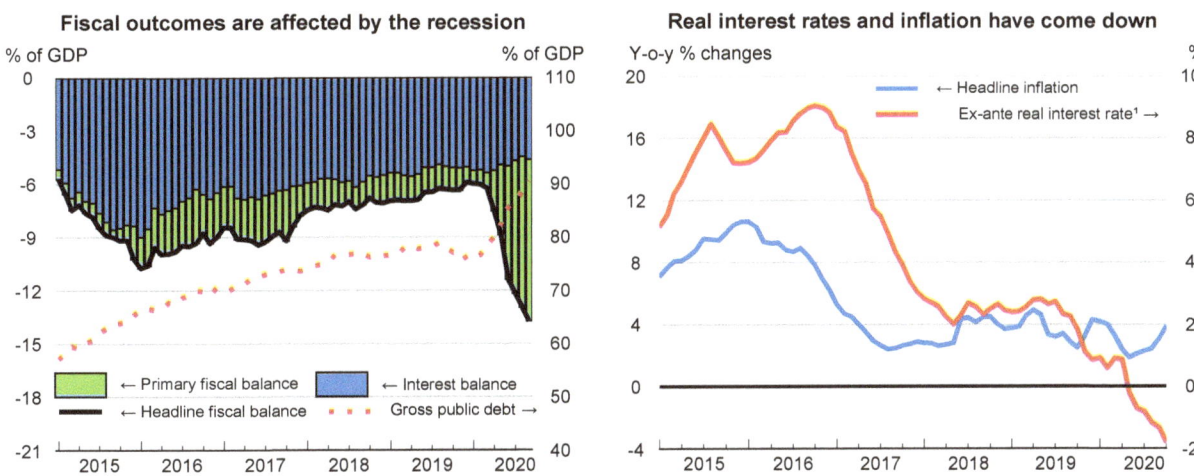

Fiscal outcomes are affected by the recession

Real interest rates and inflation have come down

1. The ex-ante real interest rate is calculated as the SELIC rate minus inflation expectations one year ahead.
Source: CEIC; Central Bank of Brazil; and Refinitiv.

StatLink https://doi.org/10.1787/888934217950

With most containment measures lifted, infections have stabilised at high levels

After the first COVID-19 case in late February, cases and deaths increased rapidly and Brazil has become one of the global hotspots of the pandemic. The health system has faced serious shortages, especially in the public sector, on which two-thirds of Brazilians depend. Many fatalities have occurred among those waiting for admission into intensive care units. New confirmed COVID-19 infections and deaths peaked in August and have declined since, but remain high. While the central government has not taken any coercive lockdown measures, state and municipal governments kept many shops and public places closed from late March through July. These restrictions have been lifted by now, with the exception of school closures. Schools are being reopened on a case-by-case basis across the country, with significant local variation, but some may not reopen at all during the 2020 school year.

The economy is recovering

Following a weaker activity drop than in other countries in the region in the second quarter, principal short-term activity indicators now point to a fairly solid and broad recovery. Even services, which include sectors highly affected by the pandemic, such as tourism, entertainment, hotels and restaurants and personal services, have seen some noticeable improvements. Confidence has rebounded among consumers and businesses alike. Credit has increased markedly since the outbreak of the pandemic. Lower employment, lower hours worked and significantly reduced earning possibilities for self-employed workers are still weighing on labour incomes and private consumption.

Fiscal and monetary policies have provided strong support to the economy

The fiscal policy response to the pandemic has been one of the strongest in the region, with discretionary fiscal measures exceeding 8% of GDP and a strong focus on the most vulnerable households, including informal workers. A new temporary emergency benefit has been paid to over 67 million informal, self-employed or unemployed workers since April, amounting to USD 120 per month, or 57% of the federal minimum wage. It has now been extended to end-2020, at half its original level. This strong support, in combination with other expanded unemployment benefits for formal workers, has reduced poverty to a 40-year low and avoided a stronger decline in incomes and consumption. Policy support for small firms includes a publicly guaranteed low-interest credit line to cover wages for employees earning up to twice the minimum wage. Additional new corporate credit lines have been created by the national development bank. Direct spending on health and transfers to states and municipalities, which have the primary responsibility for financing public healthcare services, has been increased by around 2% of GDP.

Declining inflation has been pushed down further by faltering domestic demand. Both headline and core inflation measures are now significantly below target, despite a recent uptick in food prices. Rate cuts of 250 basis points in 2020 have led to historically low nominal and real interest rates. Combined with regulatory measures that would allow additional credit extension of up to 18.5% of GDP, this will provide highly favourable conditions for private investment once confidence in the recovery strengthens and credit demand picks up.

The economy will almost recover by end-2022

Fiscal support and the end of containment measures are underpinning a partial recovery of domestic demand in 2020. The announced withdrawal of emergency social benefits will dent this recovery somewhat in early 2021, before momentum returns given the prospect of greater availability of a vaccine against COVID-19. These projections will allow activity to return close to its pre-pandemic level by the end of 2022. Exports will continue to benefit from recovering global demand for food and minerals. Manufacturing exports are limited by continuously weak prospects in neighbouring Argentina, the major destination for such exports. Import demand will pick up in line with domestic demand. A fairly stable current account deficit will continue to be covered by foreign direct investment inflows. Unemployment will peak in 2021 at almost 14%, before receding slowly amid a return of previously discouraged workers to the labour market. Inflation is projected to remain clearly below target until 2022 when the target is lowered to 3.5%. This will likely call for a gradual withdrawal of the current strong monetary support in 2022.

Besides a resurgence of COVID-19 cases, stalling reform progress would be a major risk for growth and fiscal outcomes. The pandemic is expected to add 20 percentage points to the gross public debt ratio, which will reach 100% of GDP by end-2022. Against this complicated background, fiscal sustainability hinges on keeping the pandemic-related fiscal measures temporary and on resuming the fiscal adjustment in train before the pandemic. This in turn will require mandatory spending floors and other budget rigidities to be addressed, while reviewing staff spending, subsidies and tax expenditures. The political challenge behind these reforms is not trivial, but a failure would imply breaking the 2016 expenditure rule, one of the driving factors behind growing confidence and declining interest rates before the pandemic. Social discontent that affected several South American neighbours could also affect Brazil, possibly compounded by deteriorating social conditions from the pandemic and by corruption scandals that have eroded faith in public institutions. On the upside, faster reform progress or stronger growth in main trading partners, particularly the United States and China, would accelerate the recovery.

Given limited fiscal space, structural reforms are a key policy lever

Productivity-enhancing structural reforms can go a long way to support the recovery. Better domestic regulation and closer integration into the global economy could boost competition, while simultaneously reducing the cost of intermediate and capital goods. Productivity could also benefit from better contract enforcement through a more efficient judiciary and lower tax compliance costs through a substantial overhaul of the fragmented indirect tax system, with a view towards a unified value added tax. Better and more professional training would allow workers to seize new opportunities arising from ongoing structural changes in the economy and facilitate the reallocation of resources. Social protection could be strengthened cost-effectively by building on existing cash transfer schemes. With higher participation thresholds and benefit levels, and a more rapid inclusion of new applicants, these could be transformed into a universal means-tested social safety net, including for informal workers. This would also allow reductions in non-wage labour costs of formal jobs and foster formalisation, because cash transfers are financed through general taxation rather than labour charges. Preserving valuable natural assets such as the Amazon rainforest for future generations will require stronger efforts to enforce existing laws, building on past progress in enforcement.

Bulgaria

The first COVID-19 outbreak was smaller in Bulgaria than in many countries and the economy less severely impacted by confinement measures than expected in the first half of 2020. An economic contraction of 4.1% is expected in 2020 to be followed by a recovery, with growth of 3.3% in 2021 and 3.7% in 2022, driven by rising domestic demand and a moderate rebound in exports. Fiscal support for households and firms and high public investment are central to the strength of the recovery. Private investment will remain subdued given substantial uncertainty.

Low public debt and high fiscal reserves, together with EU financial resources, will allow the government to sustain and expand its fiscal assistance. The government's wage subsidy scheme will keep unemployment down, and rises in public wages and social benefits in 2021 will provide a boost to household incomes. With effective planning and implementation, the large EU-funded public investment programme has the ability to increase potential growth. Reforms to ease access to insolvency and firm rehabilitation proceedings have taken on an added urgency.

COVID-19 cases surged in autumn 2020 from an initially low level

Bulgaria avoided the worst of the initial COVID-19 outbreak, with a comparatively low number of cases and deaths. Following the easing of confinement measures, new cases began to increase in July and a surge in infections occurred from October. While the country benefits from having a large number of acute care hospital beds, the sharp rise in infections is proving a challenge for the health system. The government responded at the end of November by closing hospitality establishments, shopping malls, and education facilities. Education has been moved online where possible.

Bulgaria

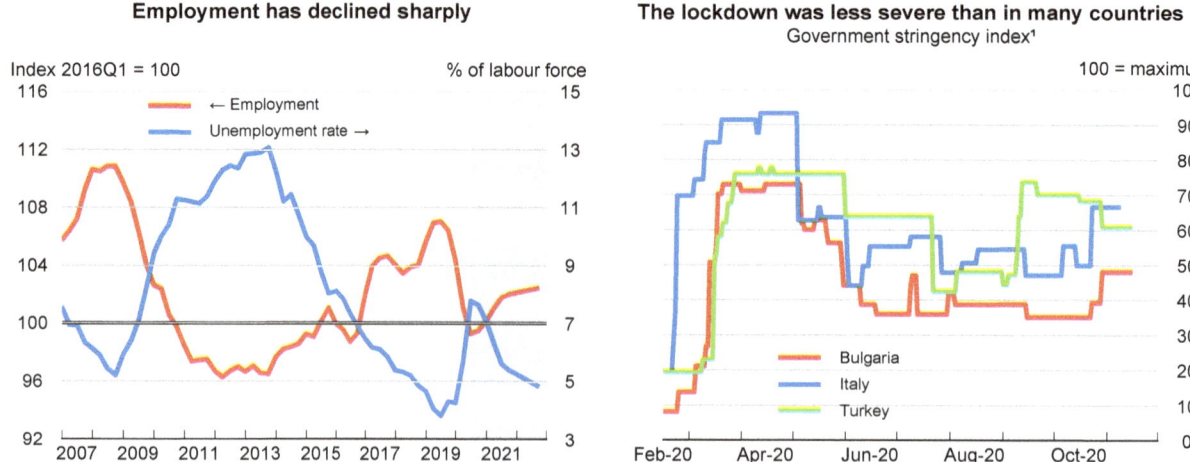

Employment has declined sharply

Index 2016Q1 = 100 / % of labour force

The lockdown was less severe than in many countries
Government stringency index[1]

100 = maximum

1. A composite indicator based on nine sub-indicators including school closures, workplace closures, and travel bans.
Source: OECD Economic Outlook 108 database; and European Center for Disease Prevention and Control (ECDC) though Our World in Data, Oxford COVID-19 Government Response Tracker.

StatLink https://doi.org/10.1787/888934217969

Bulgaria: Demand, output and prices

Bulgaria	2017	2018	2019	2020	2021	2022
	Current prices BGN billion	Percentage changes, volume (2015 prices)				
GDP at market prices	102.3	3.1	3.7	-4.1	3.3	3.7
Private consumption	61.6	4.4	5.5	-0.7	2.7	3.1
Government consumption	16.0	5.3	2.0	4.1	3.7	3.0
Gross fixed capital formation	18.8	5.4	4.5	-8.4	5.8	4.4
Final domestic demand	96.4	4.8	4.6	-1.4	3.5	3.4
Stockbuilding[1]	1.6	1.1	0.0	-2.6	-0.3	0.0
Total domestic demand	97.9	5.8	4.6	-4.2	3.1	3.4
Exports of goods and services	68.9	1.7	3.9	-10.7	6.0	5.7
Imports of goods and services	64.4	5.7	5.2	-9.9	6.1	5.3
Net exports[1]	4.4	-2.5	-0.7	-0.8	0.2	0.5
Memorandum items						
GDP deflator	–	4.0	5.3	1.6	1.5	1.9
Consumer price index	–	2.8	3.1	1.6	1.4	1.8
Core consumer price index[2]	–	2.1	1.8	1.2	1.4	1.8
Unemployment rate (% of labour force)	–	5.2	4.2	6.4	6.1	5.1
Household saving ratio, net (% of disposable income)	–	1.2	1.0	1.6	-2.6	-4.3
General government financial balance (% of GDP)	–	2.0	1.9	-4.4	-4.5	-2.6
General government gross debt (% of GDP)	–	31.8	29.9	34.4	38.6	40.7
General government debt, Maastricht definition (% of GDP)	–	22.3	20.2	24.6	28.9	31.0
Current account balance (% of GDP)	–	1.0	3.0	3.1	2.9	3.1

1. Contributions to changes in real GDP, actual amount in the first column.
2. Consumer price index excluding food and energy.
Source: OECD Economic Outlook 108 database.

StatLink https://doi.org/10.1787/888934217988

The economic contraction was milder than expected

Confinement measures have been less severe and the fall in economic activity lower than in many OECD countries, with economic output having shrunk by 5.2% year-on-year in the third quarter of 2020. The reopening of businesses and the relaxation of containment measures were accompanied by a recovery of activity that took on momentum in July. Manufacturing had almost returned to December 2019 activity levels by September 2020, and goods exports have started to recover. Services, including tourism, passenger transport and retail, have been slower to bounce back. Employment fell sharply and unemployment has increased from pre-crisis record lows. Inflation fell, driven not only by the fall in international energy prices, but also by the slowdown in core inflation and the cut in regulated natural gas and heating prices. The surge in the pandemic has affected the recovery and economic activity is expected to slow down substantially in the fourth quarter due to the growth in the number of cases from October and as the lockdown hits at the end of November.

The fiscal response has moderated the rise in unemployment

The government implemented fiscal measures to assist firms and households in March and has extended support as the impact of the pandemic endured. Financing of the measures, estimated to be about 3% of GDP for 2020, has come from national and EU resources. The government's wage subsidy scheme has prevented a sharper rise in unemployment. It protected jobs of around 7% of the labour force in the second quarter of 2020, while helping the most impacted firms with their labour costs. Support programmes are expected to remain in place for 2021 and further increases in public wages and social benefits are to be introduced. EU funding is due to be high with strong investment expected at the beginning of the next programming period in 2021 and substantial resources, of about 10% of pre-crisis GDP, to come from the EU Recovery and Resilience Facility.

Continued fiscal support is critical for the strength of the recovery

A recovery is underway, but its path remains uncertain, particularly given the current large rise in COVID-19 infections. The economy is expected to shrink by 4.1% in 2020, but is projected to recover to its pre-crisis level in 2022. Fiscal support will determine the strength of the recovery, with a large shift from pre-crisis fiscal surpluses to projected deficits of over 4% of GDP in 2020 and 2021. The surging pandemic will weigh on business confidence and private investment, and sporadic outbreaks will hold down growth until vaccination against the virus becomes general. Strong public investment, financed by EU resources, will then drive the revival of investment. Trade is set to recover gradually, contributing positively to growth in 2021 and 2022. The reintroduction of confinement measures is a significant downside risk that would constrain the normalisation of domestic demand.

Substantial EU resource flows represent an opportunity

Low public debt and high fiscal reserves, and EU financial assistance, put Bulgaria in a solid position to avoid withdrawing fiscal assistance prematurely. Firms may require additional credit support, particularly if the current debt moratorium is not extended. Resources should be targeted to liquidity-constrained, but otherwise viable, enterprises. Progressing rapidly with the reforms identified to improve access to insolvency and rehabilitation proceedings has become an even greater priority. Continued focus on increasing competition, reducing the cost of red tape for businesses and fighting corruption remains critical for increasing potential growth. The large planned increase in public investment, due to EU resources, represents an opportunity to close the gaps in housing efficiency and transport infrastructure, increase innovation and speed up the transition to a more digitalised and less carbon-intensive economy. It will be important to strengthen capacity to ensure an effective and rapid use of the available EU funding.

Canada

Recovery from an output decline of 5.4% in 2020 will be muted by drag from regional restrictions to combat COVID-19 outbreaks and continued disruption to travel, hospitality and related sectors, leading to output growth of 3.5% in 2021. These developments will be echoed by a slow labour market recovery and low consumer price inflation. With vaccination against the virus set to become general in the latter half of 2021, diminished restrictions and a recovery in hard-hit sectors will support growth in 2022. Growth of the public debt burden will slow.

Federal, provincial and territorial governments, along with the central bank, have been appropriately reactive to the evolving economic conditions. Going forward, governments need greater emphasis on encouraging employment and business recovery, including through green investment and through tackling long-standing structural issues that impede Canada's business sector. Ensuring that the enhancement of employment insurance is adequate following the termination of the Canada Emergency Response Benefit (CERB) also needs to be a priority. The Bank of Canada should stand ready to provide further liquidity support if required.

Restrictions are tightening across provinces and territories

Recorded daily cases in the second wave of COVID-19 have surpassed those reached in the first wave, while fatalities have remained comparatively low. Provinces and territories have been individually extending and reimposing limits on activity as well as strengthening public health requirements and testing capacities. Recent measures in provinces have included the suspension of some activities (such as organised sports and leisure activities), early-closing rules for bars and restaurants and limits on social gatherings. Age remains the dominant factor in determining who is most severely affected; around 90% of COVID-19-related deaths have been among those aged over 70 years.

Canada 1

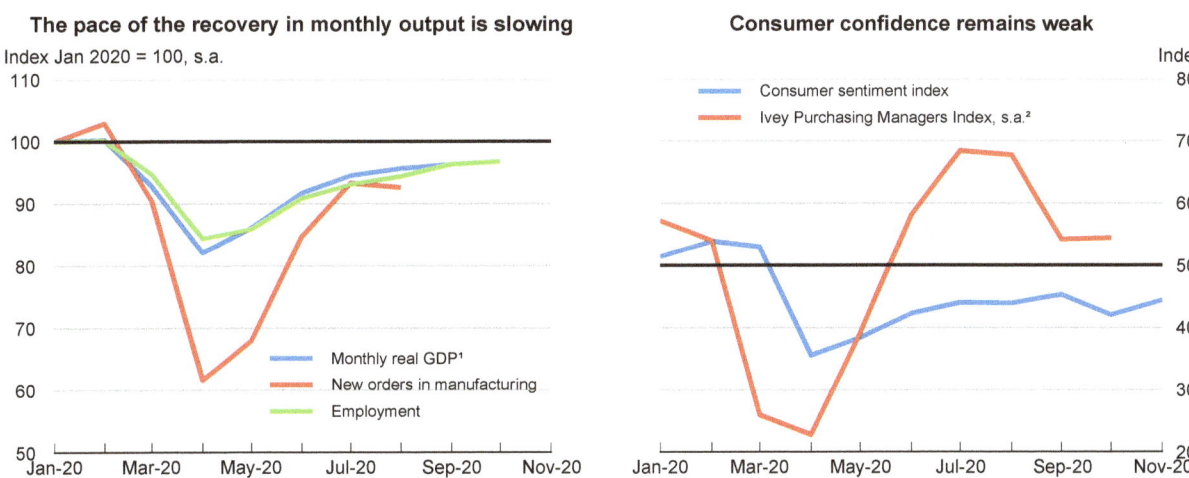

The pace of the recovery in monthly output is slowing

Consumer confidence remains weak

1. First estimate for September 2020.
2. The Ivey Purchasing Managers Index measures month-to-month changes in dollars of purchases as indicated by a panel of purchasing managers from across Canada.
Source: Statistics Canada; Ivey Business School; and Refinitiv.

StatLink ᵐˢᴾ https://doi.org/10.1787/888934218007

Canada: Demand, output and prices

Canada	2017	2018	2019	2020	2021	2022
	Current prices CAD billion	Percentage changes, volume (2012 prices)				
GDP at market prices	2 141.1	2.0	1.7	-5.4	3.5	2.0
Private consumption	1 240.4	2.1	1.6	-6.1	4.4	2.1
Government consumption	444.1	3.0	2.1	-0.1	2.0	1.3
Gross fixed capital formation	486.8	1.2	-0.4	-6.4	2.1	2.2
Final domestic demand	2 171.3	2.1	1.3	-4.9	3.4	1.9
Stockbuilding[1]	17.2	-0.2	0.1	-2.0	-0.5	0.0
Total domestic demand	2 188.5	1.9	1.4	-6.8	2.9	2.0
Exports of goods and services	672.5	3.1	1.3	-8.5	5.1	2.0
Imports of goods and services	719.9	2.6	0.6	-12.8	3.1	2.0
Net exports[1]	- 47.4	0.1	0.2	1.6	0.5	0.0
Memorandum items						
GDP deflator	_	1.8	1.9	-0.1	0.4	1.0
Consumer price index	_	2.2	2.0	0.6	0.7	1.2
Core consumer price index[2]	_	1.9	2.1	0.9	0.3	1.2
Unemployment rate (% of labour force)	_	5.8	5.7	9.6	8.7	7.7
Household saving ratio, net (% of disposable income)	_	1.7	2.9	15.0	8.5	5.4
General government financial balance (% of GDP)	_	-0.4	-0.3	-15.6	-11.3	-5.8
General government gross debt (% of GDP)	_	93.8	94.3	121.5	131.2	135.4
Current account balance (% of GDP)	_	-2.5	-2.0	-1.9	-1.7	-1.7

1. Contributions to changes in real GDP, actual amount in the first column.
2. Consumer price index excluding food and energy.
Source: OECD Economic Outlook 108 database.

StatLink ⟨⟩ https://doi.org/10.1787/888934218026

Canada 2

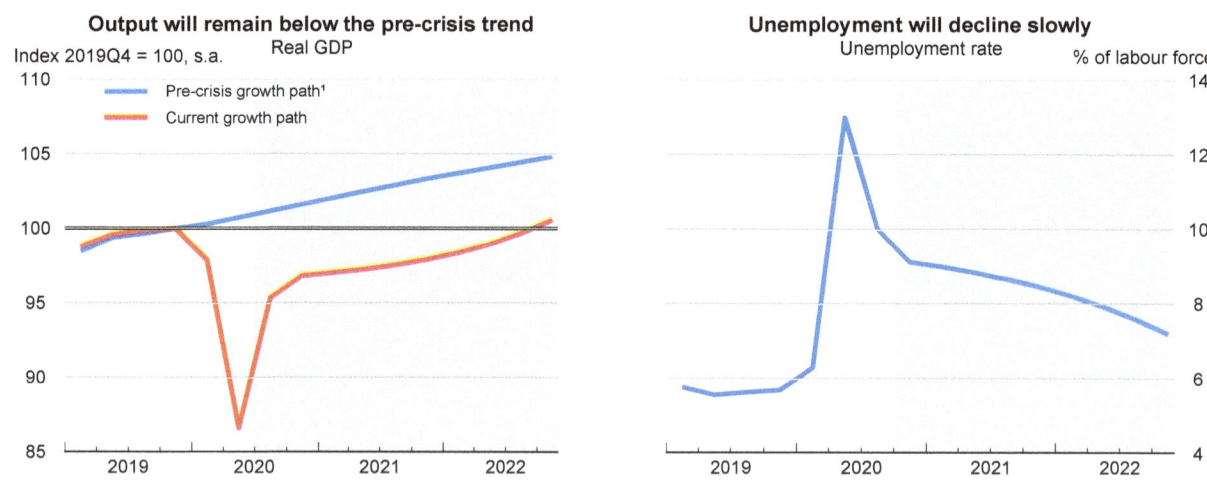

1. The pre-crisis growth path is based on the November 2019 OECD Economic Outlook projection, with linear extrapolation for 2022 based on trend growth in 2021.
Source: OECD Economic Outlook 106 and 108 databases.

StatLink ⟨⟩ https://doi.org/10.1787/888934218045

Recovery has initially been rapid

Economic activity picked up sharply following the start of de-confinement in May. Monthly GDP troughed at 18% below pre-crisis levels in April; by July, the gap was only around 6%. Activity in some sectors, including retail and wholesale trade, is already back to pre-crisis levels. The large injection of support to household incomes has played a substantial role; indeed, the income increase outstripped consumption and the household saving rate has risen substantially. A partial rebound of global oil prices helped the resource sector. However, the pace of the recovery in output and employment is slowing, demand is weak in some sectors and there are signs of a fall in consumer confidence. National accounts data show that activity in the arts, entertainment and recreation sector and in the accommodation and food services sector are still well below pre-crisis levels. In addition, structural shifts prompted by the pandemic, such as the accelerated shift to online retailing (e-commerce sales approximately doubled during lockdown), are bringing adjustment costs. The Bank of Canada's Business Outlook Survey shows business sentiment to have improved in the third quarter but remain negative. Consumer price inflation continues to be subdued. Meanwhile house price growth has been strong with housing purchases boosted, in part, by lower interest rates. Also, government support for households and banks' provisions for mortgage-payment deferrals will have limited downward pressure on prices from forced sales.

Monetary and fiscal support is evolving

Fewer monetary and financial market measures are being used, but the degree of monetary policy support remains substantial. The Bank of Canada has been able to withdraw support partially as some specific risks have receded, for instance support for the financing of provincial governments has been terminated. However, interest rates remain ultra-low (the Bank's policy rate is 0.25%) and the Bank's purchases of federal government securities continue.

Government support is also evolving. Provisions allowing tax payment deferral have ended, and the Canada Emergency Response Benefit (CERB), the major income support programme introduced for households, was retired at the end of September. However, CERB's termination is not bringing an abrupt halt to support. Many recipients are eligible to switch to unemployment insurance and substitute programmes have been introduced for certain groups. The other major programme, CEWS, which provides a wage subsidy of up to 75% to employers for up to three months, has been extended to mid-2021 with an estimated outlay of CAN 80 billon (around 3% of GDP). Employers must demonstrate a drop in revenue to access the subsidy, and the amount of subsidy is linked to the revenue drop. Rental support for business, credit support and loan guarantees are also being extended into 2021. Total federal government outlays on measures for the 2020-21 budget year are estimated at 11% of GDP. Provincial governments are retaining special provisions in safety nets and additional support for business, though the dollar value of support is expected to remain small compared with that from federal government.

The economic recovery is expected to slow considerably

The projections envisage that localised containment measures will weigh on growth until vaccination against the virus becomes general. Activity in the travel, leisure and hospitality sectors will remain significantly below pre-crisis levels. Uncertainty about economic prospects will damp household consumption and business investment. Consumer price inflation is expected to remain below the 2% target. The fiscal deficit will decline in 2021 and 2022 as tax revenues recover and need for household and business support declines. Nevertheless, there will be a further increase in the ratio of public debt to GDP.

Risks will remain elevated. As elsewhere, there are uncertainties on the scale and economic impact of future containment measures and the timing of a vaccine rollout. These issues will particularly affect the pace of recovery in the hard-hit sectors, such as travel and hospitality. Another key uncertainty is the extent to which households will unwind the elevated saving ratio through consumption or hold back due to caution about future prospects. For Canada, the future path of oil price and demand is also a key source of uncertainty and risk. Canada's economic recovery from the COVID-19 crisis will depend as well on developments in the United States given the close economic ties between the two countries. In financial markets, while a liquidity crisis has been averted so far, risks remain. The economic crisis arising from the pandemic has heightened vulnerabilities in the corporate bond market and risks from high levels of household debt through mortgage borrowing.

Economic policy now needs to nurture business opportunities, job creation and well-being

Nurturing recovery in the business sector should be a key priority. Support should focus on viable segments of those sectors heavily scarred by the crisis, but also on reallocation by encouraging positive shifts in the structure of economic activity, including through employment-intensive green investment projects and retraining programmes. Structural issues that have long held back the productivity and competitiveness of Canada's business sector, such as non-tariff barriers to trade across provinces and territories, should be addressed. In addition, the coverage, responsiveness and effectiveness of social welfare programmes should be improved. The CERB scheme was, in part, introduced because of gaps in the coverage of federal employment insurance and modest safety net welfare benefit provisions in many provinces and territories. The follow-up measures to the withdrawal of CERB address some gaps, including support for the self-employed, but the broad issue of modest support remains. Further progress in improving access to affordable childcare and housing should also be made and there should be a push to include prescription drugs in the public healthcare basket ("Pharmacare"). Preparations should begin for tackling the public debt burden when the economic recovery is well underway. A more tightly defined medium-term federal fiscal target should be considered to help guide budgeting and strengthen the credibility of fiscal management. There is headroom in the goods and services tax should additional revenues be needed.

Chile

Chile is set for a gradual recovery over the next two years, with activity returning to its pre-pandemic levels in late 2022. GDP growth will be 4.2% during 2021, after a contraction of 6% in 2020. Private consumption will be a main driver of the recovery, initially sustained by measures implemented by the government to support households, a gradual improvement of the labour market sustained by hiring subsidies and withdrawals from pension funds. Investment will regain momentum at a slow pace, conditional on the evolution of the pandemic, driven by public infrastructure plans, supportive financing conditions and tax incentives. Recovering global demand will also be beneficial.

Solid fiscal and monetary policy frameworks allowed the authorities to pursue bold measures, which prevented a deeper contraction and are avoiding deeper scars from the pandemic. Continuing with an ambitious structural reform agenda, in particular planned reforms to bolster pensions and female participation in the labour force, would sustain an inclusive recovery. Additional public investment, especially in education, the lifelong learning system, active labour market policies, and digital and transport infrastructure, would help strengthen the recovery further.

The country has been hit hard by the pandemic

Chile has been hit hard by the pandemic, with one of the highest numbers of deaths per million inhabitants. The cases have been concentrated in the Santiago metropolitan area, with scattered outbreaks in other regions of the country. Local quarantines, mobility restrictions and night-time curfews have been applied across the country. The city of Santiago and other large cities were put under a strict lockdown in May, with most containment measures lifted progressively in mid-July, when infections started declining. A state of emergency, declared in March to impose containment measures, has been extended until the end of the year.

Chile

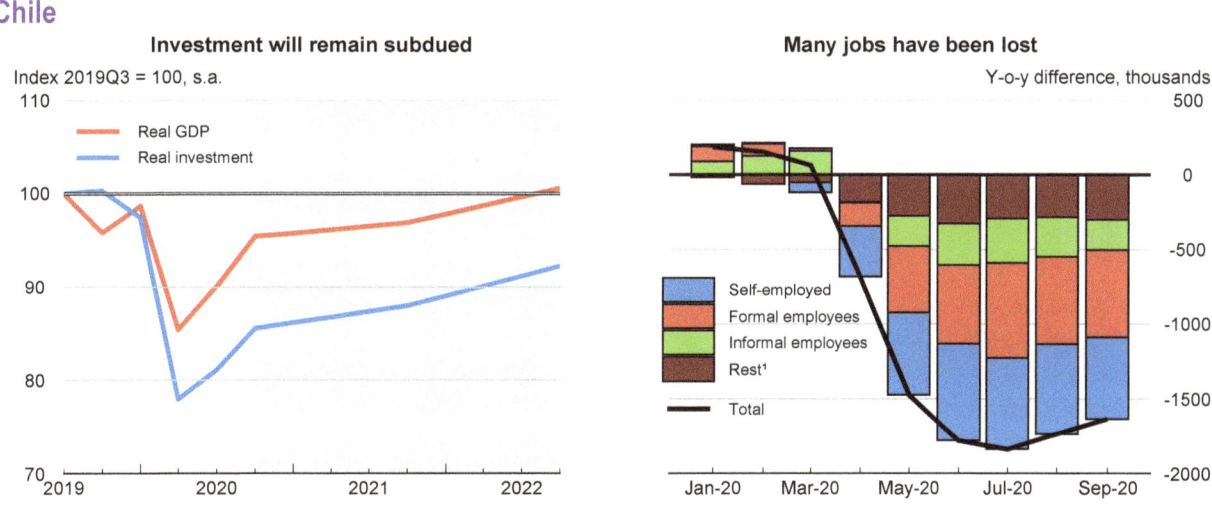

1. The rest includes employers, domestic workers and unpaid family workers.
Source: OECD Economic Outlook 108 database; and INE.

StatLink 🔗 https://doi.org/10.1787/888934218064

Chile: Demand, output and prices

Chile	2017	2018	2019	2020	2021	2022
	Current prices CLP billion	Percentage changes, volume (2013 prices)				
GDP at market prices	179 891.3	4.0	1.0	-6.0	4.2	3.0
Private consumption	113 983.7	3.7	1.1	-7.7	7.5	3.4
Government consumption	25 363.3	4.3	0.0	-2.1	5.5	1.5
Gross fixed capital formation	37 761.9	4.8	4.2	-13.9	1.8	4.1
Final domestic demand	177 109.0	4.0	1.6	-8.3	5.9	3.3
Stockbuilding[1]	697.7	0.7	-0.6	-1.3	-1.4	0.0
Total domestic demand	177 806.7	4.7	1.0	-9.6	4.5	3.3
Exports of goods and services	51 007.3	5.1	-2.2	-0.7	7.2	4.1
Imports of goods and services	48 922.7	7.9	-2.3	-13.4	8.4	5.6
Net exports[1]	2 084.6	-0.7	0.0	3.6	0.0	-0.2
Memorandum items						
GDP deflator	_	2.4	2.6	6.7	3.6	2.5
Consumer price index	_	2.4	2.6	2.9	2.6	3.0
Private consumption deflator	_	2.6	1.9	3.1	2.7	3.0
Unemployment rate (% of labour force)	_	7.4	7.2	10.8	9.8	8.7
Central government financial balance (% of GDP)	_	-1.6	-2.8	-8.7	-4.7	-3.8
Current account balance (% of GDP)	_	-3.6	-3.9	0.3	-0.2	-0.7

1. Contributions to changes in real GDP, actual amount in the first column.
Source: OECD Economic Outlook 108 database.

StatLink 𝖆𝖎𝖘𝖑 https://doi.org/10.1787/888934218083

Economic activity has started to recover

After the social protests in late 2019, the COVID-19 outbreak has pushed the economy into its deepest recession since 1982. Employment has reached a historic low after almost 25% of the labour force lost their jobs. Around 10% of firms are using the job retention scheme, which now covers nearly 17% of all dependent workers. With containment measures being relaxed gradually since July, short-term indicators suggest that economic activity has started to recover, particularly retail sales and manufacturing output, while tourism and hospitality continue to be weak. Business sentiment has improved considerably and consumer confidence has lately picked up as well. Inflation remains contained due to the strong contraction of demand.

Bold policy reactions will limit the economic scars of the pandemic

The monetary policy stance has been highly expansionary, with record-low policy rates and unconventional measures ensuring both financial stability and credit expansion. These policies should be maintained as planned to support the recovery. The fiscal response was among the largest in the region and included cash transfers for informal and vulnerable households and the middle class, a job retention scheme, tax deferrals and reductions, and liquidity provisions and guarantee measures to help firms. Furthermore, an agreement between political parties led to a temporary emergency plan to support the recovery of the economy for the coming two years and a commitment to fiscal consolidation thereafter. This agreement, based on hiring subsidies, measures to support low-income households, public investment and tax incentives for firms, will help the recovery and make it more inclusive. Measures to speed up and streamline regulations and private investment projects are also being implemented.

A gradual recovery is underway in an uncertain environment

Economic recovery will be gradual and uneven in the next two years. Private consumption will be the main driver of the recovery, due to formal employment gains supported by hiring subsidies, but precautionary saving will remain high. Private investment will start to recover only slowly, given high uncertainty, and is conditional on the evolution of the pandemic. Mining exports have been resilient and Chile will further benefit from recovering global demand, especially from China and the United States. Additional virus outbreaks are the main risk to the outlook, until an effective vaccine becomes widely deployed, and could require persistent limits to international travel, bans on large public events, and restrictions on bars and restaurants. The ongoing constitutional review, a series of elections during 2021 and renewed social protests could further increase uncertainty and dampen investment. Exports and job creation would benefit from a potentially stronger global recovery than anticipated.

An ambitious structural reform agenda would strengthen inclusive growth

Public debt is increasing rapidly, but is expected to remain sustainable provided that the temporary fiscal measures are phased out once the recovery is fully underway. The authorities should focus on efficiency-enhancing reallocation of public spending, for example through the reduction of tax exemptions. Continuing to strengthen the fiscal framework, including the fiscal rule and the already successful Autonomous Fiscal Council, would reinforce the credibility of fiscal plans. The second wave of extraordinary withdrawals from pension funds will decrease and, in many cases, deplete individual retirement savings and could potentially be disruptive to financial markets, while having only a small positive impact on demand. Direct public support for those in need would be better to strengthen demand while preserving future old-age pensions.

Continuing with an ambitious structural reform agenda will be the key policy lever to boost inclusive medium-term growth. Addressing long-standing barriers to productivity growth will require better spending in education and ensuring that firms are more exposed to competition and innovation. Streamlining regulation on concessions in the communications sector would foster the deployment of digital infrastructure and help reduce connectivity gaps. A full revision of employer-provided training programmes could increase the quality and the targeting of these programmes on vulnerable workers, improving their prospects of finding formal jobs in expanding sectors. The current bill to streamline and simplify bankruptcy procedures would promote a faster reallocation of capital.

China

Following the steepest quarterly dive and subsequent surge on record in the first and second quarters of 2020, respectively, and then stabilisation in the third quarter, activity is projected to return to its past trajectory, with growth of about 8% in 2021 and 4.9% in 2022. New COVID-19 cases have reappeared sporadically, but the coronavirus outbreak seems largely under control in most of the country. Investment, in particular debt- and stimulus-fuelled infrastructure investment, has boosted growth in 2020. Real estate investment has also remained strong. Exports have boomed on the back of pent-up demand for masks and other COVID-19-related materials and equipment as well as teleworking-related goods. Consumption is still to recover from the hit caused by the outbreak. Even though sales of luxury goods are booming and box office revenues have reached new highs, the lack of a recovery in employment and falling household incomes mean that prospects for a full consumption recovery are not bright. Inflation is easing, despite elevated pork prices.

Monetary stimulus, which was needed during the outbreak, is now being withdrawn as the recovery is gaining momentum. Shadow banking has also picked up following a few years of decline. Increasing corporate defaults have sharpened risk pricing. Fiscal policy will remain supportive, with a number of tax cuts and extensions of social benefits promoting consumption amid weak consumer confidence. However, more ambitious structural reforms in the area of social protection, and a more equitable provision of public services, are needed for consumption to rebound. Infrastructure investment will remain robust, mainly benefitting state-owned enterprises as entry restrictions are being relaxed only slowly.

China 1

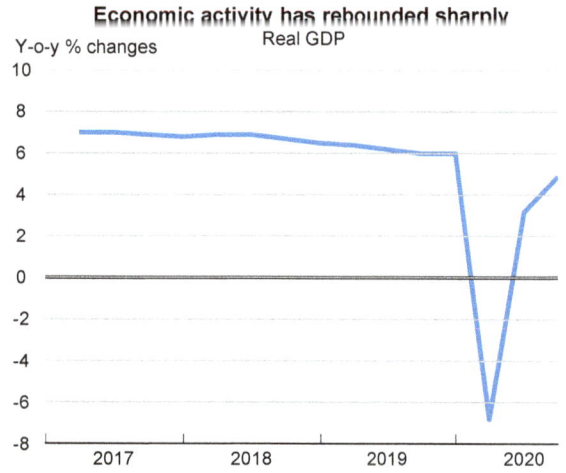

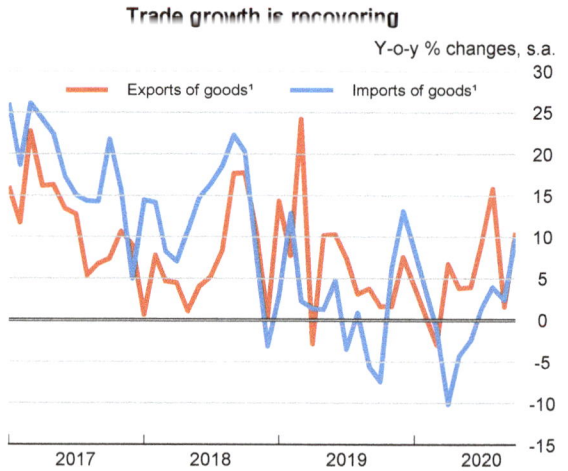

1. In nominal terms.
Source: CEIC.

StatLink 🔗 https://doi.org/10.1787/888934218102

China: Demand, output and prices

China	2017	2018	2019	2020	2021	2022
	Current prices CNY trillion	Percentage changes, volume (2015 prices)				
GDP at market prices	83.2	6.7	6.1	1.8	8.0	4.9
Total domestic demand	81.7	7.2	5.9	1.3	7.2	4.8
Exports of goods and services	16.4	3.7	2.0	-3.7	7.5	5.5
Imports of goods and services	14.9	5.7	0.2	-7.2	2.1	4.6
Net exports[1]	1.5	-0.2	0.4	0.5	1.1	0.4
Memorandum items						
GDP deflator	_	3.5	1.6	0.9	1.6	2.0
Consumer price index	_	1.9	2.9	2.8	2.3	2.1
General government financial balance[2] (% of GDP)	_	-3.0	-3.7	-6.9	-6.2	-5.2
Headline government financial balance[3] (% of GDP)	_	-2.6	-2.8	-3.5	-3.0	-3.0
Current account balance (% of GDP)	_	0.2	1.0	2.5	3.5	3.5

1. Contributions to changes in real GDP, actual amount in the first column.
2. Encompasses the balances of all four budget accounts (general account, government managed funds, social security funds and the state-owned capital management account).
3. The headline fiscal balance is the official balance defined as the difference between revenues and outlays. Revenues include: general budget revenue, revenue from the central stabilisation fund and sub-national budget adjustment. Outlays include: general budget spending, replenishment of the central stabilisation fund and repayment of principal on sub-national debt.

Source: OECD Economic Outlook 108 database.

StatLink ᓂ᷒ᔑᒲ https://doi.org/10.1787/888934218121

China 2

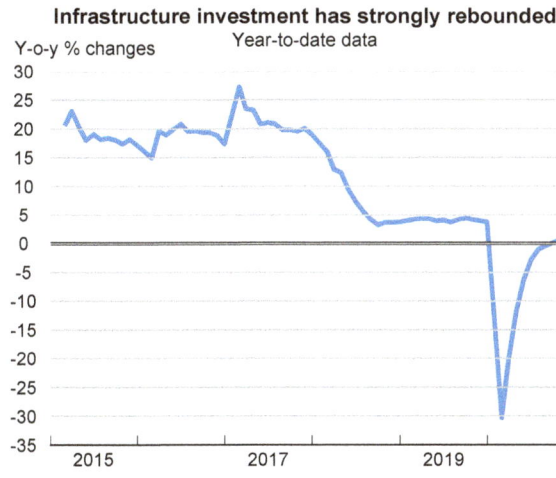

Infrastructure investment has strongly rebounded

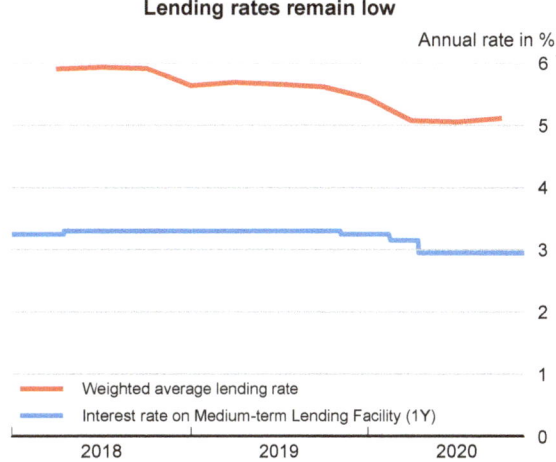

Lending rates remain low

Source: CEIC.

StatLink ᓂ᷒ᔑᒲ https://doi.org/10.1787/888934218140

The COVID-19 pandemic has retreated

China has implemented strict sanitary and non-sanitary measures to regain control of the outbreak. Even though clusters of COVID-19 cases have reappeared sporadically in various parts of the country, and are likely to continue doing so, the proven tracing, testing and isolation system prevents them from posing a major risk to economic activities. Hundreds of millions of people have been tested by the nearly 4 000 testing institutions countrywide. The coronavirus pandemic appears to have been brought under control in most of the country, but there is an unknown number of asymptomatic carriers of the virus and citizens returning from abroad also bring it back, so quarantines and hygienic measures have continued.

The sharp drop in economic activity was followed by a rapid rebound

As of early autumn, almost all activities had restarted and exceeded pre-pandemic levels in seasonally adjusted terms. Industrial production has also risen and capacity utilisation is increasing. Similarly, services have been growing, though unevenly: finance and IT services continue to perform very well, while catering and accommodation value added is shrinking. An upturn in infrastructure investment has helped growth to resume and is lifting the output of a number of midstream manufacturing industries and imports of raw materials such as iron or copper. Tourism services imports, however, have been suspended by COVID-19-related immigration measures around the world. Exports are driven not only by COVID-19-related goods, but also by goods required for teleworking, such as IT equipment and home appliances. Consumption is lagging behind as employment is slow to recover and incomes fell in urban areas in the first three quarters of the year compared with the same period a year before.

Fiscal policy continues to support growth, while monetary policy has become more neutral

Monetary policy supported the economy by lowering the costs of financing but, as the recovery gained momentum, it has turned more neutral, leaving the benchmark interest rate unchanged for over half a year. This was needed to avoid further stimulus to the already hot real estate market. Smaller banks, hit harder by the outbreak, continue to face relatively high interest rates in the interbank market. In addition to the support provided earlier in the year, such as lower reserve requirements and lower loan-loss provisioning coverage ratios, they can now use part of the special treasury bonds - introduced to support economic recovery - to replenish their capital. Shadow banking has picked up after shrinking for several years, helping private businesses obtain funding. Recent defaults of wealth management products will sharpen risk perception. Corporate debt, mainly accumulated by state-owned enterprises, jumped by 10 percentage points in the first quarter of 2020, the latest data available. Deleveraging should restart once the recovery is on a stable path.

Fiscal policy has continued to support the recovery. Special and general local bonds, as well as special treasury bonds, are financing an infrastructure investment drive, with local government investment vehicles still playing an important role. Local governments may be pushed to reduce spending on important public goods including health, education and social assistance, as the burden of COVID-19-related spending and the costs of the summer floods are high. While physical investment, in particular in certain types of infrastructure such as suburban rail, is crucial for an inclusive recovery, soft investment in education, health and social security should also be stepped up. Once the recovery is fully established, potential revenue sources to finance new social spending include a progressive income tax and a recurring tax on the ownership of real estate. In addition, increasing submission of state-owned enterprise profits and dividends to the budget could become a more important source of finance. Active involvement of local government investment vehicles in the infrastructure drive will likely push up corporate debt and, potentially, contingent liabilities at the local government level.

Growth has rebounded, but is not inclusive and unlikely to be sustainable

The return of investment as the main source of growth implies an interruption of multiple rebalancing processes that were putting the economy on a more inclusive and sustainable path prior to the outbreak. These processes include a shift from investment to consumption, from industry to services and moving people from rural to urban areas. Consumption will not recover fully without more robust employment creation, the reversal of falling urban household incomes and stronger social security. Equally, the transition to a services-based economy will not make major progress without strong consumer demand. The fastest growing services, such as finance and IT, do not create as many jobs as the shrinking ones, such as catering and accommodation. A third process, urbanisation, has also stalled as the number of new migrants fell in the first three quarters of the year. These important processes should be restarted to avoid a further build-up of imbalances in the economy.

Moratoria on debt repayment for borrowers heavily hit by the crisis will limit bankruptcies this year, though defaults on bond issues have slightly increased. Allowing more indebted, unviable state-owned enterprises and other public entities to go bankrupt would sharpen risk perception. The lowering of the loan-loss coverage ratio for small banks also increases their vulnerability to serial bankruptcies of smaller firms. Bankruptcies would spur unemployment, both in urban areas and among migrants. Continuing lockdowns in other countries could disrupt value chains, hitting China's parts and components producers and assemblers, although their reliance on imported inputs is decreasing. A faster-than-expected recovery from the virus crisis in Asian countries would boost not only exports, as these are the fastest growing markets, but also employment, as export-driven firms account for nearly a quarter of total employment. A prolonged trade conflict would likely entice further protectionist measures and take a toll on global trade and growth. The new regional trade agreement (Regional Comprehensive Economic Partnership), in contrast, will boost trade and provide better access to third markets.

More support to individuals and small firms hit by the outbreak is needed for a robust recovery

The COVID-19 crisis should be used as an opportunity to initiate reforms to reduce the out-of-pocket share of health costs and strengthen social protection to reduce precautionary saving and encourage consumer spending. Abandoning growth targets for good would help avoid incentives to pursue growth at any price and hence make growth more sustainable. Acceleration of the reform of the household registration system to grant access to public services to all would also work in that direction. Rebalancing from investment to consumption will continue only with those structural reforms. The private sector needs to be provided with a level playing field to expand investment opportunities and reverse the shrinking share of private investment. Allowing private entry to railway investment is a welcome step and should be widened to all sectors. Corporate deleveraging should restart and shadow banking should continue to be reined in once the recovery is on a stable path.

Colombia

Growth has rebounded in many sectors of the economy, with the notable exception of tourism and entertainment. Unemployment is already starting to see a moderate decline. After a fall of 8¼ per cent in 2020, GDP is projected to rise by 3½ per cent in 2021 and 3¾ per cent in 2022, helped by low interest rates and fiscal stimulus. Inflation will be contained, owing to substantial spare capacity.

Macroeconomic policies have responded to the crisis in a bold and timely manner. Additional healthcare spending, income support to households, wage subsidies and extended credit lines have been facilitated by a temporary suspension of the fiscal rule. Public debt will rise substantially, but will remain manageable under the authorities' plans, which include higher revenues and spending cuts from 2022. Monetary authorities have provided ample liquidity, with interest rates reduced to record lows. Fostering formal employment through lower payroll taxes will be key to raise productivity and make growth more inclusive.

COVID-19 has hit Colombia hard, but signs of recovery are emerging

Colombia has been hit hard by the pandemic. New infections and COVID-19-related deaths peaked in July and August, and have since stabilised at a high level. A nationwide lockdown lasted from late March to early September, and was subsequently replaced by targeted and selective measures. Strong efforts to increase intensive care capacity have alleviated the severe strains on the health system and allocated additional resources to the health sector.

Colombia

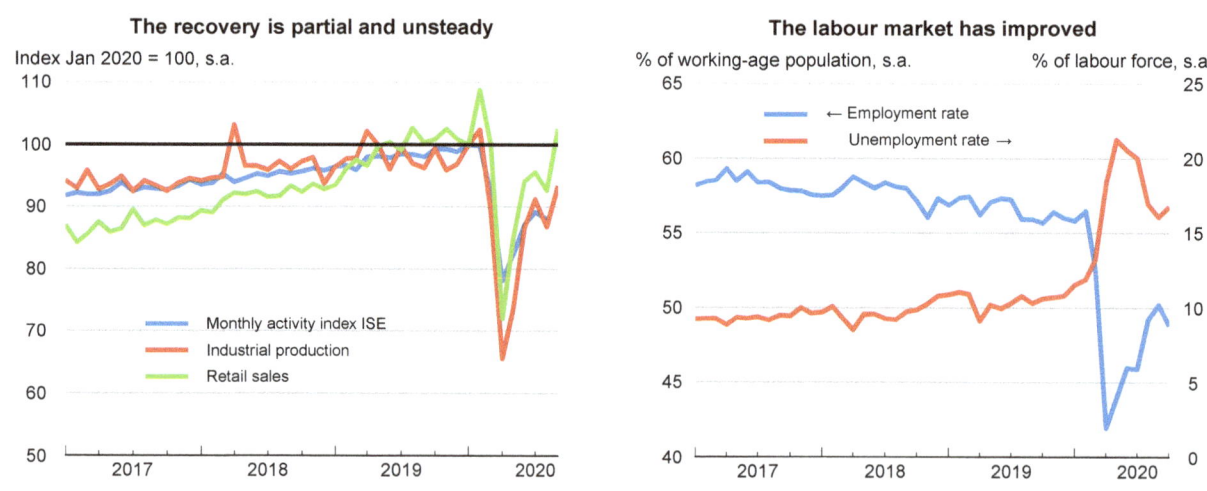

Source: Refinitiv; OECD Main Economic Indicators database; DANE (Colombia); and Banco de la República (Colombia).

StatLink ᴍᴧˢᴾ https://doi.org/10.1787/888934218159

Colombia: Demand, output and prices

Colombia	2017	2018	2019	2020	2021	2022
	Current prices COP trillion	Percentage changes, volume (2015 prices)				
GDP at market prices	920.5	2.5	3.3	-8.3	3.5	3.7
Private consumption	630.6	3.0	4.5	-7.6	3.1	4.0
Government consumption	137.0	7.0	4.3	2.7	3.8	1.1
Gross fixed capital formation	200.0	1.5	4.3	-18.6	7.9	6.0
Final domestic demand	967.6	3.3	4.4	-8.4	4.1	3.9
Stockbuilding[1]	- 1.1	0.1	-0.1	-0.1	0.3	0.0
Total domestic demand	966.4	3.4	4.3	-8.5	5.1	3.9
Exports of goods and services	139.4	0.9	2.6	-18.9	0.1	5.6
Imports of goods and services	185.4	5.8	8.1	-17.5	7.4	5.8
Net exports[1]	- 46.0	-1.0	-1.3	0.9	-1.5	-0.5
Memorandum items						
GDP deflator	_	4.5	4.3	1.3	3.0	3.1
Consumer price index	_	3.2	3.5	2.5	2.4	3.0
Core inflation index[2]	_	3.9	3.3	2.0	2.3	3.0
Unemployment rate (% of labour force)	_	9.7	10.5	16.1	14.8	13.0
Current account balance (% of GDP)	_	-4.0	-4.2	-3.9	-3.9	-3.7

1. Contributions to changes in real GDP, actual amount in the first column.
2. Consumer price index excluding primary food, utilities and fuels.
Source: OECD Economic Outlook 108 database.

StatLink ⫘⫘ https://doi.org/10.1787/888934218178

The relaxation of containment measures has given rise to a gradual recovery

Exacerbated by a large share of informal jobs and small businesses, the lockdown, and lower oil prices, took a strong toll on economic activity in the second quarter of 2020. Since late May, a limited relaxation of the lockdown has allowed a rebound in some sectors, as evidenced by increases in activity, retail sales and industrial output. Consumer and business confidence measures have also improved. Sectors that continue to be subdued include entertainment, recreation, retail, transport and accommodation. Despite incipient declines in the unemployment rate, employment remains more than 10% below its January level. Inflation continues to be well below target.

A strong and timely macroeconomic policy response supported the economy

A strong macroeconomic policy response has cushioned the decline in domestic demand and is helping to contain long-term scars from the pandemic. The government provided additional healthcare spending, cash transfers to poor families through existing programmes, a new programme to support informal workers and families not previously covered, payroll subsidies for affected firms and extended credit lines, particularly for small firms. This additional spending of around 3% of GDP was made possible through a temporary suspension of the fiscal rule for 2020 and 2021, and significant fiscal policy support will continue in 2021. Public debt will rise by almost 15 percentage points to above 60% of GDP by 2022. The monetary authorities cut rates by 250 basis points and provided substantial extra liquidity in domestic and foreign currencies, which helped to protect payment systems and stabilise stressed foreign exchange and asset markets.

Growth will recover to almost 4% in 2021 and 2022

With substantial contractions in domestic and external demand, output is projected to decline by around 8¼ per cent in 2020. A significant public investment programme, including in infrastructure and publicly-supported housing, will promote the recovery in 2021, when GDP is projected to grow by 3½ per cent. Private consumption will recover only slowly at first, especially in services. A weak external environment will not provide much support in 2021 and 2022. A renewed rise in infection rates, or delays in the availability of a vaccine, could require further restrictions, causing activity to decline again. Failure to implement planned revenue measures and raise public spending efficiency, including through better targeting of public subsidies and the elimination of numerous tax exemptions, could jeopardise future compliance with the fiscal rule and make debt sustainability more challenging. On the external side, Colombia remains vulnerable to adverse developments in already low commodity prices, especially oil. On the upside, better global prospects would allow a faster return to pre-pandemic output levels.

Policy support should continue, while social protection can be improved

Fiscal and monetary policies should continue to provide ample support to the economy in 2021. A solid institutional framework and a fairly comfortable starting position in 2019 can keep fiscal risks under control despite higher public debt, provided that fiscal policy returns to compliance with the fiscal rule once the recovery is firming. Monetary policy can equally remain highly accommodative until 2022, as subdued domestic demand and a weak labour market make an earlier resurgence of inflationary pressures unlikely. Expanding social protection by building on existing well-targeted cash transfer programmes can help to contain the long-term social impact of the pandemic at manageable cost. Improved incentives are needed to promote formal job creation, including through lower payroll taxes and lower costs of registering firms. Fewer trade barriers and stronger competition could support necessary reallocation processes. This would make the economy more resilient and promote productivity and equality, especially when combined with well-designed professional training programmes.

Costa Rica

Costa Rica experienced a surge of infection cases in the second half of 2020, which delayed the easing of confinement measures. After a deep recession this year, GDP is projected to recover gradually in 2021 (by 2%) and gain momentum in 2022 (by 3.8%). As confinement measures are progressively lifted, domestic demand will recover, but remain subdued due to high unemployment. Uncertainty related to high public debt will weigh on investment. The rebound of the US economy will help exports recover, particularly of medical supply and business services.

In reaction to the pandemic, the authorities have appropriately increased health and social protection spending, after having suspended the fiscal rule. However, once the recovery is underway, putting public debt on a declining and sustainable path is key for macroeconomic stability, and hence fiscal prudence and the fiscal rule should be reinstated at that stage. Ensuring that social spending primarily reaches those who need it the most would support incomes, reduce poverty and raise spending efficiency. Reducing regressive tax exemptions could help to increase revenues. Lowering the administrative burden for starting and formalising businesses would raise investment and formal job creation.

Daily infection cases have started to decline from high levels

Confinement measures prevented the spread of the virus from March until June. In late June, daily infection cases started to rise rapidly, leading to a prolongation of confinement, and a tightening in strongly affected regions. However, since September, many services with client interactions have been allowed to reopen with up to 50% of their capacity, and only a minor share of activities remains closed. International travel restrictions have been relaxed, but limited restrictions on domestic vehicle traffic and social distancing measures remain in place. Since early November, daily infection cases and COVID-19-related deaths have started to decline.

Costa Rica

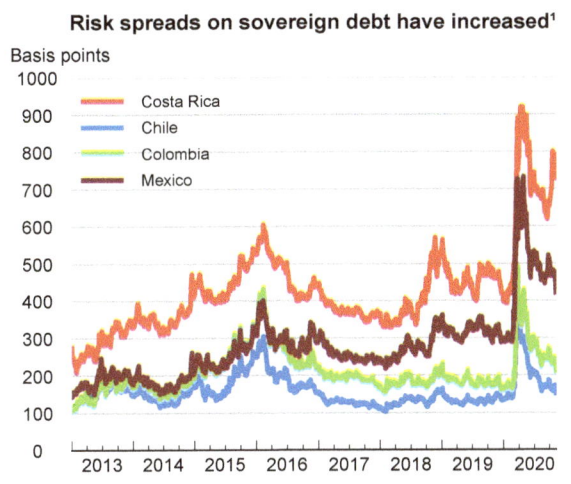

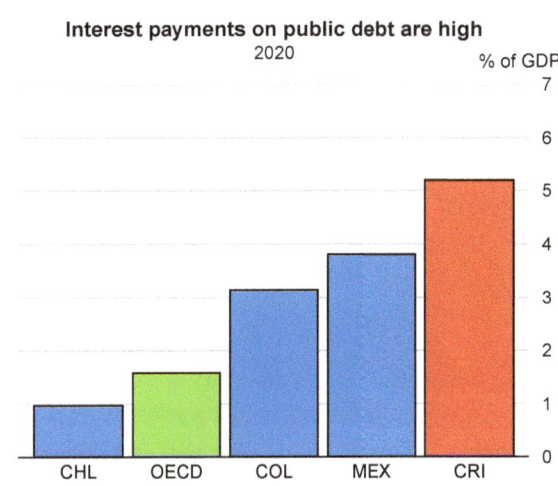

1. Risk spreads refer to the yield difference of sovereign bonds compared to U.S. treasury bonds.
Source: Refinitiv; Ministerio de Hacienda; and IMF World Economic Outlook.

StatLink https://doi.org/10.1787/888934218197

Costa Rica: Demand, output and prices

Costa Rica	2017	2018	2019	2020	2021	2022
	Current prices CRC trillion	Percentage changes, volume (2012 prices)				
GDP at market prices	33.2	2.7	2.1	-5.6	2.0	3.8
Private consumption	21.2	2.0	1.8	-6.8	1.8	4.4
Government consumption	5.7	0.5	4.9	1.7	1.2	-0.8
Gross fixed capital formation	5.7	3.0	-8.1	-5.1	0.2	3.9
Final domestic demand	32.6	1.9	0.5	-5.0	1.4	3.3
Stockbuilding[1]	0.7	-0.7	0.8	1.2	-0.1	0.0
Total domestic demand	33.3	1.1	1.1	-4.1	1.5	3.4
Exports of goods and services	10.9	4.7	2.7	-14.3	4.1	8.8
Imports of goods and services	11.0	0.1	-0.1	-10.0	2.4	7.1
Net exports[1]	- 0.1	1.6	1.0	-1.4	0.5	0.4
Memorandum items						
GDP deflator	_	2.5	1.8	0.6	1.3	1.7
Consumer price index	_	2.2	2.1	0.7	1.5	2.0
Core inflation index[2]	_	2.1	2.4	1.2	1.6	2.0
Unemployment rate (% of labour force)	_	10.3	11.8	19.9	19.3	14.6
Current account balance (% of GDP)	_	-3.3	-2.2	-2.6	-2.6	-2.7

1. Contributions to changes in real GDP, actual amount in the first column.
2. Consumer price index excluding food and energy.
Source: OECD Economic Outlook 108 database.

StatLink ▒▒▒ https://doi.org/10.1787/888934218216

A gradual recovery is underway

After a strong drop in economic activity in the second quarter of 2020, the spread of the virus and the prolongation of confinement measures have postponed the recovery. High unemployment is weighing on household incomes and private consumption. Confinement measures and lower demand have particularly affected labour-intensive services sectors, such as hotels and restaurants, retail, transport services, domestic services and construction. Recent episodes of road blockades around port areas temporarily disrupted economic activity further. However, activity in free trade zones has bounced back, driven by strong export demand for medical supplies and IT and business services from the United States. Employment is starting to recover, and the unemployment rate has fallen slightly from a historical high of 24.4% in July to 23.2% in August. Due to sovereign financing needs of 15.7% of GDP in 2021 and high uncertainty about the fiscal strategy, risks of near-term financing stress have increased. Sovereign bond spreads have recently picked up further, weighing on business confidence and investment. The authorities have initiated consultations with the IMF on a three-year financing assistance programme.

Social spending has helped to protect those most in need

The authorities have appropriately increased health and social protection spending to mitigate the adverse effects of the pandemic. A direct cash transfer programme supports individuals who lost their job or face reduced working hours, including informal and self-employed workers. A loan programme provides working capital finance for firms. Payments of value added, income and tourism taxes, customs duties and social security contributions have been deferred towards the end of the year. The central bank has reduced the policy rate to 0.75% and created additional loan facilities to support firms and households. The temporary reduction of countercyclical buffer provisions for banks has created space for the reprofiling of credit repayments of distressed borrowers.

The recovery will be partial and gradual

GDP is projected to grow by 2% in 2021 and 3.8% in 2022. Exports will continue to lead the recovery, driven by rising demand from the United States. The gradual easing of confinement measures supports strongly affected services sectors. Private consumption will slowly improve, but high unemployment continues to weigh on household incomes. The economic contraction has led to a significant loss of government revenues, exacerbating an already vulnerable fiscal situation. The fiscal deficit is set to widen to around 9½ per cent of GDP in 2020, and the ratio of central government debt to GDP will rise to around 80% over the coming years. Investment and confidence will remain subdued until fiscal uncertainty dissipates. Downside risks relate to political gridlock leading to a failure to pursue needed fiscal reforms. Severe new COVID-19 outbreaks may require retightening of confinement measures on a regional basis. Upside risks relate to a stronger recovery in the United States and increasing export demand.

Pursuing structural reforms is key for the recovery

Buttressing the health system and targeting fiscal support to those hit hardest by the recession should continue to be the short-term priority. Eliminating regressive tax exemptions and improving public spending efficiency, including through a public employment reform, could provide more fiscal space and set the basis for a medium-term fiscal strategy that puts public debt on a sustainable path. Continuing the implementation of structural reforms, such as those aimed at strengthening domestic competition, is key to support formal job creation. A comprehensive strategy to reduce informality, including by lowering social security contributions for low-wage workers, and constructing a social safety net for all workers, combined with improvements in the quality of education and training, would make growth more inclusive. Continuing to develop country-wide tracking and testing capabilities would help to reduce risks of new virus outbreaks.

Czech Republic

GDP is estimated to contract by 6.8% in 2020, and projected to recover slowly, by 1.5%, in 2021. The economy has been hit hard by lockdown measures and a drop in trade. Additional containment measures, high uncertainty and weak sentiment amid the second outbreak will delay economic recovery until an effective vaccine is widely deployed towards the end of 2021. Fiscal support will help maintain household consumption, but investment will take longer to rebound. The unemployment rate will rise from low levels and inflation will slow.

The authorities reacted swiftly to the pandemic, supporting incomes, employment and liquidity. This supportive stance should be maintained. The central bank can further ease monetary policy in case of persistent weakness, beyond the conventional measures already implemented at the beginning of the crisis. Gradual fiscal consolidation is planned following a supportive budget for 2021. Care should be taken not to tighten fiscal policy too soon. Active labour market policies should be boosted to facilitate labour reallocation.

The Czech Republic is experiencing a strong second wave

The number of cases as well as the number of deaths have risen steeply after the summer, well beyond the numbers in the first wave. A state of emergency has been declared, and a national lockdown reintroduced in October. The government also increased restrictions on certain activities, banning events and gatherings, closing education establishments and severely limiting activity in the hospitality and retail sectors.

Czech Republic

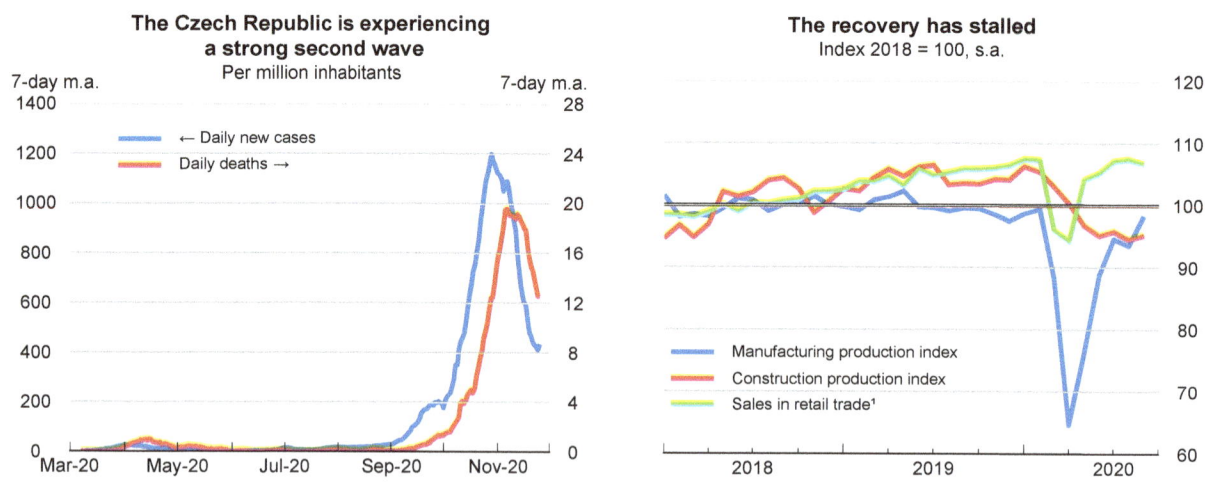

1. Sales in retail trade, except of motor vehicles, constant prices.
Source: European Centre for Disease Prevention and Control (ECDC); Czech Statistical Office; and OECD calculations.

StatLink 🛒 https://doi.org/10.1787/888934218235

Czech Republic: Demand, output and prices

Czech Republic	2017	2018	2019	2020	2021	2022
	Current prices CZK billion	Percentage changes, volume (2015 prices)				
GDP at market prices	5 117.4	3.2	2.3	-6.8	1.5	3.3
Private consumption	2 422.0	3.5	3.0	-4.0	1.1	2.2
Government consumption	958.7	3.8	2.3	2.9	1.9	0.7
Gross fixed capital formation	1 275.7	10.0	2.1	-6.6	-1.6	9.1
Final domestic demand	4 656.4	5.3	2.6	-3.4	0.6	3.6
Stockbuilding[1]	73.1	-0.5	-0.2	-1.6	-0.6	0.0
Total domestic demand	4 729.5	4.7	2.4	-4.9	0.0	3.7
Exports of goods and services	4 048.4	3.7	1.2	-12.9	8.1	4.7
Imports of goods and services	3 660.5	5.8	1.3	-10.9	6.2	5.5
Net exports[1]	387.9	-1.2	0.0	-2.2	1.5	-0.2
Memorandum items						
GDP deflator	–	2.6	3.9	3.7	1.7	1.8
Consumer price index	–	2.1	2.8	3.3	2.2	2.0
Core inflation index[2]	–	2.4	2.5	3.6	2.5	2.0
Unemployment rate (% of labour force)	–	2.2	2.0	2.6	3.6	3.6
Household saving ratio, net (% of disposable income)	–	7.4	7.6	8.1	5.6	4.5
General government financial balance (% of GDP)	–	0.9	0.3	-7.7	-4.8	-3.6
General government gross debt (% of GDP)	–	39.7	37.7	45.7	50.0	52.7
General government debt, Maastricht definition (% of GDP)	–	32.0	30.2	38.2	42.6	45.2
Current account balance (% of GDP)	–	0.4	-0.3	2.0	2.5	0.6

1. Contributions to changes in real GDP, actual amount in the first column.
2. Consumer price index excluding food and energy.
Source: OECD Economic Outlook 108 database.

StatLink https://doi.org/10.1787/888934218254

The recovery has stalled amid elevated uncertainty and renewed restrictions

Activity picked up soon after the sharp contraction in the first half of 2020. Manufacturing production, retail sales and tourism bounced back, but at the end of the summer the recovery stalled amid the resurgence of the pandemic. The Prague stock exchange PX index and the koruna exchange rate lost value from August to October, after the summer gains. The unemployment rate started to rise from low levels, and wage growth eased markedly. Inflation on the other hand has remained above the upper boundary of the tolerance band (1-3%) for most of the year. While greater slack and lower oil prices have had a dampening effect, the koruna depreciation and rising food and administered prices put upward pressure on prices.

The authorities have appropriately eased policies to support the economy

To help the economy during the crisis, the government introduced job retention schemes, benefit payments to the self-employed, income support to workers caring for children and tax deferrals. Moreover, a COVID-19 loan and guarantee programme has been launched to boost firm liquidity, and deferrals of rent and loan repayments have been offered. Some of these programmes are now being extended due to the renewed outbreak. The government has submitted to parliament a supportive budget for 2021, with large spending increases on healthcare and investment to promote the recovery. Monetary policy also moved quickly to accommodate the drop in activity and support liquidity by cutting policy rates (from 2.25% to 0.25%) and by lowering the countercyclical capital buffer (from 1.75% to 0.5%). The central bank also broadened the scope of its liquidity-providing operations.

The recovery will be slow

The continuation of the pandemic, containment restrictions, and low foreign demand will delay and weaken the economic recovery. Assuming a six-week lockdown in the fourth quarter of 2020 and some continuing restrictions in the first half of 2021 on activities requiring close proximity, GDP is projected to grow by 1.5% in 2021 and 3.3% in 2022 after a vaccine becomes deployed in the latter half of 2021. High uncertainty will dampen private consumption and business investment. Firm bankruptcies are expected to rise in 2021 due to prolonged economic weakness and a gradual withdrawal of some support measures. The unemployment rate is expected to continue rising in the first half of 2021. Thereafter, once the pandemic is better controlled globally and locally, economic growth will gather pace on the back of rising trade and domestic demand.

Uncertainty regarding the projections remains high. In case of a prolonged lockdown, private consumption, investment and trade will drop again to low levels. Protracted adversity would significantly increase bankruptcies, and the unemployment rate would surge. The highly open Czech economy is exposed to disruptions in international trade or new trade barriers. On the upside, the current substantial government support could have a stronger positive impact on the economy.

The supportive policy stance remains warranted

The central bank has limited room for further monetary easing using conventional measures. However, in case of prolonged economic weakness, it could consider further reducing interest rates, undertaking asset purchases and longer-term financing operations. According to a new medium-term fiscal framework, the government plans a gradual fiscal consolidation starting in 2022. However, enough flexibility should be preserved to avoid tightening fiscal policy too strongly too soon. Active labour market policies and reskilling programmes should be boosted and insolvency procedures accelerated to facilitate resource reallocation from declining to growing sectors.

Denmark

The economy is projected to contract by around 4% in 2020, followed by a gradual recovery of nearly 2% in 2021 and 2½ per cent in 2022. Domestic demand is underpinned by a strong rebound in consumption and employment, following a smaller initial hit from the COVID-19 containment measures than elsewhere. Nevertheless, tightened restrictions during autumn and the weak external environment will hold back the recovery.

Targeted fiscal measures remain in place to support firms and workers facing restrictions. A welcome withdrawal of broad support schemes combined with strong institutions for re-skilling should push and pull the reallocation of resources forward. The release of special mandatory holiday savings to households and elevated public investment will provide ample stimulus to domestic demand. Further advancement on structural reforms, notably the envisaged greener tax mix, could serve both short and long-term goals with well-designed implementation.

Controlling new virus outbreaks has proven difficult

The pandemic has so far remained milder than in most OECD countries. Patient hospitalisations have stayed well below capacity limits and total mortality rates have not exceeded levels in previous years. Nonetheless, Denmark has experienced a resurgence of COVID-19 cases since late summer and the government has therefore gradually tightened containment measures. In November, public gatherings were limited to 10 people, mask-wearing became mandatory in all indoor public places, and restaurants and bars had to close at 10 p.m. Teleworking and limiting the number of social contacts have been encouraged. Rapid spreading of coronavirus in mink farms and fear of mutations led to culling of all minks in the country and a partial lockdown of seven north-western municipalities in November.

Denmark

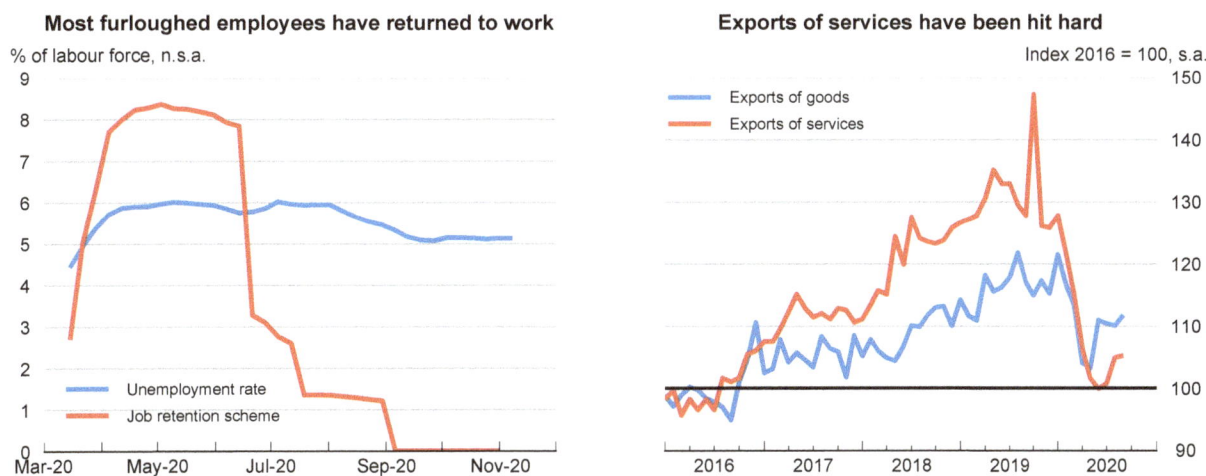

Source: Danish Business Authority; Danish Agency for Labour Market and Recruitment; and Statistics Denmark.

StatLink https://doi.org/10.1787/888934218273

Denmark: Demand, output and prices

Denmark	2017	2018	2019	2020	2021	2022
	Current prices DKK billion	Percentage changes, volume (2010 prices)				
GDP at market prices	2 192.9	2.2	2.8	-3.9	1.8	2.5
Private consumption	1 016.6	2.7	1.4	-4.3	3.4	2.5
Government consumption	535.4	0.3	1.2	1.4	1.5	0.7
Gross fixed capital formation	465.5	4.8	2.8	-0.3	0.0	2.5
Final domestic demand	2 017.5	2.6	1.7	-1.8	2.0	2.0
Stockbuilding[1]	18.1	0.3	-0.3	0.2	0.0	0.0
Total domestic demand	2 035.6	2.9	1.4	-1.5	2.0	2.0
Exports of goods and services	1 207.8	3.2	5.0	-11.5	3.8	5.2
Imports of goods and services	1 050.5	4.8	2.4	-8.9	4.4	4.5
Net exports[1]	157.3	-0.5	1.6	-2.1	-0.1	0.7
Memorandum items						
GDP deflator	_	0.6	0.7	1.2	0.4	0.8
Consumer price index	_	0.8	0.8	0.4	0.7	0.9
Core inflation index[2]	_	0.6	0.8	0.9	0.7	0.9
Unemployment rate (% of labour force)	_	5.1	5.0	5.7	6.2	5.7
Household saving ratio, net (% of disposable income)	_	6.2	3.7	7.7	6.7	5.9
General government financial balance (% of GDP)	_	0.7	3.8	-3.9	-2.9	-1.8
General government gross debt (% of GDP)	_	51.0	51.7	62.5	58.5	59.2
General government debt, Maastricht definition (% of GDP)	_	34.0	33.3	44.1	40.1	40.9
Current account balance (% of GDP)	_	7.0	8.9	7.6	6.8	7.1

1. Contributions to changes in real GDP, actual amount in the first column.
2. Consumer price index excluding food and energy.
Source: OECD Economic Outlook 108 database.

StatLink https://doi.org/10.1707/888934210000

The economy initially rebounded quickly but the recovery has now slowed

Most economic sectors had reopened by early summer after a comparatively soft shutdown. Mobility data and consumption covered by credit card transactions had returned to the levels in 2019 by June. International travel restrictions gave a boost to domestic tourism, and the housing market rebounded strongly with prices and sales exceeding pre-pandemic levels. Consumer price inflation has picked up in recent months, driven by an increase in tobacco duty rates. Half of the 3% drop in dependent employment during spring had been restored by August. Since then, the recovery has slowed according to daily unemployment figures. Weak external demand is also holding back the recovery, notably in services exports, while a high share of pharmaceuticals and food products partly cushions goods exports.

Large stimulus measures and targeted support will continue

Fiscal policy reacted strongly and next year's budget envisages further stimulus of about 1% of GDP. The government has successfully replaced broad and large-scale subsidy schemes created during the shutdown by targeted measures. The job retention scheme, protecting more than 8% of workers at the peak, was rolled back by the end of August to cover only firms forced to close. Suspension of local governments' expenditure ceilings in 2020 and energy renovation of social housing will stimulate demand through 2022. The government boosted household gross incomes by up to 2.6% of GDP in October by releasing special mandatory pension savings from a recent reform of employees' holiday payment schemes. Income taxation of the freed funds improves the public budget in 2020 by almost 1% of GDP.

A prolonged and fragile recovery is projected

The resurgence of the COVID-19 pandemic makes the near-term outlook particularly uncertain. The economy is set to recover gradually as authorities need to tackle local virus outbreaks until a vaccine becomes generally available in the latter part of 2021, leaving economic activity below its pre-pandemic level until mid-2022. The job retention scheme has protected household incomes, which along with freed holiday savings and high wealth will bolster private consumption. High uncertainty will keep business investment subdued through 2021, although the high content of R&D in medical and green technologies is shielding the setback. The speed of recovery depends critically on international trade coming back, not least since Denmark's exports increasingly reflect trade of goods produced and sold abroad by Danish multinationals without crossing Danish borders. The United Kingdom is a key trading partner and a hard Brexit without a trade agreement with the European Union is a large downside risk to the projections. On the upside, better tracking and effective use of the enormous test capacity (more than 1% of the population per day in November) could accelerate the recovery by removing the need for many costly containment measures.

Structural reforms should continue

Firms and workers would benefit from clear guidance on likely containment measures and compensation schemes to plan for an uncertain future. Liquidity support, loan guarantees and targeted subsidies should be the main measures to get through the pandemic. In case of renewed shutdown needs, the short-time work scheme agreed with the social partners in August will provide backing with fewer distortionary costs than the job retention scheme being phased-out. Through 2020, the government has maintained its structural reform agenda, notably on climate change. This should continue and would help to facilitate the needed reallocation of resources from some services losing demand towards expanding sectors, such as environment protection activities.

Estonia

With a milder contraction than initially feared, GDP is set to fall by 4.7% in 2020, before rebounding by 3.4% in 2021 and 3.3% in 2022. Consumption is expected to strengthen as households regain confidence and draw down large savings set aside at the peak of the pandemic. Investment will also regain momentum on the back of improved expectations for industrial production, exports and the services sector. Inflation will remain subdued in 2021 before stabilising somewhat above 2%.

The various employment support measures put in place have helped to cushion the hit to the labour market, but unemployment is expected to remain well above its pre-crisis level in the next two years. As a result, the large group of low-skilled workers recently integrated in the labour market may have difficulties finding new jobs. Interventions should be maintained as long as unemployment remains high, while training and active labour market policies should be strengthened to avoid losing the social benefits of reforms made in recent years.

Efforts have been made to bring the epidemic under control

Estonia has managed to slow the spread of the virus throughout its territory, avoiding so far a resurgence. The infection rate remains the second lowest in Europe, and on average fewer than 10 patients have been in intensive care since the end of September. As a result, domestic confinement measures have been fully relaxed. However, international travel restrictions remain in place, with mandatory quarantine for all travellers upon arrival on Estonian soil with exception of those coming from the Baltic States and Finland, for which less strict rules apply.

Estonia

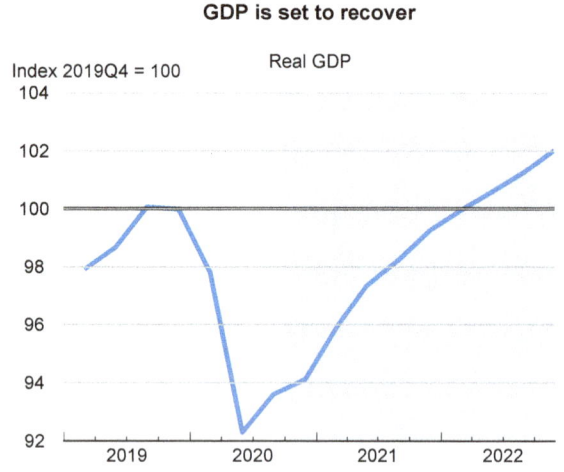

GDP is set to recover

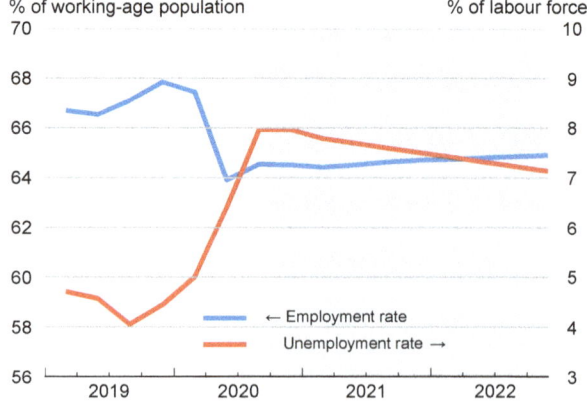

Unemployment and employment rates will not return to their pre-crisis levels

Source: OECD Economic Outlook 108 database.

StatLink https://doi.org/10.1787/888934218311

Estonia: Demand, output and prices

Estonia	2017	2018	2019	2020	2021	2022
	Current prices EUR billion	Percentage changes, volume (2015 prices)				
GDP at market prices	23.8	4.4	4.9	-4.7	3.4	3.3
Private consumption	12.0	4.6	3.4	-5.5	1.2	2.8
Government consumption	4.7	0.6	3.1	2.4	2.7	1.3
Gross fixed capital formation	6.0	3.3	11.1	-9.5	3.6	5.5
Final domestic demand	22.7	3.7	5.4	-5.0	2.1	3.1
Stockbuilding[1]	0.2	0.5	-0.3	-1.7	-0.3	0.0
Total domestic demand	22.9	4.0	4.9	-6.7	1.9	3.1
Exports of goods and services	18.1	4.0	6.2	-10.3	6.2	5.1
Imports of goods and services	17.1	5.6	3.8	-12.7	5.1	5.9
Net exports[1]	1.0	-1.0	1.9	1.2	1.1	-0.1
Memorandum items						
GDP deflator	_	4.2	3.4	-1.2	1.3	1.5
Harmonised index of consumer prices	_	3.4	2.3	-0.7	1.3	2.1
Harmonised index of core inflation[2]	_	1.7	2.4	-0.1	0.8	1.9
Unemployment rate (% of labour force)	_	5.4	4.4	6.8	7.6	7.3
Household saving ratio, net (% of disposable income)	_	6.2	9.6	17.2	17.8	16.2
General government financial balance (% of GDP)	_	-0.5	0.1	-7.3	-6.5	-4.0
General government gross debt (% of GDP)	_	13.0	13.4	23.8	29.5	33.9
General government debt, Maastricht definition (% of GDP)	_	8.2	8.4	18.8	24.5	28.9
Current account balance (% of GDP)	_	0.8	1.9	5.7	7.5	7.1

1. Contributions to changes in real GDP, actual amount in the first column.
2. Harmonised index of consumer prices excluding food, energy, alcohol and tobacco.
Source: OECD Economic Outlook 108 database.

StatLink ᵐˢ🔗 https://doi.org/10.1787/888934218330

Activity has rebounded quickly

The decline in activity in the second quarter of 2020 was less sharp than expected, not least due to containment measures being less strict than elsewhere and an early control of the COVID-19 outbreak. Retail trade rebounded quickly and in June was already 7.3% higher than a year earlier. Manufacturing, which did not have time to recover from a pre-crisis slump in external demand, suffered the largest hit but was well on its way to recovery after the summer. The tourism sector has been particularly impacted, with 78% fewer overnight tourists compared with last summer, although hospitality services account for a small share of the economy. High-frequency indicators signal that consumption has not yet fully recovered, with card spending and cash withdrawal frequencies remaining five percentage points below last year's level in the third quarter.

Large and effective economic support has now stopped

The pandemic-related fiscal stimulus, containing state guarantees, loans, income support and tax measures, has been large, at 4.1% of GDP. In particular, the job retention scheme, with its generous eligibility conditions, has helped to contain the effect of the pandemic on the labour market. However, given the sanitary situation and the absence of strict confinement measures, temporary support has ended and there is no discussion at the moment about further action.

A gradual recovery is projected

Like other Baltic and Nordic countries, Estonia has suffered a milder contraction than the rest of the euro area. With a strong rebound expected in 2021, Estonia should return to its pre-crisis GDP level at the beginning of 2022. Consumption is expected to strengthen as households regain confidence and draw down large savings set aside at the peak of the pandemic. Expectations for industrial production, exports and the services sector have improved, suggesting a continued recovery in 2021. Investment should also strengthen, as foreign demand improves.

Estonia entered the pandemic with the lowest public debt ratio in the OECD, and the fiscal exemption clause has been used to support the economy. Reflecting these fiscal measures, the budget deficit will decline only moderately during the projection period, as the gradual recovery will not bring tax receipts back to pre-crisis levels in the coming two years. However, with recent institutional reforms and a proven track record of credible fiscal management, the public debt trajectory remains sustainable, provided growth returns to its potential and interest rates remain low. Apart from a resurgence of the pandemic, a persistently high level of unemployment weighing on private consumption is a key risk to growth.

Additional policy measures are needed to strengthen the recovery

Given the integration in the labour market of many low-skilled workers in recent years, the crisis could leave permanent scars on vulnerable groups and unwind the social benefits of past reforms, as unemployment is set to remain well above pre-crisis levels until 2022. The job retention scheme should be extended as long as unemployment remains high, and active and passive support rapidly provided to job seekers, in contrast to past practices in Estonia. This support should be targeted to those weakly attached to the labour market and therefore at risk of remaining unemployed in the long term. Improving unemployment insurance coverage could also give the unemployed better access to training and stronger incentives to participate. The crisis has also amplified the relevance of digital skills and there is an opportunity for Estonia, a front-runner in digital technologies but with a quarter of adults lacking basic computer skills, to upskill and reskill parts of the population by increasing adult education and training. This would allow low-skilled and displaced workers to strengthen their links with the labour market while allowing firms to reap further productivity benefits from digitalisation. At the same time, some of the EU funds should be directed towards digitalisation, in particular its diffusion across firms, to strengthen growth potential.

Euro area

After a projected GDP decline of 7½ per cent in 2020, growth of 3½ and 3¼ per cent in 2021 and 2022, respectively, will bring output back to its pre-pandemic level only at the end of 2022. Persistent virus outbreaks and accompanying containment measures will continue to hamper activity until a vaccine is widely implemented. Private consumption and investment will be affected the most by pervasive uncertainty and low confidence. Unemployment is projected to rise until mid-2021, approaching double-digit rates, and fall only gradually afterwards. Fiscal support and subdued activity will keep Maastricht public debt above 100% of GDP. Failure to promote reallocation from declining activities towards those likely to expand would durably worsen growth prospects.

With inflation set to remain well below the ECB objective by end-2022, monetary policy should ensure that borrowing costs for the public and private sectors remain durably very low while the pandemic-induced crisis lasts. To avoid a premature tightening that could derail the recovery, national fiscal policies should also remain supportive over the coming two years, taking advantage of very low interest rates and sizeable financing under the EU recovery plan. However, as the pandemic will likely have a durable negative impact on some sectors, the composition of fiscal measures needs to shift from an emphasis on income support to the promotion of labour and capital reallocation. At the EU level, steps to reduce financial fragmentation are also key for improving resilience, *inter alia* through greater cross-border lending. Efficient vaccine distribution and further development of testing and tracing capabilities are needed to minimise the impact of future virus outbreaks.

Euro area 1

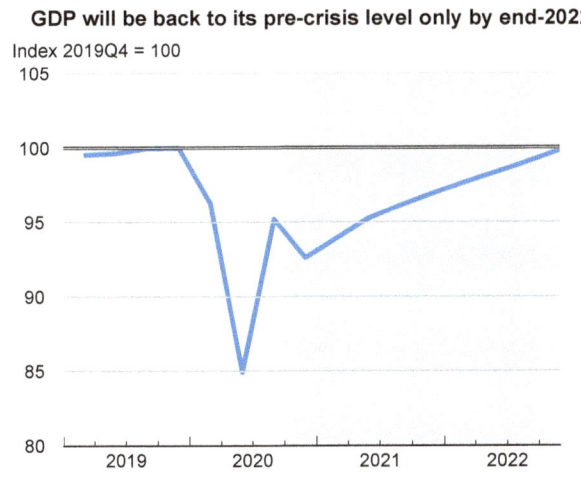

GDP will be back to its pre-crisis level only by end-2022

Index 2019Q4 = 100

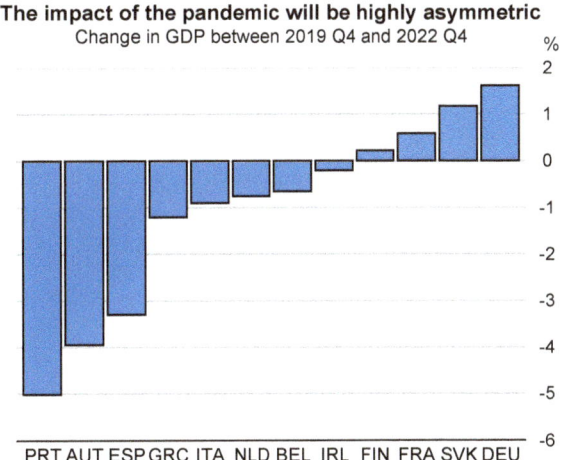

The impact of the pandemic will be highly asymmetric

Change in GDP between 2019 Q4 and 2022 Q4

Source: OECD Economic Outlook 108 database.

StatLink 🔢 https://doi.org/10.1787/888934218349

Euro area: Demand, output and prices

Euro area	2017	2018	2019	2020	2021	2022
	Current prices EUR billion	Percentage changes, volume (2015 prices)				
GDP at market prices	11 190.4	1.9	1.3	-7.5	3.6	3.3
Private consumption	6 024.9	1.5	1.3	-8.3	4.4	3.5
Government consumption	2 296.7	1.2	1.8	1.8	2.7	0.4
Gross fixed capital formation	2 305.3	3.2	5.8	-10.7	2.1	4.8
Final domestic demand	10 626.9	1.8	2.4	-6.7	3.5	3.1
Stockbuilding[1]	78.8	0.1	-0.5	-0.2	-0.3	0.0
Total domestic demand	10 705.7	1.9	1.9	-6.9	3.2	3.1
Net exports[1]	484.7	0.1	-0.5	-0.8	0.6	0.3
Memorandum items						
GDP deflator	_	1.4	1.7	1.6	0.9	1.0
Harmonised index of consumer prices	_	1.8	1.2	0.3	0.7	1.0
Harmonised index of core inflation[2]	_	1.0	1.0	0.7	0.7	0.9
Unemployment rate (% of labour force)	_	8.2	7.5	8.1	9.5	9.1
Household saving ratio, net (% of disposable income)	_	6.4	6.7	14.3	11.4	9.2
General government financial balance (% of GDP)	_	-0.5	-0.6	-8.6	-6.5	-4.1
General government gross debt (% of GDP)	_	102.5	103.6	119.4	122.2	122.9
General government debt, Maastricht definition (% of GDP)	_	87.7	85.9	101.8	104.5	105.1
Current account balance (% of GDP)	_	3.5	3.1	3.0	3.4	3.5

Note: Aggregation based on euro area countries that are members of the OECD, and on seasonally-adjusted and calendar-days-adjusted basis.

1. Contributions to changes in real GDP, actual amount in the first column.
2. Harmonised index of consumer prices excluding food, energy, alcohol and tobacco.
Source: OECD Economic Outlook 108 database.

StatLink https://doi.org/10.1787/888934218368

Euro area 2

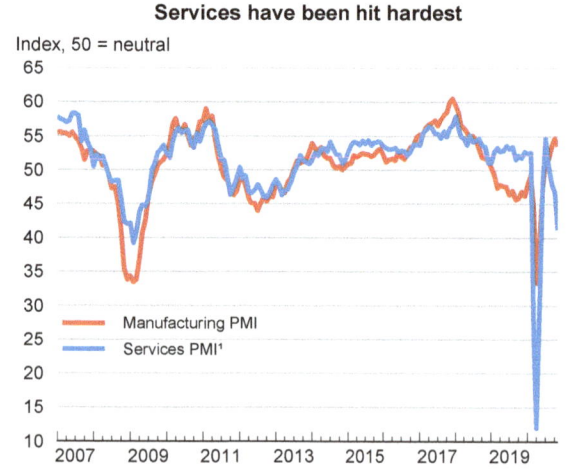

Services have been hit hardest

Index, 50 = neutral

- Manufacturing PMI
- Services PMI[1]

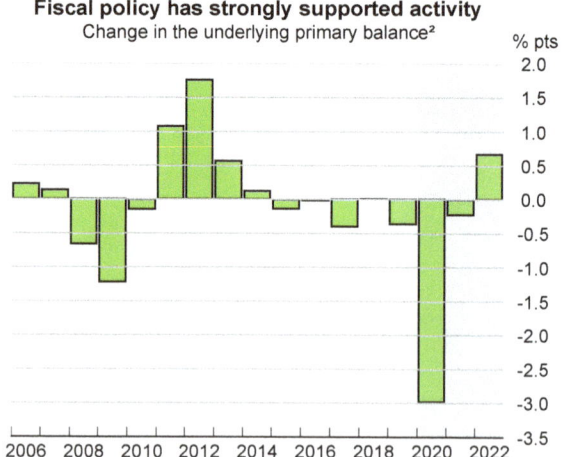

Fiscal policy has strongly supported activity

Change in the underlying primary balance[2]

% pts

1. Private service sector firms.
2. Measured in percent of potential GDP.
Source: IHS Markit; and OECD Economic Outlook 108 database.

StatLink https://doi.org/10.1787/888934218387

The epidemic has strongly resurged

After a marked epidemiological improvement from May to July, COVID-19 infections have flared up again across Europe, placing a heavy burden on healthcare systems. There has been widespread introduction of targeted containment measures aimed at reducing personal interactions, such as curfews or closing of bars and restaurants, especially in areas with a high risk of contagion, and some countries have reimposed country-wide lockdowns. These, however, have tended to be less strict than in spring: schools have often remained open, and more firms have been allowed to operate than during the first lockdown. As diverse cross-border travel restrictions have re-emerged, the European Union adopted a recommendation to member states on a coordinated approach to the restriction of free movement, based on common criteria for assessing the epidemiological situation in countries or regions of origin or destination.

After a strong rebound, activity is declining again, hampered by the resurgence of the pandemic

Following the end of lockdown measures, activity rebounded vigorously until mid-summer, although the performance in different sectors varied widely. Retail sales caught up to, and even exceeded, pre-pandemic levels, partly reflecting pent-up demand. In contrast, the recovery in industrial production remained incomplete, especially in capital goods, due to considerable investment weakness. The rebound in services relying on travel or direct personal contact was more muted, as illustrated by a very weak tourist season, especially in places mostly reliant on international travel. Differences in sectoral specialisation, and especially in the economic weight of international tourism, are a key driver of the asymmetric impact of COVID-19 across the euro area, with southern countries generally hit hardest and, among them, Spain more affected than Italy. Cross-country variation in the length and strictness of containment measures and in the extent of discretionary fiscal support also help explain the asymmetry in impacts.

With the resurgence of the pandemic in the autumn and new measures restricting activities, a reversal of the recovery is likely in the fourth quarter of 2020. High-frequency indicators based on internet searches often point to a decline in activity, while business surveys show diminishing confidence in services. The magnitude of the decline in output, however, is much smaller than in the second quarter.

Strong EU support has increased fiscal space at the national level

Decisive action at the EU level has created very favourable financing conditions for sovereigns. Following a series of policy announcements between March and June, the ECB has continued to provide abundant liquidity and conduct wide-scale asset purchases, while signalling its willingness to step up support if needed. In line with the recent decrease in, and subdued outlook for, inflation, ECB policy rates are assumed to remain unchanged over the coming two years. SURE, a EU lending facility to support national short-time work schemes, has become operational and witnessed strong take-up, with loans approved to 17 member states, almost exhausting the facility's EUR 100 billion envelope. Furthermore, in July the European Council reached an agreement on Next Generation EU, a recovery plan envisaging EUR 750 billion of financing (about 5.5% of EU27 2019 GDP), mainly in the form of loans (EUR 360 billion) and grants (almost EUR 380 billion) to member states. A substantial part of these grants will be allocated to member states most affected by the pandemic, thus increasing their fiscal space. As a result of these actions, sovereign spreads in the euro area have narrowed substantially.

National fiscal policies have provided substantial support to activity, backed by the temporary lifting of Stability and Growth Pact constraints until end-2021, which is welcome. Successive measures have been announced throughout 2020, leading to a discretionary stimulus of close to 3 percentage points of euro area GDP, though considerable uncertainty surrounds these estimates. A broadly neutral fiscal stance is expected in 2021, followed by moderate budget consolidation in 2022. In these years, national budgets will benefit from Next Generation EU grants, supporting investment and reforms set out in national recovery and resilience plans. These plans, assessed and approved at the EU level, are also designed to contribute to the broader priorities of digitalisation and climate change mitigation.

A mild recovery with important risks

GDP is projected to grow only moderately over the coming two years, hampered by the recurrent need for containment measures for the next six to nine months and the ensuing high uncertainty and depressed confidence until vaccination is generally deployed. Investment will remain far below its pre-pandemic levels, but the recovery of private consumption is also projected to be sluggish, held back by high unemployment, modest wage growth and precautionary saving. Though a bit more dynamic, export growth will be constrained by the subdued recovery in international trade. After declining in 2020, inflation will return to around 1%. As in 2020, the impact of the pandemic is projected to remain asymmetric across the euro area, potentially widening the gap in prosperity between countries.

Worse-than-expected virus outbreaks or unexpected delays in implementing effective vaccination, threatening to overwhelm healthcare systems, could force governments to impose stricter or longer-lasting confinement measures, resulting in higher output losses. Failure to overcome quickly current disagreements over the required legislation for Next Generation EU could delay public investment and reignite market tensions. A no-deal Brexit at the end of 2020 would further weaken trade and confidence. The expected increase in non-performing loans (NPLs), particularly in the sectors hit hardest by the pandemic, could threaten financial stability in some countries. Moreover, protracted NPL disposal would hamper the reallocation of bank credit and thus weaken investment further. Likewise, failure to foster labour reallocation through reinforced active labour market policies and increased investment would worsen the scarring effects of the pandemic. On the upside, swift production and distribution of vaccines, coupled with more effective testing, tracing and isolation strategies, would minimise future virus outbursts and thus bolster activity and confidence. Prompt and efficient implementation of the EU recovery plan could enhance structural reform implementation and help the euro area achieve stronger productivity growth.

Policies need to support resource reallocation

National fiscal policies should continue to support aggregate demand, and avoid premature budget consolidation. In this context, governments should start to implement recovery and resilience plans swiftly, regardless of procedural lags that may slow down the receipt of Next Generation EU grants. Public investment and reforms should promote resource reallocation from activities that may face long-lasting subdued demand towards those likely to expand. An example of the latter is residential retrofitting for higher energy efficiency, which is essential to meet decarbonisation targets. Electric vehicles, another avenue for a green recovery, offer huge potential for innovation and investment. Fostering labour and capital reallocation requires enhanced training opportunities and speedier and more harmonised insolvency regimes. At the EU level, reducing financial fragmentation would also strengthen resilience and more efficient resource allocation. Welcome steps would include common deposit insurance, a European asset-management company to facilitate NPL disposal, and freer movement of capital and liquidity across borders within banking groups.

Finland

Recovery from the COVID-19 hit to the economy began in the second half of 2020, led by consumption and exports. GDP is estimated to have fallen by 4% in 2020 and is projected to expand by around 1½ per cent in 2021 and 1¾ per cent in 2022. Investment will be slow to recover owing to surplus capacity and uncertainty about the economic outlook. The unemployment rate will peak in 2021, but will remain high by the end of 2022. The main risk to the outlook is that virus infection rates rise again in Finland and its trading partners before an effective vaccination is implemented, delaying the recovery.

If the recovery is delayed, fiscal stimulus should be extended and temporary income support measures prolonged. To encourage employers to limit use of the temporary layoff scheme to viable jobs, they should contribute to the benefit costs of their furloughed employees. Once the recovery is firmly established and the pandemic has subsided, fiscal prudence will be required to stabilise the debt-to-GDP ratio. Reforms to close early retirement pathways would make a significant contribution to fiscal consolidation.

The first COVID-19 wave was mild, but a second wave has arrived

Finland has had a relatively low incidence of COVID-19 cases by international comparison since the onset of the pandemic. Hospitalisations of people with coronavirus-related illnesses soared during the first wave, but large reductions in mobility and timely containment measures cut the tally to low levels during the summer. Since then, a second wave of infections has developed, with the source of infection being unknown in more than half of new cases, impeding contact tracing. While hospitalisations have again increased markedly, they remain well below the levels reached during the first wave. To slow the spread of the virus, the government recently strengthened capacity and opening-hour restrictions on bars and restaurants, but devolved their implementation to regional authorities based on local epidemiological conditions, and tightened border entry restrictions.

Finland

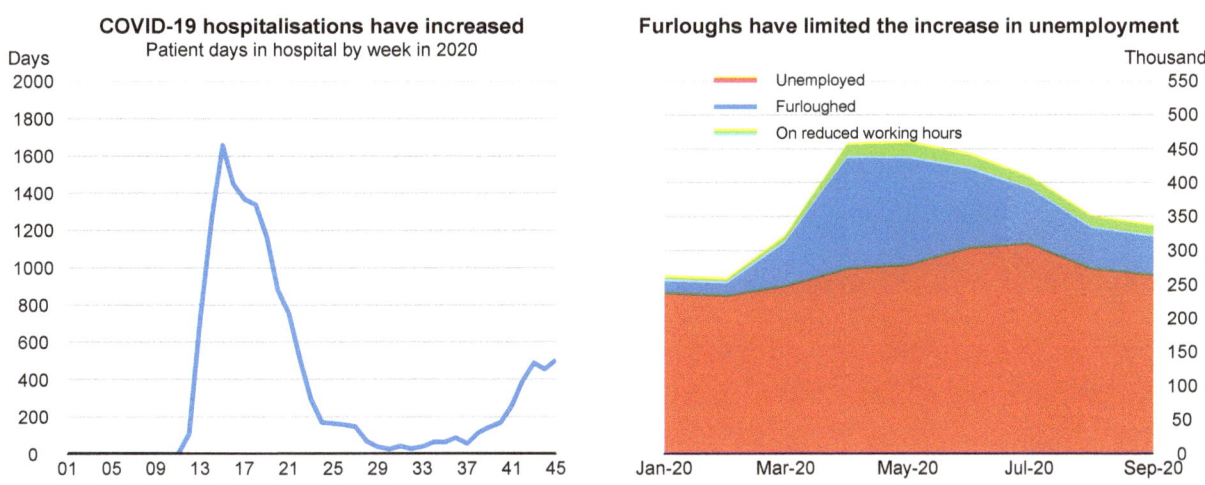

Source: Ministry of Social Affairs and Health; and Statistics Finland's Px Web databases.

StatLink ᵐˢᵖ https://doi.org/10.1787/888934218406

Finland: Demand, output and prices

Finland	2017	2018	2019	2020	2021	2022
	Current prices EUR billion	Percentage changes, volume (2010 prices)				
GDP at market prices	225.9	1.5	1.1	-4.0	1.5	1.8
Private consumption	120.3	1.8	0.8	-4.9	3.8	2.1
Government consumption	51.6	1.6	1.1	2.0	0.7	-1.5
Gross fixed capital formation	52.9	3.9	-1.0	-1.9	-0.6	3.3
Final domestic demand	224.7	2.3	0.5	-2.6	1.9	1.5
Stockbuilding[1,2]	1.1	0.5	-0.9	0.8	0.1	0.0
Total domestic demand	225.8	2.9	-0.4	-1.7	2.0	1.5
Exports of goods and services	85.0	1.7	7.7	-11.7	2.4	4.7
Imports of goods and services	84.9	5.4	3.3	-8.8	2.5	3.7
Net exports[1]	0.1	-1.4	1.7	-1.2	-0.1	0.3
Memorandum items						
GDP deflator	_	1.9	1.8	2.4	1.5	1.5
Harmonised index of consumer prices	_	1.2	1.1	0.5	1.0	1.4
Harmonised index of core inflation[3]	_	0.3	0.7	0.5	0.9	1.4
Unemployment rate (% of labour force)	_	7.4	6.7	7.9	8.3	7.7
Household saving ratio, net (% of disposable income)	_	-0.8	0.4	6.6	1.6	1.4
General government financial balance (% of GDP)	_	-0.9	-1.0	-7.5	-5.1	-3.7
General government gross debt (% of GDP)	_	72.7	72.7	79.1	86.0	91.2
General government debt, Maastricht definition (% of GDP)	_	59.6	59.3	63.8	68.5	72.3
Current account balance (% of GDP)	_	-1.7	-0.2	-0.3	-0.3	0.0

1. Contributions to changes in real GDP, actual amount in the first column.
2. Including statistical discrepancy.
3. Harmonised index of consumer prices excluding food, energy, alcohol and tobacco.
Source: OECD Economic Outlook 108 database.

StatLink https://doi.org/10.1787/888934218425

The economy has shrunk and forward indicators have recently turned down

Real GDP contracted by 4.5% in the second quarter, much less than in most other OECD countries. Accommodation, tourism and food and beverage services experienced the largest falls in activity. The trend employment rate has declined, reversing most of the gains since 2017, and the unemployment rate increased to 7.6% in September, 1.7 percentage points higher than a year earlier. Consumer and business confidence fell in August-September, largely offsetting earlier summer gains. Capacity utilisation in industry has fallen sharply, as have the volumes of construction underway and building permits issued, pointing to falls in business and housing investment.

The government has provided substantial income support

The government has provided substantial support to limit both household and business income losses caused by the crisis. The temporary layoff scheme, under which laid-off workers are paid unemployment benefits, has protected many jobs and limited the increase in unemployment. Stand-down periods before receiving unemployment benefits were eliminated and eligibility for unemployment benefits was extended to entrepreneurs and the self-employed. The government has also provided support for SMEs and hard-hit industries, such as air and sea transportation, restaurants and cafés. It also reduced firms' tax burdens and social security contributions temporarily. Mainly because of the crisis response, the structural budget deficit is estimated to have increased by 3.5% of GDP in 2020. With special measures unwinding and planned consolidation in the event that the economic recovery is sustained, the structural deficit is projected to decline by 1.7% and 0.7% of GDP, respectively, in 2021 and 2022.

Consumption and exports will lead the recovery

The economic recovery began in the summer, but following the initial rebound is set to slow somewhat owing the second virus wave in Finland and its trading partners. The recovery will be led by consumption and exports. Rising employment and the running down of savings accumulated during the pandemic will support private consumption, with export market growth underpinning rising exports. The unemployment rate will peak in 2021 as many temporary layoffs become permanent, and slowly decline to 7¾ per cent in 2022. Inflation should rise as the output gap shrinks but remain moderate. The recovery would be delayed if the recent resurgence of coronavirus infections is not soon reined in, the rollout of an effective vaccine is delayed, external demand remains weak owing to a prolonged global pandemic or banking losses were greater than expected, leading to tighter credit conditions.

Further measures may be needed to sustain the recovery

In the event that the economic recovery is delayed, the government should extend temporary income support measures beyond the end of 2020 and reinstate the temporary limitation on creditors' rights to petition for bankruptcy. The government should also create a default unemployment insurance fund into which uninsured employees are automatically enrolled to expand coverage of earnings-related unemployment benefits. To encourage employers to limit temporary layoffs to jobs they believe can be restarted, employers should be required to contribute to the unemployment benefit costs of their furloughed employees.

France

Activity is projected to fall by 9.1% in 2020 and expand by 6% in 2021 and 3.3% in 2022. After a second national lockdown at the end of 2020, the sanitary situation is assumed to improve only slowly. Despite sporadic local virus outbreaks, the easing of containment measures and the prospective rollout of an effective vaccine would still allow for a gradual reduction in precautionary saving and, eventually, a catch-up in the most affected sectors (tourism and leisure services). As export markets recover, external demand and investment will pick up. The unemployment rate will peak around end-2021 and remain above its pre-crisis level in 2022. By the end of 2022, public debt is expected to increase to 120% of GDP.

Temporary emergency measures and the medium-term recovery plan provide strong fiscal support, balancing measures on the supply and demand sides. The gradual phasing-out of short-time work schemes and loan programmes for firms will encourage the reallocation of resources across firms. To ensure a gradual recovery, the government should continue to target new support measures to firms directly impacted by temporary national and local restrictions. Prioritising and speeding up testing capacities would also help in identifying and isolating infected people more rapidly, helping to control the epidemic and boost economic activity.

France 1

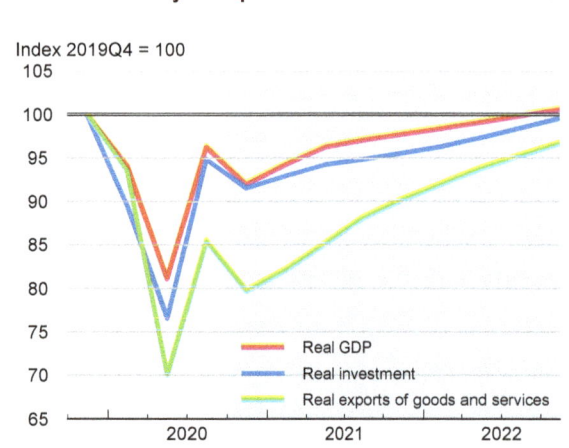

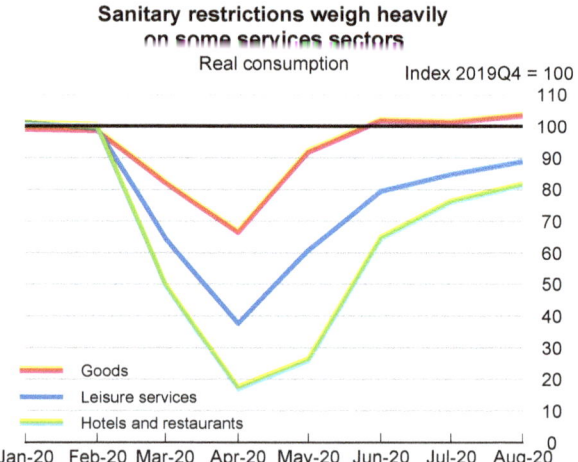

Source: OECD Economic Outlook 108 database; and INSEE.

StatLink https://doi.org/10.1787/888934218444

France: Demand, output and prices

France	2017 Current prices EUR billion	2018	2019	2020	2021	2022
		Percentage changes, volume (2014 prices)				
GDP at market prices	2 298.6	1.8	1.5	-9.1	6.0	3.3
Private consumption	1 241.1	0.8	1.5	-7.9	6.5	3.8
Government consumption	543.4	0.9	1.7	-3.1	6.5	0.4
Gross fixed capital formation	517.3	3.2	4.3	-10.9	7.2	3.7
Final domestic demand	2 301.7	1.4	2.2	-7.5	6.6	3.0
Stockbuilding[1]	21.6	0.0	-0.4	0.2	-0.5	0.0
Total domestic demand	2 323.4	1.4	1.8	-7.3	6.0	2.9
Exports of goods and services	711.6	4.6	1.8	-18.7	5.2	9.3
Imports of goods and services	736.4	3.1	2.6	-12.7	5.3	7.5
Net exports[1]	- 24.8	0.4	-0.3	-1.8	-0.2	0.3
Memorandum items						
GDP deflator	_	1.0	1.2	2.5	1.0	1.0
Harmonised index of consumer prices	_	2.1	1.3	0.5	0.4	0.8
Harmonised index of core inflation[2]	_	0.9	0.6	0.7	0.5	0.8
Unemployment rate[3] (% of labour force)	_	9.0	8.4	8.4	10.5	10.2
Household saving ratio, gross (% of disposable income)	_	14.0	14.3	20.6	16.6	15.1
General government financial balance (% of GDP)	_	-2.3	-3.0	-9.5	-7.4	-5.6
General government gross debt (% of GDP)	_	121.7	124.4	142.0	143.2	144.8
General government debt, Maastricht definition (% of GDP)	_	98.0	98.1	115.7	116.8	118.5
Current account balance (% of GDP)	_	-0.6	-0.7	-2.4	-1.9	-1.4

1. Contributions to changes in real GDP, actual amount in the first column.
2. Harmonised index of consumer prices excluding food, energy, alcohol and tobacco.
3. National unemployment rate, includes overseas departments.
Source: OECD Economic Outlook 108 database.

StatLink ⇗ https://doi.org/10.1787/888934218463

France 2

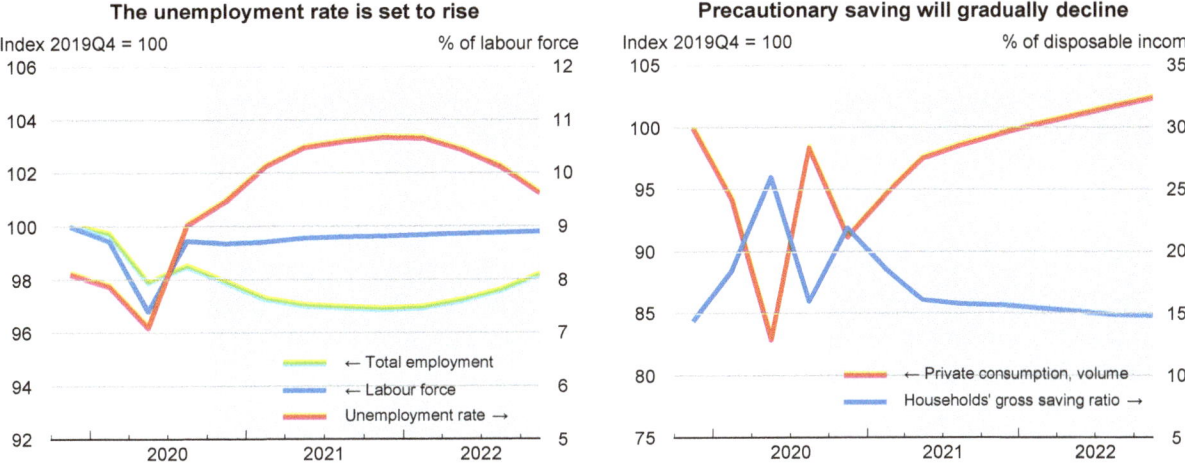

Source: OECD Economic Outlook 108 database.

StatLink ⇗ https://doi.org/10.1787/888934218482

Increasing infections led to a new lockdown

After a significant slowdown of the epidemic owing to the first nationwide lockdown, COVID-19 infections and the number of persons in intensive care increased significantly between mid-July and early November. Despite tightened sanitary regulations, such as the mandatory wearing of masks in indoor spaces, most French regions had been officially classified as highly vulnerable to the epidemic as of end-October. The renewed virus outbreak has put testing capacities in large cities, where it is most important to identify cases rapidly, under severe strains and increased bottleneck risks for the healthcare system. In September, the authorities imposed local closures of bars and restaurants and tightened rules on public gatherings in cities where infections had become problematic. They further applied curfews for non-essential activities in high-infection metropolitan areas and for most regions in mid-October and a second national lockdown two weeks later. With COVID-19 infections decreasing significantly, the authorities announced a progressive easing of the lockdown and most shops reopened at the end of November.

The resurgence of the pandemic has halted the recovery

The recovery has been highly uneven and progress has partly reversed. After the sudden initial economic stop, goods consumption, the construction sector, non-market and high-tech services as well as most manufacturing industries all recovered quickly in May and June. According to the French Statistical Institute (INSEE), economic activity in October rebounded to 4% below its end-2019 level from a decline of 31% in April. Yet, it is estimated to be 13% below its end-2019 level in November, as the sanitary situation continued to curb the demand for tourism, accommodation and transport services, and renewed restrictions sharply cut activity in those sectors. Business sentiment has worsened and the high level of delayed social contributions payments point to significant liquidity constraints for firms. The unemployment rate increased to 9% in the third quarter of 2020, and the employment rates of younger and low-skilled workers have been disproportionately affected. The rebound of new hires on temporary contracts has lost momentum and the decline in the take-up of the short-time work scheme appears to have stopped in November.

Policy responses are extensive

The authorities have taken comprehensive measures to head off macroeconomic destabilisation and support the ongoing recovery. Discretionary budgetary measures will reach about 3.9% of GDP in 2020, notably through the strengthened short-time work scheme and support for the smallest firms and the self-employed. The government also announced a EUR 100 billion medium-term recovery plan, France Relance, with fiscal measures that are set to reach 1.6% of GDP in 2021 and 1.1% in 2022. The EUR 10 billion business tax cut, hiring and car subsidies, and higher public investment, as well as additional financing for training programmes, will provide broad support for the recovery over the coming two years. Renewed emergency measures and the already planned housing and corporate income tax cuts, as well as higher financing for the health sector, will also partly damp the negative impact of the crisis on household incomes and business profit margins.

The European Central Bank's accommodative monetary policy and expanded asset purchases will continue to support aggregate demand. The Next Generation EU plan will help finance 2021-22 fiscal measures in France (France is set to receive EUR 40 billion of European grants) and in its main trading partners, thereby boosting domestic and external demand. The French authorities have also prolonged to 2021 emergency measures for badly hit sectors and firms to alleviate corporate costs, notably through tax holidays and high public coverage of the wages under short-time work agreements, and to support firm financing (via public guarantees of loans and quasi-equity long-term loans). At the same time, in most sectors, the increased cost sharing of the short-time work schemes and additional funding for training will encourage resource reallocation.

The outlook is highly uncertain

Economic activity is set to decline by 9.1% in 2020 and is projected to reach its pre-crisis level around the end of 2022. Some sectors – such as transport and hospitality, which represent around 9% of GDP – will be durably affected by the pandemic. After a weak end to 2020, the assumed slow improvements of sanitary conditions and the prospective rollout of an effective vaccine will support consumption and housing investment, with households drawing on their high savings. Yet, targeted restrictions in services sectors requiring close physical interaction will remain in the first part of 2021. High unemployment and the slow labour market recovery will keep hurting poorer and more precarious households. As demand in trading partners gains ground, exports will catch up gradually from their historically low levels. Business investment will recover only slowly, reflecting reduced profit margins and persistent uncertainty. The budget deficit and the public debt-to-GDP ratio are projected to remain at high levels, with the latter (Maastricht definition) reaching 120% of GDP in 2022.

Passenger transport, tourism and cultural activities will bear enduring scars. Demand for such services has decreased and, in addition, their opening remains only partial and highly dependent on local restrictions until the epidemic ends. Furthermore, businesses have built up sizeable debt, notably through government loan guarantees. As a result, some will face liquidity and solvency concerns, which could precipitate large-scale firm bankruptcies and dent economic prospects. A slower recovery of the main trading partners in the euro area would also delay the recovery in France. On the upside, high pent-up domestic demand, a swift use of European recovery funds and a faster-than-projected recovery in the tourism sector would raise growth.

Strengthening the recovery

The French recovery plan is set to provide well-balanced fiscal support and the current flexible approach of adapting policies to the evolution of the pandemic should be maintained. The priority is to develop healthcare further and refine testing capacities to ensure that the strategy of mass testing, isolation and local restrictions is successful. While the widespread testing is welcome, such a policy can only be efficient if results are known rapidly. Fast-track testing and giving a gate-keeping role to general practitioners to screen those who need test results urgently, as is done in Germany, could help achieve this. Specific emergency measures should also continue to target viable firms affected by renewed local restrictions or temporarily depressed demand. Allowing an efficient reallocation of workers in the aftermath of the crisis is another key challenge, as gross corporate debt has soared and unemployment and bankruptcies are set to rise. The increased targeting of the short-time work schemes is welcome, but ensuring broad access to lifelong learning for low-skilled and long-term unemployed workers, as well as an efficient implementation of quality standards for these programmes, is needed. Reviewing collective restructuring procedures and speeding up court processes would ease the required adjustments. Strengthening innovation and management training initiatives for small firms, and providing them with extended hiring support programmes, would raise economic activity by facilitating the adoption of new technologies and removing barriers to firm growth.

Germany

Activity is projected to contract by around 5½ per cent in 2020, driven by falling private consumption, business investment and exports. Growth is set to recover slowly to 2.8% in 2021 and 3.3% in 2022. Private consumption and exports initially rebounded rapidly, but demand for services will stay weak into 2021 as virus containment measures have been tightened. Further uncertainty will constrain the recovery of investment as well as demand for capital goods exports before general deployment of a vaccine increases confidence. Short-time work has cushioned the increase in unemployment, but sustained falls in the unemployment rate are not expected until after mid-2021, once employees on short-time work have been reabsorbed.

Strong fiscal support has protected jobs and firms in 2020 but the rate of fiscal consolidation needs to be carefully managed. Additional targeted support is merited in 2021 and 2022 to reduce taxes for those on low incomes, increase research and development, support job placement and training, and deliver infrastructure needed for digital transformation and the energy transition.

A resurgence in coronavirus cases has triggered national containment measures

New coronavirus cases picked up considerably from the start of October, triggering new containment measures from 2 November. A robust testing, tracking and isolation system had been successful in keeping local outbreaks well contained over the previous five months, but by late October the source of 75% of new infections could not be identified. In November, the number of COVID-19 patients in intensive care exceeded the April peak, though high capacity meant there were spare beds without drawing on emergency reserves. Restaurants, bars, entertainment and public recreation facilities were required to close, tourist stays in hotels banned and public meetings restricted. Unlike in spring, schools and kindergartens remained open, though there have been closures in the worst-hit municipalities. Other national containment measures include the cancellation of large public events until 31 December, mask-wearing requirements in shops and public transport, travel restrictions and quarantine requirements for travel from high-risk areas within the European Union and Schengen Area.

Germany 1

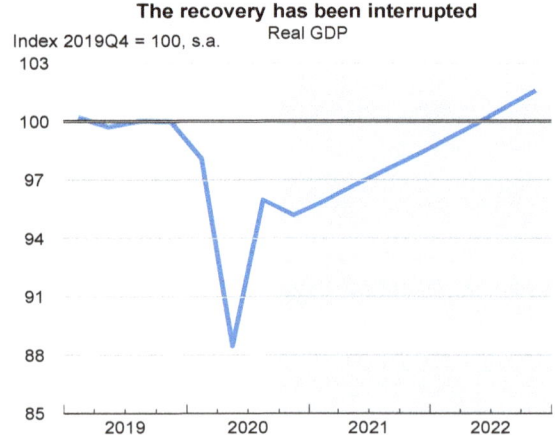

The recovery has been interrupted
Real GDP
Index 2019Q4 = 100, s.a.

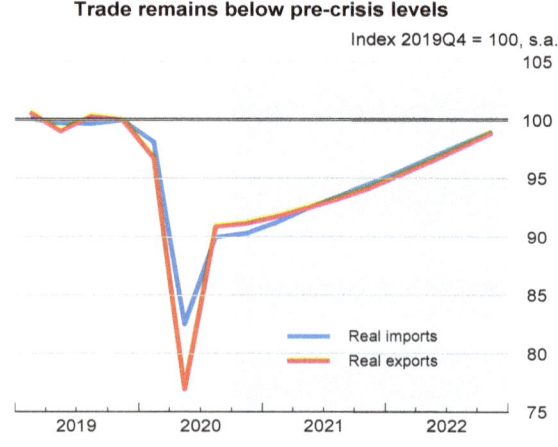

Trade remains below pre-crisis levels
Index 2019Q4 = 100, s.a.

Source: OECD Economic Outlook 108 database.

StatLink https://doi.org/10.1787/888934218501

Germany: Demand, output and prices

Germany	2017	2018	2019	2020	2021	2022
	Current prices EUR billion	Percentage changes, volume (2015 prices)				
GDP at market prices	3 263.3	1.3	0.6	-5.5	2.8	3.3
Private consumption	1 705.5	1.5	1.6	-6.2	3.2	4.0
Government consumption	648.2	1.2	2.7	4.2	1.6	0.9
Gross fixed capital formation	667.5	3.6	2.6	-4.3	2.0	3.9
Final domestic demand	3 021.2	1.9	2.1	-3.5	2.6	3.3
Stockbuilding[1]	13.1	-0.1	-0.7	-1.0	-0.5	0.0
Total domestic demand	3 034.2	1.8	1.3	-4.5	2.1	3.3
Exports of goods and services	1 541.6	2.5	1.0	-11.1	4.5	4.5
Imports of goods and services	1 312.5	3.8	2.6	-9.6	3.0	4.7
Net exports[1]	229.1	-0.4	-0.6	-1.2	0.8	0.2
Memorandum items						
GDP without working day adjustments	3260.0	1.3	0.6	-5.2	2.8	3.2
GDP deflator	_	1.7	2.2	1.4	0.8	1.2
Harmonised index of consumer prices	_	1.9	1.4	0.4	1.1	1.3
Harmonised index of core inflation[2]	_	1.3	1.3	0.7	1.1	1.3
Unemployment rate (% of labour force)	_	3.4	3.1	4.2	4.8	4.3
Household saving ratio, net (% of disposable income)	_	10.9	10.9	16.6	15.2	12.7
General government financial balance (% of GDP)	_	1.8	1.5	-6.3	-4.4	-1.8
General government gross debt (% of GDP)	_	69.5	68.1	82.5	84.7	84.3
General government debt, Maastricht definition (% of GDP)	_	61.7	59.5	73.9	76.2	75.8
Current account balance (% of GDP)	_	7.5	7.2	7.0	7.2	7.1

1. Contributions to changes in real GDP, actual amount In the first column.
2. Harmonised index of consumer prices excluding food, energy, alcohol and tobacco.
Source: OECD Economic Outlook 108 database.

StatLink https://doi.org/10.1787/888934218520

Germany 2

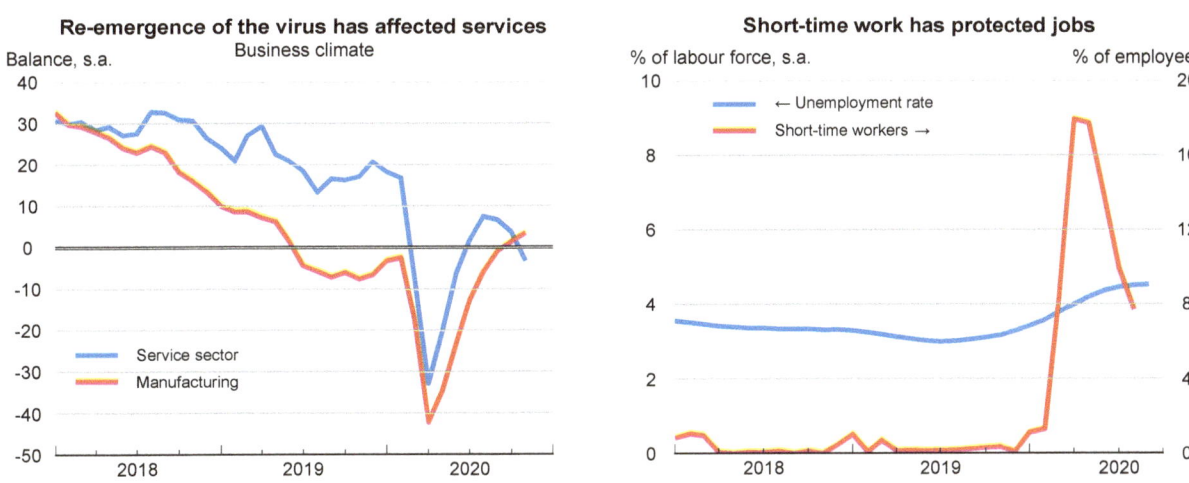

Re-emergence of the virus has affected services — Business climate

Short-time work has protected jobs

Source: ifo business surveys; Federal Statistical Office; and Federal Employment Agency.

StatLink https://doi.org/10.1787/888934218539

A rapid rebound has slowed

The sharpest decline in GDP since quarterly national accounts calculations began was followed by a rapid rebound, led first by services and subsequently manufacturing. Following a peak in disruption in April, retail turnover was already above its pre-crisis level in May. Despite substantial falls in business investment, construction activity largely continued and public investment expanded. Exports were a key contributor to the contraction as major trading partners were severely affected, with the value of exports declining by one-third between February and April. Despite significant recovery from May, in September the value of exports remained 10% lower than one year earlier and key capital goods exports, such as automotive manufacturing, were still around 15% below pre-crisis levels. Manufacturing export orders continued to increase sharply in September, even as the re-emergence of the virus in Europe saw business confidence in service industries, consumer confidence and personal mobility decline. The unemployment rate increased by 1.4 percentage points over the first six months of 2020 before levelling off, with increases tempered by widespread take-up of government-supported short-time work. Survey data indicate that a quarter or more of employees in hospitality, metal, mechanical engineering and vehicle construction were still in short-time work as of September, against less than 10% in retail, construction and finance.

Fiscal support will be removed gradually in 2021 and 2022

Two fiscal packages were announced in March and June 2020, financed by supplementary budgets of EUR 156 billion (4.5% of GDP) and EUR 61.8 billion (1.8% of GDP) respectively as the exception clause to the public debt brake was triggered. The first package focussed on protecting health, jobs and firms through health spending, cash payments to the self-employed and small businesses, social benefits, expanded access to short-time work, loan guarantees and tax deferrals. The second package contained measures to boost consumption, notably a temporary reduction in VAT rates between 1 July and 31 December 2020, a follow-up hardship fund for the self-employed, and measures to boost public and private investment in digitalisation, education, health, public transport and green energy. Exceptional fiscal support has protected jobs and assisted firms, though some measures, such as guarantees and the hardship fund for the self-employed, have been underutilised. Further support of approximately EUR 10 billion (0.3% of GDP) was added as containment measures tightened in November and a similar magnitude of additional spending and transfers is assumed in response to weak demand in 2021. Highly accommodative monetary policy and expanded asset purchases by the European Central Bank are also supporting aggregate demand.

Fiscal consolidation will initially reflect the end of exceptional support measures in 2021 such as the temporary VAT cut and hardship fund, offset to some extent by increased public investment and reduction of the solidarity surcharge to personal income taxation. The federal government's draft budget plan for 2021 includes EUR 96.2 billion (2.8% of GDP) in net borrowing, which will require the exception clause to the fiscal brake to be triggered again. Re-imposition of the debt brake in 2022 will entail further consolidation.

The crisis will continue to weigh on the economy

The rapid rebound in the third quarter of 2020 is giving way to contraction in the fourth quarter and only gradual recovery in 2021. Containment measures reduced activity in November and are assumed to ease only slightly over the rest of the winter, with service industries where physical distancing is not possible most severely affected. Strong orders, including export orders, will continue to support manufacturing growth to the end of 2020, but this will slow as the rebound in durables consumption ends. Fiscal consolidation will also weigh on growth from the start of 2021. Growth will gradually gain momentum in 2022, as the general deployment of a vaccine reduces uncertainty and hence precautionary saving by consumers, increases export demand and underpins business investment. Price inflation will in general remain low, though the end of the temporary VAT cut at the start of 2021 will cause a one-off increase in consumer prices. Unemployment is expected to rise further, reaching a peak in the first half of 2021, as slow growth constrains job creation and the reabsorption of employees on short-time work leaves less space for new hires.

The evolution of the pandemic in Germany and key trading partners is the most important risk to the projection. A further increase in cases would reduce private consumption and could require extension or tightening of containment measures if healthcare capacity is threatened. Unexpected hurdles in implementing vaccination against the virus would similarly hold down growth. Conversely, success in containing the outbreak through local measures combined with widespread testing, tracking, tracing and isolating, or faster-than-expected progress with inoculation, would support the economic recovery. Financial amplification of the crisis could lead to a protracted recession if corporate and household defaults trigger a collapse in credit availability or even insolvencies among banks, though this has been avoided to date.

The pace of fiscal consolidation should be moderated

The premature withdrawal of considerable discretionary fiscal support in 2021 and 2022 (just under 2% of GDP in total) risks derailing a recovery already impaired by the re-emergence of the virus. The extent of consolidation will depend crucially on the magnitude of discretionary support actually delivered in 2020, estimated at 4¼ per cent of GDP. Extension of expanded short-time work until the end of 2021 will provide needed support to a weak labour market, but also hinders job reallocation. Job placement assistance and training for those on short-time work or unemployed will become increasingly important. There are other opportunities for targeted fiscal measures to support demand while contributing to inclusive growth, such as reducing tax rates for those on low incomes and increasing tax incentives for research and development. Measures in the recovery package to boost infrastructure investment are appropriately targeted at key challenges facing the German economy (digital transformation and the energy transition), but need to be complemented by further steps to remove delivery bottlenecks through more funding to municipalities, bolstering local planning capacity and streamlining planning processes.

Greece

Greece's economy is set to contract by 10% in 2020 and to recover gradually in 2021, as ongoing virus outbreaks and restrictions weigh on services activity, exports, employment and investment. In 2022, the recovery is projected to accelerate, as the virus is better controlled with a vaccine having become more generally deployed, restrictions being eased globally and the government implementing new investment projects. Controlling the pandemic sooner would hasten the recovery, reducing risks of rising insolvencies, non-performing loans and declining well-being.

Extending and expanding support for households suffering income loss as the crisis continues would limit the drag on consumption and well-being, without locking workers into activities facing weak demand. Extending and better targeting liquidity support would help viable firms to stay in business. The draft 2021 budget prioritises cuts to personal income tax and social contribution rates, which will support longer-term employment growth. Strongly expanding effective training programmes would help to ensure that workers have the skills that the labour market will need after the crisis.

Infections and mortality are rising

The health impact of the first wave of the coronavirus was very limited in Greece thanks to a strong policy response. However, daily infections, hospitalisations and deaths rose from late summer, while remaining below the EU average. Responding to the rising second wave, the government first required masks to be worn in crowded and enclosed public spaces, then reintroduced strict nationwide movement restrictions, and closed businesses with high levels of physical interactions as well as schools and nurseries. Greece is continuing to expand its test, track and isolate capacity and to add facilities across the health system to manage potential pressures on healthcare.

Greece

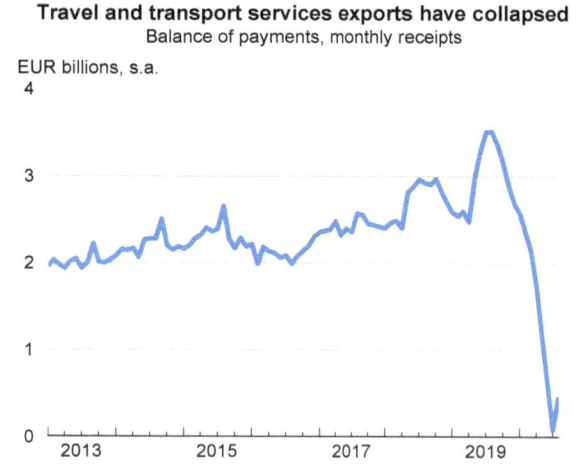

Travel and transport services exports have collapsed
Balance of payments, monthly receipts

EUR billions, s.a.

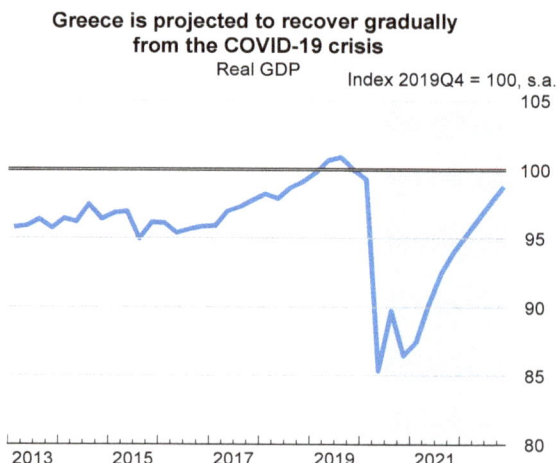

Greece is projected to recover gradually from the COVID-19 crisis
Real GDP

Index 2019Q4 = 100, s.a.

Source: OECD Economic Outlook 108 database; and Bank of Greece.

StatLink 🔗 https://doi.org/10.1787/888934218558

Greece: Demand, output and prices

Greece	2017	2018	2019	2020	2021	2022
	Current prices EUR billion	Percentage changes, volume (2010 prices)				
GDP at market prices	177.2	1.6	1.9	-10.1	0.9	6.6
Private consumption	121.7	2.3	1.9	-7.0	1.3	3.6
Government consumption	36.2	-4.2	1.2	1.3	0.5	-0.7
Gross fixed capital formation	20.8	-6.6	-4.6	-11.5	4.6	13.5
Final domestic demand	178.6	0.1	1.0	-5.7	1.5	3.7
Stockbuilding[1,2]	1.2	1.4	0.1	0.0	0.0	0.0
Total domestic demand	179.8	1.4	1.1	-5.6	1.4	3.6
Exports of goods and services	62.0	9.1	4.8	-23.8	-5.2	19.1
Imports of goods and services	64.6	8.0	3.0	-12.1	-3.1	8.2
Net exports[1]	- 2.7	0.3	0.7	-4.5	-0.5	2.8
Memorandum items						
GDP deflator	_	-0.1	0.2	-0.4	1.2	0.8
Harmonised index of consumer prices	_	0.8	0.5	-1.2	-0.2	0.8
Harmonised index of core inflation[3]	_	0.3	0.8	-1.2	-0.6	0.8
Unemployment rate (% of labour force)	_	19.3	17.3	16.9	17.8	17.2
Household saving ratio, net (% of disposable income)	_	-15.0	-11.9	-7.8	-10.7	-15.0
General government financial balance[4] (% of GDP)	_	1.0	1.5	-9.4	-7.0	-2.6
General government gross debt (% of GDP)	_	201.2	205.1	238.3	232.2	219.2
General government debt, Maastricht definition (% of GDP)	_	186.2	180.5	213.7	207.6	194.6
Current account balance[5] (% of GDP)	_	-2.9	-1.5	-5.2	-5.7	-2.7

1. Contributions to changes in real GDP, actual amount in the first column.
2. Including statistical discrepancy.
3. Harmonised index of consumer prices excluding food, energy, alcohol and tobacco.
4. National Accounts basis. Data also include Eurosystem profits on Greek government bonds remitted back to Greece, and the estimated government support to financial institutions and privatisation proceeds.
5. On settlement basis.
Source: OECD Economic Outlook 108 database.

StatLink https://doi.org/10.1787/888934218577

Very weak tourism activity is undermining the recovery

Greece's domestic consumer and services activity rebounded after restrictions were lifted in May and June. However, tourist arrivals were exceptionally weak through the peak summer season, due to uncertainty over the health situation and containment policies, and as governments in major markets required arrivals from Greece to quarantine. This has weighed heavily on demand, turnover, employment and exports. In the third quarter of 2020, accommodation and food service firms' turnover was 50% lower than a year earlier. This has reduced domestic demand, contributing to notable drops in turnover in industry and wholesale and retail trade. Weak demand has also weighed heavily on job creation, although support measures have limited job losses. Job seekers have been dropping out of the labour market, mitigating the rise in the unemployment rate.

Policy is shifting from income and liquidity support to tax cuts and investment spending

The government has budgeted spending of EUR 21.5 billion (11% of 2019 GDP) in 2020 to support workers and firms in the most affected sectors, the self-employed, the unemployed and borrowers, and to buttress firms' liquidity through deferred tax and contribution payments and subsidised lending. A one-off retroactive pension payment of EUR 1.4 billion in late 2020 also bolsters household incomes. In 2021, the government is budgeting EUR 2.7 billion to support incomes of furloughed workers and to cut the income tax wedge, and to subsidise social contributions for new hires. It will help first homebuyers and cut selected VAT rates. The government plans to supplement the public investment budget of EUR 6.75 billion with EUR 2.6 billion of Next Generation EU grants in 2021, which would more than double its 2019 investment spending. Its investment priorities are labour and social inclusion policies in education and health, green and digital projects, infrastructure and improvements to the business environment.

The continuing health crisis will curtail the recovery

The renewed strict containment measures and shutdowns are set to weaken consumer demand and services exports in the final quarter of 2020 and the first quarter of 2021. The recovery in activity later in 2021 is projected to be gradual, as the ongoing health crisis drags on consumer confidence and amplifies uncertainty in Greece and its major export markets. Weak incomes and activity are projected to damp government revenues. The health situation is assumed to improve from early 2022, as a vaccination against the virus will have become widely deployed, hastening the projected recovery in services, lifting incomes and employment, and allowing exports and government revenues to rise towards pre-crisis levels. The budget will continue to support activity and public debt is projected to decline from a peak of 214% of GDP in 2020. The ambitious public investment plans and access to low-cost financing for private investment will support domestic demand from late 2021. Investment may be stronger than projected if execution rates improve substantially and if take-up of loans from the EU Recovery and Resilience Facility is strong. Greece's services exports particularly expose its economy to a protracted health crisis, which would exacerbate business failures and non-performing loans, and reverse part of recent improvements in banks' health and ability to finance new private investment.

More targeted income support, upgrading skills and improving the investment climate would strengthen the recovery

The COVID-19 crisis underscores the need for Greece to address long-standing challenges. Weak employment adds urgency to strengthening targeted income support. Delays in tax and contribution payments to reduce liquidity pressures should come with stronger efforts to improve tax and payment compliance. The severe liquidity constraints that many firms are facing are likely to increase non-performing loans again, despite the government's extension of credit and loan guarantees and progress in implementing the 'Hercules' disposal programme. Further actions should be prepared now to strengthen banks' capital and ability to finance investment for the recovery. Measures to help activity move towards tradable and higher-innovation sectors will strengthen productivity growth. Recent progress in digitalising public services demonstrates how this can help reduce the burden of red tape. Better active labour market programmes, education and professional training would ensure that job seekers have the skills for opportunities emerging from the COVID-19 crisis.

Hungary

Following a contraction of 5.7% in 2020, GDP is projected to rebound by about 3% per annum on average in the next two years. New restrictions to contain a second wave of infections this autumn will delay the recovery. As restrictions are lifted, an effective vaccine is deployed, and global trade picks up, domestic and external demand will begin to recover from mid-2021 onwards. The labour market will improve from mid-2021 as well, while inflation will continue to be elevated.

Fiscal policy will remain supportive as social security contributions are further reduced. Monetary policy has limited room for further countercyclical action given continued inflationary pressures, which are only partly imported. Phasing out temporary measures to preserve existing businesses in a timely way is needed to enable effective reallocation. In addition to active labour market policies, a longer maximum duration of unemployment benefits (currently limited to three months) would support employment transitions to ensure a stronger recovery.

A second wave has hit the country

The number of new COVID-19 cases has been rising since September. The resurgence of infections led the government to impose new restrictions on 11 November. In consequence, hospitality and recreational facilities will remain closed at least for a month. A travel ban also remains in place. The authorities have stepped up testing and critical care capacity.

Hungary

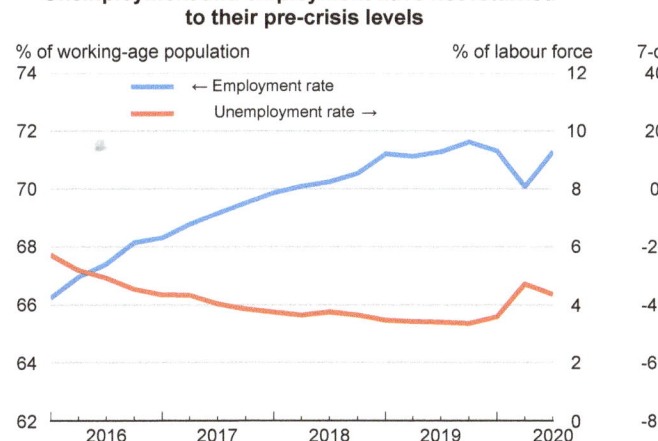

Unemployment and employment have not returned to their pre-crisis levels

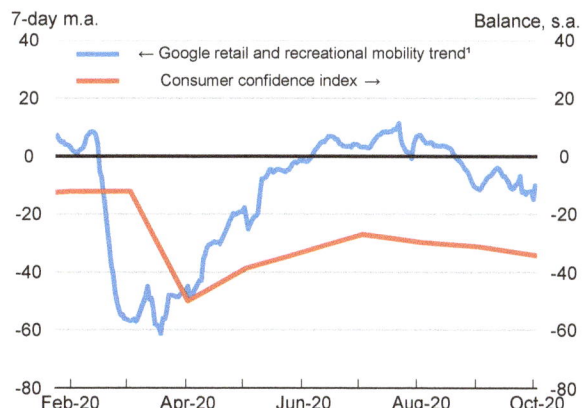

The recovery in consumer confidence has stalled

1. Deviation from the baseline. The baseline is the median value, for the corresponding day of the week, during the 5-week period January 3-February 6, 2020.
Source: OECD Economic Outlook 108 database; GKI; Refinitiv; and OECD calculations based on Google LLC, *Google COVID-19 Community Mobility Reports*, https://www.google.com/covid19/mobility /.

StatLink https://doi.org/10.1787/888934218596

Hungary: Demand, output and prices

Hungary	2017	2018	2019	2020	2021	2022
	Current prices HUF billion	Percentage changes, volume (2015 prices)				
GDP at market prices	39 233.4	5.4	4.6	-5.7	2.6	3.4
Private consumption	19 696.0	5.1	4.5	-2.6	2.6	2.7
Government consumption	7 912.9	1.7	3.5	1.0	2.2	2.0
Gross fixed capital formation	8 698.6	16.4	12.2	-9.3	0.2	3.2
Final domestic demand	36 307.5	7.1	6.4	-3.8	1.8	2.7
Stockbuilding[1]	248.3	0.1	-0.3	1.5	0.0	0.0
Total domestic demand	36 555.8	7.1	6.0	-2.1	1.9	2.7
Exports of goods and services	33 744.7	5.0	5.8	-13.7	3.3	5.0
Imports of goods and services	31 067.0	7.0	7.5	-9.7	2.4	4.1
Net exports[1]	2 677.7	-1.2	-1.1	-3.6	0.7	0.7
Memorandum items						
GDP deflator	_	4.8	4.8	2.9	3.1	3.6
Consumer price index	_	2.9	3.3	3.5	3.3	3.6
Core inflation index[2]	_	2.1	3.2	3.2	3.3	3.6
Unemployment rate (% of labour force)	_	3.7	3.4	5.0	6.4	5.7
Household saving ratio, net (% of disposable income)	_	8.1	6.3	7.3	6.1	5.8
General government financial balance (% of GDP)	_	-2.1	-2.1	-8.0	-7.5	-6.0
General government gross debt (% of GDP)	_	86.6	83.3	92.9	97.0	98.6
General government debt, Maastricht definition (% of GDP)	_	69.1	65.4	74.5	77.5	77.7
Current account balance (% of GDP)	_	0.3	-0.3	-2.5	-2.0	-1.3

1. Contributions to changes in real GDP, actual amount in the first column.
2. Consumer price index excluding food and energy.
Source: OECD Economic Outlook 108 database.

StatLink https://doi.org/10.1787/888934218615

Economic growth remains subdued

Short-term indicators show that the recovery has lost momentum. The rebound in demand slowed during the summer. Consumer confidence fell for a third consecutive month in early autumn. Industrial production bounced back fast after the historic fall in spring, but was still below its pre-pandemic level in September. Low capacity utilisation is constraining investment. The forint depreciated against the euro in spring, exerting upward pressure on inflation in summer. The unemployment rate declined over the summer before levelling off in September. The OECD's sectoral estimates suggest that the new confinement measures could lead to a quarterly output loss of just over 1% in the fourth quarter. Unemployment is set to increase due to new restrictions, which have a particularly large negative impact on the tourism and hospitality sectors.

Policy provides substantial relief

A fiscal stimulus package of 7.9% of GDP has provided relief to workers and businesses in 2020, and includes, for example, wage support and cuts to employers' social security contributions. In November, the government reintroduced wage support for furloughed workers in the most affected sectors. The fiscal expansion amounts to 3.6% of GDP after taking into account revenue-raising measures and budget reallocations. In 2021 and 2022, additional public investment will be financed partly by the inflow of EU funds, with annual commitments of up to 5.6% of GDP. The central bank reduced its main policy rate from 0.9% in May to 0.6% in July and broadened its bond purchasing programme. Furthermore, to cushion the shock of renewed restrictions, it raised the amount of loans to businesses and for corporate bond purchases by HUF 300 billion, to HUF 1 750 billion (3.8% of GDP).

The recovery is set to regain strength

After a GDP decline of 5.7% in 2020, output is projected to recover in 2021 and 2022. Government spending, including wage support and home-building subsidies, will cushion the fall in economic activity at the end of 2020 and support growth in 2021. As global trade picks up and restrictions are lifted with the gradual deployment of a vaccine, private consumption and external demand will contribute to growth from 2021. Investment is expected to rebound in the second half of 2021 on the back of stronger inflows of foreign direct investment and EU funds. A deteriorating labour market will be reflected in higher unemployment. Downside risks include prolonged containment restrictions as well as a sharp contraction of the global automotive sector well into 2022, which would hit Hungary hard given the economy's dependence on the sector. On the upside, a faster-than-expected recovery of export markets would improve the growth outlook.

Policy must support the recovery now

Fiscal policy should remain supportive until the recovery is firmly underway. The shift from broad income support towards more targeted measures to preserve jobs in the most affected sectors, notably tourism and hospitality, is welcome. In addition to supporting existing jobs, active labour market policies are a priority to improve labour reallocation for a stronger recovery. Also, the three-month maximum duration of unemployment benefits is short. Extending it would facilitate job mobility and support employment transitions. The timely withdrawal of emergency state-backed loans would help efficient reallocation to expanding sectors. Going forward, policies supporting productivity would strengthen the recovery, notably investment in local infrastructure and more competitive product markets.

Iceland

Output is set to contract by almost 8% in 2020, but is projected to expand by around 3% per annum in both 2021 and 2022, thanks to rising household consumption. Goods exports are expected to rise, although foreign tourism will take longer to gain momentum. Business investment will remain weak, but housing and public investment will pick up. Given the continued impact of the pandemic, especially on international travel, until a vaccine is deployed widely, activity will still fall short of its pre-crisis level at the end of 2022. Unemployment continues to rise and will exceed 7% in mid-2021, and wage growth will slow.

The króna has depreciated since the crisis started. Inflation expectations are rising slowly despite the downturn as wages are rising and fiscal policy is strongly expansionary. The central bank should hence remain vigilant. The government should continue to provide targeted support, including helping people and capital move to new sectors and activities. Structural reforms to strengthen competition and improve relevant skills would underpin diversification of the economy.

Containment measures have been tightened again

Iceland has gone through a comparatively mild health crisis so far. Despite a high infection rate, the number of victims has remained low thanks to effective containment measures and a well-functioning health system. Containment measures in spring were in place for a rather short period. Early mass testing helped the authorities identify infections and implement targeted health measures. The number of new infections reached a second peak in mid-October and has been declining since, while hospital capacity has remained sufficient.

Iceland

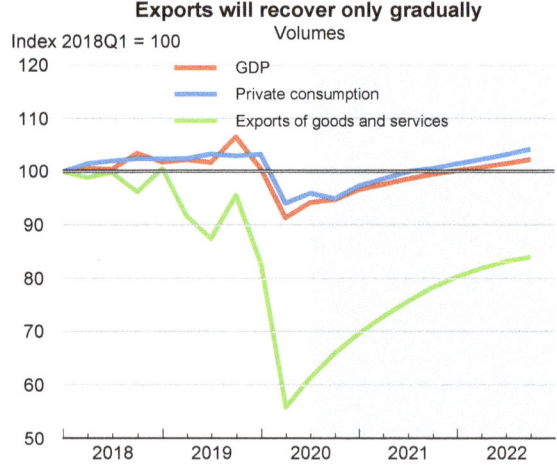

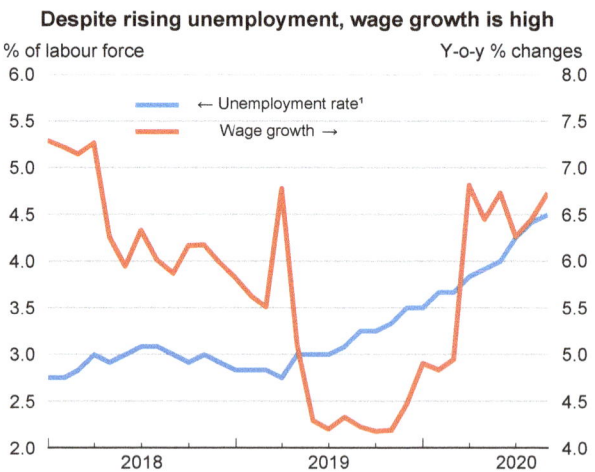

1. Twelve-month moving average.
Source: Statistics Iceland; and OECD Economic Outlook 108 database.

StatLink ⬛️🔢 https://doi.org/10.1787/888934218634

Iceland: Demand, output and prices

Iceland	2017	2018	2019	2020	2021	2022
	Current prices ISK billion	Percentage changes, volume (2005 prices)				
GDP at market prices	2 615.6	3.9	1.9	-7.7	3.0	3.2
Private consumption	1 317.5	4.7	1.3	-5.6	2.2	3.7
Government consumption	614.1	4.0	4.2	2.5	2.0	0.9
Gross fixed capital formation	574.9	-1.0	-6.6	-8.1	2.6	1.8
Final domestic demand	2 506.5	3.3	0.4	-4.0	2.2	2.5
Stockbuilding[1]	0.8	0.4	0.1	1.0	0.5	0.0
Total domestic demand	2 507.2	3.6	0.4	-2.9	2.7	2.5
Exports of goods and services	1 206.3	1.7	-4.9	-29.1	11.5	11.1
Imports of goods and services	1 097.9	0.8	-10.2	-21.7	10.2	9.0
Net exports[1]	108.4	0.4	2.2	-4.4	0.5	0.7
Memorandum items						
GDP deflator	_	2.6	4.5	3.7	0.8	2.6
Consumer price index	_	2.7	3.0	2.8	3.1	3.0
Core inflation index[2]	_	2.5	2.9	2.8	2.8	3.0
Unemployment rate (% of labour force)	_	2.7	3.5	5.4	7.5	7.3
General government financial balance (% of GDP)	_	0.8	-1.5	-14.4	-13.0	-11.2
General government gross debt[3]	_	62.1	63.2	77.9	90.1	99.4
Current account balance (% of GDP)	_	3.2	6.2	2.2	0.6	0.8

1. Contributions to changes in real GDP, actual amount in the first column.
2. Consumer price index excluding food and energy.
3. Includes unfunded liabilities of government employee pension plans.
Source: OECD Economic Outlook 108 database.

StatLink https://doi.org/10.1787/888934218653

At the end of October, the government tightened containment and mitigation measures slightly, especially by limiting gatherings further. While schools and universities remain fully operational, remote learning has become more widespread. International borders remain open to the Schengen area, and traffic has resumed at a modest level at Iceland's only international airport. All arrivals must test for COVID-19, go into quarantine and test again after a few days. Tracking and self-isolation remain the most common measures to slow the spread of the virus.

Demand is picking up slowly

Household consumption has started to increase on the back of rising wages and continued government support. Domestic tourism has more than doubled, partly replacing foreign visitors. Exports of seafood have remained largely stable, although aluminium exports have declined slightly. Overall investment remains subdued, although housing investment has picked up, reflecting some pent-up demand and improving financial conditions. Business confidence has fluctuated strongly since mid-2020, as uncertainty about the evolution of the pandemic is rising. The unemployment rate rose to 6% in September, up from 3.5% in January.

Policy continues to support households and firms

The central bank reduced the policy rate further to an all-time low of 0.75%, while continuing to provide additional liquidity to the economy. The króna has depreciated by around 20% since March, and inflation and inflation expectations are rising slowly despite the downturn. The central bank should remain vigilant to keep inflation within the target band, especially as commodity prices are increasing again. Fiscal policy has become strongly expansionary. The short-time work scheme has been extended until end-2020, and households may draw on third-pillar retirement savings. Firms with a revenue fall of more than 75% continue to benefit from direct government support. In late August, the government guaranteed a credit facility for the Icelandair Group. Public investment, especially in digital infrastructure, has expanded.

The economy will recover gradually

GDP is projected to grow by around 3% per annum in both 2021 and 2022. Business investment will remain weak as uncertainty about the evolution of the pandemic persists. Household consumption will expand gradually, following government support. Exports will rise but remain below 2019 levels, with foreign tourism expected to recover only slowly as a vaccine is implemented gradually around the world. Public investment, as planned by the government, will add additional momentum from 2021.

With slowing wages and a declining labour force, the unemployment rate will rise to close to 8% in 2021 before declining in 2022. The budget deficit will reach 13% of GDP in 2021 and 11% in 2022. Gross public debt will climb to almost 100% of GDP in 2022, above levels reached after the 2008-09 financial crisis. Specific risks to the projections include a slower recovery of tourism and disruptions to global value chains that could dent goods exports.

Structural reform could help accelerate reallocation

Structural reforms could help accelerate an inclusive recovery. Temporary simplifications of the insolvency framework should become permanent to facilitate a fresh start for firms once the crisis is over. Strengthening competition, in particular in the construction and tourism sectors, and levelling the playing field between domestic and foreign firms, could help create new businesses and diversify the economy. Investment in education, research and innovation, and green growth could improve the skills required for workers to venture into new sectors and activities.

India

After experiencing one of the world's tightest lockdowns and recording the deepest GDP contraction among G20 economies in the second quarter of 2020, the Indian economy is recovering, albeit with some hesitancy. While agriculture has benefited from favourable weather conditions, manufacturing and services are penalised by remaining containment measures and uncertainty. Significant social hardship persists and the fall in the unemployment rate must be seen against the background of declining labour force participation. Supply chain disruptions have pushed inflation above the target range of the central bank. GDP is set to shrink by 10% in fiscal year (FY) 2020-21, with household consumption sluggish and investment largely unresponsive to easier monetary conditions. Despite a projected rebound of around 8% and 5% in FY 2021-22 and FY 2022-23, respectively, due to base effects and returning confidence, the GDP loss will be substantial.

COVID-19 is exacerbating pre-existing vulnerabilities related to poverty, high informality, environmental degradation and lack of employment opportunities. To increase resilience, the government has responded with three stimulus packages, but additional fiscal measures are needed to mitigate the damage, together with a credible medium-term consolidation plan. The reform effort has continued, notably in the areas of agriculture and employment. However, poor performance of public banks, a pervasive regulatory burden, and understaffing of the judiciary hinder the proper allocation of resources needed for inclusive growth.

India 1

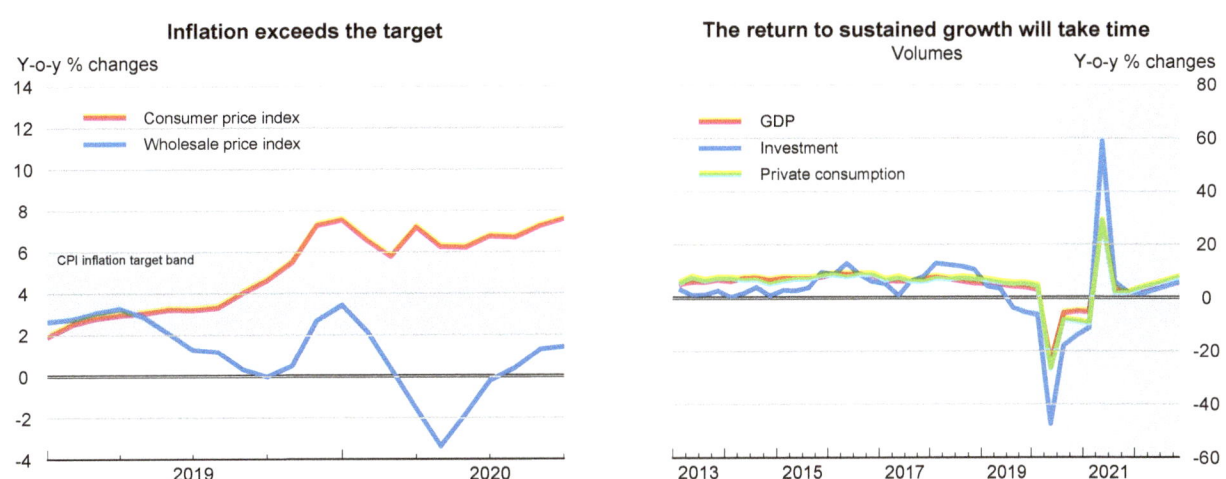

Source: National Statistical Office; Ministry of Commerce and Industry; and OECD Economic Outlook 108 database.

StatLink https://doi.org/10.1787/888934218672

India: Demand, output and prices

India	2017	2018	2019	2020	2021	2022
	Current prices INR trillion	Percentage changes, volume (2011/2012 prices)				
GDP at market prices	171.0	6.1	4.2	-9.9	7.9	4.8
Private consumption	100.9	7.2	5.3	-13.3	7.8	6.5
Government consumption	18.4	10.1	11.8	12.5	6.8	1.2
Gross fixed capital formation	48.0	9.8	-2.8	-22.9	12.9	4.8
Final domestic demand	167.3	8.2	3.6	-12.9	8.9	5.2
Stockbuilding[1,2]	9.1	0.4	0.0	-1.9	0.0	0.0
Total domestic demand	176.4	5.5	3.2	-13.5	9.0	5.2
Exports of goods and services	32.1	12.3	-3.6	-10.7	5.8	4.1
Imports of goods and services	37.5	8.6	-6.8	-27.8	12.0	6.1
Net exports[1]	- 5.4	0.4	0.9	3.9	-0.9	-0.3
Memorandum items						
GDP deflator	–	4.6	2.9	1.5	3.2	1.0
Consumer price index	–	3.4	4.8	5.9	4.6	4.6
Wholesale price index[3]	–	4.3	1.7	-1.2	3.2	3.7
General government financial balance[4] (% of GDP)	–	-6.2	-6.1	-8.3	-6.7	-6.1
Current account balance (% of GDP)	–	-2.1	-0.8	0.9	0.5	-0.4

Note: Data refer to fiscal years starting in April.
1. Contributions to changes in real GDP, actual amount in the first column.
2. Actual amount in first column includes statistical discrepancies and valuables.
3. WPI, all commodities index.
4. Gross fiscal balance for central and state governments.
Source: OECD Economic Outlook 108 database.

StatLink 🔗 https://doi.org/10.1787/888934218691

India 2

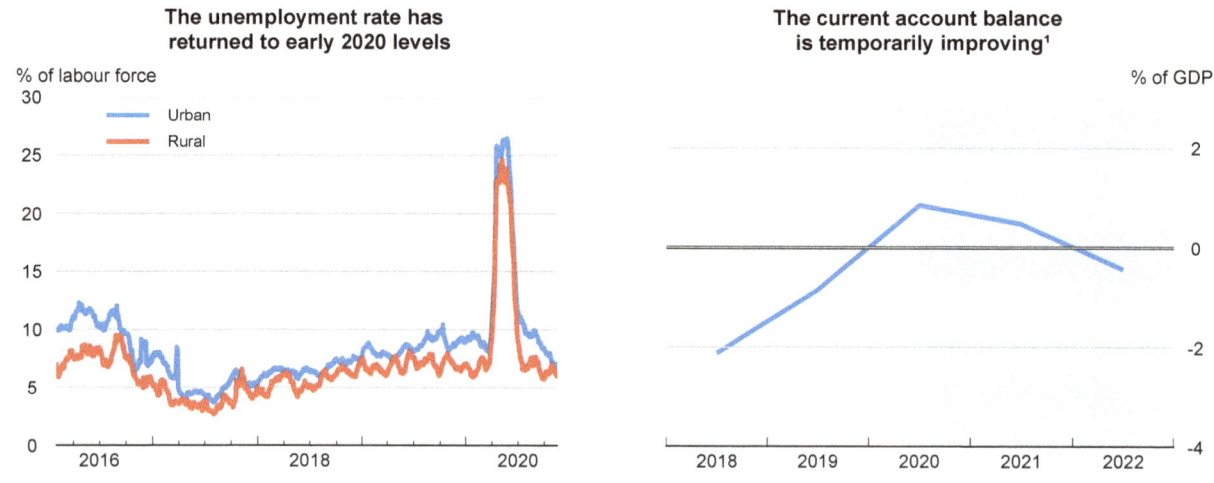

The unemployment rate has returned to early 2020 levels

The current account balance is temporarily improving[1]

1. Data refer to fiscal years beginning on April 1.
Source: Centre for Monitoring Indian Economy (CMIE); and OECD Economic Outlook 108 database.

StatLink 🔗 https://doi.org/10.1787/888934218710

A tight containment regime has slowed but not halted the virus spread

One of the world's earliest and toughest lockdowns helped to slow the diffusion of the virus. While India has recorded the world's third-largest number of COVID-19 deaths in absolute terms, the rate per capita is considerably lower than in most other large countries. The lifting of the lockdown began on 1 June and has been organised in five phases. Both the number of new infections and the number of deaths were at their highest in the first half of September and started declining rapidly afterwards. In Unlock 5.0, currently in place, the main remaining restrictions concern schools (a preference for online/distance learning), some recreational activities (such as indoor swimming and cinema halls) and worship places, while tighter lockdowns are imposed in selected locations (so-called containment zones).

The growth revival after the collapse has been hesitant

The economy is still struggling to return to the activity levels prevailing before COVID-19 hit and available indicators send conflicting signals. The rate of activity resumption, as proxied by high-frequency mobility data and more traditional real economy indicators, was vigorous until late August but has since cooled. Power demand, car sales, railway freight and the manufacturing PMI indicate ebbing momentum. Some industries, such as producers of capital equipment, keep contracting. Others are taking advantage of shifts in consumer preferences, like the one towards cars and two-wheelers that are deemed safer than public transport. On the bright side, financial markets have been extremely buoyant since the March-April trough. The current account surplus rose to 3.9% of GDP in the June quarter. Labour market data are harder to interpret, with the recent decline in the unemployment rate contrasting with the participation rate still inching down. Urban poverty is seen as worsening and the number of school dropouts surging, especially among first-generation pupils from disadvantaged households. The disruption of the cooked meal programme, and of the mid-day school meal scheme in particular, could worsen child malnutrition.

Monetary policy has done much of the heavy lifting to support the economy

Monetary easing, fiscal stimulus and supportive financial regulation have countered the effects of the lockdown and of the income shock. The Reserve Bank of India cut the policy repo rate from 5.15% to 4%, introduced mandatory credit repayment moratoria and one-off debt restructuring with upfront provisioning. The initial fiscal support amounted to about 6.9% of GDP (of which 4.9% were off-budget measures designed to support businesses and shore up credit) and was followed by a 0.2% of GDP additional package focused on household consumption ahead of the Diwali festivities and a third intervention in November of around 1.4% of GDP spanning several fiscal years. Some structural reforms were also approved, notably to liberalise the notoriously rigid formal labour market and to support synergies between agriculture and agribusiness.

With a fiscal deficit around 16% of GDP, largely due to tax revenue losses rather than substantially higher growth-enhancing expenditure, and swelling public debt, there is scant room for further fiscal expansion and the FY 2021-22 Budget is expected to be cautious. On the other hand, the recent RBI forward guidance signals its accommodative stance is set to continue. While the scope for further relaxation is currently limited by headline inflation in excess of the target range, food-related supply-side pressures are expected to abate. Against this background, additional cuts in the policy rate are projected around the turn of the fiscal year.

Prospects are uncertain and risks are mostly on the downside

Following a projected GDP contraction of 10% in FY 2020-21, economic growth is on course to rebound. Although confidence will return, the scars to the economy and society are lingering and it may take almost two years for GDP to get back to pre-pandemic levels. Inequality will rise, also in response to protracted school closures and reliance on online learning. In addition, weak balance sheets call for debt deleveraging in the private corporate sector, while the financial sector, including non-bank lenders, deals with its bad loans – a combination that will weigh on investment, with the possible exception of digital technologies.

The assumption that all COVID-19-related restrictions will be lifted by 2022 hinges on access to and rolling out of a safe and effective vaccine, even though the immunisation campaign will be an immense logistical and operational challenge and the cost substantial. Other risks are equally on the downside. Most sectors are operating far below capacity and this short-term frailty might produce scarring effects and eventually morph into a permanent decline in trend growth. On the inflation side, the 2020 surge may not reverse as swiftly as expected if some supply chain bottlenecks persist, such as producers in the informal sector that fail to restart activity after the pandemic, which would put pressure on prices. On the upside, an earlier-than-expected roll-out of a vaccine or effective treatment and the ensuing uptick in global growth would translate into faster domestic growth.

Policies should focus on sustainability and efficiency

The COVID-19 crisis is a vivid manifestation of the vulnerability of the poor to shocks, especially if they are unskilled, women, children, migrants or disabled, and the crisis is already reversing some of the well-being progress of the past decade. At a minimum, policies should protect workers, particularly in the informal sector, through portable welfare instruments that cater to both rural and urban populations, and guarantee food and cash support across state boundaries. Better targeting of energy and fertiliser subsidies, as well as tax expenditures, would free resources for pro-poor fiscal policies. Equally important is to make it easier for capital, labour, technology and talent to move towards their most productive use. Reforms aimed at this, which invariably entail reducing privileges and rents, should focus on the governance of state-owned enterprises, insolvency and bankruptcy legislation, and the professionalism of the judiciary. Further trade and foreign investment opening, including reducing and simplifying tariffs and liberalising trade in services, would also increase competition on the Indian market and boost economic growth.

Indonesia

The economy contracted sharply in the first half of 2020 and GDP is set to shrink by 2.4% this year, the first recession since 1998. The 2021 rebound, provided containment measures are lifted, will be only partial. With lingering concerns about the health situation and consumer and business confidence remaining low, growth is projected to remain below trend in 2021, with severe consequences on incomes and living standards, before picking up to 5% in 2022. Trade prospects, however, are supportive, as key Northeast Asian markets recover and new agreements including the Regional Comprehensive Economic Partnership (RCEP) come into force.

In a few months, the pandemic reversed some hard-won advances in well-being, with poverty, malnutrition, and even hunger rising fast. The credibility built up by the central bank over the years through wise use of its independence – a fragile achievement that must be preserved – has permitted an unconventional policy mix of rate easing, liquidity injection and asset purchases. Fiscal policy has been relaxed, within the structural limits of extremely low tax revenue. The policy imperative is to protect citizens from sudden further shocks: devote more resources to assistance programmes, improve targeting and monitoring, and establish a proper unemployment insurance system. In the longer run, further improvements in well-being and growth require ambitious reforms to boost human capital formation. Reform momentum is returning, as shown by the Omnibus Bill on Job Creation passed in early October.

Containment measures have slowed but not halted the spread

Indonesia has recorded a seemingly low number of COVID-19 cases and fatalities, considering its population, although some care must be taken when interpreting data since the number of tests performed as a share of the population is also the lowest among G20 economies. Large-scale social restrictions were loosened in June, only to be reintroduced in Jakarta in September due to a rising number of COVID-19 cases and high hospital bed and ventilator occupancy rates. However, mobility restrictions were more moderate in this phase.

Indonesia 1

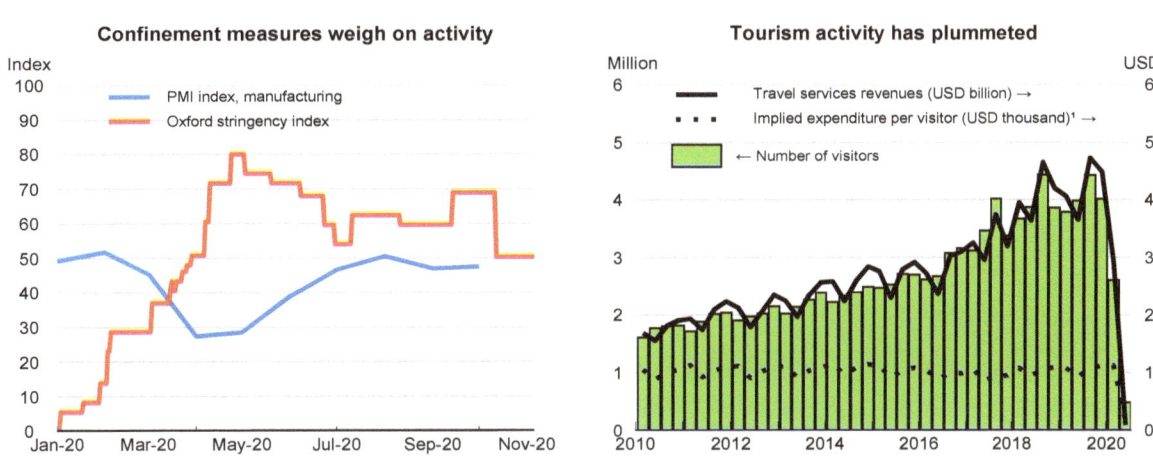

1. Implied expenditure per visitor is computed by dividing travel services revenues by the number of visitors in the same time interval.
Source: Bank of Indonesia; CEIC; Oxford COVID-19 Government Response Tracker, Blavatnik School of Government; and Markit.

StatLink 🔗 https://doi.org/10.1787/888934218729

Indonesia: Demand, output and prices

Indonesia	2017 Current prices IDR trillion	2018	2019	2020	2021	2022
		Percentage changes, volume (2010 prices)				
GDP at market prices	13 589.8	5.2	5.0	-2.4	4.0	5.1
Private consumption	7 783.7	5.1	5.2	-3.0	3.7	6.2
Government consumption	1 239.5	4.8	3.2	4.4	5.6	3.2
Gross fixed capital formation	4 370.6	6.6	4.4	-4.6	3.1	5.7
Final domestic demand	13 393.7	5.6	4.8	-2.9	3.6	5.7
Stockbuilding[1]	60.4	0.7	-1.0	-0.9	0.0	0.0
Total domestic demand	13 454.0	6.2	3.6	-3.8	3.6	5.7
Exports of goods and services	2 742.1	6.5	-0.9	-6.7	3.0	3.8
Imports of goods and services	2 606.3	11.9	-7.7	-14.3	1.2	7.4
Net exports[1]	135.8	-0.9	1.4	1.3	0.4	-0.4
Memorandum items						
GDP deflator	–	3.8	1.6	-0.4	2.3	3.0
Consumer price index	–	3.2	3.0	1.9	2.0	3.0
Private consumption deflator	–	3.3	3.2	1.9	2.3	3.0
General government financial balance (% of GDP)	–	-1.6	-2.2	-6.5	-5.8	-4.2
Current account balance (% of GDP)	–	-3.0	-2.7	-1.0	-0.4	-0.9

1. Contributions to changes in real GDP, actual amount in the first column.
Source: OECD Economic Outlook 108 database.

StatLink https://doi.org/10.1787/888934218748

Indonesia 2

Despite monetary easing, credit growth is lacklustre
Consumer confidence remains weak

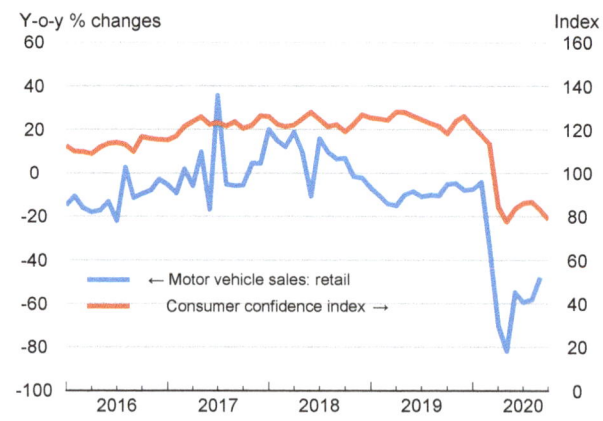

Source: Bank Indonesia; and CEIC.

StatLink https://doi.org/10.1787/888934218767

The recovery path has been uneven

The easing of restrictions since the end of the second quarter boosted activity in the third quarter, as evidenced by the recovery in the manufacturing PMI during the summer. The return of restrictions weighed on production and the manufacturing PMI has worsened again since September. Consumer surveys similarly point to improving confidence until August and a deterioration since then. Exports of goods recovered in September but fell again in October. Imports declined further in October to nearly 27% lower than a year earlier, bringing the January-October trade balance to a surplus of USD 17 billion (from a deficit of USD 2 billion in 2019). Despite a fall in services exports, due to the precipitous decline in tourism, the current account balance reached a surplus of 0.4% of GDP in 2020Q3, as against a deficit of 2.7% in 2019. Consumer price inflation moderated through 2020 to 1.4% in October (year-on-year). Survey evidence suggests a surge in poverty and malnutrition.

Low tax revenues constrained the fiscal policy reaction

The government reacted gradually as the crisis escalated with a series of fiscal packages, totalling around 2.5% of GDP. This is a substantial effort, as the ratio of tax revenues to GDP is the lowest amongst G20 countries. The 3%-of-GDP constitutional limit on the government deficit was temporarily lifted. Initially addressed to the tourism industry, government support expanded to include extra resources for the health sector, in-kind and cash transfers to the poor, tax exemptions and rebates for employees and businesses, state financial guarantees for new capital loans, and capital injections in state-owned enterprises.

Bank Indonesia (BI) cut its policy rate four times in 2020 to an all-time low of 4%. The central bank also enacted additional measures in May, such as reducing the reserve requirement ratio by 200 basis points and increasing the macroprudential liquidity buffer ratio by the same amount. In September, it extended to mid-2021 its policy of requiring lower reserves for banks that lend to small and medium or export-oriented businesses. In addition, BI has entered into a burden-sharing scheme with the government, and has bought government bonds directly, bearing the interest cost. BI's post-1999 independence is challenged by a recent parliamentary proposal to assign decision-making powers to a new monetary policy council in which the government would have voting rights.

Prospects are uncertain and risks mostly on the downside

In 2021-22, growth is projected to be driven by consumption as pent-up demand is met, but the level of GDP will remain far below its pre-pandemic trend, and therefore insufficient to prevent social distress. The projected recovery of exports will contribute to a further significant narrowing of the current account deficit. Inflation is set to edge up to 3%, the mid-range of the BI target, by 2022. The fiscal deficit is expected to shrink but will still exceed 3% of GDP in 2022.

Risks are multiple and mostly on the downside. While the deployment of a safe and effective vaccine would allow the complete lifting of COVID-related restrictions, the logistical, operational and financial challenges of rolling out an immunisation campaign are significant. The loss of growth momentum that was already manifest before the pandemic may hold back investment, thus leaving open existing gaps, notably in infrastructure. Household consumption may remain sluggish if the implementation of the economic relief programme is too slow to rebuild confidence. An upside risk to the projections is that a smoother-than-expected vaccine campaign would bring back international tourists sooner than anticipated. The investment and employment boost of the Omnibus Bill might also beat expectations, especially after the signing of the Regional Comprehensive Economic Partnership.

Making the recovery more inclusive, sustainable and efficient

For the first time in 15 years, progress in eradicating poverty and deprivation has halted, while substantial swathes of the middle class are struggling to prevent the erosion of their living standards. In the recovery phase, it will be fundamental to monitor the quality of growth, in particular for those who are most vulnerable such as women, children, migrants and the disabled. The Omnibus Bill is an important reform, which will make the labour market more flexible by reducing provisions that discouraged firms from offering long-term contracts, and will help to attract new investment by simplifying business procedures. If properly implemented, it can help bring about an inclusive recovery that generates decent jobs and respects the environment. A sustainable recovery requires additional action in fighting deforestation, reducing existing subsidies and incentives for dirty energy, and accelerating the transition to renewables. Last but not least, removing the numerous regulatory obstacles to resource allocation would make the recovery more efficient as well as fairer, since anti-competitive regulations often breed corruption.

Ireland

After suffering a sharp fall in activity during 2020, the economy is projected to recover in 2021 and expand at over 4% in 2022. Positive contributions to growth from the external sector mask domestic weaknesses, particularly in investment. Public support for employees and businesses is helping to hold up domestic demand while the authorities grapple with bringing the coronavirus under control. As recently imposed and possible future sanitary restrictions are lifted, with an effective vaccine being rolled out, and uncertainty about future trading relations is clarified, domestic demand is set to strengthen gradually.

Faced with the ongoing pandemic and the prospect of a hard Brexit, policy needs to remain supportive and be ready to cushion further shocks until sanitary restrictions and trade uncertainty are eased. Fiscal measures have rightly become more targeted. Helping unemployed workers back into employment, while facilitating the reallocation of resources across the economy, will minimise the persistence of the shock to households.

The pandemic has proven difficult to control

A resurgence of COVID-19 cases that was beginning to stretch the capacity of the health sector led the authorities to impose a second lockdown in late October for six weeks. The new restrictions included closing non-essential retail businesses and limiting the hospitality sector to take-away services. Geographical mobility for individuals was also restricted, although schools and most businesses have remained open.

Ireland

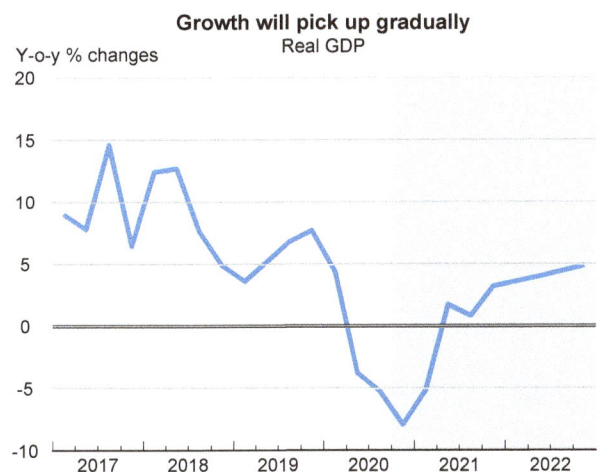
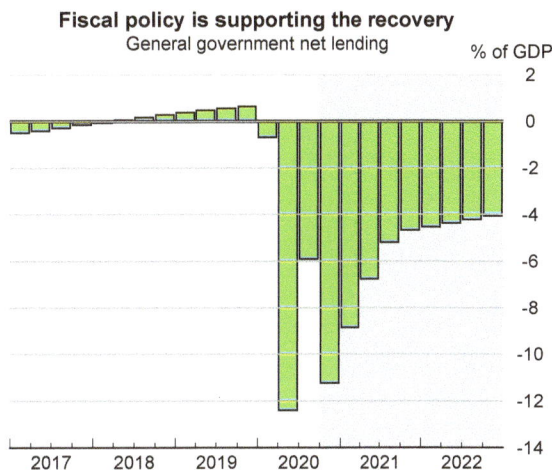

Source: OECD Economic Outlook 108 database.

StatLink 🔗 https://doi.org/10.1787/888934218786

Ireland: Demand, output and prices

Ireland	2017	2018	2019	2020	2021	2022
	Current prices EUR billion	Percentage changes, volume (2018 prices)				
GDP at market prices	298.6	9.3	5.9	-3.2	0.1	4.3
Private consumption	94.0	2.6	3.2	-13.2	1.5	4.3
Government consumption	36.6	5.7	5.8	12.3	0.1	-4.7
Gross fixed capital formation	97.0	-5.6	75.2	-35.8	-24.0	5.3
Final domestic demand	227.6	0.0	30.0	-22.1	-9.3	2.7
Stockbuilding[1]	5.6	-0.9	0.5	1.4	-0.2	0.0
Total domestic demand	233.2	1.2	31.6	-20.2	-9.1	2.6
Exports of goods and services[2]	359.1	11.2	10.6	1.8	4.2	3.8
Imports of goods and services	293.8	3.1	32.1	-10.4	-1.7	2.6
Net exports[1]	65.3	10.4	-16.9	13.9	7.1	2.5
Memorandum items						
GVA[3], excluding sectors dominated by foreign-owned multinational enterprises	_	4.7	4.5	-11.5	0.0	4.6
GDP deflator	_	0.3	2.7	2.3	-0.1	0.8
Harmonised index of consumer prices	_	0.7	0.9	-0.4	0.4	1.0
Harmonised index of core inflation[4]	_	0.3	0.9	-0.1	0.3	1.0
Unemployment rate (% of labour force)	_	5.7	4.9	5.3	8.0	7.8
Household saving ratio, net (% of disposable income)	_	6.9	7.5	22.8	16.5	13.1
General government financial balance[5] (% of GDP)	_	0.1	0.5	-7.4	-6.4	-4.3
General government gross debt (% of GDP)	_	75.0	69.4	78.3	85.1	86.6
General government debt, Maastricht definition (% of GDP)	_	62.9	57.3	66.2	73.0	74.5
Current account balance (% of GDP)	_	6.0	-11.4	4.0	8.1	10.2

1. Contributions to changes in real GDP, actual amount in the first column.
2. So called "contract manufacturing" (exports of goods produced abroad under contract from an Irish-based entity) by multinational enterprises is assumed to remain at the 2020 level in 2021 and 2022.
3. Gross value added. Data for 2018-2022 are OECD 's estimates.
4. Harmonised index of consumer prices excluding food, energy, alcohol and tobacco.
5. Includes the one-off impact of recapitalisations in the banking sector.
Source: OECD Economic Outlook 108 database.

StatLink ᴹᴵˢᴸ https://doi.org/10.1787/888934218805

Export strength masks a weaker domestic economy

The initial lockdown hit the domestic economy hard, but multinational companies largely weathered the storm. In particular, exports of pharmaceutical products and medical technology surged. Ireland's important position in trade of COVID-19-related medical goods provided a bulwark against the precipitous drop in international trade experienced elsewhere. The domestic economy fared less well. While the official unemployment rate has been creeping up only gradually, this has masked substantial numbers who are not working and not classified as unemployed, accounting for around another 10% of the labour force. In addition, heightened uncertainty about Brexit damped business investment. Nonetheless, there were some signs that the economy was faring better before sanitary restrictions were reintroduced, notably retail sales were rebounding strongly.

Fiscal policy has reacted robustly

Fiscal policy has reacted promptly and robustly, with temporary wage subsidies and income support measures for workers laid off due to COVID-19. For the business sector, tax deferrals, loan schemes and other measures supporting firms' cash-flows aimed to prevent mass insolvencies, especially among smaller enterprises. The authorities introduced an additional stimulus package worth EUR 5.2 billion in July, largely based on additional spending to get businesses back on their feet, following the easing of containment measures. The package enhanced the flexibility of the wage subsidy scheme (opening it to seasonal workers), temporarily reduced the standard VAT rate by two percentage points, provided support to the accommodation and food sector and extended income tax relief to self-employed workers. As a result, the general government deficit for 2020 is estimated to have ballooned dramatically. The 2021 budget also envisages a substantial deficit, continuing support for those affected by COVID-19, increasing spending on healthcare, boosting government investment and setting aside funds to mitigate Brexit-related shocks.

The outlook is beset by uncertainty

While short-term prospects are particularly uncertain, the Irish economy is set to recover gradually as sanitary restrictions are lifted, an effective vaccine is rolled out and clarity about future trading relations emerges. The economy will be supported by fiscal measures, which will be progressively pared back as employment recovers. Export strength is likely to continue while imports will remain relatively subdued given low rates of business investment. Inflationary pressures are quiescent.

The OECD projections assume that trade talks between the European Union and the United Kingdom reach an agreement. A hard Brexit would create a significant shock to the Irish economy. This represents the main downside risk to the outlook, in addition to further surges in coronavirus infections until immunisation is attained. Substantial increases in unemployment, particularly if accompanied by widespread business failure, could lead to scarring effects that would weigh on future growth.

Avoiding long-lasting scars

Policy over the next year, as the 2021 budget signals, needs to remain ready to cushion Brexit-related shocks and further surges in coronavirus infections. Once the economy is again recovering, helping workers back into employment quickly or to acquire new skills to improve employment possibilities and continuing to help viable businesses and new businesses emerge as reallocation occurs will be important. Progress on these fronts will avoid long-lasting negative legacies from the current shocks, pushing up unemployment and causing people to drop out of the labour force.

Israel

After a decline of around 4¼ per cent in 2020, GDP is projected to grow by around 2¼ per cent in 2021 and 4¼ per cent in 2022. Increased unemployment, and the likely rise in insolvencies after the second national lockdown, will weigh on the recovery of consumption and investment, despite government support to households and firms. From the second half of 2021, domestic and external demand will gain some strength as an effective immunisation against the virus is implemented. Unemployment will decline slowly but remain above pre-crisis levels at the end of 2022.

Macroeconomic policy should remain supportive and adapt to changing circumstances. The prolongation of some exceptional support measures until mid-2021 is welcome, but should be accompanied by more training and job-search assistance to help the unemployed transition to new jobs. Boosting investment in infrastructure and pre-school education can strengthen the recovery and help reduce socio-economic disparities.

Israel

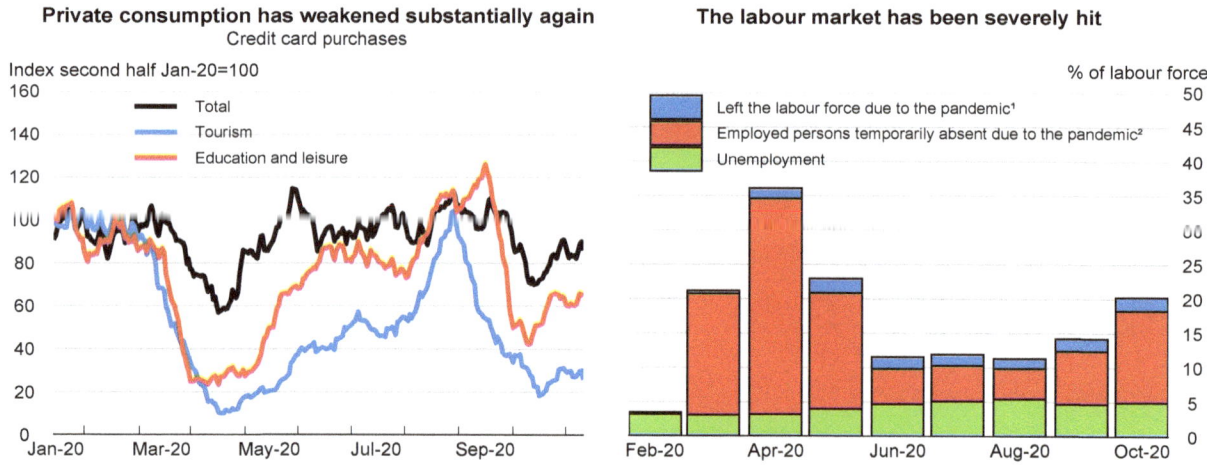

1. Series includes persons not in the labour force who stopped working due to dismissal or closure of the workplace since March. Data not available before March 2020.
2. This includes employees on unpaid leave, employees who were absent during the week due to reduced workload, work stoppage or other reasons related to the pandemic and excludes quarantined persons.
Source: Bank of Israel; and Israel Central Bureau of Statistics.

StatLink 🔢 https://doi.org/10.1787/888934218824

Israel: Demand, output and prices

Israel	2017	2018	2019	2020	2021	2022
	Current prices NIS billion	Percentage changes, volume (2015 prices)				
GDP at market prices	1 269.4	3.6	3.4	-4.2	2.3	4.2
Private consumption	694.6	3.6	3.8	-11.5	6.3	6.0
Government consumption	286.5	3.9	2.8	2.5	2.5	-0.1
Gross fixed capital formation	262.9	5.3	2.4	-10.2	-1.7	4.6
Final domestic demand	1 244.1	4.0	3.3	-7.9	3.6	4.1
Stockbuilding[1]	10.2	-0.6	0.2	0.3	-1.4	0.0
Total domestic demand	1 254.2	3.4	3.5	-7.6	2.1	4.1
Exports of goods and services	366.1	6.6	4.0	0.8	2.7	4.4
Imports of goods and services	350.9	6.3	4.1	-10.9	5.0	4.0
Net exports[1]	15.2	0.1	0.0	3.2	-0.4	0.3
Memorandum items						
GDP deflator	_	1.2	2.3	0.7	0.3	1.2
Consumer price index	_	0.8	0.8	-0.5	0.3	0.7
Core inflation index[2]	_	0.6	0.7	-0.2	0.3	0.7
Unemployment rate (% of labour force)	_	4.0	3.8	4.7	5.8	4.7
General government financial balance (% of GDP)	_	-3.6	-3.9	-12.9	-10.5	-8.1
General government gross debt (% of GDP)	_	60.9	60.0	75.0	83.6	87.6
Current account balance (% of GDP)	_	2.1	3.4	6.1	5.7	5.7

1. Contributions to changes in real GDP, actual amount in the first column.
2. Consumer price index excluding food and energy.
Source: OECD Economic Outlook 108 database.

StatLink ᴍᶳᴾ https://doi.org/10.1787/888934218843

The economy is gradually reopening after a second national lockdown

Amid rapidly increasing infection rates in the summer, the government re-tightened several containment measures in July and eventually introduced a second national lockdown from mid-September to mid-October over the Jewish holiday period. As the number of new cases has fallen, a gradual re-opening of the economy has begun. Movement restrictions have been lifted, and pre-schools, lower school grades, retail street shops and businesses that do not receive customers have been allowed to reopen except in localities with high infection rates.

Economic activity is subdued

The economy rebounded strongly in the third quarter of 2020, driven by private consumption and exports. High frequency mobility and credit card purchase data suggest a sharp drop in activity during the second lockdown albeit to a lesser extent than in the first lockdown. Consumer and business confidence also weakened again in October. The broadly-defined unemployment rate, which includes temporarily laid-off workers and people who left the labour force due to the pandemic, increased markedly again to around 20% in October. Consumer price inflation remains negative.

Fiscal and monetary support has been substantial

The monetary and fiscal authorities have taken extensive measures to support the most vulnerable households and firms. The central bank broadened its asset purchase programme to include corporate bonds in July, and expanded in October its government bond purchase programme by NIS 35 billion to NIS 85 billion (6% of GDP) and its credit facility for SMEs via banks. Approved discretionary fiscal measures amount to around 7% of GDP in 2020, including broadened eligibility to unemployment benefits for workers on unpaid leave. By end-October, about 65% of the spending had been implemented. To cushion the shock of the second lockdown, eligibility conditions for firm support have been temporarily eased further, and subsidies have been made available for firms to retain workers. A budget for 2021 has not yet been submitted, but several emergency measures, such as grants to hard-hit businesses and expanded eligibility to unemployment benefits, have been extended until June 2021, contingent on the economic situation. An additional NIS 5 billion (0.3% of GDP) has been allocated to public investment projects over the period 2020-25.

The recovery from the pandemic will be slow

The projections assume a more gradual exit from the second lockdown compared to the first one. GDP will recover only modestly by 2.3% in 2021 before expanding by 4.2% in 2022 as an effective vaccine is rolled out. High uncertainty, increasing unemployment in the near term, and a likely rise in insolvencies once government support is withdrawn will weigh on consumer demand and investment. Demand from Israel's main trading partners will only pick up gradually. Unemployment will start to fall slowly in 2021 but remain above pre-crisis levels at the end of 2022. The fiscal projections include the announced extension of several measures for next year, but assume overall lower fiscal support compared to 2020 as other emergency measures are phased out. A deterioration of the health situation requiring new nationwide lockdowns would delay the recovery further until immunisation becomes general. Growth could also be weaker in the event of heightened geopolitical tensions or renewed internal political uncertainty. Growth could be stronger if the government approves more substantial fiscal support than assumed.

Policy should support the recovery

Fiscal and monetary policy should remain supportive in the near term. Approving a budget for 2021 as soon as possible would reduce uncertainty and improve fiscal transparency. As the recovery progresses, it will be important to shift policy from broad income and liquidity support to more targeted measures that facilitate the reallocation of capital and workers from sectors facing extended lower demand to expanding sectors. In this respect, Israel has scope to step up active labour market policies, such as retraining and job-search support, to help the unemployed transition to new jobs. As some emergency measures are phased out, there is also an opportunity to channel funds into areas that help boost demand in the short term, improve productivity and narrow Israel's socio-economic gaps. Further infrastructure investment is needed, as well as additional funding to build new childcare capacity and to improve its quality, particularly in lagging regions. Strengthening existing in-work benefits would support the households most in need and improve work incentives for low-skilled workers.

Italy

After falling sharply in 2020, GDP is projected to expand by 4.3% in 2021 and 3.2% in 2022. Lockdowns and uncertainty are weighing on activity, although government support has mitigated the effects on firms and households. Substantial job creation, especially for the low-skilled, women and youth, will return only in 2022, when an effective vaccine is expected to have been deployed widely, stimulating consumption, and easing precautionary saving. Investment and exports are expected to recover gradually alongside the manufacturing sector. Supportive fiscal policy is resulting in rising public debt levels, but interest rates are projected to remain low. Higher growth is needed to improve the fiscal position in the medium term.

The government's adjusted budget envisages faster, greener, digitalised and more inclusive growth. Stimulus must be accompanied by continued structural reforms and their effective implementation. The regulatory regime can be simplified, delays in the courts system addressed and worker training outcomes improved. Tax, procurement and spending policy reforms can complement efforts to raise public infrastructure spending capacity. With financial, bankruptcy and competition reforms, these public sector reforms would support the expansion of new and small businesses, raise productivity and reduce informality and persistent inequality.

Italy 1

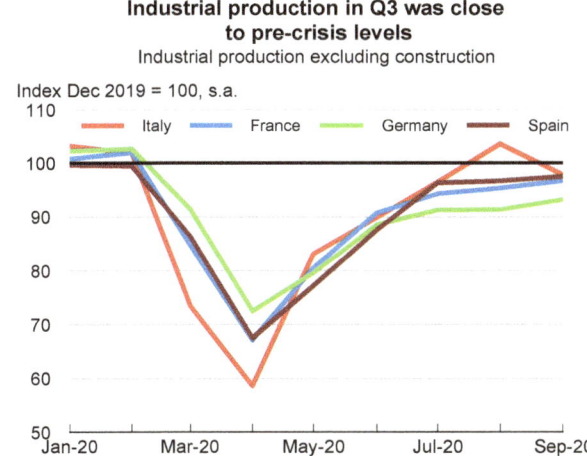

Industrial production in Q3 was close to pre-crisis levels
Industrial production excluding construction

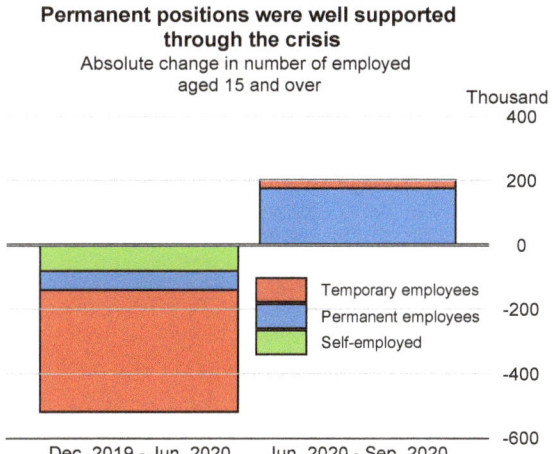

Permanent positions were well supported through the crisis
Absolute change in number of employed aged 15 and over

Source: OECD Main Economic Indicators database; and ISTAT.

StatLink https://doi.org/10.1787/888934218862

Italy: Demand, output and prices

Italy	2017	2018	2019	2020	2021	2022
	Current prices EUR billion	Percentage changes, volume (2015 prices)				
GDP at market prices	1 738.4	0.8	0.3	-9.1	4.3	3.2
Private consumption	1 046.1	1.0	0.5	-9.2	4.9	2.3
Government consumption	327.0	0.2	-0.2	2.1	1.0	-0.3
Gross fixed capital formation	304.1	2.9	1.6	-14.6	4.3	9.5
Final domestic demand	1 677.2	1.2	0.5	-8.0	3.9	3.0
Stockbuilding[1]	11.5	0.0	-0.7	0.1	0.0	0.0
Total domestic demand	1 688.7	1.2	-0.2	-7.9	4.0	3.1
Exports of goods and services	535.9	1.6	1.3	-17.8	5.4	6.6
Imports of goods and services	486.2	2.9	-0.4	-15.0	4.2	6.6
Net exports[1]	49.7	-0.3	0.5	-1.4	0.4	0.2
Memorandum items						
GDP deflator	_	1.0	0.7	1.2	0.9	1.2
Harmonised index of consumer prices	_	1.2	0.6	-0.1	0.4	0.8
Harmonised index of core inflation[2]	_	0.6	0.5	0.6	0.6	0.8
Unemployment rate (% of labour force)	_	10.6	9.9	9.4	11.0	10.9
Household saving ratio, net (% of disposable income)	_	2.6	2.5	10.2	7.1	5.6
General government financial balance (% of GDP)	_	-2.2	-1.6	-10.7	-6.9	-4.4
General government gross debt (% of GDP)	_	147.8	155.8	178.7	178.3	177.3
General government debt, Maastricht definition (% of GDP)	_	134.5	134.7	159.8	158.3	158.2
Current account balance (% of GDP)	_	2.5	3.0	2.8	3.0	3.1

1. Contributions to changes in real GDP, actual amount in the first column.
2. Harmonised index of consumer prices excluding food, energy, alcohol and tobacco.
Source: OECD Economic Outlook 108 database.

StatLink ᐊᵐˢᒥ https://doi.org/10.1787/888934218881

Italy 2

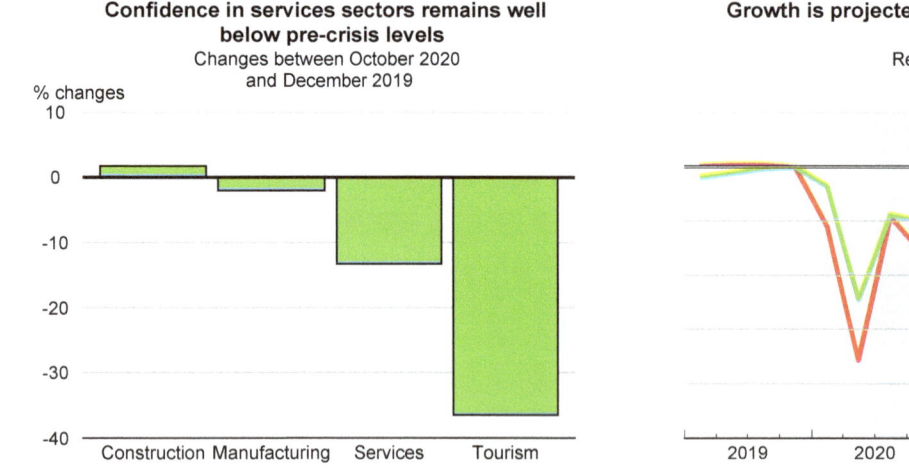

Confidence in services sectors remains well below pre-crisis levels
Changes between October 2020 and December 2019

Growth is projected to recover gradually

Real GDP

Source: ISTAT; and OECD Economic Outlook 108 database.

StatLink ᐊᵐˢᒥ https://doi.org/10.1787/888934218900

New national COVID-19 restrictions complemented with stricter local regulations

COVID-19 infection rates rose sharply from mid-October, with infection hotspots geographically dispersed and the national state of emergency extended into 2021. The country imposed a three-tier, regionally-based, system of controls that increases in intensity alongside pandemic threat levels. The controls focus on reducing social interactions, whilst allowing economic activity and schooling to continue as far as possible. Additional support of approximately EUR 10 billion has been announced in a series of three packages to help firms and workers affected by the new restrictions. Some of this will be funded by savings from the earlier COVID-19 support package, as well as by budget reallocations.

Rising infections have curtailed the sharp rebound in activity

The rise in infections, restrictions on activity and uncertainty have halted the sharp recovery in activity in the third quarter. Generous liquidity support has helped firms, with COVID-19-related guarantees and bank repayment moratoria extended to over EUR 300 billion in loans. Industrial, construction and retail sales activity recovered in the third quarter, reaching levels close to those in December 2019. Short-time work support helped protect against job losses. Job creation returned in the third quarter, but did not rebound as quickly as activity, weighing on consumption. Young workers, who are more likely to be on temporary contracts, women and the self-employed have suffered most from the deterioration in the labour market. Confidence has improved, but ongoing outbreaks reduce the potential for a fast rebound in 2021. Business confidence in the services sector, particularly tourism, has recovered more slowly than in the manufacturing sector. Precautionary saving rates remain elevated.

Extensive fiscal support is helping to cushion the impact of the crisis

The government's fiscal support totals around EUR 100 billion (6% of GDP), after the support package in the summer added a further EUR 25 billion to earlier initiatives, and measures announced in November targeted sectors hardest hit by new restrictions. Most of this spending is expected to take place in 2020, and relies extensively on existing instruments. Substantial measures to protect households include wage support, childcare allowances, extended leave, loan deferrals (in particular for first time homebuyers), as well as the deferral of tax payments. Firms have received liquidity support with grants to specific sectors, tax deferrals, social security contribution holidays and loan guarantees for new and existing loans, including small and medium-enterprises and exporters. The measures have mitigated potential business closures and job losses.

The extraordinary packages to support incomes of workers, the ban on firing workers and easier terms to extend fixed-term contracts will continue into 2021. The adjusted budget for 2021-2023 proposed further fiscal support for households and firms in 2021 that, whilst less generous than 2020 levels, is more targeted. The level of support is likely to increase should restrictions last longer than currently envisaged by the authorities. The adjusted budget also outlines tax reforms to improve efficiency and transparency, to raise employment in southern regions and to reduce the labour tax wedge and provide income support to middle and lower-income workers. In addition, the adjusted budget increases public investment using the EU Recovery and Resilience Facility from the latter half of 2021 to support greener, digitised and more inclusive growth. These proposals could set growth on a sustained higher trajectory if coupled with structural reforms that enable labour and capital to move to the most productive firms, helping narrow the gap between Italy's most and least productive firms.

The recovery will be slow and unequal

Lockdowns and uncertainty about the pandemic will weigh heavily on activity, investment and employment until general immunisation has been attained. The unemployment rate will pick up during 2021 and remain high in 2022. Consumption growth is projected to recover, but household precautionary saving will remain elevated. Investment is expected to recover in 2022, as public investment rises and firms in more resilient sectors such as manufacturing begin to undertake replacement investment. The services sector, by contrast, will recover more slowly as domestic demand and tourism remain weak until an effective vaccine is widely deployed. This will exacerbate labour market and regional inequalities. Bankruptcies and non-performing loans will rise, as in other countries. Exports recover only partially, reflecting weak global demand, including for tourism. Fiscal support is raising net borrowing in 2020, which will decline in 2022 as growth and revenues recover, and EU Recovery and Resilience projects become more significant. Interest rates are projected to remain low. The pace of growth will have a large bearing on the evolution of government debt ratios, which will remain elevated, at just below 160% of GDP (Maastricht definition).

Downside risks to the projections are significant. Delays in public investment spending and a slower recovery in private sector investment would reduce the pace of recovery in 2022. Whilst the banking sector is much stronger than a decade ago and has so far withstood the impact of the crisis, it could be negatively affected by extensive bankruptcies. There are also upside risks to the projection. Effective immunisation against the virus may come faster than anticipated. Households may save less than projected. Export performance may return to pre-pandemic levels if firms take advantage of shifts towards more regional global value chains. Rapid firm adaptation to consumers' increased use of digital technologies could raise productivity and growth, particularly since prior to the crisis, Italy lagged peer countries. This effect may be especially important in increasing market access for smaller companies. Firms in sectors with relatively low fixed costs and barriers to entry, which are able to quickly begin hiring, could drive a sharper rebound in activity.

Complementing fiscal support with structural reform will sustain higher growth

Fiscal policy will need to remain supportive until the recovery is underway. Raising the effectiveness of public administration is critical. Public investments need to be prioritised for their individual and combined impact on growth, jobs and the long-term structure of the economy. Enhanced public employment services and improvements to existing training schemes can mitigate skills mismatch, especially for youth and other vulnerable workers. Judicial reforms, streamlined regulatory frameworks and risk-based enforcement of tax and other regulations can balance the costs and fair execution of the law. Improvements to the composition and complexity of the tax regime, as well as public sector capacity to prioritise and manage infrastructure projects, would raise the growth impact of fiscal policy. Harnessing digitalisation can reduce informality, broaden the tax net and improve targeting for social benefits. Ongoing efforts to strengthen the balance sheet and governance of the banking sector and implement bankruptcy reforms, along with greater competition, would improve the allocation of capital and labour across firms, and improve the resilience of the economy to future shocks. Sustained faster growth would lower public debt levels and interest payments.

Japan

The COVID-19 shock in early 2020 triggered a major recession and real GDP is projected to shrink by around 5¼ per cent this year. The economy is gradually strengthening although growth remains sluggish. Ongoing difficulties in bringing COVID-19 infections under control hold back domestic demand. As restrictions are lifted in the near term, consumption is expected to recover, supported by government subsidies and incentives. In addition, recovering external demand, as the sanitary situation of trading partners improves, will sustain export growth. On the other hand, private investment is set to remain relatively subdued. Overall, GDP is projected to expand by 2¼ per cent in 2021 and 1½ per cent in 2022, assuming further economic stimulus.

Fiscal policy reacted forcefully to the sanitary shock, and has subsequently been balancing the needs of protecting households by keeping infection rates low with reactivating businesses adversely affected by the pandemic. However, without any action beyond the measures currently in place, the recovery may slow. A resilient and sustainable economic expansion will require further policy support and structural reforms.

Japan 1

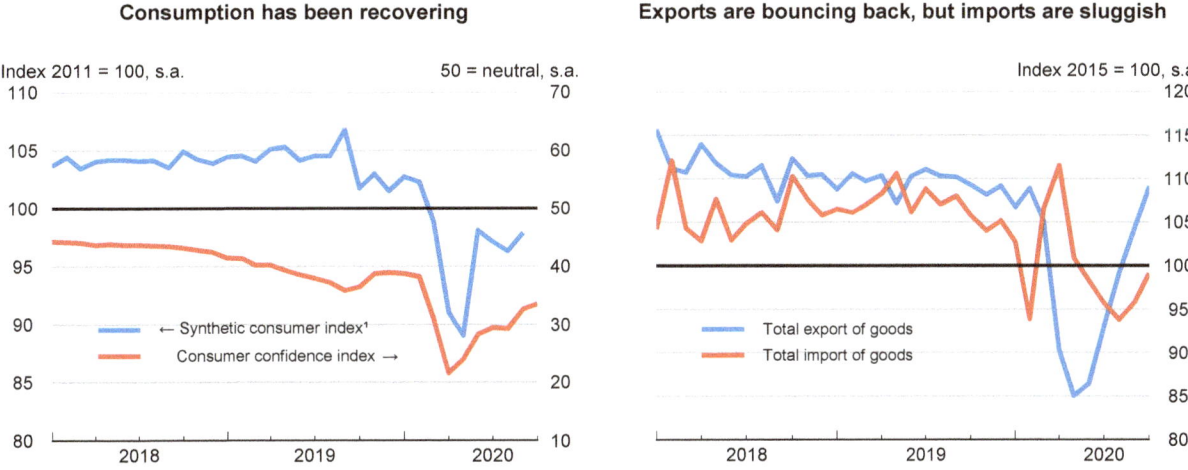

Consumption has been recovering

Exports are bouncing back, but imports are sluggish

1. The synthetic consumer index is calculated by the Cabinet Office to show monthly macro-level private consumption trends by using both demand and supply side statistics. The consumer confidence index is the average of four sub indicators for overall livelihood, income growth, employment, and willingness to buy durable goods, on a scale of 1-100.
Source: Cabinet Office; and Bank of Japan.

StatLink ᵐˢ⁴ https://doi.org/10.1787/888934218919

Japan: Demand, output and prices

Japan	2017	2018	2019	2020	2021	2022
	Current prices YEN trillion	Percentage changes, volume (2011 prices)				
GDP at market prices	545.9	0.3	0.7	-5.3	2.3	1.5
Private consumption	302.6	0.0	0.1	-6.1	2.6	1.4
Government consumption	107.1	0.9	1.9	1.9	1.5	-0.4
Gross fixed capital formation	129.9	0.6	1.3	-4.7	0.2	2.4
Final domestic demand	539.6	0.3	0.8	-4.1	1.8	1.2
Stockbuilding[1]	1.2	0.0	0.1	0.0	0.0	0.0
Total domestic demand	540.8	0.3	0.8	-4.1	1.8	1.2
Exports of goods and services	96.9	3.5	-1.6	-14.4	5.2	4.8
Imports of goods and services	91.8	3.7	-0.7	-7.6	0.9	1.7
Net exports[1]	5.1	0.0	-0.2	-1.2	0.7	0.5
Memorandum items						
GDP deflator	–	-0.1	0.6	0.9	0.4	0.6
Consumer price index[2]	–	1.0	0.5	0.2	0.2	0.4
Core consumer price index[3]	–	0.2	0.5	0.2	0.1	0.4
Unemployment rate (% of labour force)	–	2.4	2.4	2.8	2.9	2.8
Household saving ratio, net (% of disposable income)	–	4.3	5.3	7.1	4.6	4.5
General government financial balance (% of GDP)	–	-2.3	-2.6	-10.5	-5.5	-3.5
General government gross debt (% of GDP)	–	224.2	225.3	241.6	243.3	243.9
Current account balance (% of GDP)	–	3.6	3.6	3.0	3.6	3.9

1. Contributions to changes in real GDP, actual amount in the first column.
2. Calculated as the sum of the seasonally adjusted quarterly indices for each year.
3. Consumer price index excluding food and energy.
Source: OECD Economic Outlook 108 database.

StatLink https://doi.org/10.1787/888934218938

Japan 2

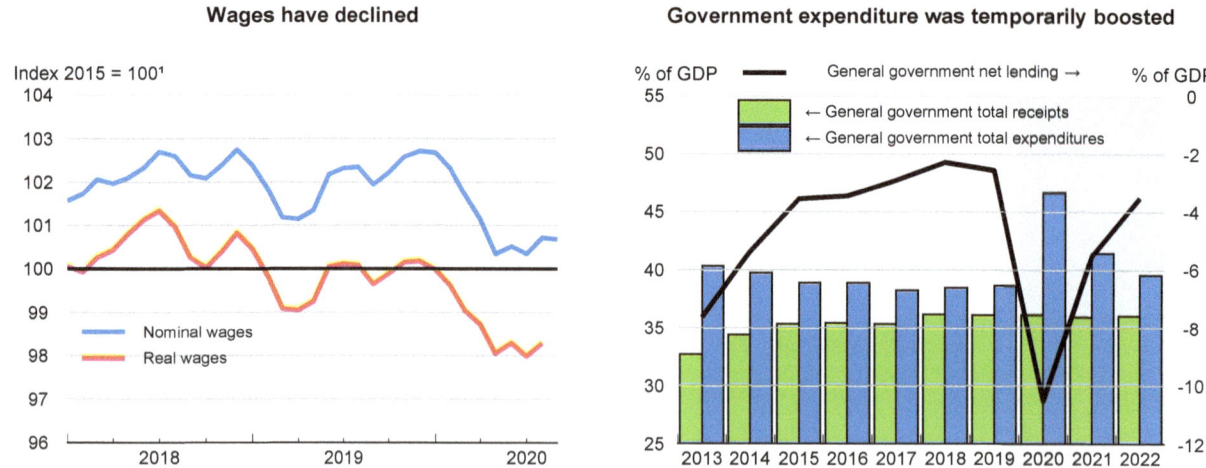

Wages have declined

Government expenditure was temporarily boosted

1. Nominal wages refer to total cash earnings per employee. Real wages are nominal wages deflated by the consumer price index of all items less imputed rent. Three-month moving average.
Source: Ministry of Health, Labour and Welfare; and OECD Economic Outlook 108 database.

StatLink https://doi.org/10.1787/888934218957

After a state of emergency, the economy is gradually reopening

Confronted with the first wave of COVID-19 infections in March, the Japanese government declared a state of emergency from 7 April to 25 May. This enabled prefectural governors to order school closures, restrict the use of public facilities and request non-essential businesses to close. Even though confinement was not legally imposed, economic activity dropped dramatically as businesses closed or shifted to telework and households shielded themselves. This helped bring the spread of the coronavirus under control while the capacity for testing and medical care was stepped up. A second wave of infections between late-July and mid-August saw a limited rise in new cases of COVID-19 and a comparatively low death rate. While limiting the number of infections considerably below the health system's capacity to cope with them, central and local governments gradually lifted the restrictions on large-scale events and other activities involving close personal interaction. Against this backdrop, it is assumed that the government will not need to impose comprehensive confinement measures and that the health situation will improve with the advent of a vaccine.

Consumption and exports are recovering, but investment is lagging

Consumption appears to have recovered well with consumer sentiment picking up. Due to the rapid recovery of large trading partners, Japan's exports have also started to recover, while imports have so far remained sluggish. Due to government subsidies for firms and employees, the unemployment rate has barely risen. However, wages have plummeted for many workers and will take time to recover, while job creation remains anaemic. Notwithstanding a recovery in industrial production, forward-looking indicators suggest continued weakness in investment, due to a low capacity utilisation rate and huge uncertainty about future growth. Consumer price inflation will be zero or slightly negative in the near term because of low demand, but is projected to edge up and turn positive as consumption and employment improve.

Government measures are protecting businesses and supporting households

Since the onset of the pandemic, the government has launched several supplementary budgets, with a wide range of measures to support households and protect businesses and employment. These include cash handouts of JPY 100 000 to every resident, cash transfers to heavily affected business owners, expanding the Employment Adjustment Subsidy which provides firms with financial support to cover the cost of special paid leave, additional cash benefits for single-parent households and a rent subsidy to help heavily affected firms. The Bank of Japan has also acted to support the economy, expanding its policy to ensure financial stability by providing smooth and adequate financing through enhanced purchases of various assets and introducing interest-free loans against private debt as collateral. In addition, some public financial institutions provide interest-free loans to firms.

The supplementary budgets also finance distinct measures for the recovery stage, including subsidies to support domestic services, and funding for digital transformation and supply-chain adjustments. For example, the authorities started promoting domestic tourism by providing coupons to households or reimbursing fixed amounts as digital cash. Furthermore, the government expanded the programme from October, by including dining in restaurants, visiting local shopping areas and travelling to and from Tokyo, which had been excluded thus far.

The outlook is uncertain

Following a sharp contraction in 2020, the economy is projected to recover slowly, with annual growth of around 2¼ per cent in 2021 and 1½ per cent in 2022. The recovery of major trading partners is set to support exports, whereas weak real income growth is likely to hold back private consumption. In addition, the Tokyo Olympic and Paralympic Games in summer 2021 are assumed to go ahead, which will temporarily boost consumption and exports though by less than anticipated earlier given the decline in international travel. Currently, the authorities are managing to limit the number of infections, but the risk of a larger-scale resurgence remains elevated. The sanitary situation will weigh on consumer sentiment until a vaccine becomes widely deployed, and will determine the size of the potential onsite audience for the Olympic and Paralympic Games. On the other hand, the recently signed Regional Comprehensive Economic Partnership (RCEP), through the effects of tariff reductions and rules of origin simplification, will support stronger trading relationships between members.

The OECD projections assume an additional fiscal impulse worth around 0.5% of GDP in 2021-22, which would avoid an even sharper decline in public demand Without additional fiscal support from the supplementary budget, the recovery would be slower. However, the additional fiscal support will further push up public debt, which has reached unprecedented levels, exceeding 240% of GDP. The projections also assume that the Bank of Japan will maintain its stance, holding down interest rates on government bonds, until its inflation target is achieved.

Enhancing resilience, productivity and sustainability

The immediate priority for policy is to support the recovery and react to further sanitary shocks to shield households and businesses. In designing policies, the government should focus on structural reforms that will enhance resilience, productivity and sustainability, as the economy continues to recover but remains exposed to pandemic-related threats. For those purposes, policies that promote flexible working styles are essential. This will require actions to adjust the social security system to allow for more flexibility in work and childcare, to reinforce the education system and to strengthen investment. Digitalisation, one of the new government's main targets, can support these ambitions. Actions to facilitate teleworking and allow individuals to easily access online education and government services, including social security benefits, will support investment and job creation while enabling households to minimise their exposure to the pandemic. These actions should be inclusive and ensure that they cover the most vulnerable and those severely affected by COVID-19. In the longer term, action will still be needed to address underlying fiscal trends. The review of the government's economic and fiscal framework in 2021 will be an opportunity to take stock of the impact of the coronavirus on the public finances and review progress to meeting mid-term targets. Finally, fiscal policy during the recovery ought to support reductions in greenhouse gas emissions, notably through increased research and development, use of renewable energy and energy efficiency.

Korea

Effective measures to contain the spread of COVID-19 have limited the estimated fall in GDP to just over 1% in 2020, the smallest decline in the OECD. Activity is picking up on the back of a rebound in consumption, bolstered by large government transfers to households, and a recovery in exports, led by semiconductors. The sizeable digital and green investments of the New Deal will buttress the recovery. GDP is projected to grow at about 3% per annum in 2021 and 2022, but the recovery remains vulnerable to a further spread of the virus in Korea or abroad until an effective vaccine is deployed in the latter half of 2021.

Policies need to continue supporting households and businesses until the economy is on a firmer recovery path. Relatively low public debt allows an expansionary fiscal policy and the announced fiscal rules will help reinforce long-term sustainability in the face of rapid ageing. Beyond an immediate stimulus to the economy, the New Deal constitutes an opportunity to boost productivity, inclusiveness and green growth. Effective implementation is key and outcomes should be monitored closely to ensure maximum impact.

A resurgence of COVID-19 was contained, but many jobs have been lost

A resurgence of COVID-19 infections in mid-August led to stricter distancing measures for almost two months, which have stemmed the spread of the virus so far. The government eased the distancing guidelines in mid-October and higher-class attendance was allowed in all schools. The Google mobility indicator for retail and recreation rebounded following a sharp contraction in late August and September. However, in November, distancing rules were tightened for the operation of facilities such as bars and restaurants and school attendance was limited in some areas.

Korea

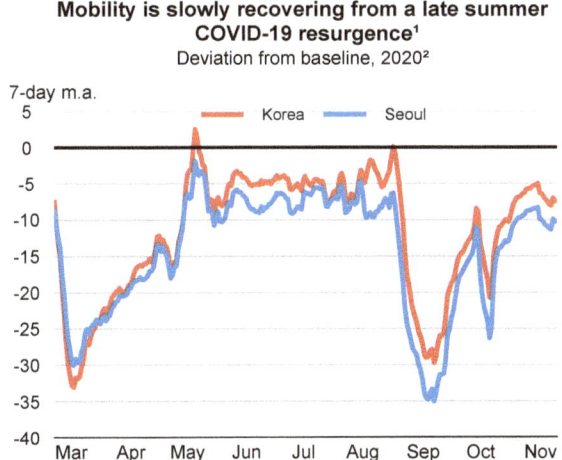

Mobility is slowly recovering from a late summer COVID-19 resurgence[1]
Deviation from baseline, 2020[2]

Exports have bounced back

Exports of goods, USD value

1. Mobility trends for places like restaurants, cafés, shopping centres, theme parks, museums, libraries, and movie theatres.
2. Deviation from the baseline. The baseline is the median value, for the corresponding day of the week, during the 5-week period from 3 January to 6 February, 2020.
Source: Google LLC, *Google COVID-19 Community Mobility Reports*, https://www.google.com/covid19/mobility/.; and Kore Customs Service.

StatLink https://doi.org/10.1787/888934218976

Korea: Demand, output and prices

Korea	2017	2018	2019	2020	2021	2022
	Current prices KRW trillion	Percentage changes, volume (2015 prices)				
GDP at market prices	1 835.7	2.9	2.0	-1.1	2.8	3.4
Private consumption	872.8	3.2	1.7	-4.1	3.2	1.9
Government consumption	283.0	5.3	6.6	5.5	6.1	5.4
Gross fixed capital formation	578.5	-2.2	-2.8	2.1	1.5	3.4
Final domestic demand	1 734.3	1.7	1.1	-0.5	3.2	3.1
Stockbuilding[1]	14.3	0.3	0.1	-0.7	-0.5	0.0
Total domestic demand	1 748.5	2.0	1.1	-1.1	2.7	3.1
Exports of goods and services	751.4	4.0	1.7	-3.9	4.0	3.2
Imports of goods and services	664.3	1.7	-0.6	-4.2	4.3	3.1
Net exports[1]	87.1	1.0	1.0	0.0	0.0	0.2
Memorandum items						
GDP deflator	–	0.5	-0.9	1.2	1.1	0.6
Consumer price index	–	1.5	0.4	0.5	0.6	1.1
Core inflation index[2]	–	1.2	0.7	0.4	0.6	1.1
Unemployment rate (% of labour force)	–	3.9	3.8	3.8	3.6	3.2
Household saving ratio, net (% of disposable income)	–	7.2	7.1	11.5	8.5	8.1
General government financial balance (% of GDP)	–	3.0	0.9	-4.2	-3.8	-3.0
General government gross debt (% of GDP)	–	41.9	40.9	43.9	46.3	48.1
Current account balance (% of GDP)	–	4.5	3.6	3.8	3.9	4.0

1. Contributions to changes in real GDP, actual amount in the first column.
2. Consumer price index excluding food and energy.
Source: OECD Economic Outlook 108 database.

StatLink ⟹ https://doi.org/10.1787/888934318005

The economy is recovering gradually

Private consumption is gradually recovering, and a 31% surge in online shopping in September compared with a year ago has boosted retail sales. The alleviation of distancing recommendations, along with government support to households, has propped up labour-intensive services, such as tourism, hotels, restaurants and culture, where activity nevertheless remains relatively low. About 421 000 jobs have been lost economy-wide over the 12 months to October. Exports have bounced back, led by semiconductors and automobiles. Investment has held up relatively well so far, despite weak demand and high uncertainty.

Expansionary policy has damped the COVID-19 shock

The government has introduced massive policy support, totalling KRW 285 trillion (about 15% of GDP) so far, including extra budget easing, liquidity provisions and credit guarantees, to mitigate the COVID-19 impact. The national assembly passed four supplementary budgets, worth KRW 67 trillion (3.5% of GDP), of which about 70% will be debt-financed. General government net lending is expected to move from a surplus of 0.9% of GDP in 2019 to a deficit of 4.2% of GDP in 2020, and gross public debt is projected to rise above 48% of GDP in 2022. This fiscal expansion is appropriate given economic conditions. At the same time, the recently planned introduction of fiscal rules limiting the general government deficit to 3% of GDP and gross government debt to 60% of GDP from 2025 onwards is welcome, especially as ageing will push up welfare spending. The Bank of Korea has maintained the policy rate at 0.5% since May 2020, following cuts totalling 75 basis points earlier this year, and provided ample liquidity. Headline inflation rose to 0.1% and core inflation fell to 0.3% (year-on-year) in October, calling for monetary policy to remain accommodative.

Steady economic growth is projected over the next two years

GDP is projected to increase by 2.8% and 3.4% in 2021 and 2022 respectively. The easing of distancing rules with the rollout of an effective vaccine will allow a gradual recovery of services, which will lift employment. Strong growth in government consumption and transfers provide a major boost to the economy, and the "New Deal" will support investment. Exports are expected to expand further as the global economy picks up, and a potential easing in US-China trade tensions would impart additional momentum. The recently signed Regional Comprehensive Economic Partnership agreement will also support exports. The accelerated pace of digitalisation worldwide is set to boost demand for semiconductors and electronic products. Nevertheless, uncertainty remains unusually high, especially regarding the strength of the demand for exports, which are crucial to the Korean economy.

The recovery is still vulnerable to the global environment

Some households, notably those comprising non-regular workers, and industries, especially in services, still face very challenging conditions. Support to households needs to be targeted towards those most in need. Temporary support to companies, such as tax and social security deferrals and reductions, may need to be extended. However, some jobs and companies are likely to disappear permanently, as the crisis has affected demand patterns durably and accelerated ongoing trends, in particular digitalisation. Hence, encouraging the restructuring of firms and investing in training and upskilling is essential to make the most of the "New Deal" and foster digital, green and inclusive growth.

Latvia

GDP is set to contract by 4.3% in 2020, before growing by 2.4% in 2021 and 4.0% in 2022. Activity rose rapidly in the third quarter of 2020 after containment measures had been withdrawn. However, the recovery has been interrupted by the recent tightening of containment measures in response to a renewed virus outbreak, and is projected to resume at a slow rate when the restraints are relaxed. Private consumption will strengthen as household confidence and net disposable incomes increase. Investment will also gradually regain momentum. The labour market has been quite resilient. However, unemployment will remain elevated in 2021 due to a slow recovery in labour-intensive sectors.

Fiscal policy helped to prevent a more severe downturn, and will continue to support the recovery. The strong fiscal position leaves room for the government to provide further help to households and businesses, if needed. To facilitate the reallocation of workers and capital, training programmes should be enhanced and insolvency procedures should be made more effective.

New restrictions have been imposed to combat the second wave

Incidence and mortality rates related to COVID-19 have been low compared with other European countries so far. However, the number of confirmed cases has risen rapidly from mid-September and a state of emergency took effect on 9 November. No more than two households can gather at private events, public recreation facilities are closed, and restaurants can only provide takeaway services. Other national containment measures include wearing masks in public transport and stores, and allowing only certain retailers to open during weekends. Unlike in the spring, elementary schools and kindergartens remain open. Google data indicate that mobility to places like restaurants and shopping centres, while higher than most OECD countries, was about 17% below pre-COVID-19 levels in mid-November. Midweek traffic congestion in Riga has declined since mid-October.

Latvia

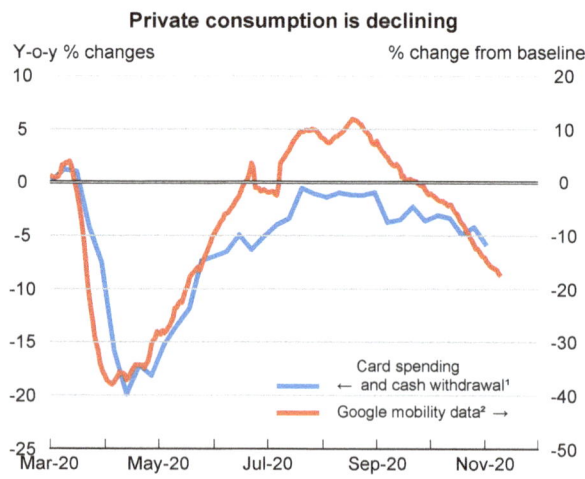
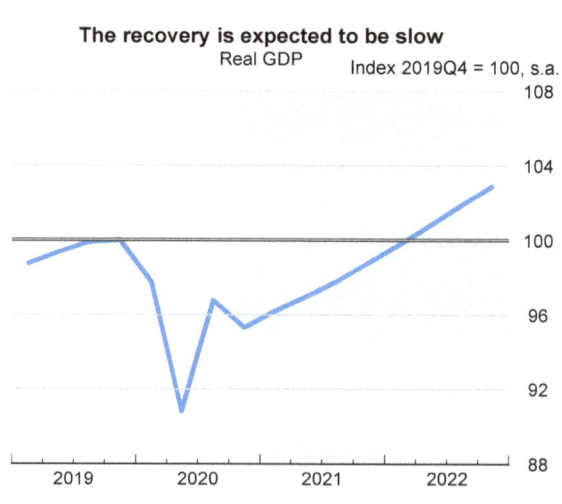

1. Weekly year-on-year percentage change. Average over past 4 weeks.
2. Google retail and recreation community mobility trend. The baseline is the median value, for the corresponding day of the week, during the 5-week period January 3-February 6, 2020. Average over past 14 days.
Source: OECD Economic Outlook 108 database; Google LLC, *Google COVID-19 Community Mobility Reports*, https://www.google.com/covid19/mobility/ ; and Swedbank.

StatLink https://doi.org/10.1787/888934219014

Latvia: Demand, output and prices

Latvia	2017	2018	2019	2020	2021	2022
	Current prices EUR billion	Percentage changes, volume (2015 prices)				
GDP at market prices	27.0	4.0	2.1	-4.3	2.4	4.0
Private consumption	16.3	2.6	2.2	-11.2	2.8	5.9
Government consumption	4.9	1.6	2.6	2.6	2.7	2.4
Gross fixed capital formation	5.6	11.8	2.1	-2.4	0.1	2.9
Final domestic demand	26.7	4.3	2.2	-6.7	2.1	4.5
Stockbuilding[1]	0.4	1.6	0.6	1.6	0.0	0.0
Total domestic demand	27.1	5.5	2.6	-5.2	2.2	4.5
Exports of goods and services	16.6	4.3	2.1	-6.0	1.8	4.4
Imports of goods and services	16.8	6.4	3.0	-7.5	1.4	5.2
Net exports[1]	- 0.2	-1.4	-0.5	1.0	0.3	-0.5
Memorandum items						
GDP deflator	_	3.9	2.4	0.2	1.4	1.9
Harmonised index of consumer prices	_	2.6	2.7	0.1	0.4	1.5
Harmonised index of core inflation[2]	_	1.9	2.2	0.9	0.9	1.6
Unemployment rate (% of labour force)	_	7.5	6.3	8.4	8.8	8.1
Household saving ratio, net (% of disposable income)	_	-1.3	-3.0	5.6	1.0	-2.3
General government financial balance (% of GDP)	_	-0.8	-0.6	-5.5	-3.8	-2.2
General government gross debt (% of GDP)	_	46.3	47.7	54.6	56.4	57.4
General government debt, Maastricht definition (% of GDP)	_	37.1	36.9	43.8	45.5	46.6
Current account balance (% of GDP)	_	-0.3	-0.6	3.1	3.1	2.3

1. Contributions to changes in real GDP, actual amount in the first column.
2. Harmonised index of consumer prices excluding food, energy, alcohol and tobacco.
Source: OECD Economic Outlook 108 database.

StatLink https://doi.org/10.1787/888934219033

Effective containment enabled a swift recovery from the first wave

A sharp fall in private consumption led to a GDP contraction of 9% in the second quarter of 2020 compared with the same quarter of 2019, but data for the third quarter point to a strong rebound across most sectors, including manufacturing and retail. The swift recovery owes in part to less stringent restrictions and effective policy responses that limited the early spread of the virus. The seasonally adjusted unemployment rate had increased by about two percentage points at its peak in July, but already declined to 8.4% in September despite the end of the job retention scheme. Wage growth for full-time employees has slowed but remains above zero. Card spending and cash withdrawals are below last year's levels and have recently begun to decline.

The fiscal response has focused on boosting investment

The government took significant steps to support firms' cash flow, the health system and jobs in companies hit hard by the crisis, with measures that amounted to 4¾ per cent of GDP. However, limited demand for some of the programmes, particularly loan guarantees, and some delays in implementation have led to lower spending than expected. The income support measure for inactive workers closed at the end of June, but was reintroduced in November. Compared with neighbouring countries, Latvia's fiscal response has focused more on boosting investment, and the European Recovery Facility has potential to achieve further progress. The 2021 draft budget proposes a structural deficit of about 2% of GDP, excluding EU grants. The government plans to reduce the structural deficit to about 1% of GDP in 2022. It also intends to raise the monthly minimum wage from EUR 430 to EUR 500 as of January 2021. In addition, social security contributions will be reduced by one percentage point and the threshold for personal income tax will be increased by 50%. Accommodative ECB monetary policy is mitigating the recession through low borrowing costs.

A slow recovery lies ahead as health risks remain

A slow recovery is projected as virus containment measures are assumed to ease gradually from December. GDP should recover to its pre-crisis level during the first half of 2022. Higher minimum wages and a lower tax wedge for low-income workers will improve households' disposable income and foster consumption. Nonetheless, restrictions on several activities, and high precautionary saving, until an effective vaccine is deployed, will moderate private consumption until consumers regain confidence. Business investment will pick up slowly, supported by low interest rates and declining uncertainty. Exports will recover slowly as economic activity gradually improves in Europe. Unemployment will remain high as long as labour-intensive sectors, such as tourism, cannot operate normally. High public investment is projected to support the labour market recovery and offset some of the possible negative employment effects of the minimum wage increase. Inflation will edge up only slowly due to significant spare capacity. Failing to contain the spread of the virus until a vaccine becomes available would reduce private consumption and further slow the recovery in the short term. Conversely, a swift use of European recovery funds could lead to a stronger rebound.

Policies should support the reallocation of workers and productivity

Measures to improve relevant skills and support the reallocation of workers and capital should complement higher public investment. Latvia's rental housing market offers few affordable choices, reducing opportunities to match workers to jobs. Increasing spending on active labour market policies and reforming the private rental market would ease labour reallocation. To strengthen access to housing, Latvia should expand the competencies of municipal housing companies and facilitate the development of non-profit or limited-profit providers. Improving insolvency procedures would help restructure viable firms and liquidate unprofitable ones more rapidly. Accelerating the digital transformation has become more urgent; in particular, training to improve digital skills would encourage greater uptake of digital technologies.

Lithuania

Following a relatively mild contraction, GDP is projected to grow by around 3% in 2021 and 2022 on average, as confidence strengthens and investment picks up slowly with the rollout of an effective vaccine. Unemployment has risen in the wake of the crisis and, despite some gradual decline, it will remain above the pre-pandemic level. Inflation will move upwards in tandem with the revival of economic activity.

A comprehensive package of fiscal and financial measures averted a sharper GDP contraction in 2020. The short-time work scheme and support for non-standard workers, along with increases in social benefits, mitigated the impact of the crisis on jobs and poverty. Targeted support should continue given the uncertain outlook. Structural measures, especially effective skilling and re-skilling programmes, are essential for the reallocation of workers and stronger long-term growth.

The resurgence of the epidemic triggered new containment measures

Lithuania dealt successfully with the outbreak of the pandemic in the spring, recording low fatality rates. However, since early August, COVID-19 infections have been rising again, prompting the government to introduce new measures to contain the spread of the virus. These entailed, at an initial stage, tighter requirements for mass events, mandatory registration of visitors at catering and other facilities, changes to the closing times of businesses and lockdowns at the municipality level. A nationwide partial lockdown came into force in early November, including restrictions on the operation of some businesses, such as restaurants and gyms, and a ban on gatherings of more than five persons in public places. Secondary education is taking place remotely or combining distance and school-based learning, while vocational and tertiary education is provided only remotely.

Lithuania

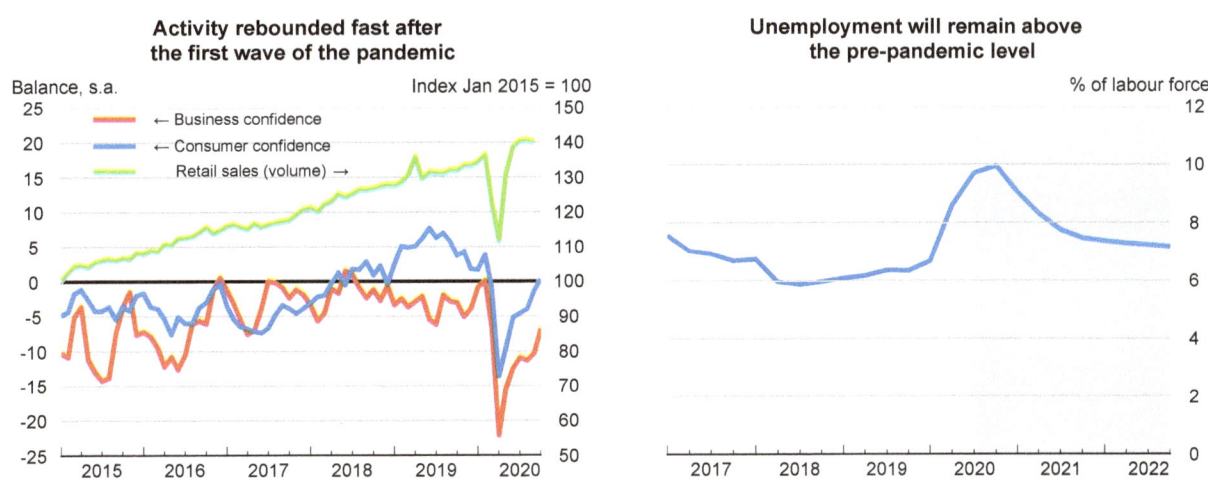

Source: OECD Economic Outlook 108 database; and OECD Main Economic Indicators database.

StatLink https://doi.org/10.1787/888934219052

Lithuania: Demand, output and prices

Lithuania	2017	2018	2019	2020	2021	2022
	Current prices EUR billion	Percentage changes, volume (2015 prices)				
GDP at market prices	42.3	3.9	4.3	-2.0	2.7	3.1
Private consumption	26.3	3.7	3.4	-3.2	2.8	3.0
Government consumption	6.9	0.2	0.1	5.9	4.7	1.1
Gross fixed capital formation	8.5	10.0	6.2	-6.6	3.8	4.3
Final domestic demand	41.7	4.4	3.4	-2.4	3.4	2.9
Stockbuilding[1]	- 0.4	-1.1	-1.5	-0.9	0.2	0.0
Total domestic demand	41.3	3.3	2.0	-3.4	3.8	3.0
Exports of goods and services	31.1	6.8	9.5	-4.7	3.7	4.9
Imports of goods and services	30.1	6.0	6.3	-6.9	5.5	5.0
Net exports[1]	1.0	0.7	2.5	1.4	-0.9	0.3
Memorandum items						
GDP deflator	_	3.5	2.8	1.1	1.5	1.8
Harmonised index of consumer prices	_	2.5	2.2	1.2	1.5	1.8
Harmonised index of core inflation[2]	_	1.9	2.3	2.7	1.6	1.8
Unemployment rate (% of labour force)	_	6.1	6.3	8.8	8.1	7.3
Household saving ratio, net (% of disposable income)	_	-3.6	0.6	6.9	5.6	4.3
General government financial balance (% of GDP)	_	0.6	0.3	-8.9	-5.4	-3.9
General government gross debt (% of GDP)	_	40.7	44.5	53.6	58.1	60.7
General government debt, Maastricht definition (% of GDP)	_	33.7	35.9	45.0	49.5	52.1
Current account balance (% of GDP)	_	0.2	3.5	5.2	3.9	4.2

1. Contributions to changes in real GDP, actual amount in the first column.
2. Harmonised index of consumer prices excluding food, energy, alcohol and tobacco.
Source: OECD Economic Outlook 108 database.

StatLink https://doi.org/10.1787/888934219071

The confinement-related decrease in activity was relatively mild

Economic activity contracted in the second quarter of the year amid containment measures, heightened uncertainty and a deterioration of the external environment. The dip was short-lived, however, with retail sales and consumer confidence rebounding quickly once the confinement measures started to be eased in mid-April. Crisis-related measures to protect jobs and incomes have sustained private consumption. Unemployment rose sharply in the wake of the health crisis, but the rise was mitigated by a short-time work scheme. The economy faces headwinds from the new containment measures due to the resurgence of the pandemic and the associated increase in uncertainty. Investment remains weak, despite increased public spending, as business confidence is still low.

Fiscal policy continues to support the recovery

The government swiftly provided fiscal and financial support to households and firms to alleviate the economic consequences of the crisis. Total fiscal measures account for over 6% of GDP in 2020. The 2021 draft budget envisages continued, yet less comprehensive, support to the recovery. Some of the measures introduced during the confinement period, including the short-time work scheme and the temporary job seeker's allowance, will be extended into 2021. Additional initiatives include higher social benefits and higher wages for some public employees, such as doctors and educational staff. The draft budget also gives special attention to the acceleration of investment programmes, including through the co-financing of climate-related projects. Fiscal support remains appropriate in a context of still weak activity and the resurgence of the pandemic.

The economy is set to recover

After a comparatively mild contraction in 2020, growth is projected at 2.7% in 2021 and 3.1% in 2022. Stronger confidence and policy measures will support the recovery. Investment will pick up gradually, aided by the faster implementation of EU-funded projects and a stepping-up of the multi-annual public investment programme covering a wide range of areas. While declining from its crisis peak, unemployment will remain above the pre-pandemic level. Prolonged effects of the pandemic on domestic demand and weaker-than-expected growth in Lithuania's trading partners could slow the recovery. On the upside, a swifter-than-expected use of EU recovery funds could foster stronger output growth.

Policies should support the vulnerable and promote reallocation

High poverty rates before the onset of the crisis underline the need to protect vulnerable groups more effectively. Higher social spending and a better tailoring of social benefits and services to individuals' needs are essential in this regard. Policies should also facilitate the reallocation of workers and capital from declining to expanding sectors. This will require further progress on skills, including by strengthening vocational education and re-skilling and up-skilling programmes for adults. The rise of new technologies further heightens the need to improve digital skills and encourage firms to adopt these technologies. Moreover, lower administrative burdens could provide a welcome boost to business dynamism.

Luxembourg

After a 4.4% contraction in 2020, the economy is projected to expand by a moderate 1.5% in 2021 and by 3.8% in 2022. The introduction of lockdowns in neighbouring countries will significantly restrain exports in the fourth quarter of 2020, causing the economy to contract. GDP will start growing again in the first quarter of 2021. The recovery will gather pace in the following quarters on the back of more dynamic external demand and greater confidence of domestic consumers and firms due to a rollout of an effective vaccine. The unemployment rate is expected to peak at the beginning of 2021 at around 7.2% and to decline to 6.2% at the end of 2022. Risks to the projections are to the downside and include less favourable epidemiological developments, persistent labour market weakness, and increased distress in financial markets. On the upside, a faster disappearance of the pandemic, associated with efficient vaccine distribution, could lead to a stronger rebound in private consumption and investment.

Policy support should focus on valuable industries that are still affected by the downturn (such as transport, hotels and restaurants). Active labour market policies and training programmes should be extended to workers under job retention schemes (such as "*chômage partiel*") to speed up job relocation if displacement occurs. A strengthening of labour activation policies should be envisaged in the light of the expected termination of job retention schemes in June 2021.

A second wave of infections is building up

The containment measures adopted by the government succeeded in limiting the outbreak until the end of June. However, the number of new infections started to increase again in July. In the autumn, the daily number of new infections relative to the population became high with respect to other EU countries, although intensive care units continued to operate without capacity constraints. The projection assumes that the current virus outbreak will be managed with a further tightening of the restrictive measures (possibly including the prohibition of indoor services by restaurants and bars), but without the re-introduction of a full, country-wide lockdown. A widespread COVID-19 testing strategy has allowed a relatively accurate and timely tracking of the pandemic.

Luxembourg

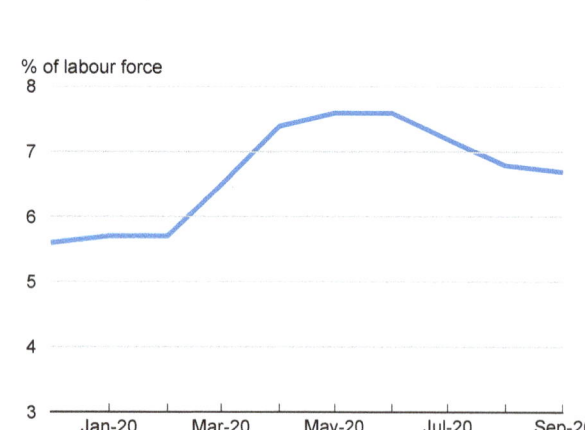

The unemployment rate has started to decline

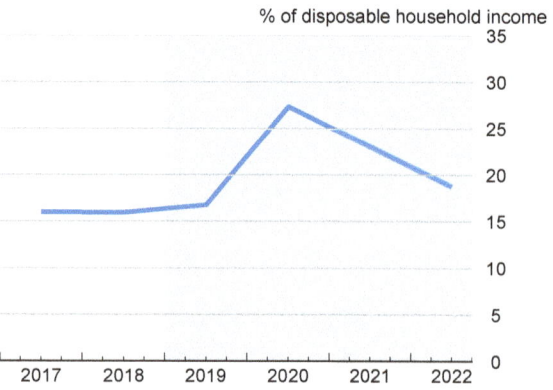

Household saving has increased to unprecedented levels
Household net saving ratio

Source: Eurostat; and OECD Economic Outlook 108 database.

StatLink ⟍ https://doi.org/10.1787/888934219090

Luxembourg: Demand, output and prices

Luxembourg	2017	2018	2019	2020	2021	2022
	Current prices EUR billion	Percentage changes, volume (2010 prices)				
GDP at market prices	56.8	3.1	2.3	-4.4	1.5	3.8
Private consumption	16.9	3.3	2.8	-12.4	2.7	5.7
Government consumption	9.4	4.0	4.9	4.0	2.2	1.0
Gross fixed capital formation	10.7	-6.1	4.0	-17.5	5.1	6.5
Final domestic demand	37.0	0.8	3.7	-9.3	3.1	4.4
Stockbuilding[1]	- 0.1	1.0	-0.2	-0.2	0.0	0.0
Total domestic demand	36.8	2.3	3.4	-9.5	3.1	4.4
Exports of goods and services	123.5	0.5	0.8	-1.2	2.5	3.5
Imports of goods and services	103.6	-0.3	0.9	-2.4	3.1	3.7
Net exports[1]	20.0	1.7	0.2	1.6	-0.2	1.1
Memorandum items						
GDP deflator	_	2.5	3.4	3.2	1.6	1.2
Harmonised index of consumer prices	_	2.0	1.6	0.1	0.9	1.3
Harmonised index of core inflation[2]	_	0.9	1.8	1.2	1.1	1.3
Unemployment rate (% of labour force)	_	5.5	5.4	6.4	7.0	6.4
Household saving ratio, net (% of disposable income)	_	16.0	16.8	27.4	23.1	18.8
General government financial balance (% of GDP)	_	3.1	2.4	-6.1	-6.1	-4.7
General government gross debt (% of GDP)	_	28.9	30.0	35.3	42.8	49.4
General government debt, Maastricht definition (% of GDP)	_	21.0	22.0	27.3	34.9	41.5
Current account balance (% of GDP)	_	4.8	4.6	2.7	2.7	3.5

1. Contributions to changes in real GDP, actual amount in the first column.
2. Harmonised index of consumer prices excluding food, energy, alcohol and tobacco.
Source: OECD Economic Outlook 108 database.

StatLink 〽️ https://doi.org/10.1787/888934219109

The economic rebound has been interrupted

In the second quarter of 2020, the economy shrank by 7.2% quarter-on-quarter, on the back of a steep decline in private consumption and investment. This was the largest-ever GDP drop over a single quarter, but smaller than in most other EU economies. This is partially thanks to the relative resilience of the financial sector and its large role in the economy. From May onwards, a gradual relaxation of containment measures enabled an economic rebound. Industry purchasing managers' index (PMI) and retail sales have recovered from the lows in April, and the labour market has continued to improve, with the unemployment rate declining from its peak of 7.4% in May. However, in line with the deterioration in the epidemiological situation in Europe, and as a consequence of the introduction of new strict containment measures in some key trading partners, such as France and Germany, the economy is estimated to have contracted in the last quarter of 2020 and the recovery is to resume only in 2021.

The policy support has been strong

A number of tax, expenditure and financial measures have been put in place to reduce the impact of the pandemic and related containment measures on the economy. Tax and social security charge deferrals were introduced to alleviate the liquidity situation of businesses and the self-employed during the lockdown. Eligible companies benefited from repayable advances which aimed to support SMEs affected by the COVID-19 outbreak. This adds to the six-month moratorium on debt repayments voluntarily agreed by banks in April. At the same time, to facilitate new lending, the government set up a loan guarantee facility of EUR 2.5 billion for new credit lines until the end of 2020. The short-time work scheme ("*chômage partiel*") has been extended until June 2021.

The recovery will gather pace from mid-2021 but risks persist

After an estimated GDP contraction in the fourth quarter of 2020, driven by a steep decline in exports, the recovery will resume in early 2021. It will gain momentum throughout that year, on the back of more dynamic external demand and greater confidence of domestic consumers and firms. GDP is projected to grow at 1.5% in 2021 and 3.8% in 2022, assuming that the pandemic gradually gets under control with the implementation of an effective vaccine. After a large fiscal expansion in 2020, the fiscal stance will be slightly contractionary in 2021 and 2022. The unemployment rate is expected to peak in the first quarter of 2021 at 7.2% and to decline to 6.2% at the end of 2022. Favourable financing conditions and funds provided through the EU Recovery and Resilience Facility will support investment in 2021. Risks to the projections are to the downside and include a worsening of the epidemiological situation and prolonged weakness in some employment-intensive industries, such as hotels and restaurants. Subdued external demand can weigh on the economy for longer, and possible increased distress in the financial sector could derail the recovery. On the upside, a faster control of the current virus outbreak, or better-than-expected outcomes in the development and distribution of vaccines, could lead to a stronger rebound.

Policy support should become better targeted

To prepare for the expected termination of short-time work schemes, labour activation policies should be expanded and extended to workers in job retention schemes (such as "*chômage partiel*") to speed up re-employment. Should the recovery be delayed further, a selective extension of short-time work schemes beyond mid-2021 should be considered in sectors particularly hit by the crisis but with longer-term viability (i.e. transport, restaurants and hospitality).

Mexico

After the sharp decline in 2020, GDP is projected to grow at 3.6% in 2021 and 3.4% in 2022. Economic growth will be led by exports, particularly from manufacturing firms integrated into global value chains. Private consumption will strengthen mildly, aided by robust remittances, a slowly improving labour market and a boost in confidence as an effective vaccine is rolled out. Ample spare capacity will keep inflation contained. The pandemic is causing significant increases in poverty, inequalities and gender gaps.

Macroeconomic policies need to foster the recovery. Despite limited fiscal space, the severity of the recession warrants stepping up fiscal policy support. This could include income and training support for the hardest-hit workers, both in the informal and formal sectors, while temporary payroll tax reductions could help more SMEs and support the creation of formal jobs. Bolstering private investment will be key for a stronger recovery, which calls for reducing regulatory burdens and regulatory uncertainty.

After having stabilised at a high level, cases are resurging in some states

Mexico recorded the first COVID-19 cases in late February. Transmission became widespread, making Mexico one of the OECD countries with the highest human toll. New cases, hospitalisations and deaths stabilised at a high level. Localised new outbreaks have recently emerged in several states. Mobility restrictions started to be relaxed as of end-May, and activities deemed essential, such as those in automotive, construction and mining sectors, reopened. Social activities remain restricted in most states and schools continue to be closed in all states.

Mexico

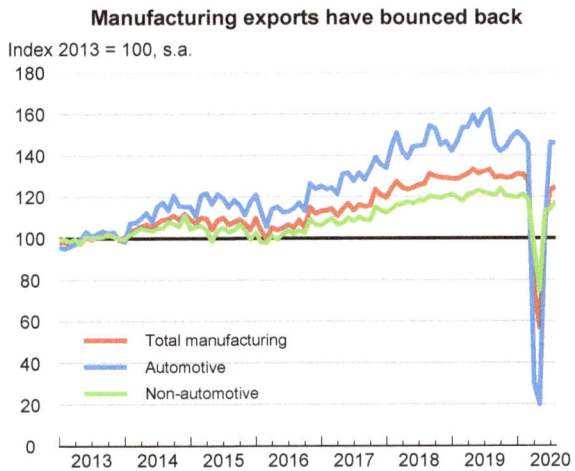

Manufacturing exports have bounced back

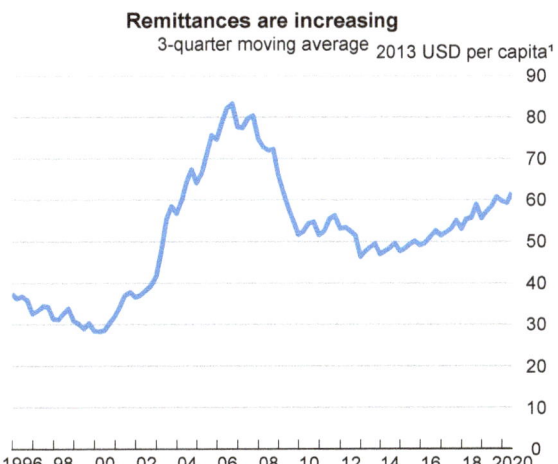

Remittances are increasing

1. Population figures projected from 2020Q1 onwards.
Source: INEGI; OECD Population Statistics; and Bank of Mexico.

StatLink ᐅ https://doi.org/10.1787/888934219128

Mexico: Demand, output and prices

Mexico	2017	2018	2019	2020	2021	2022
	Current prices MXN billion	Percentage changes, volume (2013 prices)				
GDP at market prices	21 934.2	2.2	-0.3	-9.2	3.6	3.4
Private consumption	14 305.3	2.4	0.4	-10.9	2.3	2.9
Government consumption	2 548.0	2.8	-1.4	2.4	-2.4	0.4
Gross fixed capital formation	4 845.7	1.0	-5.1	-20.5	4.2	6.2
Final domestic demand	21 699.0	2.1	-1.0	-11.3	2.1	3.2
Stockbuilding[1]	632.7	-0.1	-0.2	-0.1	0.1	0.0
Total domestic demand	22 331.7	2.0	-1.3	-11.5	2.3	3.3
Exports of goods and services	8 258.6	5.9	1.4	-15.7	6.5	6.8
Imports of goods and services	8 656.1	5.9	-0.9	-17.5	6.5	6.5
Net exports[1]	- 397.6	0.0	0.9	0.6	0.1	0.2
Memorandum items						
GDP deflator	–	4.9	3.3	2.6	3.1	3.0
Consumer price index	–	4.9	3.6	3.4	3.2	3.0
Core inflation index[2]	–	3.8	3.7	3.8	3.3	3.0
Unemployment rate[3] (% of labour force)	–	3.3	3.5	5.3	5.0	4.8
Current account balance (% of GDP)	–	-2.1	-0.3	-0.2	-0.5	-0.9

1. Contributions to changes in real GDP, actual amount in the first column.
2. Consumer price index excluding volatile items: agricultural, energy and tariffs approved by various levels of government.
3. Based on National Employment Survey.
Source: OECD Economic Outlook 108 database.

StatLink ᵐˢᴾ https://doi.org/10.1787/888934219147

The economy has started to recover

After a deep contraction in the second quarter, activity has started to recover. Manufacturing production, particularly in the automotive sector, is picking up. Construction has also started to recover, while services and retail sales have dropped about 10% since February 2020. According to short-term indicators, investment remains 17% below its level in 2019. Exports have bounced back, driven by the rebound in the United States. The labour market has also started to improve. The labour force declined by 12 million people in the second quarter, but it has increased by around 8 million people since then. However, the recovery in female labour participation has been more muted. Formal employment, which contracted by over one million during the first seven months of the year, has started to grow, particularly in those states with stronger links to global value chains. Employment in services related to finance and hospitality continues to contract.

A wide range of fiscal, financial and monetary policy measures have been taken

Health spending has increased thanks to a substantial effort to reallocate spending. This allowed the hiring of 50 thousand additional health workers and pre-purchasing of vaccines to cover around 90% of the population. Other key fiscal measures include loans, front-loaded social pension payments, accelerated procurement processes and VAT refunds. The fiscal measures, although smaller in size than those taken in advanced and major emerging-market economies, go in the right direction. Efforts to continue reallocating spending are assumed to endure over the coming two years. The central bank has reduced interest rates by 400 basis points since mid-2019, to 4.25%. It has also supported the functioning of financial markets and provided additional liquidity, up to 3.5% of GDP, to foster credit provision. Bank accounting regulations have also been adapted to facilitate credit restructuring.

The recovery will be moderate and uncertain

GDP growth is projected at 3.6% in 2021, partly reflecting the carryover from the rebound in the second half of 2020. Exports of the manufacturing sector, strongly linked with US growth prospects, will be robust. An infrastructure plan, mainly financed by the private sector, and lower interest rates will contribute to a partial recovery of investment. The projections assume localised new virus outbreaks during 2021, requiring the persistence of some containment measures, which will weigh particularly on services requiring social interactions. The assumed rolling-out of a vaccine will boost confidence and consumption. Due to the economic contraction and the peso depreciation, the official measure of public debt will increase to above 55% of GDP this year, but it would decline gradually thereafter if government fiscal targets are met.

Uncertainty remains very high. In case of a significant increase in infections, which could be aggravated by the start of the influenza season, restoring containment measures would be needed, hampering mobility and economic activity. A stronger risk aversion could reduce financial flows to emerging-market economies, increasing Mexico's financing costs. The flexible exchange rate is helping the economy to absorb external shocks, with further backstops provided by ample international reserves, swap lines and precautionary credit lines. Additional disruptions in global value chains or foreign trade barriers would damage manufacturing activity. On the upside, if the recovery in trading partners is stronger than anticipated, exports and job creation could be higher. Integration in value chains could deepen further thanks to the new trade agreement with the United States and Canada.

Fiscal and monetary policies can provide more support

Containing new COVID-19 outbreaks remains the imminent priority, requiring improvements in testing, tracing and isolating, while continuing to strengthen the health system. Fiscal and monetary policies have a key role to play to support the recovery. Fiscal prudence over the past years and rigorous public debt management provide Mexico with space for additional temporary fiscal support, which should be targeted at those individuals and firms hardest hit by the pandemic. This can be facilitated by better-than-expected tax revenues, thanks to recent successes by the tax administration to combat tax evasion. In the medium term, phasing out regressive tax exemptions could strengthen revenues in an inclusive way. With inflation expectations well anchored and ample spare capacity holding back inflation in the short term, lower monetary policy rates would provide further support to investment.

Netherlands

GDP is set to fall by 4.6% in 2020 before picking up by 0.8% in 2021 and 2.9% in 2022. Consumption will rebound in 2021 as households scale back precautionary savings, while investment recovers only moderately due to lingering uncertainty. Unemployment and bankruptcies are expected to peak in the second half of 2021 when support measures will be phased out.

Fiscal policy should remain supportive. The government has extended its main support measures until July 2021, including loan guarantees, grants for small businesses, the job retention scheme and support to the self-employed. Policies should encourage the reallocation of workers and capital, while adapting to the evolving epidemiological situation. The job retention scheme should be adjusted to facilitate worker mobility and training. Public investment should help tackle structural challenges, including low productivity growth and high nitrogen and greenhouse gas emissions, complemented by the EU Recovery and Resilience Facility once available.

The Netherlands has entered the second wave of the pandemic

The number of new COVID-19 infections has increased rapidly after the summer, recording more cases between September and November than at the peak of the first wave. The number of deaths and hospitalisations were well below the levels of the first wave, but pressure on the health system rose through the autumn. As tracking the virus became more difficult with the surge in case numbers, restrictions were tightened to slow the spread of the virus. Hospitality services were shut down from mid-October, and most public places were temporarily closed in November. Group-gathering restrictions, mask wearing, customer registration and distancing requirements in retail trade have been strengthened. Restrictions are evaluated regularly and adjusted if necessary.

Netherlands

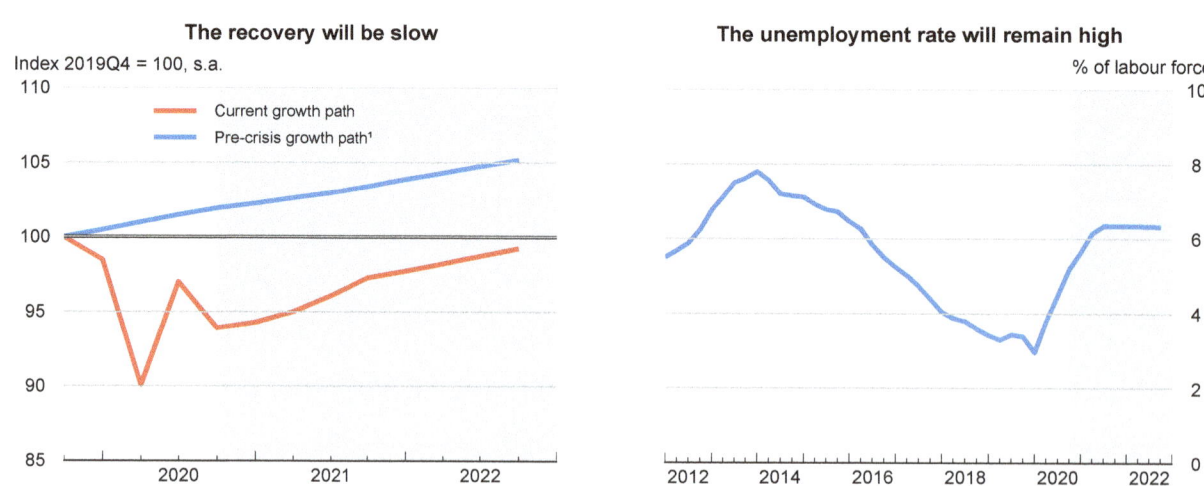

1. The November 2019 projection is based on the November 2019 Economic Outlook, with linear extrapolation for 2022 based on potential growth in 2021.
Source: OECD Economic Outlook 106 and 108 databases.

StatLink 🖳🖳 https://doi.org/10.1787/888934219166

Netherlands: Demand, output and prices

Netherlands	2017	2018	2019	2020	2021	2022
	Current prices EUR billion	Percentage changes, volume (2015 prices)				
GDP at market prices	738.8	2.3	1.6	-4.6	0.8	2.9
Private consumption	327.3	2.1	1.5	-6.7	2.7	3.4
Government consumption	179.6	1.7	1.6	-0.3	2.2	1.2
Gross fixed capital formation	148.8	3.5	4.5	-5.1	-3.2	5.0
Final domestic demand	655.6	2.3	2.2	-4.6	1.1	3.1
Stockbuilding[1]	3.7	0.1	-0.2	0.0	-0.3	0.0
Total domestic demand	659.3	2.4	1.9	-4.6	0.8	3.1
Exports of goods and services	616.3	4.2	2.6	-3.8	4.7	3.3
Imports of goods and services	536.8	4.6	3.1	-3.8	5.3	3.5
Net exports[1]	79.5	0.2	-0.1	-0.4	0.1	0.1
Memorandum items						
GDP deflator	_	2.4	2.9	2.4	1.3	0.8
Harmonised index of consumer prices	_	1.6	2.7	1.0	0.9	1.1
Harmonised index of core inflation[2]	_	1.0	1.9	1.9	1.0	1.1
Unemployment rate (% of labour force)	_	3.8	3.4	4.1	6.1	6.3
Household saving ratio, net[3] (% of disposable income)	_	9.1	10.0	18.2	16.4	13.8
General government financial balance (% of GDP)	_	1.4	1.7	-6.4	-8.0	-5.9
General government gross debt (% of GDP)	_	66.0	62.5	69.7	76.8	81.1
General government debt, Maastricht definition (% of GDP)	_	52.4	48.7	55.9	63.1	67.3
Current account balance (% of GDP)	_	10.8	9.9	9.5	9.8	9.1

1. Contributions to changes in real GDP, actual amount in the first column.
2. Harmonised index of consumer prices excluding food, energy, alcohol and tobacco.
3. Including savings in life insurance and pension schemes.
Source: OECD Economic Outlook 108 database.

StatLink https://doi.org/10.1787/888934219185

The economic environment remains fragile

Economic activity in the second quarter of 2020 recorded the largest contraction since World War II. A rapid implementation of sizeable policy support measures and allowing most economic activities to resume, subject to distancing and hygiene measures, avoided an even steeper fall. Over the summer, the economic environment turned initially more favourable, reflected in strong GDP growth in the third quarter. The rise in unemployment levelled off at the end of the third quarter, partly due to the job retention scheme (NOW) that enabled companies to retain employees. Bankruptcies are well below 2019 levels owing to financial support measures for firms. The initial recovery of producer confidence stalled in the face of the second wave and investment in tangible fixed assets continued to decline. Consumer confidence remains low and has slightly deteriorated in October. Similarly, mobility for retail and recreation has fallen steadily since the virus resurged.

Support to firms and workers is substantial

The government is maintaining generous discretionary support measures and allowing the automatic fiscal stabilisers to operate fully. The main support measures, including loan guarantees and grants for small businesses, have been extended until July 2021. The job retention scheme is also set to close in July 2021, following a gradual reduction over three phases of three months each to give businesses time to adapt. From October 2020 onwards, businesses need to apply for each phase and compensation in wage cost is subsequently reduced from a maximum of 80% to a maximum of 60% during the last phase. The income support and loan scheme for the self-employed will be complemented by training and career advice from 2021. Business taxes accrued in 2020 have been deferred up to two years, and interest on overdue taxes will remain at almost zero until the end of 2021.

The recovery will be gradual and vulnerable to infection outbreaks

Output is projected to improve gradually in 2021 and 2022. Pent-up consumption will drive the initial pick-up. However, rising unemployment, as the job retention scheme is being phased out, combined with limited wage growth and declining housing wealth, will hold back private consumption growth over 2021-22. Business investment will remain subdued, reflecting weak demand and lingering uncertainty. Government consumption and investment are projected to grow, reflecting rising healthcare expenditure, higher construction and infrastructure investment and additional capital spending from the national growth fund. Public debt will rise from 49% of GDP in 2019 to 67% of GDP in 2022. Effective treatment or effective vaccines are assumed to be widely distributed at the turn of 2021 and 2022. New effective treatment methods or earlier-than-assumed distribution of an effective vaccine is a clear upside risk. There are, however, substantial downward risks. Households' high indebtedness as well as high and illiquid housing and pension wealth add to risks from the health situation. A fall in house prices, pension cuts and an increase to pension premiums are downside risks to consumption. Some pension funds might not meet the legally required funding ratio, despite an exceptional reduction from 100% to 90% in 2020, due to persistently low interest rates. The economy is also particularly sensitive to developments in global trade, including the outcome of the trade negotiations between the United Kingdom and the European Union.

The policy stance should continue to be supportive

Fiscal policy should remain supportive and flexible to adapt to a changing environment. The crisis highlights the need to reduce tax and other incentives to hire workers on non-standard contracts. Self-employed workers on freelance or on-call contracts are particularly vulnerable to job termination as the job retention scheme mainly protected workers on permanent contracts. Although access to social benefits was eased for the self-employed, the crisis exacerbates income inequality. Fiscal stimulus should support the reallocation and adaptability of workers in vulnerable sectors by providing timely training and re-education opportunities. Public investment, in the longer term also supported by the EU Recovery and Resilience Facility, should address structural challenges, including increasing productivity growth, expanding renewable energy generation capacity and reducing nitrogen emissions from agriculture.

New Zealand

After a rebound in the second half of 2020 from the COVID-19 slump, economic growth in 2021 will average around 2¾ per cent, with rising unemployment weighing on private consumption and high uncertainty holding back business investment. Assuming that the border re-opens at the beginning of 2022 after a rollout of an effective vaccine around the world, tourism and immigration will drive further the recovery, with economic growth in 2022 of just over 2½ per cent. Until immunisation is attained, the recovery may be interrupted by intermittent localised COVID-19 outbreaks and associated containment measures.

The government should stand ready to deploy greater fiscal and monetary stimulus than currently assumed if the economic recovery falters. It should also strengthen measures to support the reallocation of workers from economic activities that are not viable in the long run to those that are.

Localised confinement was imposed to curb a potential outbreak

After eliminating domestic COVID-19 infections in June, New Zealand saw a localised outbreak in Auckland in the second half of August. The government promptly imposed containment measures in Auckland, shutting down businesses that require close physical contact and prohibiting travel to other parts of the country, while placing the rest of the country under milder restrictions. The containment measures were lifted nationwide in early October after a period without domestic infections. Daily new COVID-19 cases are likely to remain in low, single digits, and mostly involve people in quarantine facilities for international arrivals as New Zealand maintains strict border controls and a pre-emptive containment policy.

New Zealand

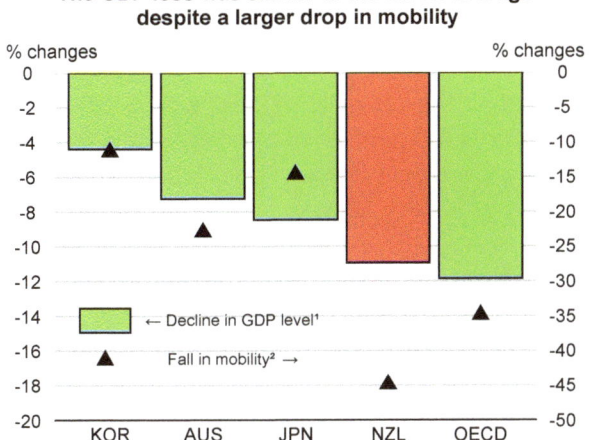

The GDP loss was similar to the OECD average despite a larger drop in mobility

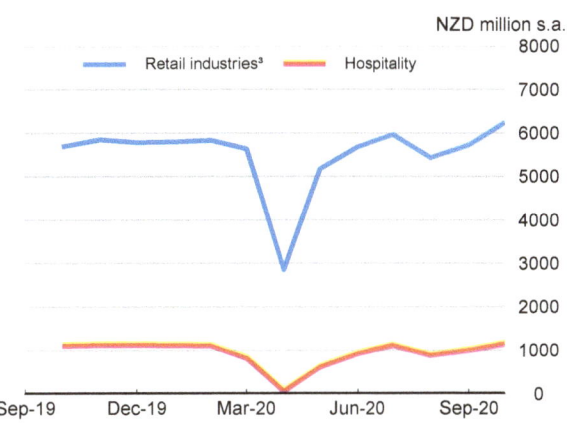

Electronic card spending rebounded

1. Values refer to percentage difference between 2019Q4 and 2020Q2 GDP levels.
2. Data refer to the fall in mobility from the baseline between 1st of March and 27th of June. The baseline is the median value of mobility during the 5-week period January 3-February 6, 2020.
3. Retail industries include retail trade, accommodation and food services (ANZSIC Divisions G and H).
Source: OECD, National Accounts database; Statistics New Zealand; and Google LLC, *Google COVID-19 Community Mobility Reports*, https://www.google.com/covid19/mobility/.

StatLink https://doi.org/10.1787/888934219204

New Zealand: Demand, output and prices

New Zealand	2017	2018	2019	2020	2021	2022
	Current prices NZD billion	Percentage changes, volume (2009/2010 prices)				
GDP at market prices	285.3	3.2	2.2	-4.8	2.7	2.6
Private consumption	164.3	3.3	2.9	-4.6	3.1	2.9
Government consumption	51.3	3.7	4.2	5.7	2.8	1.5
Gross fixed capital formation	65.2	5.6	2.5	-15.8	2.9	3.2
Final domestic demand	280.8	3.9	3.0	-5.3	3.0	2.7
Stockbuilding[1]	1.8	0.3	-0.8	-1.5	0.4	0.0
Total domestic demand	282.6	4.2	2.2	-6.8	3.5	2.7
Exports of goods and services	78.1	2.9	2.4	-11.2	2.0	6.8
Imports of goods and services	75.4	6.3	2.2	-16.7	6.2	7.1
Net exports[1]	2.6	-0.9	0.0	1.6	-1.0	0.0
Memorandum items						
GDP deflator	_	1.2	2.3	2.5	1.1	1.7
Consumer price index	_	1.6	1.6	1.6	1.1	1.6
Core inflation index[2]	_	1.2	1.8	2.1	1.3	1.6
Unemployment rate (% of labour force)	_	4.3	4.1	4.9	5.8	5.4
Household saving ratio, net (% of disposable income)	_	-0.3	1.2	4.7	3.1	1.9
General government financial balance (% of GDP)	_	1.2	-0.6	-9.1	-8.5	-5.5
General government gross debt (% of GDP)	_	34.0	32.6	43.8	48.2	53.1
Current account balance (% of GDP)	_	-4.2	-3.4	-1.6	-2.7	-2.9

1. Contributions to changes in real GDP, actual amount in the first column.
2. Consumer price index excluding food and energy.
Source: OECD Economic Outlook 108 database.

StatLink https://doi.org/10.1787/888934215223

The economy rebounded but is not yet on a firm recovery path

Despite a large drop in mobility, the fall in real GDP between the last quarter of 2019 and the second quarter of 2020 was close to the OECD average. Electronic card spending bounced back quickly from a sharp fall in April and remains robust. Consumer confidence remains low despite rapidly rising house prices and robust export commodity prices, reflecting a large increase in the number of unemployed in the third quarter of 2020. Business confidence is improving from a very low level thanks to sizeable fiscal support, a pick-up in domestic tourism as well as strong housing and construction activity.

Massive fiscal and monetary stimulus is supporting jobs and businesses

The government is providing substantial financial support to households and businesses over 2020-21, with 70% of the fiscal response package to the COVID-19 crisis (20% of GDP) to be spent by June 2021. The primary focus of the package is the retention of existing jobs. The costliest measure is the Wage Subsidy Scheme, for which NZD 14 billion (4.5% of GDP) was disbursed to businesses for retaining paid employees. Additional temporary wage subsidies were introduced for the period of heightened restrictions. This large income support scheme, covering 71% of businesses and 60% of employment at one point, was gradually reduced by tightening the eligibility conditions and expired in November 2020. The Reserve Bank of New Zealand stepped up measures aimed at boosting credit supply and lowering lending costs. It substantially increased the size of its large-scale asset purchase programme, which it estimates to have lowered 10-year government bond yields by more than 100 basis points. The mortgage interest rates have declined as well, supporting a robust housing market. In December, the Reserve Bank of New Zealand is also to start the Funding for Lending Programme, which will provide low-cost funding to banks based on their outstanding credit to domestic borrowers and increases in lending. The Official Cash Rate has remained at 0.25% since March, when it was lowered from 1%. The start date of the increased capital requirements for banks was further pushed back to July 2022.

The recovery will moderate and be subject to COVID-19-related developments

Following a rebound in activity in the second half of 2020, the recovery will moderate owing to a sustained increase in unemployment following the end of the Wage Subsidy Scheme, which will weigh on private consumption. Business investment will be anaemic as firms seek to consolidate their balance sheets and build up cash buffers to cope with the economic fallout from potential further virus outbreaks. International tourism, which represented 20% of total exports in 2019, will be constrained to nil as the border remains closed to foreign non-residents, although this impact is partially offset by increased domestic tourism. Large slack in the economy will keep inflation and wage growth low. Assuming that the border reopens in January 2022 after a global deployment of an effective vaccine, economic growth will pick up as stronger exports stimulate business investment and hiring. The economic recovery may be delayed by sporadic outbreaks of infection, necessitating localised containment measures to eradicate them, or by a worse-than-foreseen global COVID-19 resurgence that would depress export market growth. On the other hand, a faster rollout of a vaccine against COVID-19 would allow an earlier reopening of the border, possibly at first through safe travel zones.

The government should stand ready to deploy additional stimulus

Should downside risks materialise in 2021, particularly a large-scale virus outbreak that necessitates containment measures in major cities, more fiscal and monetary policy support than currently envisaged will be needed to ensure that the economic recovery remains on track. Swift implementation of the infrastructure investment component of the fiscal response package to the COVID-19 crisis and of the New Zealand Upgrade Programme in the areas of housing and green infrastructure would underpin the recovery and improve the wellbeing of New Zealanders. The government should also facilitate the reallocation of workers away from jobs that may no longer be viable, along the lines of the scheme that retrains workers in hospitality and aviation for jobs in construction, agriculture, manufacturing and healthcare. In addition, the government should strengthen support for workers during job transitions through reforms to the welfare system (Job seeker Support), introduction of unemployment insurance, or some hybrid approach.

Norway

The recovery from a decline in mainland output of 3.2% in 2020 will be muted by continued localised restrictions to tackle COVID-19 outbreaks, weak oil-sector investment and continued disruption to travel, hospitality and related sectors. Real mainland GDP is projected to increase by 3.1% in 2021 and 1.4% in 2022. Labour market recovery will be correspondingly slow and consumer price inflation will remain muted. Diminished need for restrictions as an effective vaccine is rolled out, and associated pick-ups in hard-hit sectors and rising confidence, will contribute to output growth in 2022.

The scale and timing of the monetary and fiscal policy response to COVID-19 has remained broadly appropriate. The fiscal rule that links mainland deficits to wealth-fund returns should remain firmly in place as it allows ample room to support the recovery while also providing long-term fiscal guidance. Recovery will be helped by measures proposed in the national budget 2021 to encourage further return to work, strengthen the business environment and encourage green growth.

National containment measures have been strengthened

Norway's COVID-19 case and fatality numbers remain comparatively low. Second-wave case numbers have surpassed those of the first wave, but deaths have so far remained limited. National measures have been tightened. These include, for instance, advice to remain at home as much as possible and increased restrictions on the hospitality sector. Additional restrictions apply locally, notably in Oslo. However, as of mid-November there had been no outright closure of business activities and schooling.

Norway

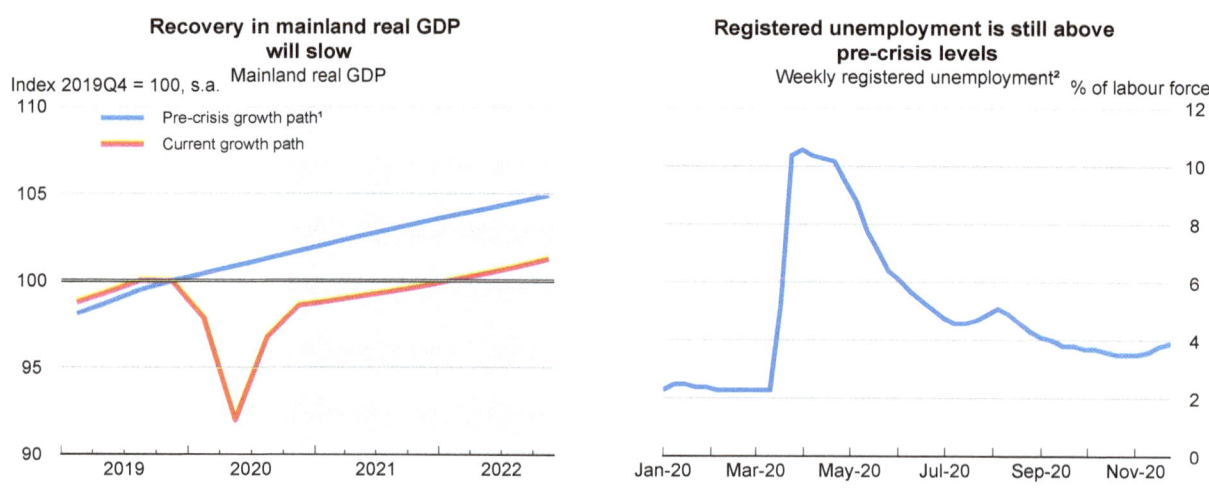

1. The pre-crisis growth path is based on the November 2019 OECD Economic Outlook projection, with linear extrapolation for 2022 based on trend growth in 2021.
2. The registered unemployment data includes temporary layoffs.
Source: OECD Economic Outlook 106 and 108 databases and Norwegian Labour and Welfare Administration (NAV).

StatLink https://doi.org/10.1787/888934219242

Norway: Demand, output and prices

Norway	2017	2018	2019	2020	2021	2022
	Current prices NOK billion	Percentage changes, volume (2018 prices)				
Mainland GDP at market prices[1]	2 792.0	2.2	2.3	-3.2	3.1	1.4
Total GDP at market prices	3 295.4	1.1	0.9	-1.2	3.2	1.5
Private consumption	1 471.7	1.6	1.4	-7.8	3.2	1.7
Government consumption	791.1	0.5	1.9	1.3	2.8	1.8
Gross fixed capital formation	809.4	2.2	4.8	-4.4	1.0	2.3
Final domestic demand	3 072.1	1.5	2.4	-4.5	2.5	1.9
Stockbuilding[2]	107.9	0.7	0.0	-0.8	0.3	0.0
Total domestic demand	3 180.0	2.1	2.3	-5.2	2.7	1.8
Exports of goods and services	1 197.3	-1.2	0.5	-0.6	4.7	2.5
Imports of goods and services	1 081.9	1.4	4.7	-12.0	2.9	3.4
Net exports[2]	115.4	-0.9	-1.3	4.0	0.6	-0.3
Memorandum items						
GDP deflator	_	6.7	-0.4	-3.6	1.8	1.9
Consumer price index	_	2.7	2.2	1.5	1.9	1.9
Core inflation index[3]	_	1.2	2.6	3.2	1.7	1.9
Unemployment rate (% of labour force)	_	3.8	3.7	4.5	5.0	4.4
Household saving ratio, net (% of disposable income)	_	5.9	8.1	16.6	12.2	11.1
General government financial balance (% of GDP)	_	7.8	6.2	-1.3	1.8	2.2
General government gross debt (% of GDP)	_	45.6	46.8	31.6	..	..
Current account balance (% of GDP)	_	7.1	4.1	3.4	4.0	3.7

1. GDP excluding oil and shipping.
2. Contributions to changes in real GDP, actual amount in the first column.
3. Consumer price index excluding food and energy.
Source: OECD Economic Outlook 108 database.

StatLink 🖼️ https://doi.org/10.1787/888934219261

The recovery is slowing

The recovery in economic activity was initially rapid. Mainland output troughed in April at 11% below pre-crisis levels; by June, it was only 6% below. However, output growth since has been lower and more recently there has been an uptick in the rate of registered unemployment. The decline and the subsequent partial recovery in the global oil price in the first months of the crisis triggered exchange rate movements in the Norwegian krone. Uncertainty about future oil price developments is weakening investment in the resource sector. Meanwhile, the housing market has been buoyant, bolstered by lower interest rates and the lifting of some mortgage regulations. Headline consumer price inflation has fluctuated below the 2% target since the crisis began. The krone value of Norway's main wealth fund has remained comparatively stable as the impact of initial international equity price falls has been offset by currency depreciation.

A comprehensive welfare system is limiting socio-economic damage

Norges Bank continues to provide substantial monetary support through a zero-per-cent policy rate and an extended loan programme for banks to the end of 2020. Norway's comparatively large public sector, comprehensive welfare system and correspondingly high taxation have meant substantial automatic stabilisation. Flexibility in the fiscal rule is allowing for expansion of the structural non-oil deficit of 4.5 percentage points of GDP in 2020.

The fiscal package to combat the economic downturn will equate to around 4% of mainland GDP. Around one-third of the outlays arises from government stepping in earlier to pay the wages of those temporarily laid off or on sick leave (the number of days employers must pay has been shortened). Large outlays are also expected for a scheme covering businesses' fixed costs, loss provisions on business loan guarantees, aviation-sector support and extensions of income security for individuals. The national budget for 2021 focuses on nurturing economic recovery, including through increased spending on research and development and further support for hard-hit sectors.

The recovery in output and employment will be gradual

Localised containment measures are expected to continue into 2021 and weigh on the economy. Activity in travel, leisure and hospitality sectors will recover slowly as will business investment in general. By the end of 2022, output will be around 4.5% below that implied by pre-crisis trend growth. The fiscal balance will deteriorate substantially in 2020 but partially recover in 2021 as revenues rebound and support measures are retired. The path of the global oil price and the prospects for non-oil trading partners will remain key uncertainties. Pre-crisis concerns for macro-financial stability linked to high levels of household debt remain.

Policymakers must remain ready to react

Norway is in a relatively good position to deal with the uncertainties ahead. However, macro-financial risks related to household borrowing must remain on close watch. Also, policy should focus on helping hard-hit businesses survive the downturn, including through transitioning to new activities. There is scope to strengthen business dynamics through better routes to recovery for businesses in difficulty. In addition, Norway should leverage the crisis to make advances in environmental policy; for instance, the 2021 budget proposes a fund for developing carbon capture and storage technologies and an increase in the carbon dioxide tax.

Poland

GDP is estimated to have fallen by 3.5% in 2020 and is projected to grow by 2.9% in 2021 and 3.8% in 2022. After a strong rebound in the third quarter of 2020, owing to pent-up consumption and government support, output is set to fall again in end-2020 as new restrictions have been introduced to contain the second outbreak of the virus. Domestic demand will regain momentum in 2021 and 2022, with the prospect and actual deployment of an effective COVID-19 vaccine. Unemployment is expected to peak in 2021 and slowly decrease afterwards.

The rollback of fiscal support in 2021 should be prudent to avoid hurting the recovery. Policy support could be better targeted to the most vulnerable households and firms. Subsidising social security contributions for low-income workers on standard contracts would make the recovery more inclusive and strengthening lifelong learning opportunities for low-skilled workers would also improve labour reallocation. Public investment to improve interregional infrastructure and to green the energy mix would simultaneously support the recovery and help to meet environmental objectives.

The epidemiological situation has worsened significantly

COVID-19 infections accelerated dramatically in the autumn, doubling over the first three weeks of October. Hospitalisations and COVID-19-related deaths have also increased considerably. The authorities have re-imposed restrictions to the whole country, in an effort to curb the rebound of COVID-19 infections. The wearing of face masks in public places has been made mandatory, most schools have moved to distance learning, gyms and eat-in restaurants have closed again, while public gatherings, the number of customers in retail shops and cultural events have been limited.

Poland

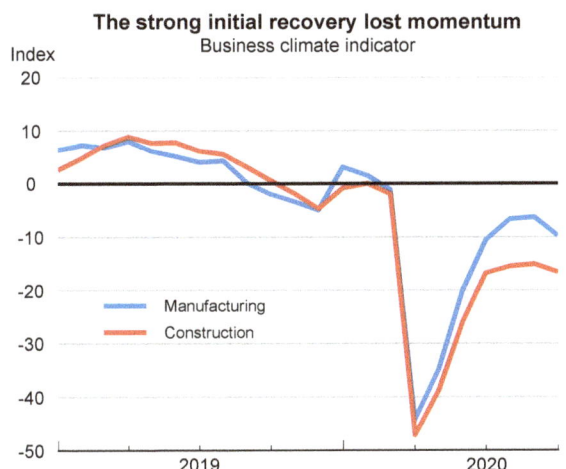

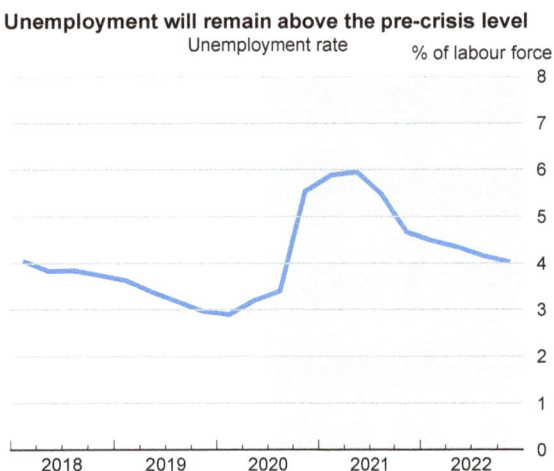

Source: Statistics Poland (2020), Monthly macroeconomic indicators; and OECD Economic Outlook 108 database.

StatLink ᵐᵖ https://doi.org/10.1787/888934219280

Poland: Demand, output and prices

Poland	2017 Current prices PLN billion	2018	2019	2020	2021	2022
		Percentage changes, volume (2015 prices)				
GDP at market prices	1 989.8	5.4	4.5	-3.5	2.9	3.8
Private consumption	1 166.8	4.5	3.9	-4.5	1.7	4.5
Government consumption	351.9	3.5	6.2	3.1	3.6	1.8
Gross fixed capital formation	348.7	9.4	7.2	-7.4	-1.6	8.2
Final domestic demand	1 867.4	5.2	5.0	-3.6	1.4	4.6
Stockbuilding[1]	47.5	0.4	-1.3	-1.3	-0.4	0.0
Total domestic demand	1 914.9	5.6	3.5	-5.0	1.0	4.6
Exports of goods and services	1 077.7	6.9	5.1	-7.0	7.9	11.3
Imports of goods and services	1 002.7	7.4	3.3	-9.6	8.4	14.4
Net exports[1]	75.0	0.0	1.1	1.0	0.3	-0.7
Memorandum items						
GDP deflator	–	1.2	3.1	3.8	-0.3	2.3
Consumer price index	–	1.8	2.2	3.4	2.3	2.6
Core inflation index[2]	–	0.8	1.9	3.9	3.3	2.6
Unemployment rate (% of labour force)	–	3.9	3.3	3.8	5.5	4.3
Household saving ratio, net (% of disposable income)	–	-1.0	1.9	13.7	12.8	9.7
General government financial balance (% of GDP)	–	-0.2	-0.7	-10.8	-6.8	-4.8
General government debt, Maastricht definition (% of GDP)	–	48.8	45.7	56.5	62.0	63.6
Current account balance (% of GDP)	–	-1.3	0.5	2.3	1.2	0.5

1. Contributions to changes in real GDP, actual amount in the first column.
2. Consumer price index excluding food and energy.
Source: OECD Economic Outlook 108 database.

StatLink ⬛⬛ https://doi.org/10.1707/000031210200

The recovery has been interrupted by the pandemic resurgence

Industrial production rebounded vigorously after the deep plunge induced by lockdown measures in spring, and exports and imports recovered quickly. Public expenditure and pent-up demand helped drive the recovery. However, the recent resurgence of the pandemic has undermined confidence and domestic demand started falling again with the renewed restrictions. The persistent uncertainty about domestic factors and the recovery in Europe is holding back private investment. The expiration of measures aimed at job protection is weighing on employment, denting household income growth.

Fiscal and monetary policies have prevented an even bigger contraction so far

Supportive fiscal and monetary policies have prevented a deeper recession in 2020. Higher social transfers, pension outlays, health expenditures and exceptional measures aimed at protecting incomes, jobs and firms' liquidity all contributed to support the economy. The minimum wage has increased by almost 16% in 2020 and another increase around 8% is planned for 2021, partly compensating for lower average wage growth. However, job and income protection measures are being progressively rolled back. Monetary policy has been highly accommodative. The central bank reduced the benchmark interest rate to 0.1% and purchased assets in the secondary market to improve banks' liquidity.

Downside risks stem from repeated waves of COVID-19

The recovery is projected to slightly accelerate in the coming two years as private investment slowly picks up. Funds stemming from the Next Generation EU package are assumed to support public investment. Higher minimum wages, supportive monetary and fiscal policies, together with higher service costs related to sanitary measures and local disruptions in production chains, are feeding into higher inflation. Higher unit labour costs and terms of trade will lower the contribution of exports to GDP growth in 2021-22. Downside risks stem primarily from new waves of COVID-19 and new containment measures if there are delays in immunisation, as Poland's testing capacity remains low. On the upside, a large-scale deployment of an effective vaccine in 2021 could accelerate the pace of recovery by boosting external demand and investors' confidence.

Targeted structural reforms could help support the recovery

Additional stimulus, if needed in the light of the uncertain pace of the recovery, should specifically target the most vulnerable workers and firms to limit fiscal costs. Strengthening lifelong learning opportunities for low-skilled workers would improve the re-employment chances of displaced workers. At the same time, it would also foster labour reallocation towards the most resilient sectors of the economy. To ensure that the recovery is sustainable and inclusive, the authorities could also reduce social security contributions for low-income workers on standard employment contracts, which offer higher stability. Planned public investment to boost aggregate demand could focus on improving cross-regional infrastructure to help smaller firms that struggle to access foreign markets. In addition, investment that develops more sustainable energy alternatives can simultaneously generate employment and help Poland to meet its long-term environmental goals.

Portugal

GDP is set to fall by 8.4% in 2020 before recovering by 1.7% in 2021 and 1.9% in 2022. The pick-up in 2021 will mainly be supported by pent-up demand. Afterwards, a broader recovery is projected to unfold, notably in the most affected sectors such as tourism and hospitality, under the assumption of an improved sanitary situation as an effective vaccine is deployed. The unemployment rate will peak in 2021 and remain above its pre-crisis level through the end of 2022. Public debt (Maastricht definition) is expected to reach 139% of GDP in 2022.

The fiscal deficit is projected to decrease in 2021-22 as the economy rebounds and some discretionary fiscal support is withdrawn. To avoid derailing the recovery, a return to fiscal prudence should take place only after the recovery is firmly underway. Scaling up lifelong learning programmes and strengthening work-based learning can facilitate reallocation of workers in the economy. Promoting market-based non-debt instruments to over-leveraged but viable firms would fasten their growth potential.

Virus infections are again increasing fast

Daily infection cases are again increasing fast. Tensions in the hospital system are less severe than in the spring virus outbreak. At the beginning of November, the government re-imposed a partial lockdown. A "state of emergency" in the face of mounting COVID-19 cases was declared and a curfew introduced in municipalities with high infection rates. Moreover, gatherings are limited to five people, mask-wearing is compulsory in all public spaces, and teleworking is encouraged.

Portugal

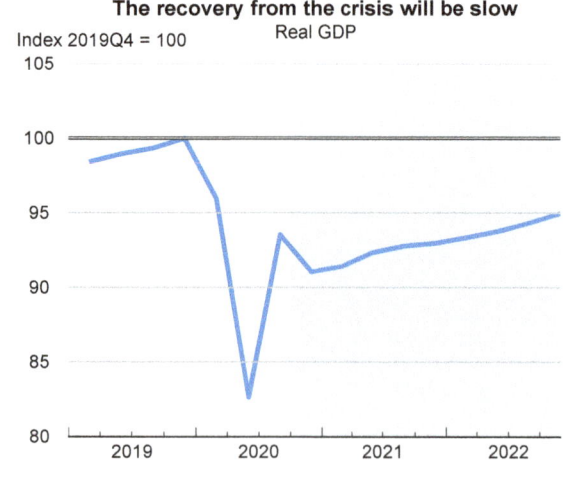

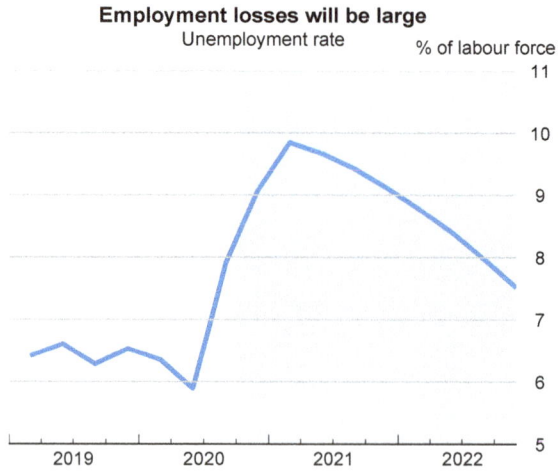

Source: OECD Economic Outlook 108 database.

StatLink https://doi.org/10.1787/888934219318

Portugal: Demand, output and prices

Portugal	2017	2018	2019	2020	2021	2022
	Current prices EUR billion	Percentage changes, volume (2016 prices)				
GDP at market prices	195.9	2.8	2.2	-8.4	1.7	1.9
Private consumption	126.5	2.6	2.4	-7.3	1.1	2.8
Government consumption	33.7	0.6	0.7	-0.3	3.5	0.7
Gross fixed capital formation	32.9	6.2	5.4	-4.2	0.1	2.5
Final domestic demand	193.1	2.9	2.7	-5.5	1.3	2.3
Stockbuilding[1]	0.9	0.3	0.1	-0.4	0.0	0.0
Total domestic demand	194.0	3.2	2.7	-5.9	1.4	2.3
Exports of goods and services	83.7	4.1	3.5	-21.3	3.6	5.8
Imports of goods and services	81.7	5.0	4.7	-16.1	2.5	6.9
Net exports[1]	2.0	-0.3	-0.5	-2.3	0.4	-0.5
Memorandum items						
GDP deflator	_	1.8	1.7	3.0	0.3	0.5
Harmonised index of consumer prices	_	1.2	0.3	-0.2	-0.2	0.3
Harmonised index of core inflation[2]	_	0.8	0.4	-0.2	-0.3	0.3
Unemployment rate (% of labour force)	_	7.0	6.5	7.3	9.5	8.2
Household saving ratio, net (% of disposable income)	_	-2.5	-2.2	8.2	6.3	3.0
General government financial balance[3] (% of GDP)	_	-0.3	0.1	-7.3	-6.3	-4.9
General government gross debt (% of GDP)	_	137.8	136.8	155.7	159.3	158.3
General government debt, Maastricht definition (% of GDP)	_	121.5	117.2	136.1	139.7	138.8
Current account balance (% of GDP)	_	0.4	-0.1	-0.4	-0.6	-0.7

1. Contributions to changes in real GDP, actual amount in the first column.
2. Harmonised index of consumer prices excluding food, energy, alcohol and tobacco.
3. Based on national accounts definition.
Source: OECD Economic Outlook 108 database.

StatLink 🔗 https://doi.org/10.1787/888934219337

The recovery has been uneven across sectors

Economic activity and confidence indicators bounced back in the summer but the strength of the recovery differed across sectors. Construction activity had hardly been affected by the past containment measures. Retail sales picked up quickly and credit card payments reached pre-crisis levels in July. The recovery in the tourism sector remains incomplete. The number of tourists in August was 68% smaller than one year ago. The number of employees on the short-time work scheme remains high. Survey indicators show that bankruptcy levels are low but insolvencies have increased by 64% in August compared with the last year. The recent resurgence of the pandemic reversed the tepid recovery trend in the travel and tourism sector in the third quarter of 2020. Finally, high-frequency data from credit card purchases show that domestic demand started falling again with the renewed restrictions. In the last quarter of the year, the resurgence of infections and the weakening of external demand are weighing on the economy.

Policy support is significant

Fiscal policy is supporting the economy through two plans, the medium-term budget plan and the national recovery plan. The budget plan has a strong focus on protecting workers' income and revamping the health sector. Key labour market policies include wage increases for healthcare workers and employees with incomes below the poverty line and increases in unemployment benefits. In addition, the government is planning to extend the job retention scheme beyond the end of 2020. The national recovery plan is dedicated to support businesses, deepen digitalisation and increase investment efforts, especially those related to climate change. An effective implementation of the national recovery plan will help with structural reforms to boost productivity, create jobs and improve environmental outcomes. In addition, the European Central Bank's accommodative monetary policy and expanded asset purchases will continue to support aggregate demand. The Next Generation EU plan will help finance 2021-22 fiscal measures as Portugal is expected to receive EUR 13.2 billion (3.8% of GDP).

Activity will recover gradually

GDP growth is projected to reach 1.7% in 2021 and 1.9% in 2022, but GDP will remain below its pre-crisis level at the end of 2022 due to long-lasting effects of the pandemic on the productive potential of the economy. High uncertainty about the evolution of the pandemic and the high share of tourism in GDP will mute the speed of recovery until an effective vaccine is in place. Business investment will pick up, supported by low interest rates and EU funds. The budget deficit and public debt are projected to remain high, with the latter reaching 139% of GDP in 2022 (Maastricht definition).

A slower-than-expected recovery in tourism and trading partners' growth would limit exports further. Weak growth could also magnify the spillover effects in the financial sector, via a significant rise in non-performing loans in most affected sectors, such as tourism. Contingent liabilities arising from loan guarantees might also pose an additional burden for public finances. On the upside, an early and effective containment of the pandemic, boosting confidence, and a faster absorption of EU funds could help to foster a stronger-than-projected economic performance.

Further well-targeted policies could facilitate the reallocation of resources

The government should ensure a progressive withdrawal of support measures only once the recovery is well underway. At the same time, it should avoid supporting non-viable firms and ensure that resources go to the most productive firms to allow a progressive restructuring of the economy. Promoting access to market-based financing, such as equity, could help recapitalise firms while at the same time mitigate debt overhang. This crisis has weakened the tourism sector's medium-term prospects, and measures should help affected businesses and their workers to shift to sectors that promise better opportunities. Key to improved reallocation will also be a faster dispute resolution system, higher efficiency of the justice system, scaling up lifelong learning programmes, and more work-based learning in vocational education and training. Finally, public employment services should be strengthened. Faced with a likely surge in the number of job seekers, they need to be supported in finding jobs in new occupations, sectors and regions.

Romania

After a 5.3% decline in 2020, GDP is projected to grow by 2% in 2021 and 4.4% in 2022. The pandemic will have long-lasting negative effects on the economy. Until an effective vaccine is widely deployed in the latter half of 2021, sporadic virus outbreaks and related containment measures will weaken trade prospects and continue to hit activity in the most affected sectors, such as transport and hospitality. EU programmes will sustain investment and help to contain increases in unemployment, but the deterioration of labour market conditions and a likely surge in bankruptcies in 2021 will hamper the recovery.

Fiscal policy needs to remain accommodative, but the composition of public spending has to be reviewed. Recent changes to the pension system should be reconsidered since they limit fiscal space for measures needed to accelerate the recovery and undermine the sustainability of public finances. Supporting investment in digital technologies in both the private and public sectors is a priority to improve the resilience of the economy against future COVID-19 shocks. Spending on education, health and social protection should increase to counter rising risks of poverty and social exclusion. Accelerating the absorption of EU funds for greener growth is a priority.

The pandemic has gained momentum

The number of COVID-19 cases has increased fast in the autumn, with an estimated infection rate currently exceeding three per thousand inhabitants in large cities, including Bucharest. The capacity of the healthcare system improved in response to the rise in hospitalisations, but shortages of medical staff remain a major issue. Containment measures were gradually lifted from May, and schools and indoor restaurants reopened in September, but the second virus outbreak has led to new restrictions. From 9 November, schools have been closed, a curfew introduced, opening hours of shops restricted, and mask-wearing made mandatory in all public spaces. Some cities were placed under quarantine. Containment measures are projected to remain in place until the beginning of 2021.

Romania

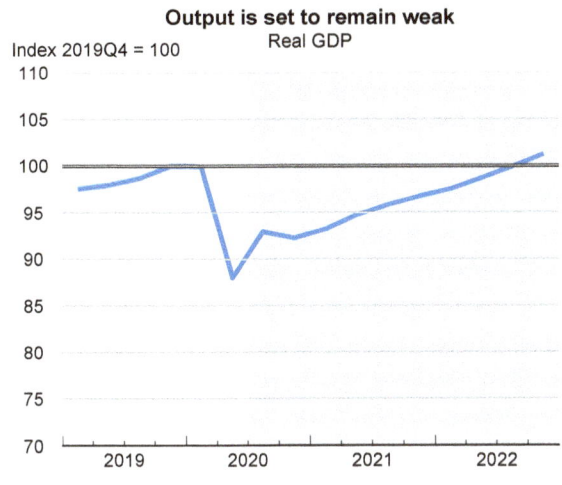

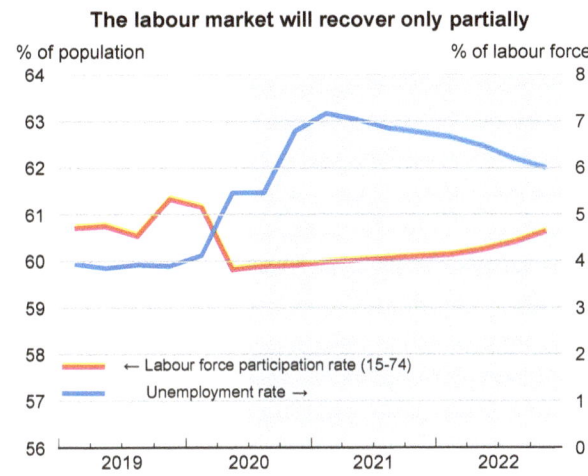

Source: OECD Economic Outlook 108 database.

StatLink https://doi.org/10.1787/888934219356

Romania: Demand, output and prices

Romania	2017	2018	2019	2020	2021	2022
	Current prices RON billion	Percentage changes, volume (2010 prices)				
GDP at market prices	857.9	4.5	4.2	-5.3	2.0	4.4
Private consumption	543.3	7.7	5.5	-7.3	2.6	5.1
Government consumption	134.8	3.3	6.0	3.4	3.5	1.0
Gross fixed capital formation	192.2	-1.1	17.8	-0.9	2.0	6.3
Final domestic demand	870.3	5.1	8.3	-3.5	2.7	4.6
Stockbuilding[1]	8.7	0.8	-2.9	0.0	-0.4	0.0
Total domestic demand	879.1	5.9	5.2	-3.4	2.4	4.8
Exports of goods and services	360.5	5.3	4.0	-15.6	3.3	5.4
Imports of goods and services	381.7	8.6	6.5	-9.9	4.3	6.2
Net exports[1]	- 21.2	-1.6	-1.3	-1.9	-0.6	-0.6
Memorandum items						
GDP deflator	_	6.2	6.9	2.9	2.6	2.6
Consumer price index	_	4.6	3.8	2.8	2.2	2.1
Core consumer price index[2]	_	2.8	3.2	3.7	2.3	2.1
Unemployment rate (% of labour force)	_	4.2	3.9	5.5	7.0	6.3
Household saving ratio, net (% of disposable income)	_	-6.4	-5.5	0.8	-2.8	-4.1
General government financial balance (% of GDP)	_	-2.9	-4.4	-9.0	-9.4	-7.1
General government gross debt (% of GDP)	_	43.6	44.3	53.9	62.0	66.4
General government debt, Maastricht definition (% of GDP)	_	34.7	35.3	44.9	52.9	57.4
Current account balance (% of GDP)	_	-4.4	-4.7	-4.6	-4.9	-4.8

1. Contributions to changes in real GDP, actual amount in the first column.
2. Consumer price index excluding food and energy.
Source: OECD Economic Outlook 108 database.

StatLink https://doi.org/10.1787/888934219375

The virus surge is undermining the recovery

After a rather quick resumption of activity following the easing of containment measures from May, the recovery has lost momentum. Droughts have negatively affected agriculture. High spare capacity in manufacturing reflects weak external demand. Retail sales almost reached pre-crisis levels, but lost momentum. The increasing number of cases and political turbulences have weighed on confidence and the economic sentiment remains well below historical levels. Labour market conditions have deteriorated with a decline in job vacancies and a rise of the unemployment rate by around 2 percentage points since January 2020.

Public finance support is limited

The future fiscal stance is uncertain due to upcoming legislative elections. It is expected to remain mildly supportive over the projection period. The 40% increase in the pension point value, voted in September, but not promulgated yet, is projected to be partly reversed due to its strong negative impact on the sustainability of the public finances. EU funds will promote public investment in transport infrastructure and finance labour market programmes, but absorption rates will likely remain relatively weak due to limited administrative capacity. Monetary policy has been supportive, with three policy rate cuts in March, June and August and government bond purchases. The central bank should continue to play its stabilising role in financial markets.

The pandemic will have long-lasting effects on the economy

GDP is set to contract by 5.3% in 2020, before expanding by 2% in 2021 and 4.4% in 2022. A weak external environment, especially in the European Union, will limit export prospects and business investment. After a 70% decline in the first eight months of the year, foreign direct investment will continue to be low. Possible sporadic virus outbreaks will continue to require targeted local containment measures and limit demand for services requiring physical proximity until immunisation is widespread. High job losses, slower wage growth, lower remittances and reduced fiscal stimulus will weigh on households' purchasing power. Public debt (Maastricht definition) is set to increase fast, to 57% of GDP in 2022, due to high budget deficits. The main downside risks to the projections relate to fiscal policy. Full implementation of the 40% increase in pensions could push the budget deficit up to 11% of GDP. This could result in a downgrade of Romania's sovereign debt rating, undermining access to financial markets. By contrast, a faster absorption of EU funds and increased political stability could stimulate investment and job creation.

Improving spending efficiency can enhance economic potential and well-being

A reallocation of spending to areas supporting economic potential, especially education, health and infrastructure, could pave the way to a sustainable recovery. The priority is to contain the pandemic by implementing fast testing, strict tracing, tracking and isolation, and by providing sufficient resources to the healthcare sector. Public support for those in need should be strengthened. The long awaited reform of social assistance that streamlines and improves the targeting of social benefits should be pursued. Fostering the digital transformation is crucial, especially in schools to ensure all have access to online education during lockdowns and in firms to foster teleworking. Amid concerns about air quality, speeding up the transition from fossil fuels to cleaner and more affordable energy sources is urgent, as it would improve health and environment outcomes while reducing vulnerability to pandemics. Finally, streamlining the permits and licensing system can remove unnecessary barriers to business dynamism.

Slovak Republic

After contracting by 6.3% in 2020, the economy is projected to grow by around 2.7% in 2021 and 4.3% in 2022. Consumption will recover gradually on the back of higher disposable income, improving labour market conditions and increased household confidence as an effective vaccine is rolled out. Investment growth will be limited by high uncertainty, weakened corporate balance sheets and low capacity utilisation. Unemployment is set to fall gradually, but will remain above pre-crisis levels at the end of 2022. Inflation will remain subdued given considerable economic slack.

The sizeable fiscal stimulus has helped prevent a deeper contraction. Fiscal policy should remain supportive in the near term. The recovery package should stimulate short-term demand and boost the long-term growth potential. Improving the digital infrastructure, access to early childhood education and female participation in the labour market is key to strengthening the recovery and making it inclusive.

The Slovak Republic is facing a second wave of the pandemic

After successfully containing the first wave of the virus outbreak, the Slovak Republic is now experiencing a strong increase in the number of confirmed cases. Testing has become more widespread, but hospitalised cases and occupancy rates in intensive care units are also increasing. In response, the government has enhanced healthcare capacity, launched a massive operation to test the entire population and declared a state of national emergency on 1 October. All mass events have been banned, secondary schools have switched to online classes, outdoor mask-wearing has become compulsory, and restaurants can serve customers only outdoors. A partial curfew has been also imposed, but, unlike in spring, businesses have not been shut down nor have store operations been restricted.

Slovak Republic

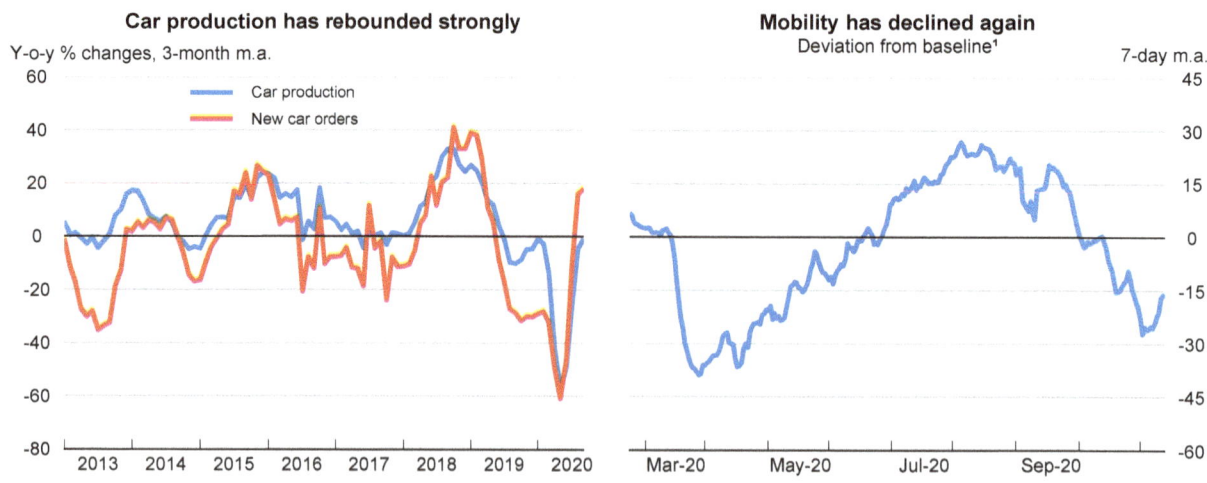

1. The graph represents a simple average of six Google mobility indicators: workplaces, retail and recreation, grocery and pharmacy, public transit stations, parks, and residential. Each indicator represents the deviation from baseline consisting of the median value, for the corresponding day of the week, during the 5-week period January 3-February 6, 2020 (i.e. the period before the COVID-19 outbreak).
Source: Statistical Office of the Slovak Republic; and OECD calculations based on Google LLC, *Google COVID-19 Community Mobility Reports*, https://www.google.com/covid19/mobility/.

StatLink https://doi.org/10.1787/888934219394

Slovak Republic: Demand, output and prices

Slovak Republic	2017	2018	2019	2020	2021	2022
	Current prices EUR billion	Percentage changes, volume (2015 prices)				
GDP at market prices	84.5	3.9	2.4	-6.3	2.7	4.3
Private consumption	47.3	4.1	2.1	-1.5	1.3	3.0
Government consumption	16.0	0.2	4.6	-1.3	3.8	1.7
Gross fixed capital formation	17.9	2.6	6.8	-13.7	-2.5	8.4
Final domestic demand	81.2	3.0	3.6	-4.1	1.1	3.8
Stockbuilding[1]	1.5	0.6	-0.3	-3.1	0.0	0.0
Total domestic demand	82.7	3.5	3.2	-7.1	1.1	3.8
Exports of goods and services	80.4	5.3	1.7	-8.7	9.1	4.2
Imports of goods and services	78.6	4.9	2.6	-9.8	7.4	3.6
Net exports[1]	1.9	0.5	-0.7	0.9	1.6	0.6
Memorandum items						
GDP deflator	_	2.0	2.6	2.0	1.5	1.8
Harmonised index of consumer prices	_	2.5	2.8	1.9	0.9	1.4
Harmonised index of core inflation[2]	_	2.0	2.0	2.3	1.1	1.4
Unemployment rate (% of labour force)	_	6.5	5.8	6.8	7.4	6.8
Household saving ratio, net (% of disposable income)	_	3.1	3.5	5.0	4.4	4.2
General government financial balance (% of GDP)	_	-1.0	-1.3	-8.2	-7.5	-5.5
General government gross debt (% of GDP)	_	63.8	63.5	73.7	79.1	81.2
General government debt, Maastricht definition (% of GDP)	_	49.8	48.3	58.4	63.8	66.0
Current account balance (% of GDP)	_	-2.6	-2.9	-1.3	-0.6	0.1

1. Contributions to changes in real GDP, actual amount in the first column.
2. Harmonised index of consumer prices excluding food, energy, alcohol and tobacco.
Source: OECD Economic Outlook 108 database.

StatLink https://doi.org/10.1787/888934219413

The second wave of the pandemic is slowing the recovery

In the first half of 2020, the economy contracted less severely than in many other European countries thanks to more resilient private consumption. Economic activity rebounded rapidly in the third quarter, driven by very strong exports growth as car production quickly recovered. Monthly data on retail sales and credit card purchases also indicate a pick-up in private consumption. While the rise in unemployment has been limited, working hours are still far below the pre-crisis level. High-frequency data suggest weakening activity since the recent tightening of confinement measures. For example, mobility data show a sharp decline in people's movement since the end of September. Consumer confidence also weakened again in October.

Fiscal support is substantial

The government has reacted promptly with a series of fiscal stimulus measures to cushion the shock. Announced discretionary fiscal measures amount to around 4.4% of GDP in 2020. In particular, the introduction of a short-time work scheme has been effective in preventing a surge in unemployment. The government has decided to extend this temporary scheme until the end of 2020. Several other temporary policies have also been extended. For instance, the deferral of loan payments for households and the benefit for families with members in need of care were prolonged until the end of the state of national emergency. The government plans to continue fiscal support in 2021. The draft budget for 2021 includes a reserve of around 1.1% of GDP for covering potential needs due to the pandemic. The budget also foresees extra spending on healthcare, education and transport infrastructure to strengthen the recovery.

The economy will recover gradually

The economy is projected to grow by around 2.7% in 2021 and 4.3% in 2022. The second wave of the pandemic will weigh on economic activity in the near term. From mid-2021, a gradually improving labour market, together with stronger wage growth and confidence gains related to vaccination against the virus, will support household disposable income and consumption. Export growth is set to weaken again in the near term given the renewed restrictions in trading partners. Investment growth will be sluggish amid high uncertainty and weak confidence, but will start to rise as demand increases. The use of EU structural funds as well as the new EU Recovery and Resilience Facility will also support investment in 2022. The general government budget deficit will narrow as economic activity picks up and some emergency measures are phased out. A faster-than-expected distribution of an effective vaccine is an upside risk to the projections. On the downside, a further deterioration of the health situation before the implementation of an effective vaccine, triggering another national lockdown, would delay the economic recovery. Supply-chain disruptions, notably for cars, and weak foreign demand, especially from Germany, also pose negative risks to exports and investment.

Measures to boost both short-term demand and productivity should be prioritised

Fiscal policy should remain supportive as planned to sustain the recovery in the near term. Going forward, strengthening public employment services is crucial to facilitate workforce reallocation. In addition, the EU funds will provide an opportunity to strengthen the growth potential of the economy and boost productivity and inclusiveness. In particular, room exists to invest in the lagging digital infrastructure to better prepare the country for the likely increase in demand for digital services that the COVID-19 crisis may bring. The government plans to expand support for pre-school education for children at the age of five. This is welcome and should be complemented with investment to enhance access to early childhood education and care for younger children as well. This would help increase female labour force participation and improve educational outcomes.

Slovenia

GDP is set to fall by 7.5% in 2020 and grow by 3.4% in 2021 as the effects of the pandemic will continue to disturb economic activity until at least mid-2021. From then until the end of the projection horizon in 2022, investment and exports will be the main engines of growth thanks to higher demand in trading partner countries, improvements in the epidemiological situation, increased household confidence due to the rolling out of an effective vaccine, and the effects of the EU stimulus plan.

Targeted sectoral support measures may need to be continued to tackle sporadic virus outbreaks, while immunisation has not been attained, and to avoid a negative long-lasting impact on the economy. Employment transitions would benefit from directing employment and training subsidies to job seekers with high assistance needs. Prolonged wage support is needed in the tourism and entertainment sectors.

The spread of the virus has gathered speed

The spread of the coronavirus has accelerated since September 2020. In addition to distancing measures, mandatory mask wearing and restrictions in schooling, the government announced new measures to contain the spread of the virus, including the restriction or prohibition of gatherings of more than six people, a ban on travel between municipalities and regions and a curfew. While remote learning is already applied in higher education, it has been extended to primary and secondary schools. Also, a two-week lockdown started in mid-November, involving – among other restrictions – the interruption of public transport services and closure of all non-essential stores.

Slovenia

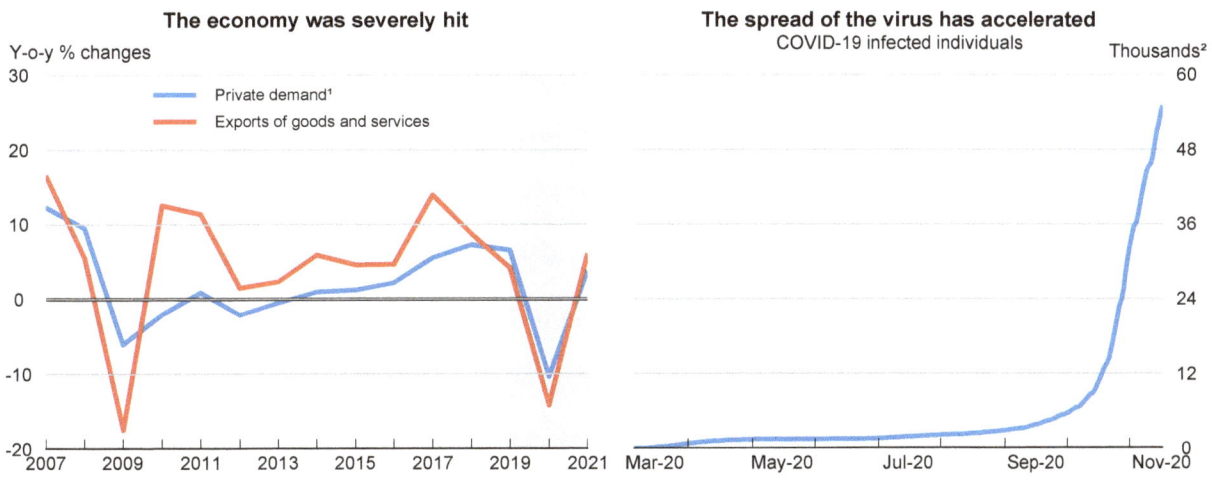

1. Private demand includes private final consumption expenditure and gross fixed capital formation.
2. Daily number of cumulative cases.
Source: Ourworldindata; and OECD Economic Outlook 108 database.

StatLink https://doi.org/10.1787/888934219432

Slovenia: Demand, output and prices

Slovenia	2017	2018	2019	2020	2021	2022
	Current prices EUR billion	Percentage changes, volume (2010 prices)				
GDP at market prices	43.0	4.4	3.2	-7.5	3.4	3.5
Private consumption	22.6	3.6	4.8	-10.8	2.2	3.4
Government consumption	7.9	3.0	1.7	3.2	3.5	2.0
Gross fixed capital formation	7.9	9.6	5.8	-11.3	2.4	7.1
Final domestic demand	38.4	4.7	4.4	-8.0	2.6	3.8
Stockbuilding[1]	0.7	0.3	-0.8	0.5	0.3	0.0
Total domestic demand	39.1	5.0	3.4	-8.0	2.4	3.7
Exports of goods and services	35.8	6.3	4.1	-13.5	5.6	6.9
Imports of goods and services	31.9	7.2	4.4	-15.0	4.7	7.7
Net exports[1]	3.9	-0.1	0.1	0.0	1.1	0.2
Memorandum items						
GDP deflator	_	2.2	2.3	2.2	1.8	1.9
Harmonised index of consumer prices	_	1.9	1.7	0.1	1.7	1.4
Harmonised index of core inflation[2]	_	1.0	1.9	1.0	1.6	1.4
Unemployment rate (% of labour force)	_	5.1	4.4	5.5	5.6	5.2
Household saving ratio, net (% of disposable income)	_	6.0	6.0	17.2	16.7	15.1
General government financial balance (% of GDP)	_	0.7	0.5	-8.3	-8.0	-5.6
General government gross debt (% of GDP)	_	84.0	86.2	98.3	105.4	108.8
General government debt, Maastricht definition (% of GDP)	_	70.3	65.6	77.7	84.9	88.3
Current account balance (% of GDP)	_	5.8	5.6	6.9	7.6	7.0

1. Contributions to changes in real GDP, actual amount in the first column.
2. Harmonised index of consumer prices excluding food, energy, alcohol and tobacco.
Source: OECD Economic Outlook 108 database.

StatLink ⟐⟐ https://doi.org/10.1787/888934219451

The pick-up in economic activity has been interrupted by the intensification of the outbreak

Economic activity picked up in the third quarter of 2020, after the end of the lockdown in mid-May. Household purchases of durables remained resilient, and firms built up inventories. The private sector's financial position continued to be favourable, as household disposable incomes declined only slightly. However, the recent acceleration in the spread of the virus has led to new restrictions that are affecting economic activity, in particular in services sectors.

Fiscal stimulus is supporting the economy

The initial fiscal package to counter the effects of the crisis amounted to nearly 4½ per cent of GDP. The measures in the supplementary budget for 2020 adopted in September result in a projected budget deficit of 8.3% of GDP. Spending on COVID-19-related measures until the end of August covered support for furloughed workers, waived social security contributions, provided income support to different categories of workers and allowed firms to defer corporate income tax payments. By the end of September, the government announced a new round of stimulus measures to support the economy. It extended the furlough scheme until the end of 2020 and introduced a basic income support for self-employed workers who have to self-isolate due to COVID-19, with strict eligibility criteria. Additional measures introduced in November, amounting to 2% of GDP, include extending the furlough scheme until the end of January 2021 and introducing a fixed subsidy scheme for businesses, doubling the amount of furlough payment workers can receive, and increasing loan guarantees for firms.

The outlook is uncertain as the virus spreads

Activity is likely to slow again as the virus spreads, and assumed sporadic local outbreaks and associated containment measures will moderate the recovery. Demand is projected to bounce back in 2021 before receding to a more stable path. Government spending and household consumption will maintain the recovery until the end of 2021, with sustained government transfers and confidence strengthening due to an effective vaccine rollout. The EU stimulus plan will also contribute to high public consumption and investment over the projection period. As the economy is highly integrated into EU value chains, the export-oriented sectors will benefit from stronger EU demand from 2021.

The outlook is highly uncertain. A further significant deterioration of the health situation could lead to prolonged restrictions that would stall the economic recovery. Continued weak external demand remains another key risk for growth. However, a bolder recovery in Europe thanks to a rapid rollout of an effective vaccine would lift growth prospects.

Targeted policy actions would increase the resilience of the labour market and the healthcare system

Unemployment is increasing, calling for reinforced active labour market policies targeted on specific groups, such as long-term and older unemployed persons. Government support to households and businesses most affected by the crisis, in particular in the tourism and entertainment sectors, should continue. However, the governance of state-owned enterprises should be improved to increase value for public money. Once the pandemics subsides, reforms to tackle spending pressures on public finances from population ageing should be advanced.

South Africa

An early and long lockdown to tackle the virus outbreak led to a significant decrease in economic activity in the first half of 2020. A substantial rebound is expected in the second half of the year, driven by high demand and favourable prices for South Africa's exports. Near-term growth will nevertheless be modest owing to subdued domestic demand. Household consumption will remain low as unemployment will remain high. Private investment will be restrained by a lack of confidence. GDP is set to contract by 8.1% in 2020 before increasing by 3.1% in 2021 and 2.5% in 2022.

Inflation will remain below the Reserve Bank's target, allowing monetary authorities to reduce policy rates further. In the event of another large virus outbreak in the near term, fiscal policy has reduced space to react. Fiscal consolidation is needed when the pandemic subsides to limit public debt growth. Recent steps in launching the auction of telecom spectrum and procuring renewable energy from independent power producers are sending positive signals to business leaders and could lift confidence if successfully concluded. Advancing structural reforms in network sectors, restructuring state-owned enterprises and boosting infrastructure investment could restore growth momentum.

The outbreak receded after a long lockdown

After the lifting of the lockdown in June, infections increased rapidly in July and August, but since mid-September the spread of the COVID-19 virus has receded, thanks to the strategy of massive testing and targeted restrictive measures. Consequently, the government lowered the alert level of the state of disaster, and partially reopened borders to travellers as of 1 October. Still, a curfew and some restrictions on gatherings, liquor sales, sports activities and entertainment remain in place.

South Africa

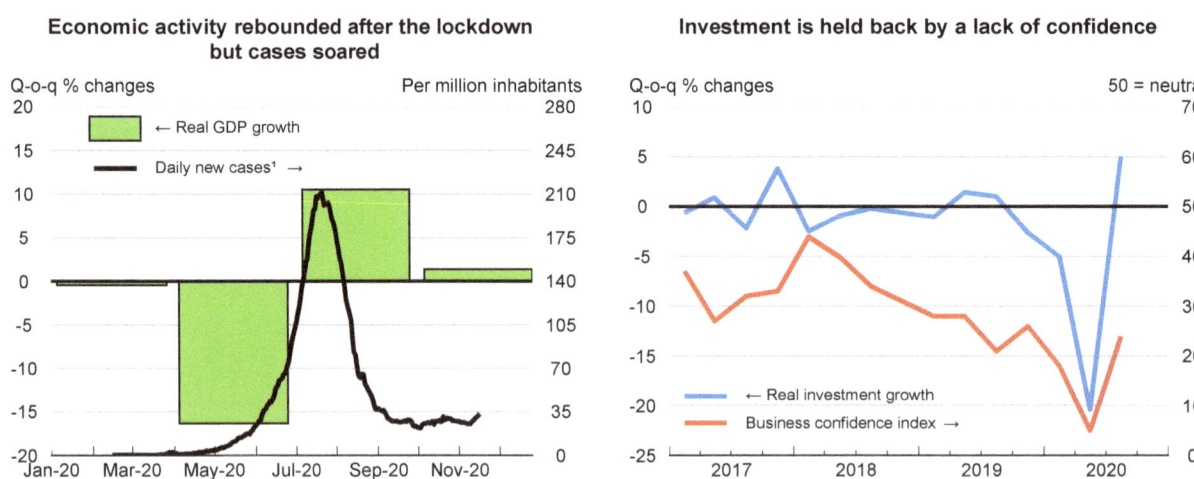

1. Seven-day moving average.
Source: OECD Economic Outlook 108 database; OECD calculations based on European Centre for Disease Prevention and Control; and Bureau for Economic Research, South Africa.

StatLink ᐧᐧᑌᔐᐧ https://doi.org/10.1787/888934219470

South Africa: Demand, output and prices

South Africa	2017	2018	2019	2020	2021	2022
	Current prices ZAR billion	Percentage changes, volume (2010 prices)				
GDP at market prices	4 659.2	0.8	0.2	-8.1	3.1	2.5
Private consumption	2 756.5	1.8	1.0	-7.0	2.0	1.7
Government consumption	967.9	1.9	1.5	2.7	3.0	1.3
Gross fixed capital formation	873.2	-1.4	-0.9	-18.1	2.5	5.9
Final domestic demand	4 597.7	1.2	0.8	-6.9	2.3	2.3
Stockbuilding[1]	1.9	-0.2	0.0	-1.4	0.2	0.0
Total domestic demand	4 599.6	1.0	0.7	-8.7	2.6	2.4
Exports of goods and services	1 378.7	2.6	-2.5	-15.1	5.4	6.8
Imports of goods and services	1 319.1	3.3	-0.5	-16.5	3.4	6.2
Net exports[1]	59.6	-0.2	-0.6	0.7	0.5	0.1
Memorandum items						
GDP deflator	–	3.3	4.2	4.1	3.7	4.2
Consumer price index	–	4.6	4.1	3.4	3.8	4.3
Core inflation index[2]	–	4.2	4.1	3.1	3.8	4.3
General government financial balance (% of GDP)	–	-3.1	-4.6	-15.3	-9.9	-8.6
Current account balance (% of GDP)	–	-3.6	-3.0	0.1	0.3	0.2

1. Contributions to changes in real GDP, actual amount in the first column.
2. Consumer price index excluding food and energy.
Source: OECD Economic Outlook 108 database.

StatLink https://doi.org/10.1787/888934219489

Economic activity picked up after the lockdown

Economic activity collapsed in the second quarter of 2020, with all sectors but agriculture registering a large fall in output. A progressive recovery started in July. Exports, mining and manufacturing rebounded strongly in the third quarter according to monthly indicators. In addition, household consumption has picked up, aided by additional government transfers to social grant recipients and wage replacement payments for workers (amounting to ZAR 51 billion, around 1% of GDP, since April). The recreation, entertainment and tourism sectors remain the most affected. In total, 2.2 million workers lost their jobs in the second quarter, while the number of discouraged workers increased by 5.6 million.

Monetary and fiscal policies are supportive

Since the beginning of the crisis, the Reserve Bank has cut the repurchasing rate from 6.25% in early March to 3.5% and provided liquidity to the banking sector. Prudential regulations were eased to help financial institutions to cope with the consequences of the crisis. On the fiscal side, the government has put in place a rescue plan amounting to 10% of GDP to support households and businesses. The initial increase in social grant amounts has been prolonged as long as the state of national disaster continues. In October, the government released a reconstruction and recovery plan aiming to mobilise ZAR 100 billion (around 2% of GDP) for infrastructure investment next year. This plan also includes an ambitious employment stimulus programme to support job creation in the public and social sectors.

The rebound following the lockdown may not last

A strong recovery is estimated to have taken place in the third quarter of 2020, almost offsetting the slump in the second quarter. Most of the recovery next year will come from the external sector as exports will be boosted by higher commodity prices and demand. In addition, the government support programme will continue helping to maintain household consumption in the short run. Investment, however, is not projected to pick up strongly next year, as business confidence will remain low.

A failure to stabilise public debt could trigger financial market turbulence and adversely affect foreign capital inflows to which South Africa is highly dependent. Disruptions to trade linked to the COVID-19 virus and persistently weak global demand could harm growth prospects. On the other hand, stronger growth in partner countries driven by a rapid vaccine distribution would lift growth.

Implementation of reforms is key to boost the economy

Targeted financial support to households and firms still affected by low activity should be continued, notably for the entertainment and tourism sectors. However, bold fiscal measures are necessary to curb public debt increases. Freezing public service wages and restructuring state-owned enterprises would limit government spending increases. Broadening competition in the economy, particularly in network industries and the transport sector, can boost the potential of the economy. Bolder implementation of government economic reform announcements is needed to lift confidence of households and businesses.

Spain

After the steep decline in 2020, GDP is projected to grow by 5% in 2021 and 4% in 2022. Localised restrictions to address COVID-19 outbreaks and continued disruption to travel and tourism will be a drag on the recovery until an effective vaccine is widely deployed. High uncertainty and adverse labour market conditions will weigh on private consumption. As external demand growth recovers gradually, exports will contribute to growth in 2021-22. The unemployment rate is projected to remain high.

The current flexible approach of adapting policies to help firms and workers to the evolution of the pandemic should be maintained, by targeting fiscal support to those most affected by the crisis. While the extension of short-time work schemes will support the hard-hit sectors, this should be accompanied by more training and stronger active labour market policies to prepare for the reallocation of resources across firms and sectors. The national recovery plan has a strong focus on digital and green investment objectives, which should be achieved through ambitious structural reforms to boost productivity, create jobs and improve environmental outcomes.

The resurgence of infections has been strong

Despite some new restrictions, such as the national closure of nightclubs and bars in August, the number of cases rose steeply in the autumn. A new state of emergency until 9 May 2021 and a national curfew were declared in October. In addition, regional containment measures, such as restrictions on non-essential activities, social gatherings and interregional mobility, partial lockdowns, the closure of hotels and restaurants and changes to closing times of businesses, have been introduced since September.

Spain

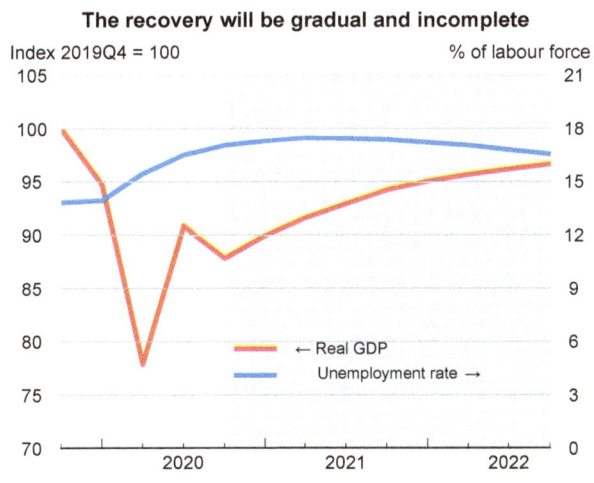

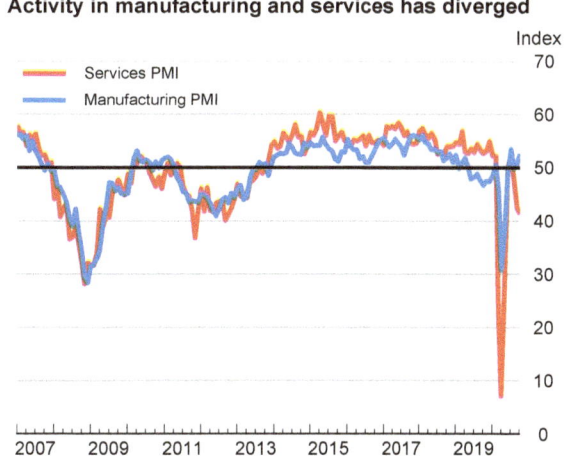

Source: OECD Economic Outlook 108 database; and IHS Markit.

StatLink https://doi.org/10.1787/888934219508

Spain: Demand, output and prices

Spain	2017 Current prices EUR billion	2018	2019	2020	2021	2022
		Percentage changes, volume (2015 prices)				
GDP at market prices	1 161.9	2.4	2.0	-11.6	5.0	4.0
Private consumption	678.1	1.8	0.9	-14.2	5.8	4.6
Government consumption	216.3	2.6	2.3	5.9	2.3	0.1
Gross fixed capital formation	216.9	6.1	2.7	-15.2	4.1	4.6
Final domestic demand	1 111.4	2.8	1.5	-10.4	4.6	3.6
Stockbuilding[1]	8.6	0.3	-0.1	-0.2	-0.1	0.0
Total domestic demand	1 120.0	3.1	1.4	-10.6	4.5	3.5
Exports of goods and services	408.4	2.3	2.3	-19.9	7.1	5.7
Imports of goods and services	366.5	4.2	0.7	-17.4	5.5	4.4
Net exports[1]	41.9	-0.5	0.6	-1.4	0.6	0.5
Memorandum items						
GDP deflator	_	1.2	1.4	0.9	0.8	0.5
Harmonised index of consumer prices	_	1.7	0.8	-0.3	0.4	0.6
Harmonised index of core inflation[2]	_	1.0	1.1	0.5	0.1	0.6
Unemployment rate (% of labour force)	_	15.3	14.1	15.8	17.4	16.9
Household saving ratio, net (% of disposable income)	_	1.4	2.0	14.2	9.8	6.3
General government financial balance (% of GDP)	_	-2.5	-2.9	-11.7	-9.0	-6.6
General government gross debt (% of GDP)	_	114.5	117.3	139.1	142.3	144.3
General government debt, Maastricht definition (% of GDP)	_	97.4	95.5	117.3	120.5	122.4
Current account balance (% of GDP)	_	1.9	2.1	1.4	1.9	1.9

1. Contributions to changes in real GDP, actual amount in the first column.
2. Harmonised index of consumer prices excluding food, energy, alcohol and tobacco.
Source: OECD Economic Outlook 108 database.

StatLink https://doi.org/10.1787/888934219527

The recovery has been uneven across sectors and regions

Despite a strong rebound in the third quarter of 2020, the level of GDP was 9.1% below that in the final quarter of 2019. The rise in infections since late summer and the introduction of travel quarantines by other countries limited the recovery in tourism-related sectors. The number of tourists in September was 87.1% smaller than a year ago and foreign credit card transactions declined by 65% in October. Manufacturing activity indicators continue to recover, but those for services registered a steeper decline, due to new containment measures. The number of workers on short-time work schemes in October was 18% of the peak in April. However, the pace of exit from job retention schemes has slowed down, with the remaining workers concentrated in sectors and regions most affected by the crisis.

Policy measures remain extensive and targeted

The short-time work schemes and the extraordinary benefit to the self-employed were extended until 31 January 2021, while the measures to help vulnerable tenants will last until the end of 2021. The new short-time work scheme is targeted to sectors directly affected by restrictions and introduces incentives to combine it with other work. In July, an additional loan guarantee facility of EUR 40 billion (3.2% of 2019 GDP) to finance new investment by firms and the self-employed and a EUR 10 billion (0.8% of GDP) fund to promote the solvency of strategic companies were created. A number of packages targeted at specific sectors (automobile, tourism, transport) were introduced during the summer. A EUR 16 billion (1.3% of GDP) COVID-19 fund was created to transfer resources to regions to help with healthcare and education expenditures. In November, to support firm solvency, the maturity period to pay the whole loan, the grace periods for the payment of the principal of the loan and the deadline to apply for loans under the public guarantees were increased, and the suspension of insolvency proceedings was extended until March 2021. In addition, the European Central Bank's accommodative monetary policy, including expanded asset purchases, will continue to support aggregate demand. The national recovery plan presented in October outlines the main areas, where the EUR 72 billion (5.8% of GDP) that Spain is expected to receive from Next Generation EU funds will be utilised. EUR 26.6 billion (2.1% of GDP) of these funds are already included in the Draft Budget 2021.

The recovery is set to be gradual and incomplete

The strong rebound in the third quarter of 2020 is set to be followed by a contraction in the fourth quarter. The adverse impact of the new containment measures on activity, especially in the hospitality sector, is assumed to ease slowly. Consequently, the recovery will be gradual and the level of GDP will remain below pre-crisis levels by the end of 2022. The increase in private consumption will be limited by the incomplete recovery of the labour market and high precautionary saving. While business investment will pick up, supported by low interest rates and declining uncertainty, still low capacity utilisation combined with weakened financial positions of firms will limit the extent of the recovery. As a consequence, the increase in economic activity will only partially reverse the rise in the unemployment rate. Downside risks include more persistent effects on household and firm solvency, restricting the recovery in domestic demand more than projected. On the upside, a faster-than-assumed recovery in tourism and trading partners' growth and a swift use of European recovery funds boosting public investment could lead to a stronger rebound.

Policies should support reallocation and productivity

In the short run, policy support to those directly impacted by new containment measures should be continued. At the same time, training should be promoted for those on short-time work schemes to improve their prospect of finding a new job in expanding sectors and firms. Public employment services should strengthen individualised support, via the aid of profiling tools, to facilitate upskilling of workers and improve labour market matching. A prolongation of the crisis can push viable firms into insolvency. Remaining gaps in insolvency regimes should be addressed to speed up out-of-court restructuring processes. There is also a need to lower long-standing barriers to productivity growth. The effective implementation of prior structural reforms addressing internal market fragmentation of product markets is key. The co-ordination and evaluation of regional and national innovation policies should be increased to raise the quality of innovation. This can also contribute to improving the structure of economic activity by facilitating adoption of digital technologies and removing barriers to firms' growth. Frontloading investment in renewable energy, energy efficiency and sustainable transport during the recovery, in line with the National Energy and Climate Plan and the national recovery plan objectives, would help the green transition as well as job creation.

Sweden

The Swedish economy is gradually recovering from the COVID-19 crisis. Overall, GDP is projected to expand by 3.3% in both 2021 and 2022. Nevertheless, high unemployment and ongoing distancing will limit the pick-up in household consumption. Low capacity utilisation and uncertainties hold back business investment. Exports will gradually pick up as the global economy recovers. Unemployment will decrease slowly despite the economic recovery, as increases in working time from low levels will precede new recruitments.

Monetary policy will remain accommodative to facilitate credit and provide sufficient liquidity to firms. The government is implementing a sizeable fiscal package to support the economy and employment as well as to tackle structural issues like green transition and regional inequality. However, additional measures may be needed to support young, low-skilled and foreign-born unemployed, as well as remote regions.

Additional containment measures can now be locally implemented

Since September, the number of COVID-19 cases has climbed up again. The number of patients in intensive care units and deaths has also increased. To contain the spread of the virus, the Swedish Public Health Agency has tightened the rules to isolate people who live in a household with an infected person: previously, they were urged to stay at home; now, they must stay at home if ordered to do so by a doctor. Furthermore, selling and serving alcohol after 10 pm was forbidden. The threshold for public events was lowered from 50 to eight people, and almost 90% of the counties have introduced additional guidelines specific to their area.

Sweden

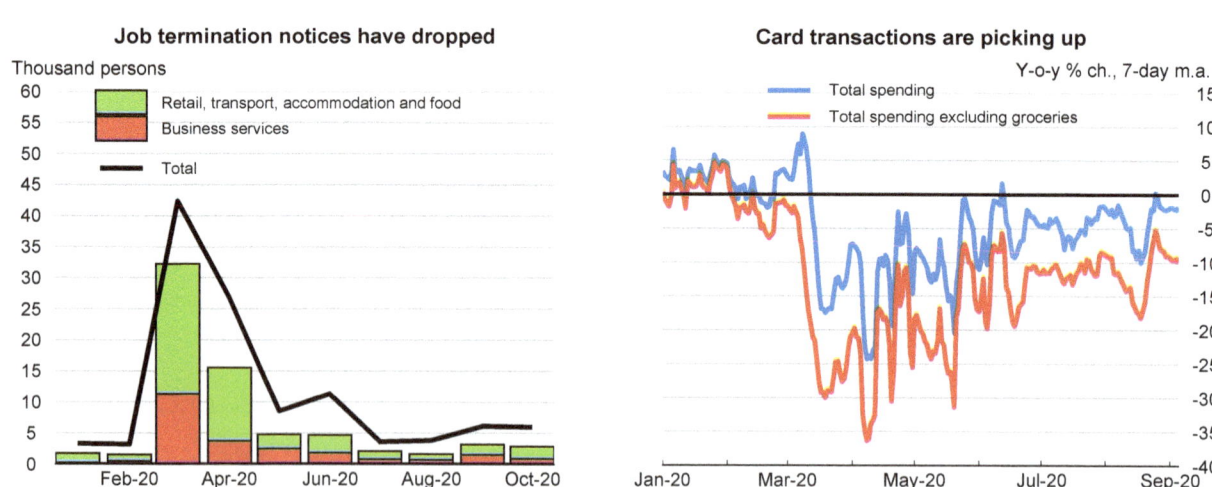

Source: Swedish Public Employment Service (Arbetsförmedlingen); Swedbank Pay; and Swedbank Research.

StatLink https://doi.org/10.1787/888934219546

Sweden: Demand, output and prices

Sweden	2017	2018	2019	2020	2021	2022
	Current prices SEK billion	Percentage changes, volume (2019 prices)				
GDP at market prices	4 624.1	2.0	1.4	-3.2	3.3	3.3
Private consumption	2 114.0	1.9	1.3	-4.6	4.0	3.0
Government consumption	1 203.4	1.1	0.3	-0.3	3.2	1.6
Gross fixed capital formation	1 163.1	1.4	-1.2	-2.2	2.8	3.8
Final domestic demand	4 480.6	1.5	0.4	-2.8	3.5	2.8
Stockbuilding[1]	27.2	0.3	-0.1	-0.6	0.0	0.0
Total domestic demand	4 507.8	1.8	0.2	-3.4	3.5	2.8
Exports of goods and services	2 021.9	4.4	3.7	-6.8	4.2	5.8
Imports of goods and services	1 905.6	4.0	1.3	-7.5	4.7	4.8
Net exports[1]	116.3	0.3	1.1	0.1	0.0	0.6
Memorandum items						
GDP deflator	_	2.4	2.7	1.4	0.9	1.2
Consumer price index[2]	_	2.0	1.8	0.6	1.1	1.2
Core inflation index[3]	_	2.1	1.7	0.5	1.0	1.2
Unemployment rate[4] (% of labour force)	_	6.3	6.8	8.6	9.0	8.0
Household saving ratio, net (% of disposable income)	_	13.4	16.1	19.3	17.4	16.9
General government financial balance (% of GDP)	_	0.8	0.5	-4.0	-3.8	-2.3
General government debt, Maastricht definition (% of GDP)	_	38.9	35.0	38.3	38.3	38.5
Current account balance (% of GDP)	_	2.5	4.2	5.4	4.8	4.9

1. Contributions to changes in real GDP, actual amount in the first column.
2. The consumer price index includes mortgage interest costs.
3. Consumer price index with fixed interest rates.
4. Historical data and projections are based on the definition of unemployment which covers 15 to 74 year olds and classifies job-seeking full-time students as unemployed.

Source: OECD Economic Outlook 108 database.

StatLink ᴍˢ₽ https://doi.org/10.1787/888934219565

Economic activity is recovering

Despite the absence of a lockdown in Sweden, sectors like hotels, restaurants and transport have been severely hit and unemployment has risen markedly, notwithstanding a generous short-time work scheme. Still, termination notices and newly registered at the public employment service have sharply decreased since the beginning of the summer, suggesting a gradual slowdown in the rise in unemployment. Domestic tourism during the summer months supported private consumption. Card transactions have increased since the end of June, including for non-grocery goods. Firms in manufacturing, retail and services are becoming less pessimistic.

Government support to the economy remains generous

The government has introduced new measures in the 2021 budget bill, amounting to SEK 105 billion (2% of GDP) in 2021 and SEK 85 billion (1.7% of GDP) in 2022. Reductions in employer social security contributions and income taxes will support employment and household purchasing power. Higher unemployment compensation, retraining and support to people weakly attached to the labour market will help reduce unemployment. Municipalities and regions will receive additional grants to cover COVID-19-related expenses and rising welfare costs. Structural measures include investments in infrastructure and the green economy. Monetary policy will remain highly accommodative: the Riksbank intends to keep the repo rate at zero at least until 2023 and has included corporate bonds in its securities purchasing programme for a total amount of SEK 10 billion (0.2% of GDP).

The economic recovery will be gradual

The household saving rate has risen and will remain very high in the near term because of increased unemployment and restrictions on social life. Nonetheless, consumption is projected to gradually regain traction, provided the number of infections remains low in most of the country and an effective vaccine is deployed. Exports are set to pick up as demand in neighbouring countries gathers momentum. However, the recovery in business investment will be slow. Firms' low capacity utilisation and the high level of uncertainty will hold back their investment, despite higher liquidity provided by government measures. Improvement in the labour market will also be slow. The increase in unemployment was damped thanks to the short-time work scheme, but it will continue for some time, as employers will first raise working hours of existing employees before hiring. A more severe spread of COVID-19, higher global trade tensions and the lack of a trade agreement between the United Kingdom and the European Union would hold back exports and investment, further delaying the economic recovery.

Additional policy action may be needed to address inequalities

The COVID-19 crisis has exacerbated inequalities among people. Unemployment has more severely hit youth, low-skilled and foreign-born persons, many of whom were working in the hospitality sector. Even though current policies will support these groups, additional measures may be needed to improve their training and help them transit to new jobs. Remote regions were already facing mounting demographic challenges, with an ageing population and the departure of young and skilled workers. Additional grants may be needed to provide adequate welfare services, especially in healthcare, elderly care and education.

Switzerland

The economy is set to contract by 4.7% in 2020 and is projected to rebound by 2.2% in 2021 and 3.4% in 2022. Activity will only reach its pre-crisis level in 2022. Private investment and consumption will be held back by low confidence and high unemployment. Exports will be hindered by subdued growth in partner countries. A strong second wave of infections heightens uncertainty, but a widespread implementation of an effective vaccine in the latter part of 2021 should improve the sanitary situation.

Budgetary support has been substantial, and monetary policy remains accommodative. Further fiscal support may be needed. As the use of the short-time work scheme decreases, many workers may need training and reskilling to match labour demand over the medium term. The procedures to start a business should be streamlined to enable better and faster reallocation of workers and capital.

COVID-19 cases have rebounded after the summer

The economy picked up at the end of April with the ending of the 6-week lockdown that involved closure of schools and many economic activities. The situation started to deteriorate again after the summer, with a sharp increase in the number of new cases in October. New sanitary measures have been implemented: wearing of masks in all closed public places is obligatory; public and private gatherings are limited; telework is recommended; and tertiary education is provided on line. Some cantons apply stricter measures; for instance, non-essential shops are closed in Geneva, and restaurants, bars, museums and theatres are closed in Jura and Vaud. Testing, tracing and isolation measures are also in place, with contact tracing carried out under the responsibility of the cantons.

Switzerland

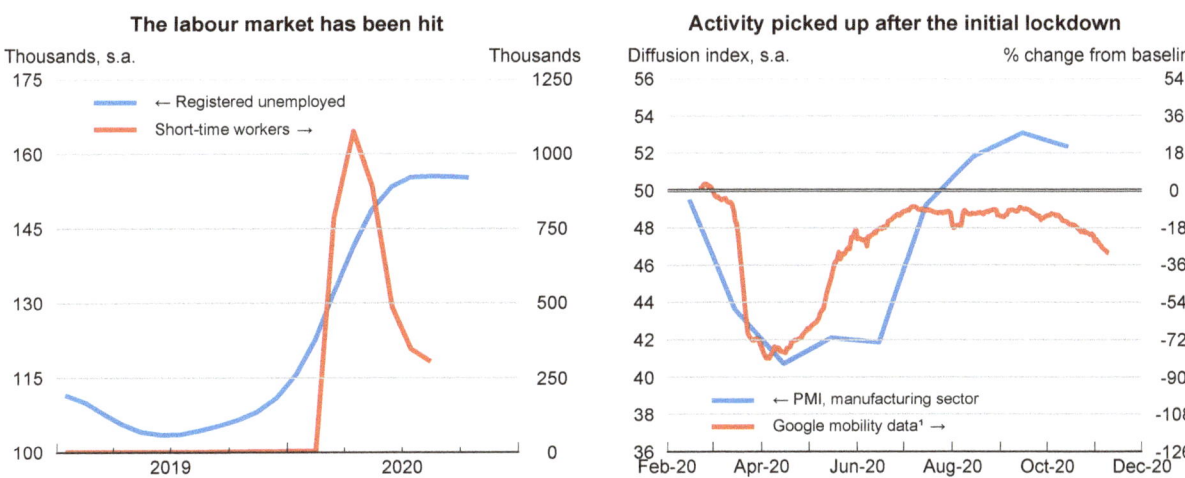

1. Seven-day moving average of the Google retail and recreation community mobility trend. The baseline is the median value, for the corresponding day of the week, during the five-week period from 3 January to 6 February 2020.
Source: State Secretariat for Economic Affairs; Refinitiv; and Google LLC, *Google COVID-19 Community Mobility Reports*, https://www.google.com/covid19/mobility/

StatLink ⟶ https://doi.org/10.1787/888934219584

Switzerland: Demand, output and prices

Switzerland	2017	2018	2019	2020	2021	2022
	Current prices CHF billion	Percentage changes, volume (2015 prices)				
GDP at market prices	694.0	3.0	1.1	-4.7	2.2	3.4
Private consumption	365.3	0.8	1.4	-6.8	1.4	1.9
Government consumption	78.6	0.9	0.9	2.2	2.0	1.6
Gross fixed capital formation	180.1	0.8	1.2	-5.2	1.9	4.4
Final domestic demand	624.1	0.8	1.3	-5.2	1.6	2.6
Stockbuilding[1]	- 6.8	0.3	0.1	-0.9	-0.9	0.0
Total domestic demand	617.3	1.1	1.4	-6.4	0.6	2.6
Exports of goods and services	452.5	3.4	-0.1	-4.4	2.2	3.3
Imports of goods and services	375.8	0.4	0.0	-6.8	0.8	3.0
Net exports[1]	76.7	2.0	-0.1	0.8	1.0	0.6
Memorandum items						
GDP deflator	_	0.7	-0.1	-0.2	0.3	0.6
Consumer price index	_	0.9	0.4	-0.7	0.2	0.4
Core inflation index[2]	_	0.5	0.4	-0.3	0.3	0.4
Unemployment rate (% of labour force)	_	4.7	4.4	4.9	5.2	4.8
Household saving ratio, net (% of disposable income)	_	17.3	17.9	22.1	20.8	20.1
General government financial balance (% of GDP)	_	1.3	1.4	-4.4	-3.8	-2.5
General government gross debt (% of GDP)	_	39.4	38.1	42.0	45.9	48.5
Current account balance (% of GDP)	_	8.6	10.9	6.4	5.8	6.5

1. Contributions to changes in real GDP, actual amount in the first column.
2. Consumer price index excluding food and energy.
Source: OECD Economic Outlook 108 database.

StatLink 🔗 https://doi.org/10.1787/888934219603

The economy has been severely impacted

The lockdown triggered a large decline in GDP in the second quarter of 2020, albeit to a lesser extent than in many other European countries. In addition to the relatively early easing of containment restrictions, the structure of the economy helped to limit the impact. Manufacturing benefited from the positive performance of the chemical and pharmaceutical industry. Meanwhile, several sectors such as accommodation, transport and construction were hit hard. Consumer confidence is rebounding, but remains below its pre-crisis level. Short-time work has concerned more than a quarter of employees since the start of the crisis, although the number of short-time workers is now decreasing. Only about half of the sharp drop in employment translated into higher unemployment as part of the working population withdrew from the labour market. Unemployment seems to have stabilised but could rebound when the use of short-time work ends or if restrictions are prolonged.

An extensive support package is being implemented

A large set of measures (amounting to around 6% of GDP, of which government guarantees account for about one-half) has been implemented to support incomes and firms. The Corona Income-Compensation Scheme has been set to compensate the loss of income for employees and the self-employed. It has been extended until mid-2021. The existing short-time work scheme coverage has been expanded to limit the impact of the crisis on employment. To avoid an increase in employees' contributions, the Federal Council provided funding to the unemployment insurance fund (around 1.7% of GDP). Government guarantees for loans and delays in the payment of some taxes were also put in place for companies in distress. Monetary policy remains accommodative with negative interest rates. Moreover, with the COVID-19 refinancing facility, the Swiss National Bank provides liquidity to banks to finance loans granted under the government's COVID-19 scheme.

The economy is slowly recovering but risks are high

The contraction in GDP should amount to 4.7% in 2020. Growth is projected to recover to 2.2% in 2021 and 3.4% in 2022. Some sectors such as transport and tourism should be affected by the impact of the crisis for longer. By contrast, the chemical and pharmaceutical industry should continue to support the recovery. Private consumption will be held back by high unemployment and low confidence levels. Exports will recover only slowly due to sluggish demand in trading partners and a strong currency. Risks are on the downside. New local lockdowns would reduce growth until large-scale immunisation is attained. Financial stability may be compromised by the continued increase in mortgage loans and residential property prices. By contrast, stronger growth in Europe would be positive for exports.

Further temporary fiscal support and streamlined regulation will help the recovery

When the use of the short-time work scheme is scaled down, a risk exists that firms disappear and many workers become unemployed. To allow better and faster reallocation, more support for training and reskilling, especially in new technologies, will be needed. Streamlining processes to start a business will be key. To help banks supply loans to firms with liquidity problems, the Swiss National Bank should be ready to extend the COVID-19 refinancing facility.

Turkey

The recovery started during the summer, driven by vigorous quasi-fiscal stimulus and external demand, now faces significant headwinds. The number of COVID-19 cases surged again in autumn. Policy support has been scaled down to contain the current account deficit, inflation and exchange rate depreciation. GDP is set to contract by 1.3% in 2020, and – absent renewed macroeconomic tensions – it is projected to grow by 2.9% in 2021 and 3.2% in 2022. Unemployment is expected to increase. Contingent liabilities and the current account deficit remain very large and high risk premia and the exchange rate depreciation have hampered the outlook. Recent stability-oriented policy measures can enhance domestic and international sentiment and support the recovery.

Physical distancing measures need to be fully enforced and additional confinement measures may be needed. Confidence in the quality of official communication on the spread of the pandemic should be restored. Improving the transparency and the coherence of monetary, fiscal, quasi-fiscal and financial policies would help improve domestic and international confidence. Reducing employment costs and promoting more flexible formal employment forms would boost job creation in the formal sector.

Turkey

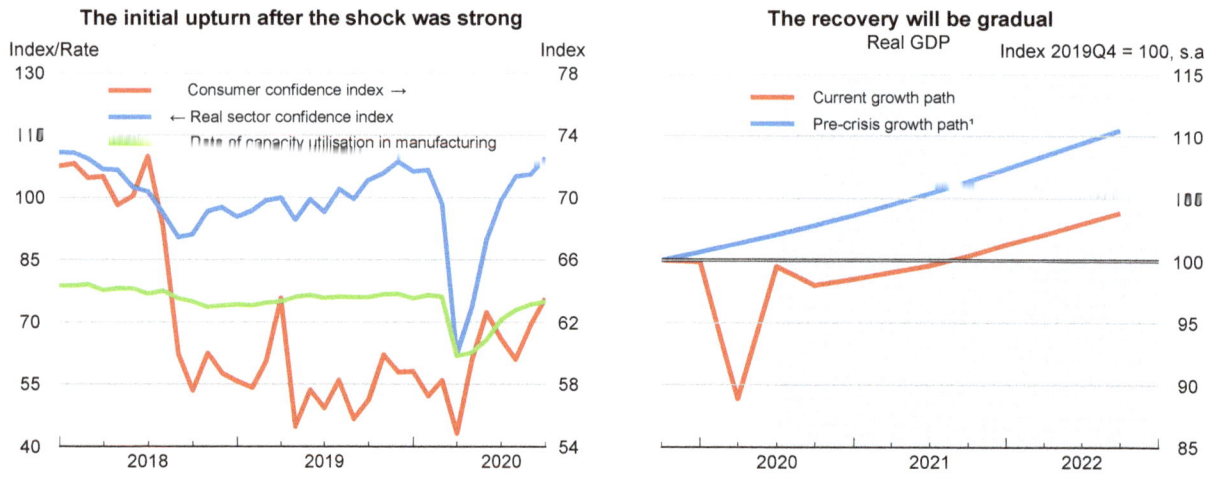

1. The November 2019 projection is based on the November 2019 Economic Outlook, with linear extrapolation for 2022 based on potential growth in 2021.
Source: OECD Economic Outlook 106 and 108 databases; Central Bank of the Republic of Turkey; and Turkish Statistical Institute.

StatLink https://doi.org/10.1787/888934219622

Turkey: Demand, output and prices

Turkey	2017	2018	2019	2020	2021	2022
	Current prices TRY billion	Percentage changes, volume (2009 prices)				
GDP at market prices	3 133.7	3.0	0.9	-1.3	2.9	3.2
Private consumption	1 836.6	0.7	1.6	-1.5	3.2	4.2
Government consumption	450.6	6.5	4.3	2.9	2.2	0.1
Gross fixed capital formation	935.6	-0.3	-12.4	-4.5	2.6	6.4
Final domestic demand	3 222.9	1.2	-2.1	-1.7	2.8	4.1
Stockbuilding[1]	26.2	-2.6	0.0	6.5	1.2	0.0
Total domestic demand	3 249.1	-1.6	-2.1	5.1	3.9	3.9
Exports of goods and services	816.0	9.0	4.9	-19.8	5.0	7.1
Imports of goods and services	931.4	-6.4	-5.3	-0.9	8.8	9.2
Net exports[1]	- 115.4	4.2	3.2	-6.2	-1.3	-0.9
Memorandum items						
GDP deflator	_	16.5	13.9	12.8	12.4	9.5
Potential GDP, volume	_	4.7	4.0	3.2	2.8	2.8
Consumer price index[2]	_	16.3	15.2	12.0	11.9	9.5
Core inflation index[3]	_	16.5	13.4	10.9	11.9	9.5
Unemployment rate (% of labour force)	_	11.0	13.7	12.5	14.8	15.3
Current account balance (% of GDP)	_	-2.1	1.2	-2.9	-2.7	-3.1

1. Contributions to changes in real GDP, actual amount in the first column.
2. Based on yearly averages.
3. Consumer price index excluding food and energy.
Source: OECD Economic Outlook 108 database.

StatLink ᵃᵐˢᴸ https://doi.org/10.1787/888934219641

The initially successful fight against the pandemic has lost its early momentum

Infections, which were relatively contained in April and May, have grown again after the relaxation of confinement measures in June. The monitoring of the health situation was difficult as only symptomatic cases have been reported until the end of November. There was a sharp escalation of infections in autumn, together with a rising number of deaths. Despite increased pressures on the hospital infrastructure, the testing, tracing and tracking system and health professionals, the saturation of intensive care capacities was avoided as of the first half of November, but tensions have augmented. Some new confinement measures were introduced in October and November and additional restrictions may become necessary.

The economy recovered sharply in the third quarter of 2020 but faces headwinds

The drastic fall in activity in the second quarter was followed by a sharp recovery. It was driven by ample quasi-fiscal and monetary stimulus and strong export demand on the back of a large exchange rate depreciation and exporters' successful diversification towards new markets. The rebound in industrial production was particularly vigorous. Business investment remained weak, but job retention programmes in the formal sector reduced employment losses. However, the unemployment rate for new entrants to the labour market and, in particular, youth is soaring. Weakness in tourism activity, which accounts for 4% of GDP and 7% of employment, has had adverse spillovers in tourist regions, despite a partial rebound in August thanks to domestic demand and visitors from certain countries such as Russia. The resurgence of infections, the weakening of external demand, regional geopolitical uncertainties, and further exchange rate depreciation and volatility in the last quarter of 2020 will weigh on the outlook.

Quasi-fiscal and monetary support is being scaled down

Monetary and quasi-fiscal support has been massive. Concessional credits to households and businesses, provided mainly by public banks, but also private banks incentivised by government guarantees and new credit regulations (backed by negative real interest rates), gave an outstanding quasi-fiscal stimulus. Resulting pressures on the current account deficit and inflation have generated concerns about financial and exchange rate stability. Faced with a surge in risk premia and exchange rate depreciation, the authorities tightened the fiscal stance in autumn and public banks drastically reduced their credit expansion. The central bank has raised policy interest rates. The earlier divergence between the effective funding costs and the official interest rate of the central bank had created investor uncertainties, raising risk premia and denting exchange rates. Recent stability-oriented economic and monetary policy announcements and measures, including the sharp increase in the policy interest rate in November, have improved investor sentiment.

The recovery will be gradual and risks persist

GDP is projected to contract in the last quarter of 2020 and recover only very gradually afterwards. The resurgence of the pandemic, the modest coverage of formal social safety nets and cash transfers, combined with firms' and households' already high debt levels, will weigh on private consumption. The subdued international trade environment will not permit exports to be buoyant. Investment will be affected by persisting uncertainties. There are both downward and upward risks. Uncertainties concerning regional geopolitical developments aside, domestic and international confidence may either weaken or improve according to developments in fiscal, financial and monetary policies. In this context, any increase in risk premia would bear on the cost of foreign financing of the high external funding requirements stemming from the large current account deficit and debt rollovers. If downward risks materialise, pressures on the exchange rate inflation and financial stability would intensify and the economy may contract again.

Rebuilding confidence in the macroeconomic policy framework and structural reforms is crucial

Room is available for above-the-line fiscal support until the recovery is firmly underway. Part of the support currently provided through public and concessional loans and loan guarantees can be converted into more transparent, targeted and temporary cash transfers. Such support should be accompanied by the implementation of a coherent and credible macroeconomic policy framework, encompassing monetary, fiscal, quasi-fiscal and financial policies, and all contingent liabilities, to improve transparency and confidence. Reducing employment costs and promoting more flexible employment forms in the formal sector would facilitate high-quality job creation.

United Kingdom

GDP is set to contract again in the fourth quarter of 2020 as virus containment measures are implemented, and to fall by 11.2% in 2020 as a whole. Growth of 4.2% in 2021 and 4.1% in 2022 is projected to be driven by a rebound of consumption, while business investment will remain weak due to spare capacity and continued uncertainty. Until an effective vaccine is broadly deployed, risks of further outbreaks will dent confidence. Increased border costs will weigh on imports and exports from 2021 as the United Kingdom leaves the EU Single Market and is assumed to enter a new, less comprehensive free trade agreement with the European Union. Labour market withdrawals and unemployment will increase even though the Coronavirus Job Retention Scheme continues to support employment. Bankruptcies are set to rise, although extensions to crisis loan schemes are set to soften the increase.

Fiscal and monetary policies should stay supportive until the recovery firmly takes hold. Closely monitoring the situation, adapting and targeting support to hard-hit areas and sectors, while allowing structural change to take place are key challenges going forward. Extending increased levels of cash support and training to the unemployed can help this restructuring. Reaching a free trade agreement with the EU is essential to limit disturbances to exporting and importing industries.

United Kingdom 1

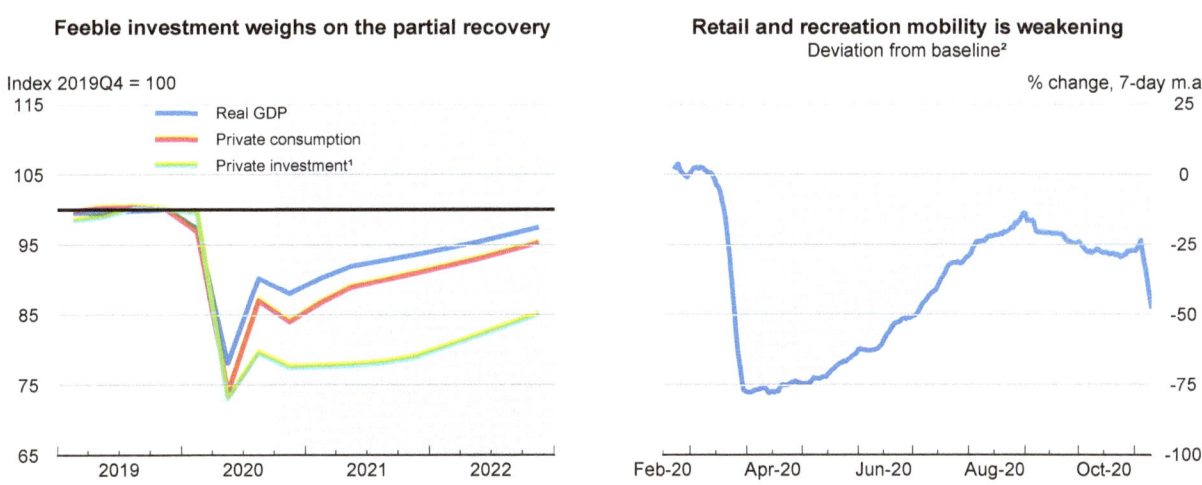

Feeble investment weighs on the partial recovery

Retail and recreation mobility is weakening
Deviation from baseline[2]

1. Residential investment is excluded.
2. The baseline is the median value, for the corresponding day of the week, during the five-week period between 3 January and 6 February 2020.
Source: OECD Economic Outlook 108 database and Google LLC, *Google COVID-19 Community Mobility Reports*, https://www.google.com/covid19/mobility/.

StatLink ᓀᔭᔥᒪ https://doi.org/10.1787/888934219660

United Kingdom: Demand, output and prices

United Kingdom	2017 Current prices GBP billion	2018	2019	2020	2021	2022
		Percentage changes, volume (2018 prices)				
GDP at market prices	2 068.8	1.3	1.3	-11.2	4.2	4.1
Private consumption	1 334.4	1.4	0.9	-14.6	4.3	5.0
Government consumption	387.3	0.6	4.1	-9.4	6.4	0.7
Gross fixed capital formation	372.3	0.4	1.5	-12.2	1.9	5.2
Final domestic demand	2 094.0	1.1	1.6	-13.2	4.3	4.1
Stockbuilding[1]	4.6	0.1	-0.1	-0.5	0.3	0.0
Total domestic demand	2 098.6	1.2	1.5	-13.9	4.5	4.1
Exports of goods and services	622.9	3.0	2.8	-13.1	-1.1	0.1
Imports of goods and services	652.8	2.7	3.3	-21.0	-0.2	0.2
Net exports[1]	- 29.9	0.1	-0.2	2.7	-0.3	0.0
Memorandum items						
GDP deflator	_	2.2	2.1	5.9	-2.9	1.0
Harmonised index of consumer prices	_	2.5	1.8	0.8	0.7	1.5
Harmonised index of core inflation[2]	_	2.1	1.7	1.2	0.8	1.5
Unemployment rate (% of labour force)	_	4.1	3.8	4.6	7.4	6.2
Household saving ratio, gross (% of disposable income)	_	6.1	6.5	19.4	17.7	15.2
General government financial balance (% of GDP)	_	-2.2	-2.4	-16.7	-13.3	-8.8
General government gross debt (% of GDP)	_	113.9	117.3	145.3	157.4	160.5
Current account balance (% of GDP)	_	-3.7	-4.3	-2.6	-3.6	-3.4

1. Contributions to changes in real GDP, actual amount in the first column.
2. Harmonised index of consumer prices excluding food, energy, alcohol and tobacco.
Source: OECD Economic Outlook 108 database.

StatLink https://doi.org/10.1787/888934219679

United Kingdom 2

Unemployment is increasing

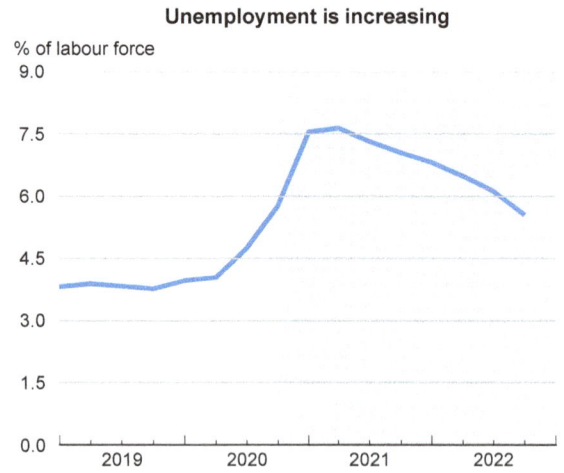

Fiscal measures increase public debt

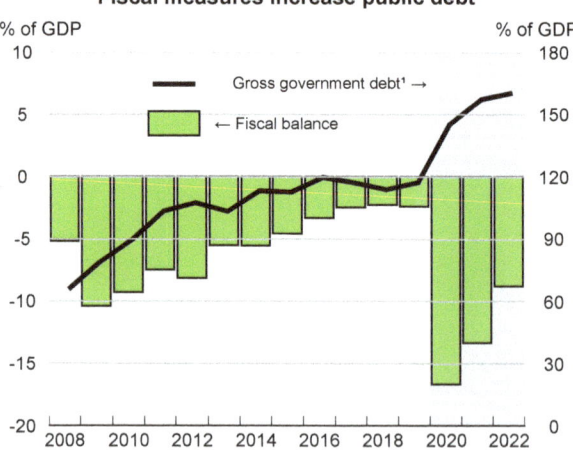

1. General government gross financial liabilities.
Source: OECD Economic Outlook 108 database.

StatLink https://doi.org/10.1787/888934219698

Confirmed COVID-19 cases have risen recently

Daily confirmed cases of COVID-19 reached new records after the summer, as propagation increased and more people were tested compared with the first wave. Hospital admissions and COVID-19-related deaths are still considerably lower than their April peaks, but pressure on the healthcare system has been rising. New national measures, including advice to stay at home and restrictions on hospitality and non-essential retail activities and socialising across households, have temporarily replaced a three-tier system of local alert levels in England. Distancing and hygiene measures continue to apply, such as rules on the use of masks and telework when possible. Devolved administrations in Northern Ireland, Scotland and Wales have all tightened containment measures, with a two-week nationwide lockdown in Wales at the end of October.

An initially strong rebound has come to a halt

A strong consumption-driven GDP rebound in the third quarter of 2020 after COVID-19 case numbers had been brought down and the lockdown lifted is set to go into reverse. As the number of cases has surged again, forward-looking indicators such as the Purchasing Managers' Index pointed to growth levelling off already before national restrictions were implemented in November. Footfall in areas of retail and recreation has declined again, and, according to the Business Impact of Coronavirus (COVID-19) Survey, the share of companies reporting falling turnover increased in October. The number of claimants to Universal Credit remained broadly constant from September to October, while the number of job vacancies increased considerably, but from a low level. Unemployment has so far only risen slowly relative to the output loss thanks to the Coronavirus Job Retention Scheme. Over 7% of the labour force was still fully furloughed on 31 August, and more than 15% of eligible employees were fully furloughed in some sectors.

Fiscal and monetary policies are supportive

The government has extended and adjusted the economic support measures put in place early on in the crisis and introduced new measures. The Office for Budget Responsibility estimates that discretionary spending to support businesses and households and strengthen healthcare and testing capacity will amount to 16% of GDP in fiscal year 2020-21. The Coronavirus Job Retention Scheme covers up to 80% of wages and has been extended until 31 March 2021. Government guaranteed loan facilities have played an important role in allowing banks to lend to firms without tying up regulatory capital. The Bounce Back Loan Scheme and the Coronavirus Business Interruption Loan Scheme have been extended to end-January, while the Covid Corporate Financing Facility, run jointly with the Bank of England, remains open until March 2021. GBP 40 billion of tax deferrals have further eased liquidity constraints.

Monetary policy has remained accommodative, easing financial stress and supporting demand. The Bank of England cut interest rates to 0.1% and increased its bond purchasing programme by GBP 200 billion at the start of the crisis, GBP 100 billion in early summer, and an additional GBP 150 billion in November, to a total of GBP 895 billion (more than 40% of 2019 GDP).

The United Kingdom is at a critical juncture

The resurgence of COVID-19 cases comes at a historic and critical moment, as the United Kingdom is preparing to leave the EU Single Market. Output is set to contract by 11.2% in 2020 before growing by 4.2% in 2021 and 4.1% in 2022. Growth will be driven by private consumption and public spending, while private investment will recover only slowly due to elevated uncertainty. The unemployment rate is projected to average at 7.4% in 2021, as the Coronavirus Job Retention Scheme continues to shield many jobs.

Government net lending will peak at 16.7% of GDP in 2020, and gross public debt is set to rise to 160% of GDP in 2022.

The projection is contingent on the health situation going forward. A deterioration could prompt additional restrictions on economic activity and lead to a slower recovery. Effective treatment or effective vaccines are assumed to be widely available at the turn of 2021 and 2022. New treatment methods or earlier than assumed distribution of a vaccine are a clear upside risk. Risks around the future relationship with the European Union compound COVID-19-related uncertainty. The failure to conclude a trade deal with the European Union by the end of 2020 would entail serious additional economic disturbances in the short term and have a strongly negative effect on trade, productivity and jobs in the longer term. By contrast, a closer trade relationship with the European Union than expected, notably encompassing services, would improve the economic outlook in the medium term.

A balance needs to be struck between protecting people and protecting jobs

Monetary policy should not tighten until there are clear signs of price pressures, and the Bank of England should stand ready to provide further support and, if necessary, expand the monetary policy toolbox to reach the inflation target. Fiscal policy should also remain supportive until the recovery is firmly underway. Policies supporting companies and jobs, such as the Coronavirus Job Retention Scheme, need to be available and adapted as needed based on epidemiological and economic developments, while not hindering the reallocation of resources towards firms and sectors with better growth prospects. Adequate cash support to displaced and low-skilled workers along with efforts to help them gain new skills and find a job would reduce their hardship and speed up structural change. Reducing the out-of-pocket cost of childcare would help parents, notably mothers, engage in paid employment and training. Public investment should address long-term challenges, notably reducing greenhouse gas emissions and boosting digital infrastructure. Plans outlined in the 2020 Spending Review to create a public-private infrastructure bank can help.

United States

The economy is recovering following the sharp fall in GDP and dramatic rise in the unemployment rate in the first half of 2020. Real GDP is anticipated to contract by 3.7% in 2020, before rising by 3.2% in 2021 and 3.5% in 2022. The unemployment rate will gradually fall, but will remain elevated compared with the pre-pandemic period. This reflects activity in some sectors, such as hospitality and transportation, continuing to be impacted by the pandemic and impediments to cross-sectoral labour reallocation. A general rollout of an effective vaccine in the latter half of 2021 will allow an easing of containment measures and strengthen confidence.

Massive monetary and fiscal responses have protected households and businesses. However, in the absence of a new substantial fiscal stimulus programme, a severe fiscal cliff would result in a rapid withdrawal of support to households, massive layoffs and a wave of bankruptcies (this is assumed to be avoided in the projection). Some state and local governments will require federal government financial assistance given a sharp drop in consumption and travel-related tax receipts. Structural reforms to promote productivity-enhancing labour reallocation should also be prioritised. For example, restrictive land use regulations should be relaxed to promote the supply of new housing and the ability for workers to move to new job opportunities. Similarly, reforming the occupational licensing system and the use of non-compete agreements in work contracts would promote labour mobility and wage growth.

United States 1

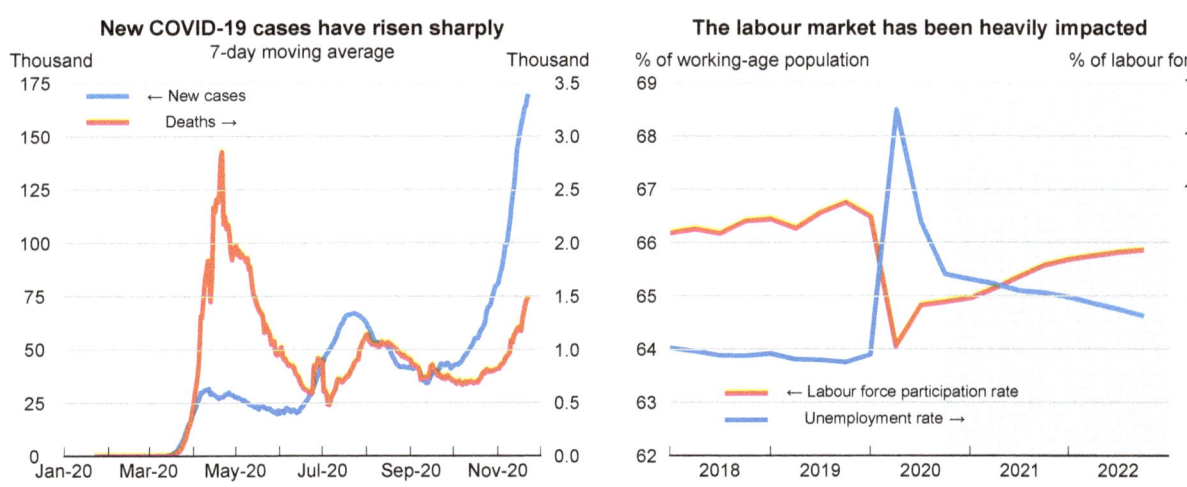

Source: OECD Economic Outlook 108 database; and Refinitiv.

StatLink https://doi.org/10.1787/888934219717

United States: Demand, output and prices

United States	2017	2018	2019	2020	2021	2022
	Current prices USD billion	Percentage changes, volume (2012 prices)				
GDP at market prices	19 543.0	3.0	2.2	-3.7	3.2	3.5
Private consumption	13 340.4	2.7	2.4	-4.0	3.4	3.6
Government consumption	2 742.7	1.5	1.8	0.6	1.2	2.8
Gross fixed capital formation	3 999.1	4.8	2.3	-1.7	3.5	4.0
Final domestic demand	20 082.2	3.0	2.3	-2.9	3.1	3.6
Stockbuilding[1]	16.3	0.2	0.0	-0.7	0.4	0.0
Total domestic demand	20 098.5	3.2	2.3	-3.6	3.6	3.6
Exports of goods and services	2 374.6	3.0	-0.1	-13.8	3.7	4.4
Imports of goods and services	2 930.1	4.1	1.1	-10.7	6.5	5.1
Net exports[1]	- 555.5	-0.3	-0.2	-0.1	-0.5	-0.2
Memorandum items						
GDP deflator	_	2.4	1.8	1.1	1.1	1.5
Personal consumption expenditures deflator	_	2.1	1.5	1.2	1.2	1.4
Core personal consumption expenditures deflator[2]	_	2.0	1.7	1.4	1.4	1.7
Unemployment rate (% of labour force)	_	3.9	3.7	8.1	6.4	5.6
Household saving ratio, net (% of disposable income)	_	7.8	7.5	16.1	14.9	13.2
General government financial balance (% of GDP)	_	-6.3	-6.7	-15.4	-11.6	-8.3
General government gross debt (% of GDP)	_	106.6	108.4	128.0	134.2	136.3
Current account balance (% of GDP)	_	-2.2	-2.2	-3.4	-4.0	-4.1

1. Contributions to changes in real GDP, actual amount in the first column.
2. Deflator for private consumption excluding food and energy.
Source: OECD Economic Outlook 108 database.

StatLink https://doi.org/10.1787/888934219736

United States 2

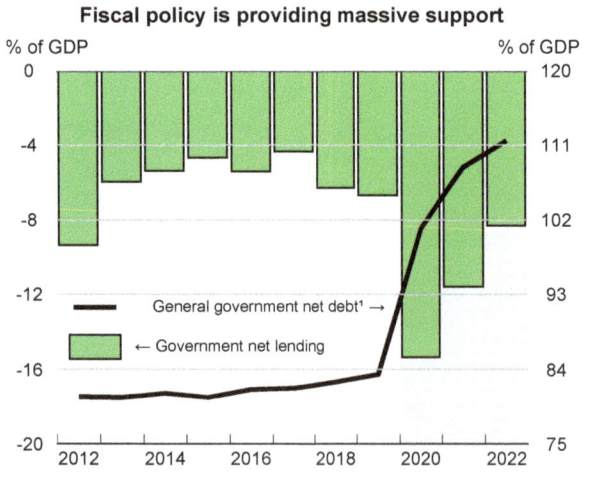

Fiscal policy is providing massive support

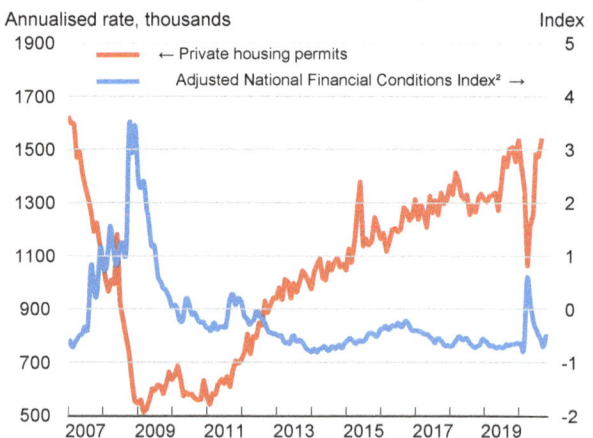

Financial conditions are supporting investment

1. General government shows the consolidated (i.e. with intra-government amounts netted out) accounts for all levels of government (central plus State/local) based on OECD national accounts. This measure differs from the federal debt held by the public, which was 79.2% of GDP for the 2019 fiscal year.
2. The Adjusted National Financial Conditions Index (ANFCI) is published by the Federal Reserve Bank of Chicago and adjusts for the state of the business cycle and the level of inflation. Positive values are associated with tighter-than-average financial conditions and negative values are associated with looser-than-average financial conditions.
Source: OECD Economic Outlook 108 database; Federal Reserve Bank of Chicago; and Refinitiv.

StatLink https://doi.org/10.1787/888934219755

COVID-19 case numbers have remained elevated

The number of COVID-19 cases has been persistently elevated since the start of the pandemic outbreak. Over 12 million US citizens have now tested positive to the virus, with more than 250 000 deaths attributed to it. Since mid-September, there has been a surge in cases. In response, new restrictions related to indoor gatherings and public spaces have been imposed in some areas. Schools in many jurisdictions have also moved back to remote learning and curfews and stay-at-home advice issued for specific locations. Nationwide testing capacity has gradually increased and the number of tests has ramped up since mid-September.

The economy is recovering, but services activity remains weak

The economy experienced its sharpest contraction in post-war history in the second quarter of 2020, with non-farm employment declining by around 22 million through March and April 2020. A subsequent relaxation of containment measures was accompanied by a discernible economic rebound, with more than half of those lost jobs added back to employer payrolls by October 2020. Indicators of spending on goods consumption have recovered strongly. Similarly, housing investment has rebounded, with low mortgage interest rates and strong pent-up demand fuelling residential sales and construction. Even so, spending on most services remains weak. Google mobility trends suggest that activity in restaurants, cafés, shopping centres and movie theatres is about 20% lower than at the onset of the pandemic. Furthermore, a high share of low-wage workers in these industries means that the crisis risks sparking a long-lasting rise in earnings inequality.

Macroeconomic policy support has been substantial

Fiscal policy reacted decisively earlier in the year once the scale of the economic impact became apparent. Comprehensive support was introduced, including supplementary unemployment insurance, one-off payments to families, financial assistance to state governments, forgivable loans with a Treasury backstop to small businesses that retain workers and increased health sector capacity. In response to the expiration of certain measures, the President issued executive orders in early August to partially extend fiscal support. However, this was funded by USD 44 billion (0.2% of GDP) from the Disaster Relief Fund and so was a temporary solution. As yet, no new broader fiscal support package has passed into legislation despite proposals from both major parties. Agreement on a new fiscal stimulus package, as assumed in these projections, is urgent to avoid a damaging fiscal cliff.

Monetary and financial market policy is also providing substantial support to the economy. At the onset of the crisis, a suite of new credit facilities were introduced and prudential regulations were eased to limit the possibility of financial institutions restricting access to finance. The Federal Reserve cut interest rates to 0-0.25% and announced the resumption of unlimited large-scale asset purchases, significantly expanding the size of the balance sheet. In September, the Federal Open Market Committee issued forward guidance that reflected the adoption of the new flexible average inflation targeting strategy. Specifically, the Committee noted that the policy rate will not increase until inflation has risen to 2%, and is assessed to be on track to moderately exceed this rate for some time, and labour market conditions have reached levels consistent with the Committee's assessment of maximum employment. Financial conditions have become highly accommodative as a result of the policies so far enacted.

The recovery will be gradual and scars will remain

GDP growth is expected to pick up through 2021, reflecting an assumed additional fiscal package that will particularly support household incomes and consumption. Improved conditions in major export markets and the fulfilment of agreed targets under the US-China Phase 1 trade deal will boost export activity at the same time. Nevertheless, until an effective vaccine has been deployed successfully in the latter part of 2021, assumed localised virus outbreaks and subsequent introduction of containment measures will temper business confidence and provide a headwind to new non-residential investment. Labour market conditions will show further steady improvement, although the unemployment rate will remain elevated compared with the pre-pandemic period. Similarly, the labour force participation rate will rise further but will not return to the levels seen in February 2020, partly reflecting early labour market exits of older workers, who have decided to retire rather than wait for the recovery, thus depriving the economy of valuable human capital. The existence of labour market slack will weigh on wage increases despite recent improvements in the pace of measured productivity growth. In turn, tepid growth in unit labour costs will keep price inflation well below the Federal Reserve's 2% inflation target.

An upside risk to the projections is that the scale of fiscal support turns out to be more expansionary than currently assumed. For example, a substantial new infrastructure package is not currently factored into the baseline projections. A downside risk is that a new fiscal package is relatively meagre in scale or takes many more months to be agreed. There is also a risk that large-scale firm insolvencies dent investment prospects. Non-financial corporate leverage has risen to historical highs, with many businesses in sectors exposed to COVID-19 confinement measures having accumulated substantial debt.

Structural reforms should accompany ongoing macroeconomic policy support

A timely fiscal stimulus should be well targeted and effective in its support of workers and businesses affected by lockdown measures. Federal government financial assistance to state and local governments should be maintained, given they may otherwise need to wind back spending due to a drop in tax receipts and balanced budget requirements. There also needs to be continued support for individuals facing difficulty in quickly re-entering employment and at risk of dropping out of the labour force. In particular, job placement and retraining services should be improved and expanded. These services will also help to reorient workers from sectors that may permanently contract in the wake of the pandemic to new growth areas of industry. Over the medium term, labour reallocation and wage growth will also benefit from reducing the scale of occupational licensing and non-compete agreements in work contracts. Similarly, restrictive land use regulations should be relaxed to promote the supply of new housing and the ability for workers to move to new job opportunities. The approval of a vaccine for COVID-19 should be accompanied by thorough planning and governance around its production and eventual dissemination to the population. A rigorous vaccination process will reduce uncertainty, benefiting the economic recovery.